Mixing, Recording, and Producing Techniques of the Pros

By Rick Clark

COURSE TECHNOLOGY
CENGAGE Learning™

Australia • Brazil • Japan • Korea • Mexico • Singapore • Spain • United Kingdom • United States

Mixing, Recording, and Producing Techniques of the Pros

Publisher and General Manager, Course Technology PTR:
  Stacy L. Hiquet

Associate Director of Marketing:
  Sarah O'Donnell

Manager of Editorial Services:
  Heather Talbot

Marketing Manager:
  Heather Hurley

Executive Editor:
  Mike Lawson

Senior Editor:
  Mark Garvey

Marketing Coordinator:
  Jordan Casey

Project Editor:
  Dan Foster, Scribe Tribe

Course Technology PTR Editorial Services Coordinator:
  Elizabeth Furbish

Interior Layout Tech/Cover Designer:
  Stephen Ramirez

Indexer:
  Katherine Stimson

Proofreader:
  Anne Smith

Cover photo courtesy of Solid State Logic. Paragon Studios, Franklin, TN–paragon-studios.com

Studio 'A' featuring an 80 channel SSL XL9000 console and DynAudio M4+ monitors

Room Design: Russ Berger Design Group–rbdg.com

Photo: Fred Paragano

Educational facilities, companies, and organizations interested in multiple copies or licensing of this book should contact the publisher for quantity discount information. Training manuals, CD-ROMs, and portions of this book are also available individually or can be tailored for specific needs.

Library of Congress Catalog Card Number: 2005927504
ISBN 13: 978-1-59200-767-7
ISBN 10: 1-59200-767-8

Course Technology, a division of Cengage Learning
25 Thomson Place
Boston, MA 02210
www.courseptr.com

Printed in the United States of America
3 4 5 6 7 11 10 09 08

Dedication

I would like to dedicate this book to my wife, Allison Black, my daughter, Sarah, and my parents, Pat and John Clark.

Foreword

Every talented recording engineer will tell you that you never stop learning the art of recording music. As a professor of recording engineering at Middle Tennessee State University, I always tell my students that we are teaching them how to learn and that it's up to them to continue learning and perfecting their art after graduation. Continuing the learning process is crucial for people in the audio field, whether they are just beginning or they have been in the trenches for decades.

It is for this reason that I am so very pleased to have a compilation of the application-oriented articles authored by Rick Clark that have appeared in *Mix* magazine over the years. I teach classes in beginning and advanced techniques of recording as well as a class in the art of soundtrack design for film. Over the past seven years of teaching, I have often required students to read Rick's articles from *Mix* as part of their homework assignments. His articles have a mass appeal, but in particular have always appealed to the beginning recording student who sometimes may feel overwhelmed by the highly technical product reviews and facility feature articles found in most trade publications. Most of the recording students with whom I work seem to come away with a better understanding of a specific topic in recording after reading one of Rick Clark's articles.

This book is a collection of interviews with the big-name folks in the audio industry. There is a sense of validity attached to an article featuring well-known engineers and producers describing important techniques of recording in their own words. Many times a student will assume that their professors are out of touch with current recording trends and that textbooks are too methodical and dated to be of any use. My hope is that once they've read this book, they'll realize that there are standard practices and techniques of recording that are tried and true, as well as a few creative tools described by these regular practitioners of audio recording.

I would like to recommend *Mixing, Recording, and Producing Techniques of the Pros* to anyone interested in learning more about the traditional aspects of audio recording, from microphone techniques to use of compression to working with artists and getting a good headphone mix. All of the topics covered in this book feature standard practices and procedures utilized by some of the best known practitioners, and these techniques are explained in their own words. I want to commend Rick Clark for compiling these articles and publishing them in a concise and easy-to-read format. I look forward to using this as a supplemental textbook in all of my recording classes.

Cosette René Collier

Associate Professor
Department of Recording Industry
Middle Tennessee State University

About the Author

Rick Clark is a producer, film music supervisor/consultant, and veteran music journalist whose work includes articles in dozens of major publications (including *Rolling Stone, Details, Musician, Billboard, The Oxford American,* and *Mix* magazine), as well as liner notes for numerous albums. His credits include producing the entire award-winning *Oxford American* music series of CDs, producing and directing video for two Emmylou Harris DVD-Audio/Video releases, and production for the latest Los Super Seven album *Heard It on the X* (which features the talents of Calexico, Lyle Lovett, John Hiatt, Delbert McClinton, Raul Malo, Rodney Crowell, Joe Ely, Flaco Jimenez, Ruben Ramos, Augie Meyers, and Rick Trevino, among others).

Contents

Introduction

First things first: This book is an update of a previous work called *The Expert Encyclopedia of Recording*. Like its previous incarnation, this edition wouldn't exist without the years of experience generously shared by the many producers, engineers, mixers, mastering engineers, and others who are featured in these pages.

I consider it a blessing to have met and learned from so many incredibly nice and talented people over the years. Many of those featured in this book have become good friends.

This book not only draws upon years of interviews I've done with hundreds of wonderfully gifted people in the recording industry, it is also a way I can sum up a huge piece of my life in one place.

The Sparks to the Heart

I fell into writing out of the pure love of music. It was the overflow from a life spent listening, playing, writing, and recording music in Memphis, my hometown.

I grew up around the old Sun 45 records when they were new and came of age when Stax and Hi Records were starting to hit. Music was everywhere and Memphis nurtured me down to my soul. It's a place that is inspiring and maddening and I have loved it enough to hate it and love it all over again. I still travel there regularly just to keep myself properly fine-tuned with its vibe and great barbecue.

Besides indigenous music, I grew up with a love for a wide variety of other musical genres.

My pre-rock musical passions were classical piano (Brahms' "Second Piano Concerto" is an all-time favorite), choral music ("Pilgrim's Chorus" from Wagner's *Tannhauser* and Bach's "St. Matthew's Passion"), ragtime Dixieland (particularly Sweet Emma and the Preservation Hall Band), and show music giants like Gershwin, Cole Porter, Rogers and Hart, and Rogers and Hammerstein.

The arrival of The Beatles totally threw me into rock and pop, and the two nights they performed on Ed Sullivan are events I'll never forget. I saw my first pop concert in 1965, which was James Brown. Every moment of that amazing show is etched on my mind. I bought my first three rock albums in one day: *For Your Love* by the Yardbirds, and *Kinda Kinks* and *Kink-Size* by the Kinks. My first 45's were the Yardbirds' *Shapes of Things*, the Kinks' *Till the End of the Day* and the Byrds' picture sleeve release of *Eight Miles High*. I still listen to these records with the excitement I felt way back then.

Plugging In

Like many kids, it was only a matter of time before I would pick up an instrument and join a band. My first paid gig was in 1969, two months after I had first picked up my first bass guitar and amp, which was a white plastic Hagstrom and a Harmony amp that had to be kicked when it would occasionally start to develop a loud crackling sound. We played at something like a Young Republicans backyard party for twenty dollars and recorded it on an early stereo Panasonic cassette recorder. I still have that tape of us butchering Booker T. & the MG's, Pink Floyd, Blodwyn Pig, and Steve Miller. It's a priceless document of innocence and joy.

From then on, I played every chance I could get. By the mid-nineties, I had performed in every imaginable venue, from the pits of chicken-wire-around-the-stage redneck dives to huge arenas, either as a band mate or sideman.

Magic in the Deep Grooves

While I loved playing live, it was always recorded music that captured my imagination. Listening to recordings has always been like hearing paintings, and I still feel that way.

Records were such mysterious things to me. You put a needle in a groove on a spinning vinyl disc and this wonderful sound came out of the speakers. Often, I would become entranced by a certain song, or part of a song, and end up playing it dozens of times in one sitting. I memorized every instrumental part, every reverb or effect and anything else that caught my ear—even the unintentional magic I experienced from seeming mistakes in the performances, production or recording.

When I wasn't playing in a band, I was working at Memphis' coolest record store, Poplar Tunes. It was also Memphis' only record store at the time, and in the late sixties and early seventies, it was a scene. Every week we had local people like Isaac Hayes, Al Green and other legends, as well as artists from all over the world hanging out in the store.

My vinyl fixation was made even more intense there, and by the time I left Poplar Tunes in 1973, I had already amassed a few thousand LPs.

Light My Fire: The First Sessions

My first studio session was in late 1969 or early 1970 in Memphis at a place called Block Six, which was owned by producer Larry Rogers. I remember sitting under the huge Altec Voice of the Theater speakers and trying to play bass on four songs: "Kansas City," "Light My Fire," "Cinnamon Girl," and an original by the organist. I was instructed that bass players needed to play with a pick, instead of using the fingers. I'll never forget the feeling of being directed like that and noticing how the pick changed the sound.

I remember pantomiming to these songs for two shows on WHBQ-TV 13's *Talent Party*, featuring host George Klein, who was part of Elvis' "Memphis Mafia." Paul Revere & The Raiders showed up on choppers and "played" and, I believe, the Vanilla Fudge were on the other time we appeared.

Shortly thereafter, I began spending time at two studios, Ardent Recording and Shoe Productions. It was at that time I met the guys in a band called Big Star and started working with Memphis power-pop artists Tommy Hoehn and Steve Burns. Warren Wagner and Wayne Crook, the owners of Shoe Productions, basically gave us the keys to the studio. We spent countless hours learning on a truly home-made console that looked like an automobile gasoline tank with slits in it for faders and metal folding chairs for stands. We did everything wrong; it was all trial and error, and of that mostly error! There were no books or teachers around to tell us not to bounce guitars on a drum track or whatever. The whole concept of an educational program for rock and rollers was a pipe dream and there was certainly no one around to mentor us. As the years passed, I continued gigging and recording in Memphis and the friendship and support from people in the studio community has been priceless.

Putting the Passion into Words

I kind of fell into writing in the eighties when Tom Graves, an editor of a new magazine called *Rock and Roll Disc*, asked me if I would write for their debut issue. I was busy as a producer, musician, and songwriter out of Memphis, and I figured that this would be merely something I did to channel my passion when I wasn't doing music. Little did I know that I would write in every issue for the life of that magazine, which turned out to be several years.

Dave Marsh and Peter Guralnick were also contributors for this publication, which was supposed to be a compact disc equivalent to the *New York Times Book Review*. The writing came from the heart and Tom was a good editor. I learned a lot and probably never made more than a hundred dollars for the total time I wrote for them. Lesson number one: you don't write for music publications if you think you are going to actually make money. Music writing is the literary world's equivalent to working in a record store. You are there because you love music. Unfortunately, publishers know this, too. Nevertheless, it put me in front of some serious readers.

Writing about music seemed natural and by the time a couple of years had passed, I had been published in *Billboard*, *Rolling Stone*, *Details*, *Goldmine*, *Guitar Player*, *Music Express* and a number of other publications. It was weird how it happened, because I never had this in mind as a career path.

I had played thousands of gigs, live and in the studio, had song cuts as a songwriter and was focused on a career as an artist.

That said, I was one who voraciously read every music magazine and book I could get my hands on. There was a time when *Rolling Stone* was required reading, as was *Musician* during Bill Flanagan's time as editor. *Mix* magazine was another I read cover to cover.

The Art of the Q&A

One thing I always loved was a good Q&A interview, and I naturally studied what made such satisfying reads. In fact, to this day, I would rather read a person's own thoughts than some writer's interpretation of them.

One book that I count as a serious influence was Bill Flanagan's thoughtful *Written in My Soul*. It was a collection of his *Musician* magazine interviews of artists discussing the creative process all compiled in one great collection. I've read it dozens of times over the years. Flanagan's interviews reflected a kind of care and thoughtfulness that taught me a lot about treating subjects with dignity.

My first interview was with jazz flautist Herbie Mann. He was in Memphis for some reason that now escapes me. He was a thoroughly charming man and I realized that I enjoyed the process of getting people to talk about their passions.

Around that time, I had already been published enough to know that I didn't really enjoy writing features on some new hot act or writing reviews. I was acutely aware of all the work and dreams that went into making recordings, and I witnessed enough pain induced by uncaring egotistical writers who should've known better. The only guideline I had in review writing was to make sure that I wrote it like I was talking to the artist face to face. That way I had to be responsible for saying what I truly meant in a constructive fashion.

Finding My Groove

Even though I had written in many departments of *Billboard*, it was Thom Duffy and Paul Verna who opened the Pro Audio section up and allowed me to dive in writing about the recording world. It was the first time I really felt charged as a writer.

The majority of producers, engineers, mixers, mastering engineers, and others involved behind the glass aren't self-involved star mentalities. With few exceptions, most are low key, approachable and generous to share their knowledge. In fact, they are often surprised that anyone would really want to interview them.

As someone who came of age in music before there were academic programs that taught about recording and the music industry, the idea of talking with those I admired for a magazine feature was like getting paid to have private tutorials.

About fifteen years ago, I began writing for *Mix* magazine. It was the beginning of a working relationship that, to this day, I cherish. My editors, Blair Jackson and Tom Kenny, are true buddies, and all the others at *Mix* are wonderful, too—George Peterson, Sarah Benzuly, Sarah Jones, Maureen Drowney, Breean Lingle, and Heather Johnson. It's quite a family. Of all the magazines in which I've been published, I'm proudest of my association with *Mix*.

Mix magazine has afforded me the chance to interview many of the people I've most admired in the world of recording. Besides feature interviews, *Mix* has let me write numerous application features that showcase pros sharing their knowledge on various topics. It is from these features that the idea of this book began. Essentially, I returned to the original interview transcripts and intros for those features and expanded upon them.

The Process

Unlike many writers, I've always had a ridiculous need to completely transcribe every single interview. Over the years, I've transcribed thousands of pages featuring hundreds of conversations with people ranging from Chet Atkins, John Fogerty, Peter Gabriel, and Mark Knopfler, to Ry Cooder, Allen Toussaint, Tony Visconti, and David Z.

I've always noticed how many conversations, especially longer ones, are often laid out like helixes. After the first five to ten minutes (when there is an urgency to get key points articulated), there is an ebb and flow where the circles of conversational thought line up and certain themes re-emerge. It is then when the key payoff happens and everything comes together.

I'm convinced that, while people might not remember their exact words, they do recognize themselves in those words chosen when they read them. I've always felt a responsibility to get it right, and that care helped those interviewed feel like their time was dignified with meaningful attention.

Out of a twenty, forty or one hundred and fifty page interview with one person, I might only use a small percentage for the feature at hand. That interview, however, would often contain a wealth of other great stuff that never made it into the magazine.

Most all of the interviews in this book have taken place over the course of the last ten years. While technology is changing so much that it is almost impossible to keep up, this book hopefully shares proven techniques, as well as creative ideas for producing, recording, mixing, and mastering music.

Some Words on This Book

I've tried to mix it up so that there is something for everyone here. Some things might sound like nonsense or seem tedious to one person but seem absolutely brilliant to another reader. Just as there are many genres of music, there is a diverse range of personalities. Just check out the selected discographies section to get a sense of the world of ecumenical offerings involving the contributors who are represented in this book.

As much as this book showcases the more technical applications of making music, I've made a point to make a lot of room for more philosophical musings. After all, this is about capturing creative sparks and paying attention to the space in between the notes.

To Those Who Made This Possible

There are many people who deserve my thanks, From my years gigging and recording in Memphis, I would like to specifically point out John Fry, Jody Stephens, John Hampton (an original Chew Head), and Skidd Mills from Ardent Recording, as well as Tim Goodwin of Memphis Sound Productions, Paul Zalesky of Stairway Recording, Steve Hauth and Ronnie Kietell for their endless hours at Steve's studio in Cleveland and Larry Lipman and Richard Ranta of the University of Memphis' fine recording program. Jon Hornyak and the Memphis Chapter of NARAS have also supplied much valuable assistance over the years.

Other Memphis friends (some of whom have moved to Nashville) include George Bradfute, Steve Ebe, Robert "Bobby Memphis" Jordan, Joe Hardy, Keith and Jerene Sykes, Carl Marsh, Greg Morrow, Ross Rice, Rusty McFarland, Jack Holder, Johnny Phillips, Gary Belz and Jesse Brownfield.

Two people who did their best to provide support through thick and thin are Debbie Edmiston and Mary Clark. I learned a lot during those years together. Thank you.

One true brother and partner in insane recording exploits at studios in Memphis and (particularly) Wishbone and Fame in Muscle Shoals is Mark Marchetti. We wrote loads of songs together and had a blast making music. Along the way, we even landed some song cuts and one that became a Billboard Top Twenty Country hit. Thanks Gail Davies! Mark now lives in Nashville, helps run Loretta Lynn's publishing company and is married to one of her twin daughters, Peggy. They have a wonderful son, Lucca. Way to go, Mark!

Another Memphis buddy who has inspired and challenged me and has been a true friend is producer, musician, songwriter and devoted family man Jim Dickinson. Jim, in more ways than he knows, held up a lens that helped me focus who I was in my culture from the Delta South and put a lifetime of feelings and understanding into something I could truly own and articulate with pride in my life and in my work.

The Nashville community has been incredibly nurturing. Special thanks to Trip Aldredge, Bob Bailey-Lemansky, Richard Dodd, Michael Wagener, Bill Lloyd, Brad Jones, Tony Brown, Bob Doyle, Brian Williams at SunTrust, Lee Swartz, Richard Bennett, Lauren Koch, Chuck Ainlay, Justin Neibank, Jim Zumwalt, Benny Quinn, John Allen, Peter Cronin, Pete Langella, Joe and Marc Pisapia, Nichole Cochran, Michael Rhodes and Georgetown Masters' Andrew Mendelson and staffers John Baldwin (Johnny eBay) and Matt Beal.

Speaking of Georgetown Masters, I have to offer special props to one of its founders, the late and truly great Denny Purcell. Since Denny passed away on August 22, 2002, a week doesn't go by without me pondering his commitment to excellence, his philosophical musings and way off-kilter humor. Months before he died, Denny would talk about how we live in the "Age of Good Enough." He saw how mediocrity was a pervasive cancer in society, and he also passionately talked about how ease of use in technology, for example, enabled us to produce a glut of "good enough" in the music industry. He is so right.

Norbert Putnam, the other co-founder of Georgetown Masters, has also been a real friend and valuable sounding board over the years. Norbert has an unstoppable drive to make concrete the things most people are too fearful to test outside of their passing dreams. He's taught me more than he realizes.

Another true believer who has opened doors for me in many areas of opportunity and understanding is my steadfast ally Brian Ahern, one of the very few I believe is a producer on the most rarified level of insight and execution. Emmylou Harris describes Brian as having a teacher's heart. No truer words can be said, and I'm grateful for his rich insights and loyal support.

Dan Goodman, who co-founded the powerhouse Vector Management with Ken Levitan, has also been right there with me through the years. He has cheered me on when I rose to the task and delivered the goods. He's also kicked my ass harder than almost anyone I know. We've been through thick and thin, and he has never wavered as an honest, straight-up, thoughtful friend. We've worked together on several projects, but our best collaboration to date has been conceiving and producing (with Charlie Sexton) the Los Super Seven album *Heard It on the X*, an homage to the spirit of Border Radio that featured the talents of Calexico, Ruben Ramos, Rick Trevino, Joe Ely, Freddy Fender, Flaco Jimenez, Augie Meyers, John Hiatt, Raul Malo, Rodney Crowell, Delbert McClinton and Lyle Lovett among others. Dave McNair, who engineered, mixed and mastered this album for the Telarc label, became a great friend over the course of this project, and I appreciate his balance of paying attention to detail, while not over-thinking things.

Middle Tennessee State University also kicked in some greatly appreciated time and energy in the assembling of this book. Cossette Collier, who teaches engineering at MTSU among other things, helped with the initial editing, before the book went to the publisher. She also contributed the nice foreword. MTSU interns, who have assisted at various stages include John Livengood, Damon Dugger, Erin Addotta, Jonathan Coomes, John Oberleas, Taner Shores and Courtney White. Belmont University interns who have also contributed include Brice Turner, Daniel Kelly and Scott Campbell.

Outside of Nashville, I need to thank Tim Monich, Tony Visconti, Allen Sides, Michael Brauer, Rudy Trubitt, John Agnello, Don Gehman, Jennifer Thiltgen, Tom Tucker, Rob Grenoble, Bob Hinkle, Rob Bowman and the great Gus Dudgeon, who is no longer with us. I loved his passion for great music and all the hours we spent in animated discussion over anything that captured our hearts. No wonder he produced such durable classics! A fond remembrance also to Hunter Thompson, who in the few times our paths crossed, provided a reminder that I should fearlessly protect the fire within.

I'm very thankful to my good buddy Bill Bentley (VP of Publicity at Warner Bros.) who did "God's work" (as Jim Dickinson calls it) by hooking me up with the late great David Briggs shortly before he tragically passed away. Briggs never gave interviews and I'm very thankful to have spent a week with him in Memphis sharing stories and eating Little Pigs barbecue. It is easy to understand, after meeting Briggs and reading his passionate quotes, why he was involved in producing Neil Young's greatest rock albums.

One late rock producer I've would've loved to have interviewed is Guy Stevens, the fiercely mercurial force behind Mott the Hoople's hardest rocking albums and the Clash's incendiary *London Calling*.

One person who has been a foundation and true support throughout the making of this book is my wonderful wife, Allison Black. Her great heart, richly nuanced intellect, incredible sense of wonder and playful humor has inspired me day after day to be more awake and attuned to the gifts in this life—my marriage to her being one of them. The day we married was one of the more perfectly realized days in my life, as was the day my daughter, Sarah Clark, was born.

I can't say enough how proud I am of Sarah and her creative mind and wise heart. I'm always amazed at how she can pack up and head to Europe or wherever, pick up work, see the world and come home— each place offering a kind of replenishment. I've always admired her self-reliance and fearless vagabond spirit. In the world of the artistic disciplines, being awake to the essence of the moment and having the wherewithal to follow it through are key in manifesting life affirming magic—real art. Thanks Sarah.

Finally, this book wouldn't have happened had it not been for Mike Lawson, a songwriter/artist in his own right whom I met in Nashville when he was trying like hell to manage a dysfunctional artist and get a music software business off the ground. Within a couple of years, Lawson was working at *Mix* running the book division, and after that, running his own publishing company, ArtistPro.

If there is one thing I've learned, it is that life re-introduces people and situations in the weirdest ways and it behooves one to be on good behavior at all times. Little did I know that this bass-playing Deadhead named Mike Lawson would end up at *Mix* wanting to do a book with me.

Within an hour of Lawson informing me of his desire for a book, I called back with the idea for this project. It took four years to get around to doing this, but I'm thankful to Mike for his patience, support and good humor throughout the process of making this happen.

All these people, as well as each person who contributed to the insights offered in this book, helped direct me in ways that gave me more depth and range in my work. Everything that is good in this book has something to do, great or small, with each of them, and to that end this is their book and I've been a grateful student. Thanks!

Rick Clark
July 2005

CHAPTER 1

Acoustic Ensemble Recording

There is nothing quite like the sound of the well-recorded musical interplay found in an ensemble of acoustic instruments. Long before "unplugged" became part of the pop culture lexicon, Nashville was mastering the art of recording all of the great acoustic country and bluegrass groups that rolled through the town. Capturing the unique individual characteristics of each instrument and understanding how to present the chemistry of the overall band sound requires skill and sensitivity to the special dynamics of the players.

I gathered a handful of Music City's finest players and producer/engineers—Chuck Ainlay, Jerry Douglas, Mark O'Connor and Bil VornDick—to discuss their thoughts on how to capture the sparks on tape. Special thanks also to Ellen Pryor and Elliot Scheiner for their supportive input.

CHUCK AINLAY

If you were searching for the archetype of a consummate engineer who has a really great vibe, it would be Chuck Ainlay. Ainlay's credits include heavyweights like Mark Knopfler (solo and with Dire Straits), Trisha Yearwood, Vince Gill, Steve Earle, Lyle Lovett, Wynonna Judd, and George Strait.

For Vince Gill's album *High Lonesome Sound* we used Alison Kraus' band for the title cut. They played on the country version with drums and everything, and we also did another version, which is bluegrass. Both versions are on the album.

If you are talking about bluegrass, the players really like to hear and watch each other. That is how they perform live. So when we did the bluegrass version, I basically used baffles laid out like a spoked wheel, where the baffles were radiating out from the center like the spokes. This created compartments where each person could look towards each other in the center, and the mics would be back sort of closer to the center pointing towards each player. That way, you could use the directional characteristics of the cardioid microphones to reject the other instruments of the other players at other areas in the other spokes. Cardioid is generally what I use. I rarely ever use omni microphones.

You don't want to get the mics too close to any sort of wall, because that would change the character of the microphone, too. So they are not right into the point of the pie, so to speak. I used baffles, because I wanted a real clean tight sound with not a lot of ambiance from the room.

Generally, for tracking the acoustic guitar, I'll usually use one mic sort of near the twelfth fret out maybe six inches from the guitar. Then I'll have another mic, generally shoulder height and out maybe two feet from the guitar, probably kind of above the bridge or the general vicinity. If I then decide to double the acoustic guitar, I usually go over the far mic, because it is just too big. The doubling already gives you that extra warmth.

I love a Neumann KM-56 or KM-54 on an acoustic. That is usually my choice of a close mic. They have a nice top end and the bottom

1

end is rolled off pretty well on them. I will also use a KM-84 Neumann. For the second mic, the one that may be located about shoulder height, I would start with maybe a Neumann U-67.

On [Vince Gill's] acoustic, I will use a 452 AKG, because the isolation is better. The polar pattern is tighter, so I can get away with using that microphone and still use the tracking acoustics. The problem with those microphones on acoustics is sometimes that they can be too brittle sounding, so you add some warmth to them in the midrange area. Yet you will need to roll out on the bottom, because when you have a vocalist, you have to mic close.

have gone to kind of cheap guitars like Takamines, because they don't have a lot of bottom end and a real rich character to them. What you are really looking for is a percussive strumming sound, rather than a filled out acoustic sound.

I'm not a big fan of DI's, and I'm also a very big fan of uncomplicated sources. That is also why I say that I'm not a very big stereo miking fan. For fiddle, I really like the C-12. It works great. Mark O'Connor, who is one of the greatest fiddle players, always carried with him an AKG C-24, which is the stereo version of the AKG C-12.

Also the Neumann M-49 is a much warmer microphone and when you get them further away

The Neumann U-67 and power supply.

U-67's are great on acoustics, if you are going for that bashing acoustic guitar sound. If you are using a Gibson acoustic that is being played hard, you can take a U-67 and mic it further away from the guitar, just straight out from the hole of the guitar and get a great sound. Naturally, it all depends on what the player is doing.

The quality of the guitar also makes a lot of difference. For just pure strumming, a lot of guys

from the instrument and they are going to sound very real.

For upright bass, I use two microphones. Usually there is one microphone about a foot and a half away from the double bass about bridge height and then the second mic is usually closer to the bass, maybe about eight to ten inches looking at the left shoulder of the bassist. That way you get the percussive wood plunk from the bass

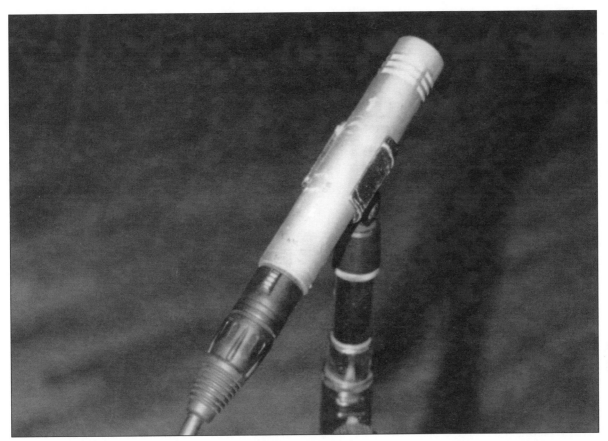

The Neumann KM-84.

there. You get your bottom end from down near the bridge.

Sometimes, depending on the bass, you have to get it closer to the "F" hole;—though some basses will have certain notes that really stick out if you get too close to the "F" hole.

Upright bass is one of the hardest things to mic. Your two microphones can cause some serious cancellation on bass, because of the low frequencies. I still try and put the upright bass in a separate room, because it is not a very loud instrument. You still want to have control and you are going to get leakage with it.

For mandolin, I rarely mic with two mics. It is just too small of an instrument. Then again, I have actually used two mics [laughs]. Again, it all depends on the mandolin. Some mandolins are richer and warmer than others. Generally the favorite position is near the "F" hole. But getting too close to the "F" hole can be too thick. If you are looking for that "woody" sound, that is where it comes from.

I don't think that there is anything all that special that we do. I always like to point out that it comes from the musicians and the music. I can't tell you how many times I've sat there and pulled up levels and it just sounded like crap and I'm tweaking knobs like crazy, trying to get it sound good. Then all of a sudden it sounds good, but it isn't because I tweaked the knobs like crazy. It is because the performance came together and all of a sudden everybody was listening to each other and they were playing tight. I think we are important people in not ruining this and making it comfortable for the musicians, but it still gets down to the players.

JERRY DOUGLAS

Producer, solo artist, and multi-instrumentalist Jerry Douglas has Alison Krauss, Del McCoury, and Lonesome River Band to his credit. Douglas has produced almost 30 albums over the course of his career.

I like the live performance vibe and keeping everything as organic as possible going down on tape. I always do first takes, because that is when all the energy is up and it is the scariest for everybody. I don't erase anything. I don't punch into live tracks. I do adjacent tracks for instruments.

If we need to fix something, then great. But if there is a chance of leaking, then we do another take or another edit possibly. This is because you don't want the chance of "ghosts," which is what you get a lot in acoustic music. When you overdub, you run the chance of still hearing the old part off of someone else's track. So it is worth doing another take.

When you are working with a bluegrass act, like Del McCoury for instance, whose band plays really dynamic bluegrass, I would try and cut live without much isolation and get some tight mics on everybody. I like to sit everybody around, so everyone can hear and see each other and not be completely dependent on headphones, but use them if they want to.

For picking out the mics in this kind of situation, I would shy away from the bigger diaphragm microphones. It is a give and take situation, because I love the old big diaphragm microphones for when these instruments are isolated, because they capture the whole sound of the instrument and not just a spot on the instrument.

We often use these big foam baffles. It is amazing how much isolation you can get from one of those things. Then it becomes easier to replace parts, if something goes wrong.

Bass and fiddle are kind of hard to track in the same room. Fiddle just takes off all over the room sometimes and bass goes to the floor and shows up in the strangest places. I try to isolate the fiddle out of the room, like I would the vocal, too.

If we are going for a real live situation, I just do two takes and edit. But if we were trying to isolate everyone, I would put fiddle in a different room and try and have an iso booth for fiddle and one for vocal.

MARK O'CONNOR

Nashville violinist Mark O'Connor has enjoyed a career that has enabled him to follow his artistic muse from bluegrass to jazz/rock fusion to more classically oriented undertakings. O'Connor (once one of the Nashville session world's most in-demand A team players) has recorded on projects like Will the Circle Be Unbroken #2, *Michael Brecker's Grammy Award winning album* Don't Try This at Home, *James Taylor's Grammy Award winning album* Hourglass *and Linda Ronstadt, Emmylou Harris and Dolly Parton's* Trio *album.*

As a solo artist, O'Connor has been nominated for seven Grammy Awards, and won a Grammy for Best Country Instrumental Performance in 1992, for his album New Nashville Cats. *Other albums are* Heroes, Liberty *and a live album of solo performances, recorded in St. Louis' Shelton Hall, called* Midnight on the Water.

When I've done bluegrass recordings, often people will want the option to replace their solos and fix parts. Obviously, it is harder to do that in recording sessions where you are all playing in the same room. So when you do a democratic project, like Strength In Numbers, you want to leave the studio knowing that you got what you wanted on tape. As a result, it made sense to be isolated. So before we were done with the song, we got the solo we wanted on there and we left and that was it. End of story.

When I did the *New Nashville Cats* album, I put everybody in the same room and said, "Trust me. I'm going to edit together pieces from different takes."

I am a much greater fan of editing, because (as the artist and producer) I can listen to takes and find out the parts that have the best musical energy. If the players got a really great solo section, but they completely botched the last head, then I can have the freedom to experiment with editing on a head from a different take for instance. That kind of flexibility is actually more musical than overdubbing.

When you overdub, the other instruments are not playing with you anymore. They are playing to another solo. So what the soloist does on the overdub is not complete musical communication. So even though the editing to a novice recording musician might sound harsh in approach, it is actually more musical, especially if the tempos are fine and the energy and intensity matches up. Then you can interchange between takes. That is what I do on most of the things that I do. It depends on how complex the music is. I think the more complex the music is, the more that you have to rely on editing.

I've recorded most every solo performance I've done for years, trying to get better and better with it. When I finally realized that I was ready to record an album of these performances for real, I picked one of my most favorite places I've performed solo: the old Shelton Hall in St. Louis, which was built in 1875. I rented it out and got the

humid climate. There are some violins that start to sound muddy or like they are stuffed with socks, in a warmer humid climate, where mine just sounds lush. Whereas when I get in too dry of a climate, it sounds too trebly and scratchy and squeaky and it just drives me crazy.

As a matter of fact, one of the halls I considered recording in for *Midnight on the Water* was a beautiful hall in Aspen that is underground.

A 2-channel Dolby SR unit.

great mics up, my old M-49 Neumanns and the old AKG C-24, and played in front of a live audience and really did it right.

For the *Midnight on the Water* recording, I used my two old Neumann M-49's in a stereo configuration. (The C-24 is very good for close miking, but not as much for accurate ambient miking, whereas the M-49's are almost like the human ear.) So when I recorded my solo performance, I was actually achieving the instrument sound and the sound of the hall, the ambiance and everything all at one time with those two mics. It really worked out.

I also used the M-49's on my *Heroes* album, so I could have completely matched sounds between me and the other guest violinists. The only difference that you were hearing between the violin sounds was the actual player and the instrument and not the way it was recorded. So each violin had one M-49, each of which were evenly matched from the same vintage year.

Temperature changes the sound and it changes the instrument. My violin is very sensitive to humidity. My violin sounds better in a warmer

When I performed my concert there a couple of years ago for the Aspen Music Festival, I loved everything except the sound of my violin. It was too dry. I thought about humidity problems and I went, "You know, I'm going to record this in the South during the summer in humidity" and so I did it in September in St. Louis in a beautiful old hall called the Shelton Hall. My violin sounds so rich on that recording, like it almost covers me. It sounds like it reaches out and embraces you almost. That is what I dreamed about. With humidity, I can make my violin sound like that.

That said, the humidity in this concert hall completely changed at night from the day. In some instances, it was as drastic as having an audience in there and not having an audience in there. It was that extreme. In most studios, you don't have to worry about that as much. But in concert halls, it's a consideration. So I realized that when I perform some of this stuff, I had to do it now in this time period, or I'd have to start all over [laughs]. That was a little added pressure.

The biggest thing is to make sure that you can play your best. If the climate is changing, but you are in a place where you feel you can play your best, then that more than compensates for the problem.

BIL VORNDICK

Bil VornDick is one of Nashville's finest engineers for understanding what it takes to make great recordings that feature acoustic instrumentation.

Among his many credits are Jerry Douglas (since the early eighties up to his latest record), Edgar Meyer, Bela Fleck (since the early eighties), Doc Watson, James Taylor, Alison Krauss, Clair Lynch, Maura O'Connell, Third Tyme Out, and a new Ralph Stanley album on the Rebel Record label called Clinch Mountain Country. *That release features an all-star cast of 32 artists, including Bob Dylan, George Jones, Vince Gill, Patty Loveless, Hal Ketchum, the Raybon Brothers and Diamond Rio.*

VornDick has engineered and/or had production credits on eight Grammy winning projects, plus 38 albums that have been nominated for Grammys.

I pick the musicians for the song, instead of just working with a normal rhythm section. I like everybody to be going down on tape at the same time. I want as many pieces to the puzzle working with each other and playing off of each other as possible, instead of starting with a click track. I go for the overall feel of a take. I'm a guy who still believes that people buy records because they feel good.

A good example: I had a number one song on a group called Third Tyme Out, and the B string was out of tune. But the person who was singing the lead vocal was doing the guitar at the same time. That was his best performance, and we couldn't re-do the guitar, because of the leakage. Maybe six or seven people have come up to me and said, "The B string is out of tune." I would say, "Yeah, we cut it quite a few more times, but the feeling and emotion wasn't there." I went with the best feeling performance that had the emotion within that helped sell the song. It still went to the top of the charts. There are some people, especially in Nashville, would go re-do the vocal and the guitar and do other things to deal with the B string on the guitar. I knew it was out of tune. Hey, it didn't hurt them. It was one of their biggest selling albums.

Currently, there is a now successful acoustic artist, whose roots were in bluegrass, cutting tracks with a click and then going back and replacing everything. As a result, you've got all of the nuances that originally went on with the little inner licks and dynamics of the song disappearing in order to be precise.

Most of the albums that I have done that have won the Grammys are all albums recorded on budgets between $10,000 and $20,000. These are not $250,000 albums. Alison Krauss' first Grammy winning record, I think, cost $12,500.

I mic everything in stereo normally, so that within those two mics I have a depth perspective on each instrument.

I'm a pretty hardcore analog guy. I would much rather paint in oils than in acrylics. You get the whole waveform in analog and in digital there are still quite a few overtones that the sampling rates are not catching. I can still hear them, but a lot of people don't give a damn. I normally cut at 30 ips with no noise reduction. If I can get into a facility that has Dolby SR, I like to cut at 15 ips with SR noise reduction. Digital may be cheaper, but analog is still the art form.

BRENT TRUITT

Before Brent Truitt became one of bluegrass and singer/songwriter folk music's most popular producer/engineers and studio owners, he earned his stripes as an in-demand session player and touring musician with Alison Krauss, The Dixie Chicks, John Hartford, Vassar Clements and others. Truitt's studio credits include Alison Krauss, Kathy Chiavola, Holly Dunn, Sweethearts of the Rodeo, Jon Randall, Gail Davies, Tom Roznowski and David Grier.

For recording acoustic music, let me also say that hopefully the person sitting in front of the mic has a good instrument. Common sense tells you that if the guitar sounds bad and won't play in tune, a great mic isn't gonna help. If I'm producing a band that may not have any real studio experience, I make sure they have their instruments tweaked up and ready to go before we get into the studio.

Sometimes people have a hard time recording the fiddle. It's easy for a fiddle to sound shrill, especially going to hard disk. My favorite fiddle mics are KM-86's. I almost always use a stereo pair in cardioid and run them through a couple of API's (smooth and warm). I usually place the mics on each side of the fiddle, maybe 10 or 12 inches apart. Try to leave plenty of room for bowing. In most cases I don't compress fiddle tracks going to tape. It seems to add that little extra harshness that you really don't want. Actually, too much compression on any acoustic instrument can be a bad thing. Use it sparingly going to tape.

As far as I'm concerned, the best mic for acoustic guitar is the KM-54 hands down. They aren't cheap or all that easy to find, but they are well worth searching out. I like to run a pair of these through a couple of Neves or API's and then into a pair of Urei 1176's. I get great results with that signal chain.

to much boom. The back mic position is almost never the same from one session to the next. Try moving the mic around while listening through the phones. The thing to watch out for is the midrange; sometimes that back mic can add an overly nasal quality to the sound.

Concerning the upright bass: this instrument is the reason my left eye twitches. It can be one of the most difficult beasts in the world to record, especially if it's not a very good bass.

By the way, there is a huge difference between a bass with gut strings and a bass with steel strings. Steel strings have more of a point to the sound, more sustain, and definitely cut through a mix a little easier. But sometimes a gut string bass, which usually has less point and more of a big bottom, is more fitting to certain kinds of tracks. For instance, I would probably go for steel string

Tube Tech compressor.

If you can't get the KM-54's, get a couple KM-84's. Even the newer KM-184 will do a great job for you. If you don't have the Neves or API's, the Avalon 737SP is a quality mic pre/comp/EQ that is affordable and really sounds wonderful on acoustic instruments. Mic placement on guitar is once again something to experiment with. I usually put one near the twelfth fret at an angle toward the sound hole being careful not to get

if the session were leaning more towards the progressive or modern side of acoustic music. But if the songs had more of an old time or hillbilly vibe, I would probably lean towards a gut string bass for that older sound.

I have been very fortunate over the years to have worked a lot with the late great Roy Huskey, one of the greatest bass players ever. He was a gut string man. Here are some details on how I cut his bass. I always used two mics on Roy. One of my favorite combos was a UM-57 (tube Neumann from the mid-fifties) on the right side, or low E side, maybe 10 inches back from the "F" hole. On the high side I put a KM-86 at about the area where he plucked the string and approximately 8 inches or so back. Both mics in cardioid and off axis or pointed kinda off centered from the sound source. Now here's where you can use some common sense. In case you don't have those mics, or that exact mic position may not sound good in your room, go out with headphones on and try moving the mics around the instrument until the sweet spot hits you. You'll know it when you hear it.

As far as mic pre-amps on Roy, I tried different pre-amps on different sessions but I always used a Tube Tech compressor at the end of the audio path. It always sounded great.

Another awesome bass player I've recorded is Todd Phillips. Todd is no stranger to anyone who knows acoustic music. He was a huge part of the early David Grisman sound. Todd is a steel string man. We usually cut Todd's bass with a KM-184 on the high side, near the area he plucks, along with the UM-57 on the low side kind of in front of the bridge and down a few inches. Both mics are in cardioid. From there we'll go into two Avalon 737SP's. The result is a very large and clear tone. Of course, Todd is a great player, giving me excellent tones to begin with, which makes it so very easy to record.

That's all great, but chances are pretty good that somewhere along the line you're going to end up recording a not so great bass. You might want to keep some pieces of foam handy to place in the tailpiece to help eliminate rattles and maybe some of the boominess. You might even try a small piece in the "F" hole to help with the boom. Sometimes you're basically just gonna have to hunt down some rattles and buzzes.

CHAPTER 2

Bass

Bass is the primal meeting ground of melody and beat. It doesn't matter whether it's a classic Motown or Stax soul groove, a four-on-the-floor country roadhouse rave-up, Paul McCartney's orchestrated four-stringed counterpoints, or Lemmy's eighth- and sixteenth-note distorto hyperdrive for speed metal band Motorhead; the bass is at the foundation of this experience we call music.

I enlisted six producers who have worked with a number of different kinds of basses: string bass, slap funk bass, rockabilly, 8- and 12-string basses and more. Once I got these six talking about it, it was apparent I could've easily filled a book. The following are a few thoughts on keeping you grounded, concerning matters of the bottom end.

NORBERT PUTNAM

Before Norbert Putnam became known as the producer of Jimmy Buffett's and Dan Fogelberg's biggest albums, as well as many other successful releases, he was one of the top session bassists in Nashville. Putnam's career as a bassist started with the classic seminal Muscle Shoals *Arthur Alexander hit, "You Better Move On."*

Over the years, Putnam's visceral, yet lyrical, bass playing has appeared on a who's who list of greats, from Elvis Presley, Henry Mancini and The Monkees to Linda Ronstadt and the Manhattan Transfer.

In the mid-sixties, the only way to record a Fender Precision bass was through an Ampeg B-15 with the bass and treble turned off and a Neumann U-87 shoved up near the speaker cone. You had the treble knob and volume full out on the Precision bass and fixed the final output level on the front of the Ampeg. Most engineers then applied two or three decibels of compression via an LA-2A or a Urei 1176. However, a few years later, almost all recordings were by direct box with the treble and volume still full out on the bass. I no longer had to haul a heavy amp. Yeah!

A little later on in the seventies, I had the Fender pickups wired directly to the output plug, bypassing the tone and volume pots. I thought this sound was cleaner and more hi-fi.

As for my acoustic bass, we recorded that two slightly different ways. One way utilized an RCA 44bx (this was for a thicker, tubby sound) placed level with the bridge and sitting in the corner of two low-rise gobos. But my favorite miking technique was the ubiquitous Neumann U-87 placed higher up near the plucking finger, about six inches above the bridge. This gave you the added attack of a heavily callused finger and the ability to use all sort of jazzy, buzzy sliding sounds. I used this placement on pop and rock sessions with Elvis, Henry Mancini, Al Hirt and hundreds of lesser gods.

My daily complement of equipment (in the sixties) was carried in the back of a 1965 Ford station wagon. Instrument cartage companies were nonexistent in 1965. So, I personally lugged my Ampeg B-15 tube amp, my 1956 Fender Precision and my 1925 Kay "plywood" acoustic bass to three or four studios a day. (I had abandoned my 200-year-old German instrument because of resonant "hot spots," which are highly resonant notes in an octave that registers and sounds much louder than the surrounding frequencies. In other words, "some notes louder than others." Not good!) I also had handy a bow and some rosin just in case an orchestra appeared.

The ability to use the inexpensive Kay bass was due to enhanced low frequencies from the close

Goodwon's bass on "Fever," which is off the new Ruby Wilson album on CDMemphis.com.

And how am I recording the electric bass today? A small Peavey amp (8" cone) and a direct box, on two separate tracks straight to hard disk. Later on in the mix room, we can listen to various "amp simulation" plug-ins if we want something different. They even have the old Ampeg B-15! Gee! It sure is easy to get great sounds these days!

The Neumann TLM 103.

proximity of the Neumann mic. Yes! That cheap old plywood "Kay" ate the hand-carved German instrument's lunch. Every note from the low E to the upper reaches of high G registered a zero level at the console. The engineers loved it! As a matter of fact, the level clear sound of that old Kay helped me pluck many accounts from my richer fellow bassists with more valuable axes.

Today, at my new studio (Cadre) in Memphis, we use a more modern Neumann TLM 103 instead of the Neumann U-87. The new Neumann has a lower noise floor to complement our new 24-bit recorders. As a matter of fact, check out Tim

DAVID Z

David Z's production and engineering credits include some of the biggest and most innovative artists of the last twenty years, particularly in the R&B/pop and blues-based music arena. For starters, Z worked on a number of classic Prince albums, including Purple Rain *and* 1999. *He shares production credits with the Purple One on the hit single "Kiss." Other credits include Janet Jackson, Etta James, John Mayall, Gov't Mule, Buddy Guy, Jonny Lang, Kenny Wayne Shepherd, Jody Watley, Big Head Todd and the Monsters, Billy Idol, Collective Soul and Leo Kottke and Mike Gordon.*

Number one, there is nothing like a good bass with a good tone. It has got to have a pure tone. There is no substitution, unless you are going to use a synth bass.

Concerning bass recording techniques, when a bass player is doing popping and funky licks, it's good to take away the middle, like 1 Hz. That kind of gives it a warm pillowy sound, yet there is a lot of high end in there, so the pops can come out, but it isn't too forceful.

I like to split the signal and use two different faders for the bass. One would be a tightly compressed signal with a lot of midrange to really sock it through, and the other would be very lightly compressed, but with a lot of bottom. I might have one with compression and one without. That way, I can EQ them totally differently. That way, I can combine the amount of each element, to make it work on lots of different sets of speakers.

Anybody can get a bass to sound huge on a big set of speakers, but you have got to have it translate to all kinds of small speakers and really horrible shitty speakers. I believe in the shitty speaker syndrome. For my home system, I have some big old KLH bookshelf speakers. They are really old and grungy, but I know what they sound like. I'm a bass fanatic; that is the thing I really fight to get right.

I love heavy bottom, but it can't be too heavy, because it makes everything a mess. Sometimes I will cut the bottom off with a filter, like below 30 or 40 Hz. Then you can boost a little more without muddying up the super sub-lows. I would probably boost it around 100 cycles. You have got to be careful, though. If you are mixing a dance record for the dance floor, you almost need the subs in there. You have got to be kind of careful, if it is going to end up in a club, or on some huge speakers. You have got to translate to that, too.

I have to mix on a lot of different systems. The big system in the studio is for the sub-lows. Then I have to switch to crappy speakers to get the midrange right. Then I might have to switch to some good NS-10 midrange and high-end speakers to get the high end right. I have a pair of these Little David speakers that are super hyped in the high end and the low end, but you get a totally different picture than an Auratone, or something like that. It is good to get it to sound right on every system you can. Bass is very elusive and you want it have power and punch, without vibrating the speakers till they rip. It is a fine balance.

SAM TAYLOR

Sam Taylor's production work has earned the respect of many in the industry, particularly with the first four critically touted King's X albums. Much of Taylor's work synthesizes the sophisticated arrangement sensibilities of his mentors George Martin and Geoff Emerick, with an assertive progressive and hard rock attitude. Taylor, a native Texan, has also produced albums for Galactic Cowboys, Atomic Opera and Bay Area band Annapurna.

Taylor likes getting as many instrument and amp choices, as well as the settings, as he can laid out in pre-production. He also prefers working with bassists who have a firm handle on their instrument and understand the concept of ensemble interaction.

I view the bass and kick drum as the basic pivotal foundation of what you anchor all of the other sounds to. I tend to approach it as one instrument. Before I go into the studio and record, I start back in pre-production making sure the bass player not only understands the concept of ensemble playing, but can play that way. If you have got four people in a band, it is not four different sounds. It is one sound. Everything has got to blend together. A lot of people don't know it, but their sound is based on the sound of everything around them. If they can figure that out, then you can come up with a really great ensemble.

For recording rock bass and drums, I like cutting 15 ips analog with Dolby SR, because of the warmth and beefy sonic quality I can achieve in that medium.

For the powerful King's X 8- and 12-string bass sound (which was played by Doug Pinnock), I employed a multiple miking set-up that enabled the bassist to switch instruments for different parts of the song, and insured sonic consistency.

When Doug started bi-amping, there might be as many as three mics capturing the high end and two mics on the low end. Those mics, plus a direct, would all be running live into the board, where we would assign them or mix them together, depending on what was sounding correct with the ensemble. I would keep the high end and the low end and the direct separate. That way I would have more control over it in the mix. I would re-compress all of those when I would use them. We would always tend to boost the high mids.

Sometimes we might change basses in the middle of a song, for a particular section. Doug might be playing a twelve and then he would switch to a four string for another section. This set-up would allow me to try and come as close to matching that, so you wouldn't feel that something had completely left.

A lot of times, with the 12- and 8-string basses, I would get Doug to double the 12- or 8-string part with his 4-string Hamer bass, which was one of the finest, cleanest basses I ever heard. It takes somebody who is really good, when you start doubling the low end of an instrument, because the sound waves are so far apart, any variation in the attack or intonation is very apparent.

Recently, I have become a big fan of engineer/designer John Cuniberti's Re-Amp, which is a super-clean tape-recorder-to-instrument-amplifier interface. The Re-Amp allows me to take a clean instrument signal (in this case, the bass guitar) and try out any number of amps and tonal settings.

The cool thing about the Re-Amp is you can plug the player in and he's ready, as long as he's got new strings on his bass and it is in tune. There is no need for any mics or to EQ his amp, he's ready to go. A bass player would be smart to have one of these. When they do a session, he can just say that this is what he uses for a direct. He plugs it into the patch bay and goes. When the track is done, he can help with the sounds and the miking of the amp. The bass player is involved in the process of getting his own sound again, without having to stand around and play a part over and over again while someone else is tweaking it. After all, we are making this together.

EDDIE OFFORD

Since the late sixties, Eddie Offord has amassed a discography that has included blues, jazz, pop, rock and practically anything else that comes to mind. It is his work with seventies art and prog rock bands that elevated him to legendary production/engineering status. He worked on the first four Emerson, Lake & Palmer albums and produced classic Yes albums, from The Yes Album *(which amazingly was his very first production) to* Relayer.

Offord has also worked with John Lennon, the Police, Dixie Dregs, Andy Pratt, Levon Helm and the RCO All-Stars, Wet Willie, David Sancious, John McLaughlin, Utopia, Tim Hardin, Thin Lizzy and 311 as well as doing film work on movies like The Last Waltz *and* Zabriskie Point.

For the well-known Chris Squire bass sound that helped give Yes much of its distinctive sound in the early seventies, we put the bass through more of a guitar amp set-up, which I think was a Sunn amp with either 10" or 12" speakers. I took it direct at the same time. On the amp, we went for lots of treble and distortion. I would just roll the bass end off of the amp, so it was all click and presence. I used the direct for the low end. I mixed those two signals together, while making sure they were in phase. By balancing the two, I could bring out the lows or focus on the treble side. I would usually bring out the upper midrange, about four or five thousand, to bring out that gritty trebly sound. By itself, the amp sounded like a piece of shit, but when mixed in with the direct, it sounded great.

Chris was the first guy I knew of that really wanted a sound that became more of a lead instrument, almost like a guitar. Before that, bass guitar was just there to provide the bottom. I still use the same principle recording bass. Of course that depends on the player and what he is looking for, too.

Whenever I can, I try to use the LA-2A tube compressors, which I think are really good. I compress the signal quite severely. For string bass, I prefer to have the player in an iso booth, if the player is amenable to the idea.

I did an album with John McLaughlin called *Extrapolation*. I put one of those hyper-cardioid pencil condenser mics really close to the bridge, so I could get the sound of the fingers on the strings. That way, I could get more presence and not so much boom. I usually place the mic an inch or two from the bridge, on the upper side of the bridge, pointing right at the strings.

GUS DUDGEON

Gus Dudgeon is best known for his work on what are considered by many to be Elton John's most critically and commercially successful albums. He also produced projects for David Bowie, XTC, Ten Years

After, Joan Armatrading, Audience, The Sinceros and The Bonzo Dog Band, among many others. Dudgeon always loved lyrical bass work, and what follows are some of this late great master's musings on the topic.

I'm a freak for bass, and I think that is because I wasn't allowed to go into any dodgy coffee bars when I was a kid. I used to hang around and listen to the jukebox outside. Most of the time you couldn't hear the voice or anything else, but you could always hear the bass. The bass would travel though the walls, the floor, and the pavement. I could recognize almost any hit record when I was a kid from just the bass line.

I hate listening to records that are bass-light. It drives me crazy if there isn't a full enough sound. A lot of bass players, when they come in sessions, will say, "I have this really great bass that's perfect for the stage, but I can never use it on sessions." I say, "Why?" And they say, "Because engineers also tell me it's too big a sound." And I say, "Get it out. Let's hear it." And nine times out of ten they play it and I go, "Thank you. That's the sound I want. I'm up for it."

During the sixties, when I was working for Decca as an engineer, damn near every bass part I ever recorded was written out by somebody. This is partially due to a certain dynamic. It was very difficult in that room to get a good bass sound. So, more often than not—in probably six out of ten sessions—it was quite normal to have two bass players on a session. One would be playing a string bass and the other would play the identical part with a pick on an electric bass. You then would combine the two sounds—the string bass sound and the click of the electric bass—and create one good sound. That was OK, but it didn't allow any freedom.

Once I got into a studio where I could get a decent bass sound, when bass players started worrying whether they were sticking straight to the bass drum I'd say, "Don't worry about it. Go somewhere else. Look for something else."

Bass players are always relegated to the back, aren't they? It's a noise to some people who look at the instrument like its only function is to hold the bottom together because the bass drum is boring and they need some notes to go with it. I could never understand that attitude.

If you were to take Herbie Flowers' part from David Bowie's "Space Oddity" and examine how many notes he played, he probably played 10 more notes than anybody else in the entire orchestra. He was constantly weaving in and out, digging around, never playing a wrong note and just looking for somewhere else to go. By the time the chord had changed, he had to go somewhere else then. It's like it's being rocket fired. It's permanently running along in the background.

Herbie Flowers and Dave Glover (bassists on Elton's *Tumbleweed Connection*) had a similar style. They always sounded like they were messing around trying to find the ideal note and were always playing great notes along the way in between. They were always looking for somewhere else to go instead of just sitting there and playing the root or the most obvious notes. It was like listening to a journey.

JIM DICKINSON

Bass has always figured as a major element in the Memphis sound, whether it be soul music, rockabilly, blues or rock and roll. Jim Dickinson has worked with all of it, as a producer and session sideman. Dickinson's production credits include Ry Cooder, North Mississippi Allstars, Sleepy John Estes, Jason and the Scorchers, Toots Hibbert, The Replacements, Big Star and John Hiatt. He has also worked with The Rolling Stones, Bob Dylan, Aretha Franklin, Primal Scream, Eric Clapton, Dr. John, The Cramps, Los Lobos and many more. Dickinson has also done extensive work on numerous films, including Gimme Shelter, The Long Riders, Paris, Texas, Crossroads, Streets of Fire *and* The Border.

A discussion with Dickinson about the role of bass in music goes beyond mere technical pointers into more philosophical areas. Like much of the great music and art from the Delta, Dickinson believes in artfully walking the line between clarity and implication.

For want of a better word, it is the mystery of the bass and the motion that I try and capture. Everyone says we are bottom-heavy in Memphis and thank God we are, because I think that is where the beat is. I don't think that the bass sound should be overarticulate. I think the bass can afford to be mysterious.

The great players of the sixties and seventies were all very mysterious. The perfect example is Bill Wyman, who is now being dismissed by some as if he were some kind of unimportant musical figure. As far as I'm concerned, the exact opposite is true. The role that he played on the early Rolling Stones records can't possibly be overemphasized. With Bill Wyman, it is the motion of his notes, more than his actual articulation that makes him special as a player.

It has been my good fortune, as a sideman and as a producer, to work with some of who I consider to be the greatest Fender P-bass players of our generation, like David Hood, Chris Etheridge, Tommy Cogbill, Duck Dunn and Tommy McClure, who to me was the greatest. There was a certain mystery to all of those players. The bass part wasn't up your nose. It was kind of floating around between your ears and behind your head somewhere. That is still the sound that I go for.

I find that the fewer times I record the ambiance of the room, the better. I will use an amp, while tracking, just deferring to the bass player. I almost never use that signal. I take the bass direct through some kind of tube pre, just to warm it a hair, and then, when I mix, I re-amp that signal in the room, and print that directly to the master. I prefer using an old B-15 or B-18 flip top Ampeg, if I can get it. It is still my favorite. Unless it is like a recorded processed sound you are after, the fewer times you record either the echo or the bass, the better off you are, as far as I'm concerned.

Another one of my preferences is to record the bass last in the control room, if the player is comfortable with the idea. I would rather record the bass last. Almost everybody overdubs bass right after the drum track. To me, if I can get a bass track I can live with, while overdubbing, I keep it. Then I let the bass player overdub last.

There is a very different focus to the performance when you are tracking. It's a different set of motives. I always tell them not to play anything that doesn't help the drummer. I am after a different kind of performance when I track, than by the end. I am definitely trying to "best" the performance of the track. That is what the record is about. Otherwise, it is just a documentary recording. Of course, I keep the live tracking bass, guitar or whatever it is, until I have bested it.

The idea of recording bass in the control room has to do with the distance between the speakers. The bass player can't hear the bottom end of his instrument through his phones anyway. I will always put the bass player in the control room, if he is up for coming, because it is the only place that he is going to hear his instrument. There is just enough physical delay, because of space and time, between the speakers and your ears, to put the bass player back in the pocket when the tempo is no longer an issue, because it is being dictated by the track when you are overdubbing, if you see what I mean.

With most music, R&B for sure, I want the bass player a little bit late, because I try to get the snare as dark as I can get it. If the bass player is dead in the pocket when we track, when I put him behind the big speakers in the control room, he's going to fall back in the pocket. I saw Sly (Dunbar on drums) and Robbie (Shakespeare on bass) do the same thing, when I produced the Toots Hibbert record Toots in Memphis. As soon as the tracking was over, Robbie walked into the control room, turned his back to the speakers and overdubbed every single bass part.

I understand the whole thing of having his back to the speakers. He was waiting for them. He simplified his parts when he overdubbed, which is one of my reasons for doing it later. With his own technique, he achieved everything that I tried to get in my process, which is get simpler and further back and down in the pocket bass parts. By playing in the control room, you can hear your notes better and articulate your overtones and all the stuff you can't possibly do, either with earphones or with a live amp in your face.

It's that not all music should have the bass on the backside of the pocket. This was especially true when we produced the Replacements' classic *Pleased to Meet Me*. Their bassist, Tommy Stinson, drove the band's groove by playing in front of the pocket. Stinson had a highly overdriven top-end-heavy sound, which presented a different kind of production approach.

Tommy Stinson played with his earphones on, because he heard the note almost instantaneously. The whole Replacements groove was in Tommy being in front of the beat and Chris Mars (drums) behind the beat and Paul Westerberg (guitar) in the middle.

Tommy played through a homemade 300-watt rig. I put the amp in the concrete equipment closet of the "B" studio in Ardent, and it was cranked all the time. I said, "Do you really need the 300 watts?" He said, "I've got 600 watts at home, man." He was trying to make that slapping roar and we were just miking that room. The room was so small, it was compressing. You could hear it all over the building. In that case, I definitely used the amp sound, as opposed to re-amping.

For acoustic string bass, I think that it is important to understand the value of finding the true bass tone out in the room.

People will jam stuff up in the bridge and up in the "F" hole and they will wrap microphones in foam and all that kind of crap. On the bridge, all you get is this little midrangey note. The big sound of the bass is coming out of the entire front and back surface. The thing people don't understand about miking an upright bass is that the sound is in the room.

A lot of the rockabilly slap bass guys had Kay basses that were basically boxes of plywood and sounded like shit. The closer you got with the mic, the more it sounded like a plywood box. If you had a good sounding room and the bottom end was coming off the floor, the further you backed off the mic, the better it got. The best bass sound you can get is from across the room, because the waveform is so long.

For the old Sun Records sound—think about how simple this is—you want the bass drum and the bass to have the same sonic space. Use the same microphone. Sam Phillips only had five microphones. He had one RCA Victor ribbon microphone in the sweet spot that was on the bass drum and the bass instrument. If he wanted more bass instrument, he got the bass player to move closer to the mic, in front of the bass drum. How easy can it be? Yet, can you get anyone to do that now? He was miking the room. All of his mics were open all the way around, sometimes with the exception of the vocal mic. He was mixing it all into mono, so there was no phase cancellation, and the sound of that room was wonderful.

CHAPTER 3

Compression

A number of years ago I was invited to spend a week visiting a well-respected boutique re-issue label and hang out with a number of renowned audiophiles and talk gear, listen to vinyl and wax about how so many re-issue CDs sound worse. I got on well with everyone and seemed to be making friends when, over a multicourse dinner in some fancy restaurant, I enthusiastically blurted out that I sometimes loved the sound of compression on drums, guitars and other things, and that, on occasion, the experience of hearing certain compressors working overtime in a recording provided a wondrous musicality to the overall sonic picture. There was silence at the table. My indiscretion was awkwardly excused, and then they reconfirmed their love for audiophile ideals.

Interestingly, only days before, several of these people professed an intense love for mid- to late-period Beatles records and the British Invasion. Imagine the Beatles' "Yer Blues" or "Revolution" without the inspired touch of monster compression causing the cymbals to roar in and out of the mix and make the bass throb the way it did.

This chapter is about compression, with no apologies, especially as it is used to turn up the rockets or provide unusual color to a soundstage. Sure, we all love meticulously miked recordings of symphony orchestras, chamber groups, jazz combos and so on, but this information is not for those purely interested in documentary recording.

KEN KESSIE

Ken Kessie is an L.A.-based producer/engineer who has worked with En Vogue, Tony Toni Toné, Brownstone, Vanessa Williams and Celine Dion. Recent credits include five songs on En Vogue's EVIII, mixing for All-4-One, and producing and engineering for L.A. buzz bands Sevensoft and Tuscaurora. His production of French superstar rapper Doc Gyneco's debut album resided at the top of the French charts for over a year.

Creative compression is all about breaking rules and doing what you're not supposed to. If you've got a deadline, you've got to go for what you know works. But when you feel that urge to step out and break new ground, try these ideas.

I sometimes make a cool faux stereo sound out of a mono one, not by time manipulation with a delay or pitch changer, but by dynamics. If you mult a single sound source to two faders, process them differently with two compressors and then pan them left and right, you'll get a sound with no additional time slop, but with space still in the center for a lead vocal. Try compressing one side really hard, while barely touching the other. With any luck, there will be some motion across the speakers. This works great on hi-hats, snare drums and other percussion instruments.

Another effective compression move involves the bass drum and bass. In a lot of the R&B mixes I do, the kick drum and bass often play at the same time. When in R&B-land, I always make the bass and kick huge—that's one reason I work a lot!—

then always have a problem fitting them both in the mix. What I do is compress the bass with the kick drum. You need a stereo compressor, with stereo linkage, and attack and release controls. So far, the Drawmer DL241 is my favorite. Send the kick drum to channel A, and slave channel B (the bass) to it. Every time the kick hits, it knocks down the gain of the bass, and by using the attack and release controls, you can get a perfect blend between the two. Settings vary for this, of course; use your ears rather than the meters.

When I'm working on an SSL board, I sometimes record through the stereo bus compressor. Here's the patch to access the compressor: In the SSL patchbay, find the section called Pre VCA and Post VCA. Using two patch cords, connect Pre VCA (top row) to Post VCA (bottom row). This bypasses the stereo compressor and the master fader. Inputs to the compressor are Pre VCA bottom row, and the outputs are Post VCA top row.

WARNING! This patch is possibly lethal to speakers or talent with headphones on. Only attempt at low volume in case of a disaster, and please note that the master fader is out of the circuit and cannot be used to lower the volume. It's worth it, though—this compressor sounds great, especially on acoustic piano.

Euphonix consoles have a dynamic filter preset called a "de-esser" in their dynamics presets. Since I don't over-EQ anymore—yeah, right!—I don't need de-essers as much, but I found that by lowering the frequency into those pesky cheap mids, the device can also act as a harshness filter, especially when there are lots of nasty midrange parts. I run it across the stereo bus, and tune it to remove just a pinch of ugly midrange when the track gets loud. It has a very smooth-sounding effect on the mix.

Many guitar stomp boxes have lots of personality, punch and, let's face it, horrible noise. Interface them with a preamp or DIs, or just plug and overload. Not only are these great for alt rock sessions, they are practically required for proper indie cred.

Look, we all know about short signal paths by now, but sometimes you gotta throw the book away. Sometimes it takes several compressors chained together to create the impact or smoothness needed for a standout sound. Sometimes one box acts as a peak limiter while the other works as

a low ratio compressor. There's no formula; just use your ears. And I do mean use your ears—compression meters are often misleading. Like Joe Meek said, "If it sounds right, it is right."

RICHARD DODD

Grammy Award-winning producer/engineer and mixer Richard Dodd's creative use of compression has won many fans who love recordings with a pulsing energy that enhances the essence of a song. Dodd's first hit project was the Carl Douglas smash "Kung Fu Fighting," (!) but he is best known for his work with Tom Petty (solo and with the Heartbreakers), Boz Scaggs, the Traveling Wilburys, Wilco, Robert Plant, the Connells, Clannad, Green Day and the Why Store.

What I go after with compression is to purely emulate the ear and a perception of sound, because obviously what a sound is and how we perceive it are two different things. Does a tree falling alone in the woods make a sound? I don't know, but if it does, I imagine it to be one thing, and in actuality it might be something else. Have you ever heard a gunshot outside, as it were? It is nothing like what we hear in the movies. It's a perceived thing. I typically use a compressor or limiter to achieve my perceived envelope—to add excitement and sensitivity or presence or change or add perspective, much in the same way that some people use reverb.

Just because you have compressed something, you don't have to use it all. If you compress something to the extreme of any perceived tolerance, it is obviously exaggerated and probably of no use. But if you then mix that in with the unaffected sound, you have something very useful. People sometimes say to me, "You use compression so well. It is so compressed, but it doesn't sound like it is compressed." The trick is that I am using both. I will have one signal that is totally pure mixed with the desired amount of the compressed signal.

What has become readily available in the digital world is multiband compression. Basically, that is of more use than an equalizer in many cases. What it has led me to realize, of course, is that even the old-fashioned analog units are actually multiband compressors, inasmuch as their inefficiencies and deficiencies, as it were, change the tonalities. They do it in an irregular fashion, and in some cases that is wonderful, and in other cases, it's a negative. The way to recover that is by mixing in either a completely uneffected signal with it, or a partially effected signal to achieve the right thing.

In other words, I may go to the compression extreme to get the effect I want, and then I will and thereby giving emphasis to another part of the sound, you can change the whole sound. By using a multiband compressor to do that, it's more like getting a sound like sticking your finger in your ear. An equalizer isn't like that. Not that an equalizer is bad, but it doesn't give that effect. All it does is change the tone. It doesn't change the envelope. If you are in the analog world and

The Urei 1176

analyze what it has done to the sound. If I need some of the purity back sonically, I'll add back some of the un-effected sound. It's no more difficult than that.

If somebody has already made the mistake of committing to digital, then I prefer to be in a hard-disk-space world, rather than a tape-based digital world. If I am already committed in the digital world for a project, then I will happily use the digital plug-ins, rather than go back to analog just to use an analog compressor. The cost of conversion isn't worth the gain. The digital multiband compressors seem to be more phase-coherent than using multiband analog equalizers. By effectively slowing down a band,

you want to do that, then there are other tricks to be able to do that, but it's more involved.

I love black 1176's, preferably with the serial number below 4,000. They are distorted in a nicer way, and they do that thing of changing the sound in a way that gives you an option, rather than a way that you immediately hate. Those 1176's have become priced beyond their worth, for the moment.

Eventually, someone will market a digital "1176-style" plug-in and everyone will believe that it is. Nevertheless, the reason they can't do it is that an 1176 is analog. By virtue of that alone, there is no comparison between analog and digital, so all this trying to be analog in a digital world is bullshit. That can't ever happen. These plug-ins might be great, and I love some of them, but they are not analog. Some might do a nice job of faking some of the effects of analog, but saying that people can't tell the difference between a digital plug-in version and an analog thing is simply not true. To get into the digital world, your whole sound has to be filtered and sampled, and in the analog world it is nowhere near as severe. End of argument. There is some fine stuff in the digital world, but it is not analog.

One other issue I would like to get into is how disgusted I get when I see a mastering person receive a digital master and reconvert it to analog so they can use some old tube limiter or some new tube limiters, or whatever. Just being old doesn't necessarily mean good. Not many people even know how to line those things up to make them operate at their best. To just convert a digital master back to analog so it can go through some analog tubes to "warm it up" is almost unforgivable in a mastering situation. This approach is rampant, just like a disease. The amount of information a mastering engineer is discarding in that extra conversion is unbelievable. It is effectively half what it used to be, regardless of whatever they have done to it. They can't add those missing samples when they have converted it, and they certainly can't keep them when they have converted it back. It's ridiculous. I have not only seen that done, I've also seen that done in 16 bit 44.1. I've witnessed this in the hands of babies, and it is frightening. If the mastering engineer was any good, he would rarely do what I just said.

MICHAEL WAGENER

Michael Wagener's engineering, producing and mixing credits run the gamut from hard rock heavies like Ozzy Osbourne, Megadeth, Skid Row, Extreme and Alice Cooper to Queen and dance-pop superstar Janet Jackson. Wagener, who has relocated from Los Angeles to Nashville, works out of his rural studio getaway, called Wire World.

There are a few ways of using compressors other than the obvious automatic level control. For instance, a compressor with a sidechain access can be used for cleaning up your bottom end. Try sending the bass through the compressor and key (sidechain/trigger) it with the kick drum, so

every time the kick hits, it pushes the bass back a little. Set the release time of the compressor so that the bass comes right back up after the kick sound stops. That's an easy way to control low-end buildup without losing punch. Just don't tell the bass player about it.

I also used to set up two compressor/limiters with a two-way frequency crossover in a way that I could send a bass or guitar, for instance, through that frequency crossover and then connect two different types of compressor/limiters to the output of the crossover—one to the low-end out and the other to the high out. The outputs of the two compressor/limiters are patched back to two line inputs of the console. That gives me the chance to use a limiter on the high end and a compressor on the low end with different attack and release times. Low frequencies don't like fast release times too much—you'll get distortion that way. On the other hand, I could ride the high fader on the console on clicks and string pops without losing the low-end content of the mix or the melody line of the bass, or I would brighten up the bass in the choruses even in the days before EQ automation.

If you happen to have one or two of the old 1176 UREIs, you can use them on the room mic(s). Push all four ratio buttons in. The compression will be immense. Patch an EQ before the 1176's, and that will take quite a bit of high end off (shelving) and then bring up a little low end—maybe 2 to 3 dB around 80 to 100 Hz—then set the attack time to a slow setting and the release to a faster setting. Then set the input level so that the needle goes back to at least –10 dB. Your drummer will not want to hear any other mics in the mix.

There are a whole bunch of different compressors out there. You don't always have to use the $10,000 Fairchild. In fact, some of the "cheap" compressors do a great job because you can hear them work. It's like with microphones—every single one has a different sound and can be used successfully on a variety of instruments. Experimenting is the secret.

MICHAEL BRAUER

New York-based mix master Michael Brauer has amassed an astounding list of credits over the years. Included in Brauer's lengthy discography are the Rolling Stones, Coldplay, Bob Dylan, Bruce

The Fairchild 670.

Springsteen, Jackson Browne, Billy Joel, Luther Vandross, Stevie Ray Vaughan, Michael Jackson, Jeff Buckley, Tony Bennett, Eric Clapton, David Byrne and many more. Brauer has also worked as a consultant for Sony Studios and has done extensive work on DVD remixing, including titles by Paul McCartney and Simon & Garfunkel. While Brauer has virtually any kind of gear at his disposal, he discusses one of the best bang for buck compressors available.

One of the most versatile compressors on the market is one designed by David Derr called the EL8 Distressor Compressor. It's the kind of compressor that can be really clean and gentle and warm and transparent. But if you want it to be vicious, there is no compressor that I know of that can get you up to 40 dB of compression, which is what it might take to get something really wicked. I always tell people to buy three, because you're going to end up using two of them in stereo and you're going to use that third one for bass or vocal or whatever.

With this unit's ability to get 40 dB of compression, you can take a regular lousy snare drum and turn it into a John Bonham kind of snare. What that means is that if you want to create your own reverb without reverb, you can! You can absolutely pull the "room" out of your snare drum.

You take the snare drum, or whatever sound you are working on, and sub-group or mult it to two channels. On the first channel, the dry or source channel, apply more gentle compression with a slow attack. By "gentle" I mean around 5 to 10 dB of compression, which is a lot on other compressors, but not on this one. The resulting sound will be this smack or really hard sound. The higher numbers on the attack knob are slower. Now, on the second channel crank the compression up to 40 dB with a very fast attack and release. When you completely remove the attack, it brings up the room ambience. So now you've got this one sound with horrendous attack punchiness to it, and another sound that captures the room reverb. You mix in the one where all the attack has been removed, you bring that up with the first fader, and you have a natural room without any reverbs, yet you hear the reverb from the snare. By the use of your compressors, you are creating your own reverb.

Now, if you are going to put in 40 dB of compression, you are going to want to crank the output gain up to make up for this extreme compression. When you crank up the output, it just becomes a different animal. That is a key function of this. With the Distressor Compressor, you won't get any buzzing or humming or crapping out. It's amazing.

The Distressor Compressor also really does a great job on vocals. It has this setting, which I guess is a midband emphasis setting, that is really designed for vocals that get thin and harsh and hurt your ears and cause you to EQ that section every time they get into that range. When you hit this setting, it automatically attenuates that area and warms it up, so you have this warm vocal all the way to the top of the range, where normally it would get very harsh. If you are dealing with a really thin voice, you can also add this DIST2 harmonic distortion setting, and it adds warmth and a little fuzz to the vocal. Depending on the application, it just sounds great.

Here is another idea, this one based on the 1176. It is called the British Setting. If you are familiar with the 1176, you basically have two knobs, an in and an out, and you have four buttons. With those four buttons, you can select your compression ratio. What you do is press them all in. Depending on the vintage of the unit, because

you can't do this on some of the newer 1176's, hitting these four buttons makes it freak. The compressor needle, or indicator, will slam over to the right. Normally, whenever there is anything going on, the needle does the opposite. This looks really weird, but as long as it slams over this way, you know that it's working. This setting gives the sound a certain sense of urgency. It strains it. It's great for a vocal that needs extra urgency. Of course, you are going to be able to control the amount of strain in the voice by the input level. In the beginning, the needle may not move at all, so you have to keep bringing the gain up until the needle starts slamming over to the left.

Here's the additional touch for this: The compressor is so wild in what it's doing with the vocal [for example], that although you don't hear the vocal coming in and out, you are hearing this intense sound. That's the best way I can describe it. Then you start bringing that second channel up to where it would normally phase out totally. Because the compression is moving this sound around, it kind of goes in and out of phase. So you back it off, just before you get to it. You have to play with this, but what that can do—especially with a vocal or instruments—is make the sound explosive.

There's a sweet spot, and you have to play around to find it. If you feel that it's starting to phase out, or it's disappearing, you might want to play with that second channel. Remember, if you bring the whole thing up out of phase, no matter what it is, it's going to disappear. But when you have that kind of compression going on, and

The Distressor Compressor.

you put it right before its cutoff—it's 180 degrees out—weird things start happening. It's pretty wild!

Obviously, it is not something you are going to want to do on a Tony Bennett record. He doesn't use any compression. It has got to be used for really aggressive rock and roll—something where you are not going to use much reverb anyway—but you are not going to create a certain intensity.

When people give me ideas and certain mix approaches for specific things like I just said, the first thing that I start thinking out is, "Wow, forget the vocal. How about doing this other thing?" There are always ideas that take off from there.

JUSTIN NIEBANK

Justin Niebank is one of Nashville's most versatile and well respected producer/engineers. Since the mid-seventies, when he started predominantly recording blues in Chicago, to the present, Niebank has worked with a wide range of artists. Niebank's credits include Johnny Winter, Delbert McClinton, Neil Diamond, Wynonna Judd, Todd Snider, Robert Cray, Blues Traveler, Keith Urban, SHeDAISY and Vince Gill among many others. For this discussion on compression, Niebank offers some thoughts on the overuse of it.

I'm getting a little tired of this "let's compress everything to death" sound that has been real popular. In the last few years of listening to records, this is the first time I've actually been distracted by the amount of compression I'm hearing. There is a way to achieving punch power, apparent volume, and intensity without having to make everything so compressed. All this over-compression is like hearing seventies era Syn-drums on recordings. It dates the music badly.

Everything's so compressed that there isn't any space for anything anymore. The problem with that kind of approach to recording is that it makes it hard to peel back those layers in the recording and find those wonderful hidden things in songs. It is hard to listen to a song twenty times and go, "I never heard that before," or "Isn't that amazing how that happened?"

When you are in different moods, you can discover things about great records. The overuse of compression to me sort of kills all that. It's like

you get it on the first listen and that's it, which I guess for some people is all right. For me, I'm disappointed and missing some of the days when recordings were little bit more orchestrated in allowing dynamics to be there.

Concerning the compression on the Beatles records, I never really heard it and said, "Oh there's the 1176 compressing everything to death". I didn't hear it as that. I heard it as the sound that made me experience something musically. These days, I'm not feeling the drummer playing hard, I'm hearing the compressor moving in front of the drummer, which is a little distracting.

CHAPTER 4

Cue Mixes

Anyone who has ever recorded in a studio knows how crucial the proper headphone or monitor mix is to a good performance. For someone cutting on the floor, an unbalanced or distorted mix can blow the vibe of a session. Inheriting a bad set of phones will sometimes be enough to hang it up for the day.

Some players and singers want real hyped sounding phones and mixes, and some couldn't care less. There are those who feel that phone volume works best at a relatively low level, while many gravitate towards turning their brains to oatmeal with wide-open volume.

Reading the dynamic of tastes and needs between different people is only part of the job an engineer has to deal with when setting up the proper phone or monitor mix to those recording.

For this chapter, we've enlisted seven world-class producers and engineers:—Brian Ahern, Chuck Ainlay, David Briggs, Terry Brown, John Guess, Clif Norrell, and Jeff Powell,—who have some very different takes on addressing the world of studio cue mixing. This chapter also includes thoughts on utilizing click tracks, since they usually happen on phones.

JOHN GUESS

John Guess is one of the hottest producer/engineers in Nashville. Guess has worked with numerous mainstream pop and country artists, including Kenny Rogers, Suzy Bogguss, and Reba McEntire. Since the late eighties, he has been in demand as engineer and mixer for country stars including Dolly Parton, Keith Urban, Toby Keith, Vince Gill, Rodney Crowell, Marty Stuart, Patty Loveless, Wynonna Judd, and George Strait.

Before moving to Nashville, Guess worked on gold and platinum pop projects by Rod Stewart, Donna Summer and Kenny Loggins, as well as projects as diverse as Captain Beefheart, Michael Omartian, Funkadelic, Luther Vandross, Frank Sinatra, Jeff Beck, Stevie Wonder, and John Fogerty, among others.

With a cue mix, I like to create as friendly an atmosphere as possible. That usually means getting a good stereo mix of everything, except for the vocal. I like the musicians to be able to control that. Most of the studios that I work at in Nashville have the individual eight fader cue mixers, made by Formula Sound, and that allows me to get a good stereo mix along with six monos for individual controls, or what we call "more me's."

With that stereo mix, I have a good mix of the band. There will be an individual one for the vocal. In the stereo mix, I will add reverb, with nothing too long or swimmy. That usually consists of some EMT 250, on one of the sends, and I'll use a Lexicon 480 on a small hall setting with a pretty healthy pre-delay. I will put that on another send. On the vocal, I just blend that with its own reverb, usually something like a Yamaha SPX-90 and feed it on its own fader.

What I usually do is set up the phones, prior to the session, with a pre-existing basic track tape that has similar instrumentation. That puts me that much further ahead in the game when the musicians walk in. That way I have a general setting of everything and I can tweak it from there.

I'm fond of the small mixer style of cue boxes that are often called "more me boxes" in Nashville. They are called that because they allow the musician to customize the cue mix with individual faders, which enables each of the players to hear more of themselves in their cue mixes.

When I set it up, I will always leave the "more me's" down on the faders out on the floor in the studio. I will go around to each station and just bring up the stereo mix to where it is comfortable for me. I will then leave it up to the individual musicians to bring the "more me's" up to his or her personal taste.

The only thing that is scary about that is, after a session, you can walk out and somebody will have his or her "more me" turned all the way up and there will be nothing else

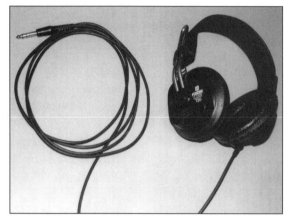

Fostex T-20 studio headphones.

on. You can usually discover that, because that person will start having timing problems during the session. If all they are hearing is themselves, they will start getting out of the pocket. I can usually tell them to back it down a little bit if we have a problem.

If you happen to be using a click track on one of the faders, and someone has it up too loud, sometimes it will bleed and you can't get rid of it later. Acoustic guitarists are famous for this. You just have to be aware of that.

For string bass sessions, it is a whole other matter. I prefer using single headphones, if they are available. That allows players to hear what is going on in the room a little better, and then they can just follow the conductor. It gives them enough to "pitch" in the phones.

Every singer is different. Some adapt to phones easily and don't have any pitch problems. Then there is the other type who sings normally until they put phones on. Then they drift sharp or flat consistently. Each individual has to experiment

and find out what works with them. They might need to pull one phone back a little bit to hear what is going on in the room.

When the "A" players come in, there is usually very little discussion about the phone mix. If there is something that needs to be adjusted, they will usually voice that right away. Since they have their own faders and pan pots, they can position that mono signal anywhere in the field that they want to.

My headphone preference, even when I am mixing and just for comparison, is the old model Fostex T-20. Not the newer ones. They are the old flat ones. I still prefer them over everything, because they don't have that real hypey high end and they are pretty smooth.

I've found that some drummers will put little earplugs in their ears before they put their phones on, just to cut down some of the level. Larrie London had his own little earphone system that he put in his ears and then put those gun mufflers or sound mufflers over his ears. If they are professional drummers, they often have their own setup.

They'll put on their small phones and then actually muffle outside sound with sound deadening devices. That way they can hear the sounds more immediately, without having to turn it up as loud.

If the session is an all-acoustic bluegrass recording, then you can often go without phones. The musicians will gather around and let the leakage happen and go for that. Most of the things that I do, however, are a more controlled situation.

I usually have the drums out in the room by themselves, with maybe the bass player. Everyone else is pretty isolated.

A number of years ago, I did have a singer one time who was never satisfied with the cue system. He could never hear anything. One day he said, "I want to hear more highs *in the lows*." I said, "I'm not sure how to go about doing that." What

I ended up doing was take a stereo graphic equalizer and set it up in front of him and ran the cue mix through the graphic and said, "Here, have at it!" I let him EQ any way he wanted to. After the session I saw how he had set it and it was pretty frightening. The level was even more frightening. Over the years, the consequences of playing phones too loud can be very alarming.

JEFF POWELL

Working out of Ardent Recording in Memphis, Jeff Powells' engineering and mixing credentials has covering everything from classic rock bands like Lynyrd Skynyrd and The Allman Brothers to more cutting edge projects like The Afghan Whigs and Primal Scream.

At Ardent, we have a system that uses an eight-channel sub-mixer that our technical department designed themselves. These sub-mixers have, on each of these channels, a separate panning control and a level control, as well as an overall volume control. They are on rolling stands with long cords on them, which makes them convenient to roll around anywhere in the studio. This means that each musician has the option to add to or take out or mix all or none of the components that are sent down these lines.

I will usually set up a stereo mix with the drummer, as we are getting drum sounds, and send that down the first two channels. As we are getting drums sounds, I will take a direct multi-track out feed into the cue amp. Anything I do in the control room will not affect what they are hearing and they have complete control over hearing how much of themselves they want to hear. I usually save back two modules, say seven and eight, to set up an auxiliary stereo effects mix. In an instant, players are then able to add as much reverb or echo as they may want to hear on their vocals or instruments. They can make it sound like they are in a bathroom or an airport hanger, or they can make it sound completely dry. I set it up to where it is completely independent of me and what I do in the control room won't affect them. That is my mode in tracking.

Usually the musicians are so happy to have the control over their own sounds that they don't ask for extra EQ, but I can provide extra, if they want it.

In overdub mode, I will usually switch things over, for ease's sake,—I will usually send just a stereo mix down one and two and I will give them what I call a "more me" track.

If the lead singer is going to blow through four tracks of him doing a song, and comp it later, I'll send him the stereo mix on one and two, which includes his voice. If he can't hear himself over the mix enough, then he can turn up his voice in the "more me" track, and add that in.

Sometimes you might run out of the eight tracks, but we cut the Allman Brothers live with two drummers, two guitar players, organ, bass, percussion and lead vocals, and it worked perfectly.

I personally prefer our Neve VR, because it has two auxiliary stereo cue sends. The SSL does, but the way our patch bay is set up, it is more user friendly, but that is more unique to our studio.

At Ardent, we use the Fostex T-20's for phones. Sometimes drummers don't like them, especially ones that move their head around a lot, because they can fly off their heads.

The sub-mixers have red overload lights. Sometimes I can go out on the floor and they will be all lit up and the phones are completely distorted. So I'll will sneak out there and tweak it up a little bit and all of the sudden they can hear. It amazes me how little importance some musicians place on headphone fidelity and mixes. The only thing I can think is that some of them are used to crappy headphone mixes.

We also have a Tascam 20-watt amplifier on top of each eight-channel mixer. We have two different rows of input holes that you can plug into. In fact, six headphones can run out of one box. It's great, if you are doing a group vocal. Anyway, there are four top row inputs and two bottom row inputs. The top inputs are connected to this 20-watt amplifier. It can get so loud that it can practically melt the phones. I've had a drummer throw the phones off one time, because they were burning his ears. He had them up so loud that they were hot as a firecracker. I've never had anybody say they weren't loud enough, even the deafest people. Drummers and lead vocalists seem to go for the highest sound pressure levels.

Back in my days as an assistant, I've seen engineers cop an attitude of "Well, tough," or make feeble attempts to fix things. When you put phones on, you can immediately tell if something is distorting. I've always believed that if a musician says there is something wrong with the phones or the mix, nine out of ten times, it's not because they are stupid, it is because there is something wrong that I can help them with. That is why I always have a headphone box by me in the control room, so I can hear exactly what they are hearing. It usually takes about two seconds to know what is the matter.

CLIF NORRELL

Clif Norrell's engineering and/or mixing credits include No Doubt, The Pixies, Saliva, Macy Gray, Jewel, R.E.M., John Hiatt, The Replacements, Indigo Girls, and Tom Petty.

As a producer/engineer, he worked with Gin Blossoms, Jeff Buckley, and Inspiral Carpets, among others.

About 50 percent of my projects use monitor wedges, as opposed to phones. This is primarily due to the fact that many of my projects are bands who need to have a gig atmosphere approximated, in order to capture the most natural performance of the band or artist.

It depends on the artist, but lots of times I will isolate the drummer and he will be the only one with headphones on. I will have everyone else use floor wedges. I try to keep everything as live as possible, except for the drums. We can usually get away with not having to baffle off too many guitar amps. I just put close mics on the guitar amps and still have a live vocal and not worry about leakage too much.

Concerning wedges, I basically don't have a preference.

We usually use whatever rentals there are available, usually JBL's or EV's. We just power them off of the headphone amplifiers and just use auxiliary sends for those. I record on a lot of old consoles. The kind of board I'm using dictates how many sends they have, but I try to send a stereo headphone mix to the drummer and then use wedges for whoever else is out there in a live band situation, which is usually what I work on.

Oftentimes I will do a standard headphone mix for everyone and I try to keep things fairly isolated when I do that.

Do I prefer using wedges over phones? I do and I don't. Sometimes the leakage gets a little critical. You have to have a good room to isolate the drums in and a big enough room to put everybody else in. You really have to have two good decent size rooms for that normally. It does work and the bands seem to like it a lot more. It is more like a gig for them. They seem to be able to hear a little bit better. It works well if you don't have a whole lot of mixes to give to them and they can stand closer to their amps. It also makes the guitars sound a little bit different, when they have some direct feedback to their amp and they can walk closer to it, or do what they need to physically do to get in touch with their amps. Sometimes, when they are off into another room, they are not going to get the kind of sustain and interplay with the amp that they need to.

I tend to do vocals in the control room sometimes. It just depends on what the artist likes and what they are used to and feel comfortable with.

With R.E.M., we generally used Sony MDR-V6 headphones for *Automatic for the People* and they liked them quite a bit, because they are a lot hypier. They have a lot more high end than most other phones. I tend to use those quite a bit and I listen through those, sometimes, when I'm mixing as well, just to check the mix.

I also like the Fostex T-20's as well. They seem to be able to get really loud, and a lot of bands like it real loud. They don't tend to blow up very often or clip out.

Even though we used phones for tracking on R.E.M., we cut some of the guitar and keyboard overdubs in the control room. Those were things where we would just put an amp out in the studio.

I recorded the Jayhawks, and we did lots of singing in the control room, instead of using phones out on the floor. A couple of times we actually had them holding their own mics and singing in the control room with no headphones to the monitors. They could go where they wanted to and they loved that and it seemed to work fine. They sang mostly through Shure SM-58's and SM-7's.

In that case, I allowed the bleed to become part of the natural mix. As long as you don't have anything on tape that is really loud, that you are not going to use, the leakage is really not a problem. I know a lot of people are probably afraid to do that, or say, "You can't do that" or "You have to put the speakers out of phase." You can do that, but it sounds weird for the people who are singing or playing to the monitors. They can't hear as well. We usually just leave the speakers in phase and turn it up for them and mainly keep it from feeding back. That works quite a bit.

I find it can help singer's pitch quite a bit, because there is some kind of psycho-acoustic pitch change that you get with headphones. I'm sure there is a technical explanation for it, but I think that it helps a lot of singers to sing with monitors.

When Amy and Emily of the Indigo Girls would sing together, we used floor monitors and that worked quite well. We would have a baffle between them, or have them looking at each other with a fairly directional mic for vocals.

I don't think [the bleed] makes it sound better, but I do think that it makes the performance so much better that it doesn't seem to affect the overall sonic quality that much. You might get a cleaner recording by not having the wedges. You could probably isolate things a little bit more and get the exact sound on the exact instrument that you want without having to worry about blend when you are using headphones, but I think the advantages from a production aspect of the performance far outweigh any kind of loss in overall sound quality.

Wedges work well for me. I think singers must feel a little uncomfortable at times with phones, because they are not hearing their own voice. They are hearing it through all the electronics and whatever kind of effects you've got on it. They may be used to that, but some of them may not. They may not be in touch with the music as they could be, if the music was coming out of the speaker, even from an overdub aspect. From the live band aspect, most bands prefer monitors.

If you are using headphones for a band session, and they have two guitar players, it seems to work a lot better to put them on stereo cues with them panned left and right, to keep it from becoming a wall of mush in the phones. That way they can hear themselves playing.

I quite often work on old Neve consoles that don't have that many sends and you've just got to make do on those. I don't usually work with the systems in some studios where you send a submix out and have the people do their own mixes. Generally, I do the mixes for them and go with what I generally think they need and go from their suggestions and change it when they need things changed.

I think the headphone mix is so critical that it is important to give the musicians and singers something that will inspire them, like a big sounding stereo mix, as opposed to something that is all cluttered. I think it deserves more attention than it gets. You should get it right, ideally, before recording. It is as critical as spending time to get good sounds to go on tape. Getting the phone mix is critical to the session, especially when you are tracking. If things aren't happening, it can seriously cause problems. When it is right, the artist's mind is freed up and you get a better performance.

I usually track a lot of people at the same time and you need to make sure that everyone is happy with their own mix. I will generally start out with the drummer on one mix and everybody else on another mix and then, a vocalist on another mix. Hopefully, we can keep it that way. If someone still isn't happy with what they are getting, you can set up another mix for them.

Sometimes a musician will ask you to turn things up until, all of the sudden you are wondering, "God, how can they listen to this?" So it is a good idea, in between takes, to go around and check their mix and make sure that everything is working right. Don't just use the control room headphones, and flip through their mixes, because their phones might be flapping out or doing something strange. You need to hear what they are hearing.

TERRY BROWN

Terry Brown is most known for his production work of ten Rush albums, among those being classic platinum selling prog rock releases like Permanent Waves, Moving Pictures, Signals, Farewell to Kings *and* Hemispheres. *Brown scored a number one hit with the first Cutting Crew record, "Died In Your Arms." Brown's engineering and mixing credits include Cirque du Soleil's* Zumanity. *He's also produced Blue Rodeo, Voivod and, among Brown's more arcane production credits, the three Klaatu albums.*

Headphone mixes are such a personal thing. You can never really be sure that you are going to keep everybody happy. I did a production with a group that was really centered around a guy in the band who did all of his writing at home with headphones. As a result, his headphone mix had very specific requirements. I had to get him a power amp to drive his headphones, which were a pair of AKG Parabolics with double drivers in each earpiece. They were seriously loud.

We had a Takamine acoustic guitar with a DI and a little chorusing and live mics and vocals. He would cut guitar and vocals as a bed track with no click and we built everything around that. Even though his requirements weren't very complicated, in terms of other instruments playing, he had to have his mix exactly right, with the right kind of reverb and decay, and he wanted the guitar in stereo. It had to fit exactly and he had to be totally comfortable with each tune, and things changed for each tune. That was a very specific thing. He could not record unless it was perfect.

Then there are situations were you have a band, and three or four different headphone mixes, because everybody's requirements are so different. From isolating different instruments, it is very difficult to give everybody the perfect feed. The guitar player always wants more guitar and the drummer always wants less guitar. With a band, you need at least three or four headphone mixes. Otherwise, it is totally impossible to keep everybody happy.

I find that with the volume that you naturally get off of drum kits, it is hard to give a drummer (especially in a very loud ambient warehouse-type room) a really good headphone mix on the drums. This is because you are hearing so much from outside of the headphones. The actual ambient volume of the drums is such that it is very difficult to create the right vibe inside the phones. In this situation, it is really a case of mainly putting hi-hat, kick, and snare in the phones and letting most of the other sounds just bleed into the phones. This problem is especially true when you are playing to clicks and you're running in sync.

You can only work at such a loud volume for an hour or two. The fatigue is dramatic if you are working at too high a volume.

Some players cannot work unless the phones are screaming loud. It can get dangerously loud sometimes. You can get a lot of distortion involved and you then aren't hearing the signal properly. Volume is definitely something that has to be watched. It can be devastating listening to a click screaming loud in your phones for a period of over eight hours. As the day progresses, it gets louder and louder, and the ears shut down. I'll sometimes set a limit on it and say, "This is it. You are not getting any more. You are going have to concentrate, or we are going to have to change the sound of the click."

Sometimes changing the sound of the click will fix things, like making it sound like a cowbell. Many drummers like to play with odd percussion elements in the phones, so they can pick up on internal beats. I usually tailor those for the drummer and find something that he is totally comfortable with.

With Rush, Neil (Pert) usually used a pair of AKG Parabolics and he would listen to them at a fairly loud volume, but he always knew his limits as far as volume was concerned.

I think the more sophisticated the player you are working with, the less of a problem playing with headphones becomes. They usually have a good handle on what they are playing and how they are playing vis-à-vis the time on the click. Moving in and out of time with a click is not a problem for them, because they have such a good internal clock that they can move around the click and always find their way back. With less experienced drummers, it can sometimes be a real problem, because they are not players with the same level of sophistication. In order to give them a little more security, the click gets louder and louder. Eventually, they are fighting to stay with the click. Volume then becomes the only real substitute for lack of finesse. It is certainly not the answer, but that is the way it tends to go I find.

I'm using this pair of Sony Professional MDR-7506's. I like those a lot. They have a really wide frequency spectrum with a very solid bottom end. I find they are great for vocalists. I don't think I would use them for drums. I did try them a couple of times, but they have such a wide frequency range that by the time you get the bass drum to a point to where it feels comfortable, they are usually bottoming out. Then, of course, you end up turning them up a little bit louder and a little louder, and then it is not a workable situation. You need a brasher type of headphone for drums, more like the gold AKG models. I forget the number of them.

I do most of my work with three or four piece bands. Normally, I create my mixes at the console, using three, four or five sub-mixes created at the console.

The SSL has got a very convenient sub-mix situation. Anything that is being done as a sort of final cut, if we are overdubbing, I'll send stereo mixes. But in terms of doing tracks, mono mixes are usually more than adequate.

The older Neves are a tough set-up. The two-pot, four button-type of syndrome. It is very hard to give a number of separate mixes on a standard old Neve. I'll usually steal the reverb send for headphone mixes in those kinds of cases. At least, then, you can do another complete set-up.

I use players in the control room so much, that the headphone mix is not really a major concern of mine. Sometimes, a guitar player will want to use phones, so he can immerse himself in sound, rather than sitting in a room and being distracted by other sounds and people talking. Bands do get a little boisterous.

It's hard to find a headphone mix that will satisfy a guitar player who desires to be in the room with a big rig feeding back and so on. In that case, I think the AKG Parabolics are the way to go. They are more than loud enough for what you need.

Unless it is a specific situation to where a guitar player needs to be in the studio with his amp, I would much prefer him sitting in the control room with me, so we can communicate quickly. That way we are hearing all the nuances in the playing that he wants to hear, coming out of the control room monitors.

Personally, I prefer having the drummer cut alone in the tracking room and having the other players recording in the control room.

Hopefully, the band is well enough rehearsed that it won't take all day to lay the tracks. That is a preferable way of doing things.

I like the idea of cutting the bass player later, as an overdub. It seems that bass finds the pocket better, when played to the control room monitors, than when the bassist is sitting in the room with the drummer and hearing drum bleed and drum signal conflicting with one another.

If you are going to cut in the room with the drums, one way to achieve a better connection to what's being played is to sit on your amp. Then you have a problem to consider, which is bleed into the drums. You are kind of stuck. Headphones for a bass player are a real tough call, especially when he is in the room with the drummer. You are, more than likely, not going to really hear what you are doing. It's a rough version of what you are playing. You don't hear the fidelity of the bass. There is no headphone in the world that can complete with that. It is much nicer to do it in an overdub situation.

CHUCK AINLAY

Chuck Ainlay has worked as a producer and recording and mixing engineer with some of the most discriminating recording artists on the planet, such as Mark Knopfler, and he has also put in years with Nashville's factory-like country music session scene. The idea of providing each player with his or her own headphone mix box might have been a cool concept, but Ainlay is quick to provide a more cautionary note on the trade-out with convenience and its possible effect on performance.

These days, everybody's got these mixers for their headphones so they can listen to whatever element they want. What ends up happening is they will turn themselves up so they can hear themselves really well, but there is a tendency to get off in their own world. As a result, people don't musically communicate as well and their dynamics don't fit as naturally.

I'm a firm believer that having everybody playing with a good stereo headphone mix makes for a more believable organic band sound and better music. It might be harder for me, because I'm trying to listen from a production standpoint and from a technical standpoint as the engineer and also make everybody happy with the headphone mix, but I really feel it contributes to the quality of things.

BRIAN AHERN

Brian Ahern is a master of nuance, and his attention to the seemingly "little" things has paid off in big ways with a body of visionary production work that has stood the test of time. It is clearly evident in his work with Emmylou Harris, Anne Murray and George Jones.

Technically speaking, a musician never plays perfectly in time, and if he or she does, then you have a bad record. When I'm recording most musicians, I don't like to use a hard click, like you get from a computer program or a drum machine. I like to use something soft and less intimidating, like a brush sound. It changes the way they feel when they are playing. They are not embarrassed if the "one" on every downbeat is vague, and they can play along and get a good feel. With a brush, they have a soft reference as opposed to a hard one where every time they miss it they are aware of it. A hard click is a hard wake-up call, rather than that reverie thing that I like. Hard clicks are out in my book.

DAVID BRIGGS

It can be easily argued that the late great David Briggs was the production force behind Neil Young's best albums, and certainly the ones that rocked the hardest and possessed the most emotional tension. Besides Young classics like Everybody Knows This Is Nowhere, After the Goldrush, Tonight's the Night, Rust Never Sleeps, Ragged Glory, *and Young's eponymous debut, Briggs also produced the brilliant swan song by the original line-up of Spirit titled* The Twelve Dreams of Dr. Sardonicus. *Shortly before his death on November 26, 1995, Briggs was producing Neil Young's* Sleep with Angels *and* Royal Trux.

Headphones are for persona non grata in my studios. There is no way in the world that you can put headphones on and work for eight hours. They are for people who want to lose the top end of their ears in about an hour.

Most musicians go into the studio, put their headphones on and do this and do that and they putz around and their energy and focus is history by the three, four or five hour mark. When you work like I do, which is without phones, I get fifteen or sixteen hours of playing a day out of bands and they love to do it. They go right back out and play some more.

I set the band up and build it in such a way that where everybody who is playing in the band has a sweet spot like you hear onstage. It's how big of a sweet spot can you get is the name of the game. When I design a stage show, it's how big of an area can everything be heard by everybody and still have everybody be able to be free to move through that area, however they feel fit. If you have a real active physical band, like Pearl Jam, or someone like that, who is bouncing all over the stage, there is not any way to cover and fill the whole stage. In most cases, however, when you take them into a studio, the physical stage movements come out of the performance and they begin to work in a smaller area. If you put them in a sweet spot with no headphones, and you get that P.A. to where it sounds great, then they don't have to work and scream their heads off. They hear everything. You don't get that feeling from phones.

I don't like wedges, but sometimes I use them for drums. Sometimes I may let the drummer use headphones. In truth, after five, six or seven hours, bashing with cymbals cutting through their heads, the drummer's top end is gone anyway. I like to use the big side fills and throw them in a big four-corners configuration, not in the room, but around the band: two coming at them and two going past them, two fronts and two backs. I surround them with the vocal. I don't put the band into the P.A. I just put the vocal up in there, except for a little bit of the kick drum, so some people can hear a little better. It is such a great way to make a record. It is infinitely less fatiguing to your ears. It is a lot more supportive for the band, because instead of having one guy out there in this lonely little dark room, with his headphones and his one instrument, censoring and editing himself as he plays along, trying to attain the perfect part, he is out there with three or four of his mates and they are all mashing and bashing. The end result is a whole different story.

CHAPTER 5

Drum Teching

Drummers can make a glorious noise, but when a noticeable percentage of the sounds hitting tape are undesirable gear squeaks and creaks cluttering up the groove, it can help wreck the vibe of an otherwise killer performance.

Drums may be made to take a beating, but like anything else, there is a point where negligence or poor maintenance will not only cause your gear to sound bad, it'll cost you jobs. It's the old what-goes-around-comes-around routine.

As a result, most producers and engineers encounter situations where it is necessary to troubleshoot drums that aren't producing optimum sounds.

I rounded up Steve Ebe, Pat Foley, Don Gehman, Robert Hall, and Craig Krampf to provide helpful tips to get the best results out of a kit, live and in the studio. In this chapter, they offer some great commonsense pointers and very creative problem solving ideas that really work.

STEVE EBE

Over the last twenty years, Nashville-based drummer Steve Ebe has performed or recorded with numerous artists from rockabilly legend Carl Perkins and fusion guitar wunderkind Shawn Lane, to roots rockers like Sonny Landreth, Sonny George and Webb Wilder; from country artists Marty Stuart, Tanya Tucker, and George Ducas and Anglo-pop/ rocker Tommy Hoehn to soul music king Steve Cropper. Ebe was also part of Human Radio, which recorded an album for Columbia Records.

The single most important thing is to have a well-maintained professional quality drum set with new heads. DW drums are the best in my opinion. They are loud, punchy, clean, and easy to tune over a wide range.

I usually muffle only the bass drum, using the hourglass shaped pillow made by DW. It attaches to the shell with Velcro, so it doesn't move around. It is low mass and low profile, so it's not soaking up any more volume than necessary.

If I find it necessary to muffle the snare, I use gaffer's tape in one of two ways. I either loop the tape with the adhesive facing out, or fold two or three waffle-like creases in the tape before applying near the rim.

Having a variety of sounds available is crucial. The drummer should always have a wide variety of sticks, brushes and bass drum beaters. A variety of heads should be handy for last minute tonal changes.

I use Aquarian heads and always have coated and clear, as well as one- and two-ply heads, on hand. The Super Kick 1 bass drum head sounds tremendous!

I have found that a handy way to carry the spare heads is to remove the center post from an old fiber cymbal case and place them in there. It is the perfect size.

When playing hard, I sometimes experience detuning, or tension rods backing out from vibration. It's no good to tune a drum if it won't stay there. To prevent this problem from happening, I use Lug Locks, or the Index Tension rods by Rhythm Tech on any problem drums. Not all drums suffer from this problem though. I have an amazing solid snare drum that won't budge.

I think a lot of people screw up by not paying much attention to the place where the cymbal sits on the stand. You should use the felt doughnut shaped pads that are situated on either side of the cymbals, but don't screw them down too tight with the wing nut. There is also a nylon sleeve or surgical tubing type of sleeve that goes over the metal post. A lot of drummers let those things wear out, or they don't use them at all. As a result, you have the cymbal touching metal, and that creates all kinds of rattles and sounds. I always keep a bunch of the sleeves in my stick bag, so when I go out and play on someone else's kit, I'm ready.

PAT FOLEY

By the time Pat Foley began working for Slingerland Drums as Director of Custom Products a number of years ago, he had already amassed an impressive list of credits as a designer of unique drums sets for the stars, including Gregg Bissonette's sets for the David Lee Roth tours (that looked like they were exploding), the Jacksons' 1984 Victory Tour, the garbage-can-looking trap set for Twisted Sister, as well as sets for Bernard Purdie, Jim Christie (Dwight Yoakam), Taylor Hawkins (Alanis Morissette) and many others.

Foley's drum tech credits include Faith No More, Los Lobos, Motley Crue and many more. As a producer, Foley has done a number of major label projects, including the Untouchables (MCA), the Redskins (London), and Laura Pallas (Island).

Microphones have no preconceptions. They don't know whether you have a big drum or a small drum in front of them. A lot of people will say, "I want a really big drum, because I want a really big sound." In fact, I have done a lot of records, where I have used very small drums that just sound huge, because with a smaller drum, you can generally tune the head lower and still maintain a little bit of tension on it. Because the bottom head responds quicker, you tend to often-times get a smaller drum to actually sound bigger. I think it would surprise a lot of people to see the kits that many of their "heroes" are playing are not nearly as big as they might suspect.

If you have a drum set and it isn't very big, I wouldn't assume that you are not going to get the sound you are looking for. A lot of times, nice small traditional sizes of drums, like 12", 13" and 16", will sound extremely large in a recording studio. I wouldn't get preconceived ideas about "You need to buy power toms to sound powerful." Those are marketing ploys basically [laughs]. That is a way to sell drums.

At Slingerland, we are sort of getting back to offering classic sizes and set-ups. The fact is, that most of the great records that you and I grew up listening to, that we loved so much, were not made with "power" toms and all of these elaborate types of super deep bass drums that drum companies offer nowadays. They were made with standard traditional sized toms that evolved because they worked very well. It has only been in the last ten years that everybody seems to think that drum purchasing is very complicated and that you have to be educated to all of the depths and diameters.

Ultimately, a drum set is one instrument. If I had to give one overall tip for tuning, I would say to think of them as one instrument, rather than a collection of instruments hanging together and tune them accordingly. If you strike your 12" tom tom, and your 16" resonates a little bit, don't be quick to dampen down that 16" to stop that resonance. Just tune it in such a way that it rings sympathetically with the 12", so that it enhances the overall sound of your set. You just want to be conscious when you tune drums of the harmonics that you are hearing, and make sure that when you strike one, and the one next to it rings a little bit, that it is basically ringing in tune. Then it all becomes one instrument and sounds much more musical, than deadening and isolating the individual components.

Most people have their own techniques of choosing the intervals that they want to use, but the important thing in tuning concerns the relationship between the top and bottom heads of the drum. If I had to give someone a quick tuning lesson, I would say to tune the tom toms with a tension that feels reasonable on the top head; snug it up and then start with your bottom head matched to the sound of the top head to where they are basically creating the same pitch. Then, once you've become tuned into what you are listening for, strike the top head and you will hear a slight waver between the top and bottom heads. That is like a phasing situation, because there is a slight delay before the bottom head responds. What I would normally do is have someone bang on that top head, while I just slightly de-tune the bottom head until I can hear those two pitches ring together. Then you will have a nice sustaining note.

Another thing that people do, if their drums don't have the sustain they want, or they don't have a big enough sound[s]; they adapt their drums to a RIMS mounting system. That is a trademarked product that happens to come standard on the drums we make here at Slingerland. It stands for Resonant Isolation Mounting System. RIMS is the most popular of these types of mounting systems. What is does, in effect, is that it suspends the drums by the tension rods, so you don't have to place a mount on the shell, which tends to restrict the vibrations.

DON GEHMAN

Since the mid-seventies, Don Gehman has produced some of the most successful albums of the popular music era, including both Hootie and the Blowfish albums, Tracy Chapman's latest platinum comeback effort, titled New Beginning, *R.E.M.'s* Life's Rich Pageant *and many of John Mellencamp's biggest releases, including* The Lonesome Jubilee, Scarecrow *and* American Fool.

One of Gehman's most unique features as a producer/engineer concerns his "Band in a Box" methodology, in which Gehman brings essentially every bit of instrument, amp, and outboard gear needed for any production. Most of the gear has been proven, over the years, to most consistently achieve the best recorded results. Gehman's success as a producer has enabled him to not only bring his favorite gear, but score endorsements from many of the manufacturers as well. For drums, Gehman is an avid fan and endorsee of DW (Drum Workshop) drums. In the spirit of the "Band in a Box" approach, Gehman works as his own drum tech for all of his production work.

Drummers who usually play live often hit cymbals way too loud in relation to the drums.

Generally speaking, it is my biggest problem in the studio as a producer/engineer. As much presence as you want to dig out of drum heads, you often wind up dragging a lot of cymbals in through the drum mics. Over the years, my problem is to try to figure out how to maintain a balance in the set where the cymbals aren't totally making noise all over the record.

DW drums are a solution. I haven't found anything that comes close. Most of that is because of sheer level. They are the loudest drums I have found so far. I have measured them on meters and they just seem to be a good 6 dB louder. It is the same way with the kick drums. It is louder. That means you are ahead right off the bat.

I carry cymbals around with me, and if a drummer is an especially hard hitter, I will go for the thinner cymbals. Zildjian has got these cymbals, which are thinner and quieter. Maybe they are called "A" customs. They are a little shorter duration, but more than anything they don't take up as much 2 kHz midrange in the area where I am boosting up the drums, and I don't pull up quite as much of that on cymbals. It kind of works itself out in the long run.

Tuning tricks are hard to describe. I am the drum tech on my session, so I usually tune drums on most sessions for the drummer. The search on each drum to find whatever sweet spot it has got is the best trick that I know. You should take them down all of the way, and then start bring them up and you can feel the spot where the drum starts to come alive. You then work both heads around that "sweet" spot and try and get the drum to speak as clearly and loudly as you can.

I like drums that are real pitch curvy. I like snares that go "boing," as well as the toms. That usually means unequal tuning between the heads, top to bottom. Generally, I set up the bottom heads lower than the top ones, which I think might be upside-down from what a lot of other people do.

I don't use any padding, except on kick drums. On kick, I will use those little DW hourglass pads. I use front heads with small holes, as small as I can get away with. I usually encounter trouble, if I have the kick drum totally sealed up. It is hard to get the resonance of the drum at the right duration. That is my biggest problem with front heads, at least for the way I put the bottom end together. They seem to eat up space that I would like the bass [guitar] to have. Drummers love it, and certainly it adds a lot of tone and action, but it is right in the heart of where I would like to put a bass guitar. It is that 150 Hz to 200 Hz area that gets gobbled up, when the front head is sealed.

Building tunnels is probably the fix that I use most of the time on drums that aren't DW's, to get the kick drum to work. I will build tunnels out in front of the kick drum to extend the front mic, so that I can get more tone and also to get me more rejection, because the drums aren't loud enough.

I will take a piece of foam, mic stands and blankets and basically extend the shell. The tunnel would be maybe two feet long. I do that usually with most drums, because you wind up with so much stuff going into the kick drum.

I usually use a mic on the front of the head, as well as one inside. That allows you to move that mic more out in front of the kick, so you can affect the resonance of the drum.

ROBERT HALL

Journeyman drummer and drum tech Robert Hall has handled the studio fine-tuning percussion chores for producers like John Hampton, Jim Gaines, Joe Hardy and the legendary Jim Dickinson. Since 1987, Hall has teched R.E.M. in the studio and periodically on the road. He has also done Little Texas, Chris Layton (Stevie Ray Vaughan) and Mickey Curry (Tom Cochrane), among numerous others. Hall also founded Robert Hall's Memphis Drum Shop, a full service operation that has attracted business from drummers all over the country, thanks to Hall's expertise.

First off, new heads are the best thing you can do to get a great sound, live or in the studio. Heads go dead just like guitar strings do, but most people don't address that nearly as often as they do their guitar strings. Generally, the stuff that comes on drums when they are new is less than the best quality to begin with, because that is a way they can keep the costs down.

The bottom or resonant heads really have almost as much to do with the overall sound of the drum as the head you are hitting on. Many drummers replace the top and still keep the bottom heads that came with the drum when they were new.

One of the most common unknowns concerns setting up the snare wires properly on the snare drum. If those aren't centered on the bottom of the drum, then it is nearly impossible to get rid of the extraneous snare buzz that goes on. It is most important to set up that snare drum with the snares (when they are engaged and tensioned up) an equal distance from each side of the drum on the bottom. If they are pulled to one side or the other, it is going to drive you crazy trying to get rid of that buzz.

When all of that is set up properly and you still have got some kind of sympathetic buzz going, you can de-tune the tension rods on either side of the snare wires themselves, the two closest to it on either side. You can actually de-tune a little bit, and a lot of the time, that'll take that buzz that one of the tom toms is causing away.

A cool trick to get resonance out of a floor tom is you can take the felt washers (like you use on cymbal stands), or you can take a little two or three inch foam square, and set it under the legs of the floor tom. By just getting it up off the ground, it just doubles the resonant factor of the drum.

Concerning the bass drum, a lot of times you will oil the hinges, but not realize that the spring itself, on the pedal, can be making a lot of noise. Sometimes newer springs and newer pedals make noise and you can literally stretch them by pulling beater forward a little bit, and doing it back and forth, before you ever put the pedal on the drum. You can stretch that spring and it gets some of the kinks of the manufacturing out of it and it'll quiet it up that way. That is without using any oil or anything.

There are a couple of heads by Aquarian that are new to the market that I think get the most incredible bass drum sound. They allow you to put the heads on without any kind of muffling inside the drums, so you don't lose the true drum roundness and the sound that the wood is producing, by filling it up with a pillow or blankets or anything like that. You can put that head on, and without any sort of muffling in the drums, get this wonderful controlled bass drum sound and it actually seems to add a little bit of low end to the sound of the bass drum as well. That is the batter side or the rear head. Those heads are made by Aquarian. One series is called Super Kick, and the other series is called Impact or Imp. Both are just terrific live and in the studio. A lot of people aren't hip to them yet, but everybody I have turned on to them has really been happy with them.

When a drummer has a whole lot of ringing in his toms that he wants to get out, but duct taping on the heads seems to choke or take the sound away too much, you can drop three or four cotton balls inside the tom toms. When you hit the drums, the cotton balls kind of come off the heads and then they settle back down and it is like this little natural muting system. It is kind of like, if you were to hit the drum and then press it with your finger, only the cotton balls are doing it without you having to touch it. You still get a really nice full round drum sound, but then it stops the ring just a little bit after the note. Naturally, the larger the toms, the more cotton balls you can put in there.

When you are using a bass drum without the front head and using a lot of packing, you get a lot of attack and punch, but you sometimes tend to lose that low end that is desirable on your bass drum sound.

In the old days, we would take a twenties or thirties style marching band bass drum, that was 26" to 28" in diameter with calf heads front and back, and set that drum in front of the drummer's bass drum and not only mic the kit bass drum, but also mic the front side of the big calfskin bass drum, which is acting like an ambient woofer. It adds all of this low end that you can mix into the final sound and really give some low end to this otherwise just punchy kind of bass drum sound. That is a trick that producer Jim Dickinson taught me about twenty-five years ago. I've used that so many times, it is crazy, but it really works great [laughs].

If you leave that front bass drum head on, you really do get more volume, resonance and more of everything out of the drum, if you can work it. From a drummer's perspective, sitting on the stool and playing, you can feel and hear so much more of the bass drum when you do that, than if you have got that front head off. If you feel good about the way your drum sounds, then you play better. You can hear it and feel it better and you

are depending less on monitor mixes and playing more acoustically with other instruments.

CRAIG KRAMPF

Over the last thirty years, Craig Krampf has drummed on over 200 albums, including 60 Top Forty hit singles, plus many movie and TV soundtracks like Clueless, The Breakfast Club, Flashdance *and* Rocky III. *These efforts have garnered over 40 Gold and Platinum awards, as well as several Grammy winning and nominated songs for various albums. Krampf's hit session credits include Kim Carnes' "Bette Davis Eyes," The Motels' "Only the Lonely," The Church's "Under the Milky Way," as well as a diverse range of releases by artists like Son Volt, Steve Perry, Alabama, Alice Cooper, Santana and many others. As a songwriter, Krampf won the prestigious BMI Million Broadcast Performances Award for co-writing Steve Perry's number three hit single "Oh Sherrie" and also won a Grammy for the* Flashdance *track "I'll Be Here Where the Heart Is," which he co-wrote with Kim Carnes and Duane Hitchings.*

When I was younger, no one seemed to know anything about bearing edges. There weren't publications out, like there are now, for younger drummers to learn about certain things.

The bearing edge is where the head sits on the drum. If that bearing edge has lumps on it, or if it is rough in one area, or that area is a little higher or lower than the rest of the bearing edge, then your head isn't seated on that drum properly.

I have known a number of people who, when they change heads, have become very fanatical about looking over that bearing edge.

If you are very careful, and don't take too much off, you can use a little light sandpaper or steel wool and maybe smooth some rough spots out. Nevertheless, there are real professionals out in drum stores who really have some great equipment and work on bearing edges. Those can always be straightened out. It's one of those little things that add up to insuring the high quality of your sound.

Around 1980, I went to using clear Remo Ambassador drum heads and I went to using a ProMark square felt beater. As a result, I am not denting my bass drum head. With round beaters you start denting the head and then it's like you start chasing your tail. For years, Dr. Scholl's Foot Pads were the famous thing to use to help prevent that problem. While I was growing up, no manufacturer made any sort of bass drum pads, so in the old days it was Dr. Scholl's Foot Pads. Nevertheless, the round beater would wear through that and you would put another on and you would just start chasing that cause you didn't want to dent or break your head. Now there are actual manufacturers out there who make special dots and special things that you can put on your head to prevent that damage.

Recording is like being under the microscope and every little thing does matter in the studio. Anytime anything is taped or stuck on top of a drum head, you are killing sound and certain frequencies. You are deadening your head. I was absolutely amazed when I went to that clear head with a square beater. My bass drum sound improved at least 60 percent. There were actual lows that engineers could show me that they were getting now on that drum, that didn't exist before. Some people maybe have a little bit of trouble since the square felt beater weighs perhaps just a little bit more. The action isn't quite as quick and, maybe if you are a real "funk drummer" or "fusion drummer," you probably couldn't get the quick action out of it. Regardless, that is one of the tips for bass drum that works for me.

If I'm doing something live, I have always been in the habit of having a spare bass drum pedal and a spare snare drum sitting right behind me onstage. It's a wretched feeling to have your bass drum pedal go down, or to break a snare head and not have a replacement. I was caught once or twice, when I was very young. In the studio, I've got 3 pedals and usually 7 to 9 snare drums that come along with me.

Even if you're playing a dive club, and you feel it might not be the greatest gig in the world, you're still playing. You should still have pride in your instrument and should take preventative measures. Just in case something would happen.

You should give the engineer enough time, before the other players get there, to get the drum sounds right. If you have the time, and the studio is available and it fits in everybody's schedule, and it is not going to cost a fortune, I love to get set up the night before and have the time to just have you and the engineer there and take the time to experiment and find the best area in that particular studio and try different mics and things. More drummers need, and musicians in general, need to be understanding of the engineer's position.

Nashville work is highly unionized and there are certain start times, like 10 a.m., 2 p.m. and 6 p.m.: three hour sessions with an hour in between. I've heard of certain drummers in town who will stroll in about ten till 10 a.m. That doesn't give the engineer time to get a drum sound. Other musicians do the same thing. Everyone is part of a team trying to work together and trying to have great sonics. People should be more giving with their time. The more time that I give, the better I am going to sound. It is for my benefit to come in an hour or two earlier, for whatever is necessary.

CHAPTER 6

Drums

Great drum sounds have been achieved with everything from mega-multi-miked set-ups to overly compressed single source cassette jam box recordings. It all boils down to capturing performance sparks that embrace the soul of the moment.

Check out all the great records in the history of popular music, from the swelling dissonant sea of cymbals and toms in The Beatles' "Tomorrow Never Knows" to the thick earthy immediacy of Al Green's "Take Me to the River," or the relentlessly ominous attack of Peter Gabriel's "The Intruder" and the floating lyricism of Tony William's solos on the classic VSOP recordings. It is amazing to hear the range of sounds that have been derived from drum trap sets.

Any engineer or producer will quickly admit the importance of getting the appropriate drum sound down right from the start.

I enlisted a handful of the industry's finest, as well as two legendary session drummers, to offer some input for maximum percussive output. Along with Kenny Aronoff, Dave Bianco, Peter Collins, John Hampton, Roger Hawkins, Skidd Mills, Nile Rodgers, Elliot Scheiner, and Dave Thoener, I would like to thank to Jim Dickinson and Jim Keltner for their assistance in helping put things together for this chapter.

DAVE BIANCO

Dave Bianco has established himself as a purveyor of audacious drum sounds. Check out his work on releases by artists like AC/DC, The Posies, Ozzy Osbourne, Henry Rollins, Motorcaster, Frank Black, and Teenage Fanclub. Bianco has also earned a Grammy for his work on Tom Petty's Wildflowers.

As you can see in the following remarks, Bianco is a fan of simplicity and enjoys learning from experimentation and happy accidents.

I think my big rule of thumb is simplicity and less phasing between microphones. I try to use as few as possible. It depends upon the acoustics. You have to figure it out. There ain't no rules. Lately, what I have been doing for drums is to try and find one microphone that will pick up the entire drum kit, like back in the day when you were working at Sun Records and recording Elvis. I try to find the best mono microphone that will get the entire kit. It should be able to get an equal amount of kick and snare. I usually put that in front of the drums. Sometimes I will use a stereo mic, like an SM-69 or a tube mic like a U-67.

Occasionally, I will apply some light compression, usually with a Urei 1176.

When I worked on Mick Jagger's solo record, *Wandering Spirit*, there were a few songs that we wanted a retro type sound. I just used the one microphone for the whole drum sound in the mix. I used nothing else and it was amazing.

With that being the core of the sound, I like futzing around the off-ceiling and the close mics. I will use D-112's on the kick or RA-20, or sometimes a 421, and outside the kick, maybe a 47FET. Sometimes I will double up on that, but I don't do that often.

I usually use an SM-57 on the snare drum. I like a 57 because it has the midrange peak and it usually can take all the abuse of the sound pressure level and not break up. It is the handy dandy.

Recently, I will "Y" the snare microphone and record it that way, top and bottom. I put a pair, so you will have a top and a bottom, which can phase and sometimes doesn't. If it doesn't, I will put a phase reversal on the bottom. I find that having both microphones coming down one line makes an extraordinary full and fat sound on a snare. That is one trick I use.

floor tom. That way you get this decay from the condenser mic.

KM-86's are my favorite choice for overheads. However, if I can get my hands on some C-12's, I'll gravitate towards them.

C-12's are fun to use, because they are so full spectrum, punchy and bright. They kind of set the tone of what the set is going to sound like at the top of the spectrum on down. The problem with those sort of microphones, though, comes from the fact that they are so wide pattern, that you can get some phasing and can get into a little

The drums.

For the toms, I normally use 421's, because I like the way they capture the low end and the attack, while having the ability to take intense sound pressure. SM-57's also work well.

Sometimes I will let the 421's get the full attack and impact of the toms and get the overtone from an 87, pulled back maybe six to eight inches above, or maybe in between two rack toms or above the

bit of a jam with them. If that is the case, then the 86's are the answer, because they are a little tighter and clearer.

I often like to shoot the room mics underneath the cymbals. Sometimes, I will have them behind the drum kit and aiming at the center of the drum kit.

Experimentation is something that I really love to do, and I get much inspiration from hearing the raw energy drum sound found on many home demos.

It is great to study about using tube this and tube that and use the cool console and all of that, but listen to what these kids do for demos and stuff on 8-track. You would be amazed, since the boom of home recording, how much wild stuff people are doing and a lot of it is being done with really cheesy compressors and microphones in really funny places. The young kids are fearless, and they don't know how things work and they just stumble upon things that are just amazing.

For the Motorcaster sessions, I re-amped a sub-grouped section of the drums back into the studio for maximum energy.

I just wanted the maximum resonance that I could get. Basically, what I did was we sent a mix, of the kick drum and the snare and the toms out in the room, through a P.A. that had a sub-woofer and about a thousand watts power. What it did was make the room resonate a bit more and we got a bit of a better room drum sound with that. There is only so much that you can do before feedback happens, but we would get the sound just under the feedback mark, where you would hit the tom and you wouldn't get a big over-ring.

We EQ'd the P.A. as much as we could to get that resonant sound out. Basically, we had more low end that way and it really made for a neat drum sound. I have done that on a few occasions. I think we had the most success here, because of the shape of the Ardent "C" room. We were able to do enough dampening to it, to make it work.

I took Motorcaster's drum sound a step further by drawing from the freewheeling home demo aesthetic. We had this SM-58 above the drums, which we ran into a Boss guitar sustainer pedal. It is a compressor that has an input/output and a sustain control. It didn't work, going right to tape, so we put the signal back through the Yamaha cassette 4-track that they recorded their demos with, and then went from the output of that to the tape recorder. I further compressed it, to get it up to a level that the tape would like to see, and it gave us this most amazing sound.

In spite of all the playful experimentation of sound, I still maintain that the key to all really good drum sounds is having a good kit that is well tuned.

We have microphones that are really good at showing you what reality is, and if you have a good sounding set of drums, you are going to sound good. If you have a bad sounding set, it is the opposite. It seems obvious, but it is really the truth.

SKIDD MILLS

Skidd Mills has made quite a name for himself as an engineer and producer who is totally attuned to the nuances of great drum sounds that have energy and exciting color. His primary studio home base is Ardent Recording in Memphis, where his session credits include ZZ Top, Riddlin' Kids, Saliva, Sister Hazel, Third Day, Spin Doctors, Killjoys, B.B. King, 2 Minutes Hate and Joe, Marc's Brother.

I take great pains to make sure that the components of the kit are the best that they can be. I also like sampling an array of snares, cymbals and other elements of the kit to insure the most appropriate tonal setting to the production at hand.

I think that the most important thing, beyond having great sounding drums to begin with, is to make sure that all of your mics are in phase. Sometimes you have to be careful. You can have a snare drum that is in phase and if you start doing something like EQ'ing your overhead mic then that phase can change. You have to stay on top of it.

For my typical trap kit mic set-up, I like SM-57's, one on top and one on the bottom. Sometimes I'll use a 421 on the bottom. My favorite kick drum mic is the AKG ATM-25, while for toms, I prefer 57's on the tops and 421's on the bottoms. RE-20's have become a mic of choice for hats, unless I'm wanting a little more top, in which case I may choose a 451 or KM-84, especially for a more "pristine" effect.

When I begin working on the drum sound, I usually start working with the overheads.

I think how good your overheads sound has a lot to do with the final overall quality and sound of the drums. From there I will bring in my kick drum and everything else after that point. You have to have some frame of reference, however, so I usually use my overheads as starters. Again, you want to make sure that all the elements are in phase with each other. It makes all of the difference in the world.

Once that is all happening, I usually like to start concentrating on my room sounds. The room itself is probably the most important thing. As far as mics, there are about three different things that I will use. I will use Neumann KM-86's in front of the drum kit, maybe five or six feet back on each corner at about chest level. Depending on how much I like the sound, I will sometimes compress it to tape. My favorite is a stereo Fairchild. Other than the KM-86's, I will sometimes use Neuman 249's. Sometimes, I will use two PZM's and tape them back to back and put them in the center of the drum kit and stick them up pretty high. I will like to sometimes blend those in with either my 249's or my KM-86's to add some "zizz." It depends a lot on what the production style is and how much of a room sound you want.

My favorite overhead mics are 414's. I will usually, depending on what kind of a record it is, put them both in a cardioid pattern and have them placed with one taking care of the hi-hat and snare and any cymbals over on the drummer's left side, while the other one would be taking care of the toms and the ride cymbal, or any other cymbals on his right. That is your basic "H" pattern. I would probably have them about three feet apart and about two or three feet off the cymbals. Those heights may change, depending on phasing.

The other way I may deal with overheads is to use two AKG-414's in an M-S stereo pattern. That is what we did on the Joe, Marc's Brother material. We used M-S stereo, which stands for "middle side." I use one cardioid mic that is suspended above the center of the kit and pointing straight down on it. I then use another 414 butted

The Shure SM-57.

right up and perpendicular to the first mic. The cardioid mic is assigned to two tracks, while the bi-directional is assigned to one track in phase and the other signal is assigned to the other track out of phase.

The whole trick to M-S is getting them decoded correctly. I have seen people decoding by eyeballing the meters, which isn't going to give you a correct stereo picture. I've seen people decode off of the monitor faders, which is not really correct. The best way to do it is to decode off of the console bus. That way, you are basically listening to the output of the console while you try to get those two bi-directionals completely out of phase. That is what you are trying to do. Once that is correct, it is a great stereo picture.

DAVID THOENER

David Thoener has enjoyed a vital recording career that has captured some of rock history's most important events (like Woodstock, Bob Dylan's 30th Anniversary Concert, the Rock and Roll Hall of Fame Concert) and albums by artists like John Mellencamp, Kiss, Santana, Matchbox 20, Brooks & Dunn, Courtney Love, Willie Nelson, Aerosmith, Jon Bon Jovi, Michael W. Smith, and Meatloaf.

It's a real art, recording drums. Drums are among the most difficult instruments to record, because there's so many drums you're encountering and you're dealing with ways to get all those drums sounding exactly like they do in the room. When the drummer comes into the control room and listens, I try to get it to sound exactly like what he's hearing when he's out in that room, not only the sonics of the drums themselves, but the ambiance, too. If I can achieve that, then I'm very happy, and usually the band's very happy.

I often like to use a minimal miking approach at first. Nevertheless, I am careful not to limit my choices as the project unfolds. One rule I've learned over the last 20 years is that anything can work and you can never dismiss any idea when it comes to recording anything.

Someone might say, "We'll just put a U-87 30 feet in front of the kit and that's the only mic we're going to use." Immediately I may think that is not a good idea, but the artist or the producer is hearing it in a way that's hard to describe, and that's the best way they're trying to describe it. You have to take what you think they want, and turn that into something that's viable on tape. Those people can change their minds, which often happens, as you start putting down overdubs, and the song turns into a beast of its own. You have to make sure that you've recorded the drums in such a way that if all of a sudden the arrangement has changed, you can still bend.

In other words, you've got five overdubs on the track, and all of a sudden that single miked drum balance that was perfect in the basic track is not quite the same balance anymore. Everything affects everything. Nevertheless, I'm a minimalist in that I will record with as few drum mics as possible, even one mic, if I can get away with it.

At the Record Plant, we used to stick drums in this first floor back area behind Studio A, where they used to put the garbage. It used to be a real drag for the drummers, because they'd have to stay out there for eight hours a day drumming with garbage around them. But everyone agreed that it was a killer sound because there was a lot of marble around and cement walls and stuff. You know, whatever you gotta do.

To me there are no rules whatsoever. I am open to everything. If someone says to me, "let's put the drum at the bottom of this stairwell and mic it on the first floor," it's like, sure, sure. Maybe something amazing will happen that will cause us to look at each other and say, "Holy shit. That sounds great."

KENNY ARONOFF

Over the last ten years, some of rock's most distinctive sounds have been the cracking snare and solid grooves of Kenny Aronoff. It's an exciting style that has restraint and taste, while conveying an ever-present sense that something explosive can happen just around the corner. Artist's whose albums are among the over 300 albums that bear Aronoff's trademark artistry include John Mellencamp, Melissa Etheridge, John Fogerty, Bob Seger, Travis Tritt, Elton John, Bob Dylan, Lisa Germano, Jann Arden and Jon Bon Jovi.

If I don't properly hear my cymbals, then I start selecting different sounding cymbals with different personalities that will allow them to speak in the kind of room I am working in. When I am playing in a room that is real bright, I will go to a darker cymbal. The converse is true, if the room is very warm or dead. In that case, I will go to brighter cymbal with more ambiance. It all comes down to what I am hearing through the speakers.

If my cymbals are getting lost in the overall sound, I address the situation by changing out cymbals that work in a frequency range that isn't shared as much by other instruments, particularly guitars.

The biggest components in getting a great drum sound are obviously the right drum equipment and the way the drummer tunes and plays his drums. That is what the drummer has control over.

Nevertheless, mic placement is everything, too. I just did a song on the new Melissa Etheridge album called "I Could've Been You" that had a real laid back bluesey feel. I used two snare drums. I played on a very small 4-inch wood drum very lightly in the verses. Hugh made that drum sound so deep and big. Then when the chorus came in, it was more aggressive sounding, like Soundgarden. That was a 6½-inch metal drum, and that drum sounded higher than the other one. The richness of that 4-inch wood drum was so amazing; of course it was tuned pretty low.

ROGER HAWKINS

Over the last thirty years, some of the greatest records of all time have benefited from Roger Hawkins' brilliant sure-footed pocket. For starters, consider such classics of Percy Sledge's "When a Man Loves a Woman," Aretha Franklin's "Respect," "Chain of Fools" (in fact most of her biggest records), the Staple Singers' "Respect Yourself" and "I'll Take You There," Paul Simon's "Loves Me Like a Rock" and "Kodachrome," Bob Seger's "Old Time Rock and

Roll," Traffic's "Shoot Out at the Fantasy Factory" and too many more to list here.

It is very important for the drummer to like the sound of his drums. If he doesn't like the sound of his drums, then he isn't going to put out a maximum performance. Sometimes session drummers, and I am sure that a lot of session drummers can relate to this, have a great sound in the booth, but they aren't hearing it correctly in the phones. You just won't put out as much. It just isn't as possible to do, because suddenly you are fighting the drums, instead of playing the drums.

It is important for the drummer and the engineer to communicate and for the drummer to not feel afraid to mention to the engineer that it isn't sounding the same to him in the phones as it is sounding in the studio. I don't think good engineers take offense to that. I think they know what I just said.

It is important for drummers to realize the effect of listening to the drums too loud in phones. The freedom offered by multi-channel personal headphone mix boxes also can lure drummers into setting up headphone sounds that unwittingly compromise their performances.

One of the things that was a little tricky to me was the multi-channel phone mixers, when I first started using them. Naturally, I turned myself up pretty loud. When I walked into the control room, I could tell that the drums weren't "singing." You are executing the parts okay, but the energy isn't there. That is something to be aware of for any drummer starting to use a multi-channel headphone mix. Keeping the level down a little bit and playing up to the music is one way drummers can approach the situation.

Ultimately, the engineer and drummer owe it to each other and the music at hand to have an open respectful dialogue. If you are not hearing what you are playing, sound-wise and level-wise in the phones, then you are pretty much going to be a sterile player. A lot of times, drummers are afraid to speak up, but if you speak up in the right way, and you are serving the project, I think it is fine. It must be done that way.

PETER COLLINS

Peter Collins, who is based out of Nashville, has produced an amazingly wide range of critically and commercially successful projects, ranging from Rush and Queensryche to Jewel, Indigo Girls and Brian Setzer.

Generally speaking, these days, I like for the listener to be able to "see" the kit in its entirety, rather than split up over the stereo system, with each component cleanly separated. I'd rather be able to "see" the drummer sitting in the room with the kit, with the kit sounding like one instrument, rather than a whole bunch of percussive elements. So when I'm recording, I want to have that vision at the end of the day.

I think that's found on most of my records over the last few years; particularly on the Brian Setzer record, which has a very natural organic sound to it that isn't hyped up.

I'm a huge fan of pre-production, so that the drummer is totally prepared and we can nail it very quickly in studio. I try and catch the early performances. They don't get better. They usually get worse. It is important to catch him while he is fresh and not "thinking." It is very important that drummers don't "think." Then you just get a natural flow of performance.

I usually like to use click tracks that are not metronomes, but actually tonal sequences that follow the chord changes. It is also helpful for everybody concerned, in terms of reminding them what the pre-production was. It gives everyone some room to breathe around it, because it isn't as rigid as a metronomic type click.

For me, a personal landmark record was *Rites of Passage* by the Indigo Girls, which we recorded with Jerry Marrota over at Woodstock. We used Bob Clearmountain's mix room, which was normally not used for recording. We had Jerry in a booth in this small room, and the drum sound was extremely present. It is the complete antithesis of the stadium rock sound.

On the last two Rush records, *Counterparts* and *Test for Echo*, I've gone for a much more organic, less hyped sound. My philosophy with Neil Pert's [Rush's drummer,] drums has changed over the years. In 1985, when I first worked with him, they wanted an ultra high-tech sound, which was very fashionable in those days; the days of Trevor

Horn, Yes and Frankie Goes to Hollywood and all those British bands. Rush specifically wanted to be in that arena, which involved a very hi-tech drum sound, if you like. It was not a particularly organic sound.

The engineer, James "Jimbo" Barton, was very much into that sort of thing; high compression on the drums and very clever use of reverbs that were very much larger than life. In those days, when we did *Power Windows* and *Hold Your Fire*, Jimbo's use of it was extremely effective. You listen to those records now and they sound a little over the top [laughs].

At the time, Neil was triggering samples of African drums and all sorts of other odd things, plus he had a small kit behind him and a big kit in front there in the studio. Together, with all his toms and percussion stuff, he would spin around in the middle of a song and play the smaller kit and then come back to the big kit.

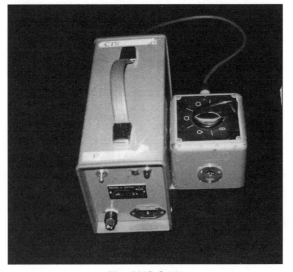

The AKG C-12.

A very good example of understated drums are the drums on the single re-make I did of Jewel's "Foolish Games," which was a Top Ten hit. The drums created a really cool momentum to the track, without you being very aware that they were there. Omar Hakim played and it was a really beautiful, subtle performance.

Overall, I think drum sounds today are so much better than they used to be. The standards are so much higher.

NILE RODGERS

During the late seventies, Chic was unquestionably the most elegant band with the deepest R&B grooves in the world of disco. One key component in Chic's artistic vision was producer/guitarist Nile Rodgers. Rodgers has since produced some of the biggest acts in popular music. One of Rodgers' production strengths come from his ability to inspire drum tracks featuring signature musical hooks as memorable as any great lyrical or melodic instrument line in pop.

Over the last year, there have been three number one rap and hip-hop hits (Will Smith, Notorious B.I.G., Puff Daddy and Mace) using grooves from Rodgers' productions. Among Rodgers' many credits are Madonna, Peter Gabriel, Duran Duran, Power Station, Vaughan Brothers, Paul Simon, Al Jarreau, Sister Sledge and David Bowie.

My philosophy, when it comes to recording drums, is pretty simple. Depending upon the style of music, and depending upon the ultimate philosophical goal that we start out with (which is also subject to change a thousand times, before the record is finished), I look at the drums as the foundation of the record, the foundation of the groove, the foundation of the song and the foundation of the mix. Everything is based around the drums.

I think of the drummer as an instrumentalist and a composer and so we are composing a drum part. We are not just playing the record. We are playing a composition with a beginning, middle and end.

Most of the time, we all play together, when we are cutting a rhythm track. Often, I'll say to the drummer, "You're the only person who counts right now. We are all subordinate to you, because we can all change our parts."

When I'm recording drums, I'm expecting some unique wonderful thing to happen on the drums, that is going to inspire me to say, "What a minute! Let's make that a hook!" That was certainly the case with Madonna's song "Like a Virgin," which Tony Thompson played drums on.

I'm not sure that I gave Tony the actual [sings the chorus drum fill] pattern, but I sure know that when I heard it, I went "Hey, I want you to do that every time at this point." It just became a hook.

In R&B music, putting hooks in the rhythm section used to be a very powerful trick. After all, when a person is singing your song, they never sing a lyric all the way through. They sing lyrics and then they sing some part of the groove.

Another song that jumps out at me is "Modern Love" by David Bowie. When we sat down and rehearsed the song, I said, "Okay, Omar, this is what your pattern is going to be." He played it and we started grooving, and while we were playing the song, I noticed that he was changing the pattern. After we finished the performance, I liked what he did so much that we then went back and changed our parts to sympathize with his parts. That is a perfect example of what I'm talking about. The arrangement that I had written and rehearsed with the band wasn't ultimately what went on the record. It was just because of the magic of that performance. After he made that performance, we didn't go, "Okay, let's cut another one and try and make it better." Instead I went, "That's the one! That's the drum performance!"

The AKG D-112

A drummer's ability to understand the beat and how to shift the feeling and vibe, to be on top of the beat or behind the beat, is incredibly essential to me in feeling comfortable with a musician. If a person doesn't understand the difference of interpreting a beat and interpreting swing feel, and isn't able to rock and groove behind and on top of beats and all of that stuff, then it isn't a person I want to play with really. I feel uncomfortable with them.

When I think about those days with Chic, we played the songs like ten, eleven, or twelve minutes at a pop with no click track. We just grooved like that. "We Are Family" has got to be like ten minutes long. When you start the record "We Are Family" at the beginning, all the way towards the end, you don't feel like there is some big groove shift.

I grew up in a vibe that was like, "the only time you speed up when you are playing is if the conductor makes you speed up." But R&B bands were all about pocket and laying and sticking right there and being able to set your watch to the tempo. We were like metronomes. We would just practice grooving. You had to be able to play the same thing, over and over and over again, and be able to keep it there for an hour, if you had to.

Nowadays, I use a click track all the time, because all the drummers I know are completely comfortable with them. As a matter of fact, I only started using click tracks when drummers I knew started requesting them.

Traditionally, it is older guys who have been playing in blues bands or more freestyle bands, who have problems with click tracks. I've been a good enough coach with these guys to make them very comfortable with them. That is because I program something that feels musical to them. It feels like part of the arrangement, and they are not just playing to a [makes a metronome sound]. Instead they are playing to something that is swinging [laughs].

If you could go into every poker game and start every hand with two aces, you would feel pretty good. So every time I walk into a recording studio, I'm trying to get in there with as many aces as possible, a great engineer, great equipment, great musicians and hopefully great songs. Then I try and make it as good as it can be.

ELLIOT SCHEINER

Elliot Scheiner has worked with many of the most successful and influential acts in pop and rock. Many of Scheiner's productions feature a drum sound that is immediate and organic, while not overwhelming the emotional thrust of the material. On radio and in critical listening environments, Scheiner's work sounds great, and the string of platinum artists, like the Eagles, Fleetwood Mac, Jimmy

Buffett, Aerosmith, John Fogerty, Billy Joel, Toto, Boz Scaggs, Stevie Nicks and Steely Dan, attest to that fact.

I go in with the attitude that I don't want the players to do what I want them to do. I want then to do what they do. Obviously, somebody saw something in them. In the case of a band, I feel that it is my obligation to capture what somebody saw. The whole trick with a lot of this is in placing the mics right.

Nine out of ten times, I find the same mics will work for most any drummer's kit. On the kick, I normally will use a 112. Occasionally, I will find a bass drum that won't work with that mic. In that case, I will go to an RA-20. It seems to be working in those situations where there is a drum that is tuned a little bit differently (usually a little lower) and where I'm not getting enough attack. The RA-20 gets me a little bit more attack on the drum.

For snare drum, I use one mic and one mic only. It is on top and I seldom use a bottom mic, unless somebody insists on it. I have always used an SM-57. It gives me the natural sound of the drum. They take a beating and they don't overload.

For the rack toms, I used to use 421's. The 421's worked great on just about anyone's toms. I did some live recordings for the Eagles and 421's worked out fine. But when I worked for Fleetwood Mac, their front of house guy was using SM-98's on the Mick's toms. (Since then, I've noticed that most of the live guys have gone to SM-98's for toms.) The live guys use them because you don't see them. They are teeny and the front of house guy gets everything he needs out of them for live stuff, but I wasn't getting everything I needed out of them for recording.

I ended up putting ATM-25's in there and those worked out great. I close miked each tom and I didn't have to use any EQ. The 98's were already in place and the front of house guy wasn't going to lose his 98's. So I had to position my mics pretty close to the 98's and pretty close to the heads. Those mics take a beating as well. I was surprised. I've been using the ATM's in the studio as well.

I never put mics underneath. I don't see the benefit. It is more phase shift that I have to worry about and it isn't adding anything. I can usually get what I want out of the tom toms from right above.

For overheads, I've always used C-12's. I keep them up fairly high. I try and get more than just the cymbals. I try to get as much good leakage as I can from the rest of the kit. I usually place them right above the cymbals, anywhere from four to six feet, depending on how many cymbals there are. I will also angle them a bit.

For hi-hat, I will mostly use a KM-81, positioned away from the drummer on the back side of the hat. If you are looking at the drummer from the side, and the top of the hat that is closest to the drummer is like twelve o'clock, then I will place the mic at about four o'clock, not too close to where his stick hits.

I've been using RA-20's as room mics, and bring them down to like chair level for somebody who is sitting down. Sometimes I will face the drums and sometimes I'll face them away from the drums. Either way, I end up capturing what I want out of the drums, with very little EQ.

I really like big live rooms to put drums in. I can always put baffles around the drummer, but I like to start with a very live room and then work down.

I've always felt that the drums and bass were the heart of the record. On most of the records I've mixed, the drums are fairly loud. With the exception of a few rock and roll records, where they are sitting back a little more; most of the records I've done are records where I can afford to keep the drums way up there, like the Eagles and Fleetwood Mac. John Fogerty loves loud drums. He had the drums louder than I have ever mixed them. I wouldn't have thought about mixing them that loud, but they definitely worked that way.

JOHN HAMPTON

Over the past twenty years, John Hampton has made a name for himself as a producer, engineer and mixer. Credits include the platinum Gin Blossoms CDs, and a wide range of other projects, ranging from B.B. King, Todd Snider and Jimmy Vaughan to the Replacements and the Cramps. Hampton's mixing skills on numerous country projects, including Travis Tritt, helped put some attitude into the genre's sound. Most recently, Hampton has been producing Who Hit John, Dragstrip Courage and the Pharaohs at his home base studio, Ardent Recording in Memphis, Tennessee.

You want to know how to record drums? First of all, as everybody knows, you have to start with a good drummer. In my personal opinion, if you mainly are recording rock, you've got to find a guy who hits the drums pretty consistently and hard, because you want a solid backbeat.

The drums they are making today, like DW (Drum Workshop), Pearl, GMS, Noble & Cooley, Ayotte and all those solid shells, are made to withstand high pressure, and they really sound better, more "rock," when you hit them harder.

In the process of all this, you can get a little more help recording drums by using analog tape. That is because there is kind of a maximum that the tape can handle, before it puts this nice smooth little bit of compression on the drums themselves. You might say that analog tape has a true zero attack time, so you don't have to worry about little peaks getting through before the compression reacts. So I like to use analog tape and I like to use good drummers and good drums. All that stuff helps and should be in place before you move microphone number one into the picture.

I like to go for a natural drum sound. The way a drum kit really sounds is probably the way they sound twenty feet away or so. Because the closer you get to them, you are so overwhelmed by the shock of the air molecules hitting your body that your concept of what that drum sound really is, is pretty distorted. Even if you put your fingers in your ears, you are still feeling the drums against your body. It is a not really what drums sound like.

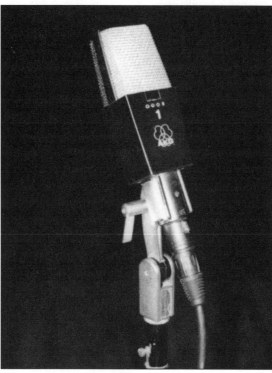

The AKG C-414.

So I tend to start with a good realistic stereo overhead picture, looking at the kit from the top. When you are doing that, you are not getting a lot of the kick drum; but it is a good place to start. When you look back at old pictures of George Martin and the Beatles, that is how everybody did it. You are looking from the top and adding the kick drum to it.

I like a fairly wide stereo picture. In that regard, I tend to shy away from X-Y stereo and, my personal taste heads toward M-S stereo, or mid-side stereo. That can give you a wider image than a normal X-Y and yet remain phase coherent. I like to use condenser mics that have a pad. I've used everything, but my favorites today are AKG 414's. They get the closest to capturing the body of the cymbal, as well as the high part of the cymbal. They usually will also give you a pretty good starting drum sound on their own, without any other microphones.

From there, I will start trying to put the kick drum into the stereo overhead picture. My choice today is the AKG D-112, but there are a lot of good kick drum mics out there. I've used Beyer 201's and Audio Technica ATM-25's, which are good sounding kick drum mics. I've even used a KM-84 and blew it up. But it sounded good for a minute.

Getting that microphone to be phase coherent into your overhead picture is pretty much a matter of hitting phase switches. You try to get the kick drum as equal in level to how loud the kick is in the overheads. Then you start hitting the phase switch on the kick drum and you'll usually find that one phase position yields a bit more low end than the other. That is the one that you want to go with. Then you EQ to taste, like dump all the midrange, but add a little 4 kHz.

My rule is W-A-R on 580 Hz, if you are using a Neve console [laughs]. Dump it when you record it and dump it when you play it back. Why? Because if you do that, then the sound you get is the sound of rock. It is "that" sound. It is the "sound" you've heard on every great rock record on the planet. Midrange on drums, to me, just sounds like cardboard. It sounds cheap. Dumping midrange is a more high tech sound.

Now we have to bring the snare drum into the picture. Normally, I will use a regular old Shure 57. I mic top and bottom. The bottom mic, for me, is optional. Sometimes you need it and sometimes you don't. It depends on how hard the person playing is hitting the drum. If the drummer is creaming it, you may need a little bit of that bottom mic, because one of the physics principles of a snare drum is that, no matter how hard you hit the drum, the snare rattle is always about the same level. So the harder you hit the snare, the quieter the sound of the bottom head relative to the top head. So the harder the drummer hits, generally the more I might need that bottom mic to get the whole sound of the drum.

Usually, a 57 is a little midrangey in the 1 kHz range and you want to get rid of some of that and add a little top to brighten it. So put in a little mid-dump and add top EQ to it and then bring that into the overhead picture and get it balanced in there about equal with the overheads and you start doing the same thing with the phase switch. You will always find one phase switch that is a bit more robust than the other.

I mix lots and lots of records that nobody got the snare drum phase in with the overheads. All of a sudden, for the first time, people are hearing their snare drum in phase with their overheads and they think I'm a genius. I'm not a genius. All I did was put your snare in correct phase.

Basically, what I just explained is what I do all the way around the kit. I do the same thing with the tom toms. I dump some mids and, usually, add a little in the 4 kHz range for stick attack, so it'll kind of cut through the wall of guitars you are going to end up with. And with all the tom toms, check the phase by putting each of them up equal in level to how loud it is in the overheads and mess with the phase, until you get it right. I usually use 57's on the toms, too.

Sometimes, some drums don't give you that 100 percent happy feeling in the resonance department. Adding a mic underneath the tom tom, usually out of phase with the top mic, adds back that boom boom you are so use to hearing. I usually use 421's for that, and I generally don't EQ. I just knock it out of phase. Knocking it out of phase will do a little bit of a natural midrange dump, because of its distance to that top mic. A lot of times, that mid-dump is proportional to the size of the drum. What I mean by that is, the bigger the drum, the further those mics are apart, and the lower that canceling frequency is, which is about right for the bigger drums. You want to go down with the frequency with the mid-dump.

For some reason it seems that whatever that canceled frequency is between those two microphones, seems to be a good frequency to cancel and that frequency obviously becomes a lower and lower frequency, the bigger the drum is, because that distance between those two mics has been increased. The wavelength of the cancelled frequency is longer, because the microphones are getting further and further apart, because the drums are getting bigger.

So you've got the kick, the snare and the toms in the picture with the overheads. At this point, I will get the guy to play for a while and kind of putz to taste to get it to where I like it. At that point, you want to listen to the balance of the drums and make sure that the ride cymbal and the hi-hat are sonically in proportion to the kit.

A lot of times, when you lean on an overhead picture like this, the ride cymbal (just by virtue of the fact that the drummer generally keeps the ride cymbal lower and closer to the drum kit than a crash cymbal) sometimes needs a little help. So although it is totally against everything I know, I'll put another mic on the ride cymbal to help bring it into the picture. The more mics, the more of a headache it becomes to keep it all phase coherent.

Now I have the distance between the ride cymbal mic and the overhead mics to contend with. Sometimes, you will find that, if you talk to that drummer, you'll find out that he or she may be able to live with the ride in a place where it is more easily heard. A lot of drummers are like that. So the first thing I'll do is say, "Hey, can we scoot this over here?" If this doesn't cause a panic, then I will do that. If it does cause a panic, because I don't want to ever mess with a player's comfort level, I'll bring in another mic.

A lot of times, you can bring in the other mic underneath the ride cymbal. This is a little helpful, because the cymbal itself becomes a sonic barrier to the crash cymbals. It can actually help isolate the cymbal by miking it in from the bottom. Although generally the ride sounds you are looking for come from the top … where the bead hits the metal. So in an ideal world, the extra mic would be on top, and you'll just live with it. Maybe you can just squeak just enough of it in to where it is in proportion, and that is it. Don't try and get it too loud, or you will open you a whole new can of worms.

For a lot of these drummers, when the hat opens and the cymbal plates are lose and banging into one another, you can't get the hi-hat low enough in the mix. Then when they tighten it up and start playing a little beat on it, you can't get it loud enough. It has always been a big headache. So I usually have a good condenser mic, probably a good KM-84 or a 451 or something that is a half-inch condenser with a 10 dB pad. On the top above the hi-hat, generally not necessarily looking at where the stick hits the cymbal, but rather in a place where it is not letting the snare drum fall into the microphone's pick-up pattern. Usually, a lot of times, you can take these mics and you don't have to aim the mic at the point where the stick hits the cymbal. You can aim it opposite the cymbal from there and, where the stick hits the cymbals, it is still within the good part of the microphone's pick-up pattern, but the snare drum is not.

So I usually have that, but I like to keep it down, unless I absolutely have to have it. Because, again, it brings in another little phase problem. The fewer mics the better.

A lot of times, in rock music especially, it kind of gets hard to keep that soundstage picture clear, and I understand that a lot of people nowadays … you kids out there … don't necessarily want it to be clear. Fine! But in case you are one of those who want to keep it a little cleaned up, usually the best way out of that is to put some of that super high 16 or 17 kHz type EQ on those overheads. It makes an artificially detailed drum picture, but it has a tendency to detail the drums in a place that

is well above the smear of electric guitar crunch stuff. The higher frequencies are not really in those guitar sounds. So those higher frequencies are a good place to go to pull the drum detail out of the guitar hash.

But then you may run into the problems of a hi-hat falling into the same frequency range of an "S" in the vocal. Now you've got a singer who is singing about "girls," instead of a "girl," and now he's got two girlfriends. That is because the hi-hat made it sound like there was an "S" after the word "girl." [sings] "You're so fine girls. Ooohh, you're so fine girls." So the guy's girlfriend hears his song on the radio and knocks him upside the head, thinking he's got a bunch of girlfriends.

My favorite reverb is a natural room, and my "favorite" favorite reverb is the room the drums are sitting in. That is actually air molecules moving around in sympathy with the drum kit. When I do set up room mics, I like to set up ROOM mics, meaning I don't mic the drum kit from the room. I mic the room. I usually have a tendency to use large diaphragm condenser mics looking away from the drum kit towards parts of the room that sound good. I'm getting what's coming off the walls and floor and ceiling. I think the reason I like that is because it enables me to maintain a detailed drum picture and yet add a room sound to it.

If you put your room mic up looking at the drum kit, you will often encounter some problems with maintaining the clarity of the drum's sonic picture.

Let's just set up a typical scenario. The stick hits the ride cymbal. The sound gets to the overhead mics in, say, 2 milliseconds. Then that sound arrives to the room mic in 47 milliseconds. Now you have smeared the definition of the drum picture. And that is happening with all of the cymbals and all of the drums and everything. But if you are just getting the reflections off the wooden walls of the tracking space, the wood doesn't contain those higher frequencies and therefore, they don't have a tendency to smear the detail of the drums.

There are some pretty bright sounding rooms out there, and Ardent's C studio is one of the brightest. But even our C studio doesn't ever get up to the point of smearing that detail. It gets pretty bright, but it doesn't do that. If I do end up mixing stuff where people had mics looking at the drum kit, I have a tendency to dump everything from about 3 or 4 kHz up out of those rooms. I then let the overheads serve as the providers of the detail and not the room mics. That is often helpful.

CHAPTER 7

Dynamic Signal Processing

Depending on which engineer or producer you are talking to, the subject of when and how to use dynamic signal processing—compressors, limiters, expanders, gates—can raise a passionate range of opinions. If you say to the wrong guy, "Hey, I really like the sound of a compressor smashing the crap out of a room drum sound," you might have permanently discredited yourself. Someone else might get enthusiastic and excitedly share his methods in achieving new levels of sonic bizarreness.

When it gets down to it, most everyone will admit that it's whatever works for your ears. Obviously, jazz or symphonic music requires a different sonic approach than rap, hard rock, folk or country.

It is generally regarded that dynamic signal processing came into being during the 1930's, with Bell Laboratories designing equipment to control the amplitude characteristics of telephone signals. It was around that time when the film, broadcasting and music recording industries picked up on this development, enabling users to have better control of excessive signal variances.

Basically, limiters kept extreme or sudden loud passages from going beyond a certain point and compressors helped contain those loud sections, while bringing up the volume of quieter passages. This enabled the signal to have more apparent loudness.

Early devices of note were the Western Electric model 1126A limiter amplifier, which was used extensively by the film world. RCA was another pioneer in dynamic signal processing. Their LA-2A, which came out in the early forties, was another classic that found much use in the film world.

Since then, there have been a truckload of signal processing devices introduced in the audio world. Most haven't endured, but names like Fairchild and Pultec elicit quite a cult of equipment personality reverence for many. As a result, the value of these vintage units has increased to phenomenal proportions.

For this chapter, I talked to Bruce Swedien, Joe Hardy, John Hampton and Bob Ludwig, who generously gave their input concerning the gear they liked best and how they use it in the studio.

JOE HARDY

Joe Hardy is the guy responsible for helping ZZ Top achieve their legendary gritty crunch. Besides engineering and mixing the multi-platinum Afterburner *and many of that Texas trio's other classic albums, Hardy's producer/engineer credits include Georgia Satellites, Steve Earle, Jeff Healey, and The Hooters.*

The term *compressor,* in and of itself, sounds pejorative. It's like, "You are compressing my voice? You are taking my big huge voice and squeezing it down to this?" It sounds like an evil thing, but compressors are our friends.

A lot of singers might get a nice thick tone, but when they go up to another note, their tone thins out a little bit. If they go up to another note, it is fucked. To a degree, compressors really help all that, because they even everything out.

To help give immediacy and presence to Billy Gibbon's voice on ZZ Top's *Antenna*, I cut with a Valley 440.

I don't think they make those anymore. They were made in Nashville. They are great vocal compressors. The Valley 440 takes the low stuff and turns it up. It still limits the dynamic range, but instead of not letting the high stuff through, it takes the low stuff and turns it up, so the dynamic range is moved up from the bottom. All of Billy's vocals are going through the Focusrite pre-amp and a Valley.

I ran Gibbon's guitar signal through a Fairchild limiter to achieve his classic in-your-face guitar skronk.

It was pretty slamming. I'd say I had 10 or 15 dB of compression at all times. I also probably compressed it some during mixing on the SSL. I compressed the mix and the mastering guy compressed the mix and then the radio station compressed the mix. People like compression.

For mixing, I use the SSL main compressor for the whole mix a lot. I usually use a 4 to 1 ratio and I don't really try to compress stuff more than about 4 dB or so. I've seen very famous mixer guys go way higher than that. I think you want to get as much compression on there as you can and still sound loud, but to where you don't start hearing breathing. The SSL is one of those compressors that (if you set it right) you don't hear it much. You want it to sound fairly smooth and to sound louder. I think the SSL compressors are really good for that. I especially like the convenience of the SSL compressors.

One reason I really use them is because everybody changes their mind so much on the mix. The computer remembers where the settings are for each channel. So it is way easier, because you know you can get the mix back to where it was, better than having to rely on notes about outboard compressors. That's why everybody likes SSL.

Generally, I go for the slowest attack I can get and the fastest release I can get.

If the attack gets fast, it really starts crunching the transients. It makes everything sound non-raucous. You want to let all the transients come

through, but if the attack time is too ridiculously slow, it never catches anything.

Compressors kill high end real fast. They can really dull stuff out and it is because they start taking the transients out. If your perception is, "The cymbals don't sparkle as much as they used to," it is because you are not getting that first big spike that screams "cymbal" or "snare drum" at you. Pianos, acoustic guitars, all those things start getting duller when they just don't have that little spike on them.

BRUCE SWEDIEN

Bruce Swedien, whose engineering credits range from Duke Ellington, Tommy Dorsey, and Quincy Jones, to Michael Jackson, feels that a producer or engineer should be very judicious with signal processing.

I do a lot of R&B music. If the music doesn't have a lot of the primitive energy in it, then it loses a lot of its appeal. To me, compression kind of takes away that extreme energy and makes things sound a bit contrived. Limiters and compression in general will tend to remove high frequencies first. I would rather have peaks that go past the limits of what we should be doing and keep the primitive energy there.

Michael Jackson's classic 1979 dance hit "Don't Stop Till You Get Enough," which I mixed, has absolutely no compression.

The absolute opposite of that approach was "Jam," the opening cut of *Dangerous*. On that track there is a lot of individual channel compression on the SSL.

Among the compressors and limiters that top my list are the Fairchild, the Urei 1176 LN and the Neve 2254, which I occasionally use slightly on Jackson's voice; it's a favorite for mixing. I also have a stereo pair of 165 A DBX limiters, as well as four DBX 160's.

I found this Neve console in Toronto. In it were these class A solid state 2254 Neve limiters. I had them pulled out and installed in my racks. I replaced the DBX 165 A's with the Neve 2254's. I didn't change anything else and made Michael (Jackson) a mix on a cassette. He called me the next day and said, "You've changed something on my voice and I love it." If that isn't a testimonial, I don't know what is. It was precisely the same gain control and the same levels, in and out, but a totally different emotional response. It was warmer. It almost sounded like more low end, but of course, it isn't. I would also used the adjectives of clearer, less fuzzy.

The Fairchild is also a classy piece of gear. The one I have is an old tube 2-channel mastering limiter. It is extremely warm and very gentle. I don't think you can even vary the attack or release. It's pre-set. If you have a choir image or something where the miking image hasn't been optimum, and you've got some tones or sounds that are a little woofy, or will present too much level to your mix without adding any impact, then the Fairchild is a wonderful choice.

Unless I am going for the specific effect of a squashed sound during the mixdown process, I will almost never put a program limiter in the chain. I can remember a couple of instances, but not very often.

JOHN HAMPTON

John Hampton, whose credits include The Replacements, Lynyrd Skynyrd, Vaughan Brothers, The Cramps, B.B. King and The Allman Brothers, as well as producing the multi-platinum body of work by Gin Blossoms, prefers dynamic signal processors that are transparent, but doesn't mind using them for effect.

I generally put limiters, like a Fairchild, on musical instruments and compressors on voices. Usually I will break out a limiter on acoustic guitars or clean sounding electrics that have a lot of dynamic range, especially when they have to compete with a wall of constant level Marshalls in the mix. However, I don't like constricting the dynamic range that much.

I use slower attacks on programming in general, including the drums. A slow attack will hold down the overall level, but it lets the little transient things pop through, which to me is a more lifelike sound.

If you want "I don't hear it" compression that does a good job of controlling level, my preference is the UA 176B. A slow attack (like 4 to 1 ratio) with a pretty quick release, but not totally quick, is almost perfect for a female singer who you don't want to notice lot of compression. With the UA 176B you can control the attack and

release times, something you can't get from old Fairchilds. Generally, I like the artifact of compression and the way it sounds on a voice. Some people don't like it, but I personally do.

The SSL compressors are perfect for giving you a hard agitated effect. If you don't necessarily want that, I will ditch the SSL from the program and use the Summit DCL 200. I'll dial the attack time and release on the Summit to where I'm kind of hearing a similar tone. Then, I'll A/B the SSL compressor to the Summit, most of the time it will be toned down a little bit and not quite as hard sounding. The Summit definitely warms things up. I use that religiously on mixes, drum kits, and a number of things.

A transistor compressor that I like is the Valley 440. You can control all of the parameters on it—the ratio, release and attack time, threshold—and you can dial up just about any kind of compression on it quickly.

Expanders work well on voices that have too much noise on poor analog recordings. I will use an expander as a kind of single ended noise reduction. They will let the voice come through, and as soon as the singer is done singing, or in between words, it kind of closes things up a little to keep the noise down. It doesn't work quite as hard as a gate, which turns the signal completely off. There is an expander in the Valley 440 that I use. There are also expanders on the SSL console.

For really weird compression, hit Listen Mic To Tape on the SSL console, and put any track in Record. Whatever that is going through the input of that compressor is recorded on tape. It's this wild crazy pumping, 60 dB of gain reduction thing that smashes everything to pieces. It's a real neat sound to add occasionally, when you are looking for a raved up sound.

Gates come in handy for a lot of things, but I never automatically gate anything. Gates on kick drums with a fast attack, and a pretty fast release, can add a whole new dynamic envelope to the drum. A lot of times you can economize the amount of low end in your mix that way, which helps the bass guitar be more intelligible.

During the eighties, mainly in metal music, a lot of people only wanted to hear the stick on the head and then let the reverb become the rest of the drum, so to speak. For that effect, gates played a big role. As a result, you could have this little drum attack, with the giant reverb attached to it. It's really no longer a drum. It's another animal. I don't know what it is. It's a thing.

I will use gates with slow attack a lot of times if I've got, for example, a real quiet passage and I've got single coil guitar buzz and I want to eliminate it in between the parts the musician is playing.

I personally tend to not use any compression at all, if there is something that has got its own natural attractive dynamic all by itself and it's not competing with too many constant level sounds. Once the overall level of everything is set, I like to let the music have its own dynamic and then ride faders as needed. After all, there are definitely times where dynamic signal processing can work against you.

When you are trying to get a record approved by a record company, you might run the mix through a compressor so it will sound like it's on the radio. Sometimes that's what it takes for some record company people to visualize the commercial potential. I try to do it always, even when I am doing rough mixes, so people will kind of get an idea what it is going to sound like when it is finished. It's going to get smashed when it comes out of the radio transmitter anyway.

BOB LUDWIG

For many years, Bob Ludwig's name has been synonymous with great mastering. His credits, which could fill a book, include The Doors, Barbra Streisand, Pat Metheny, Steely Dan, Jimi Hendrix, Madonna, Led Zeppelin, Fleetwood Mac, Bruce Springsteen, Pink Floyd, The Rolling Stones, The Police and so on and so on.

Besides his extensive work with tube and solid state sound processors, Ludwig has developed quite an expertise in digital compression and limiting.

We have four different digital domain compressors here at Gateway. We have one on the Neve DTC 1.5 console, another on our Harmonia Mundi Acustica BW/102 console and one on our Sony STP 1000. The fourth one is on the Sonic Solutions system. They all have their different characteristics, just like analog compressors do. If I were to characterize them, I would say that the Harmonia Mundi is probably the most transparent of them all. The Neve has definite sound to it, and when that sound is appropriate for the music,

there is nothing quite like it. It's best for a lot of dance stuff or generally rock music. Depending on if it is working right, you would say it glues everything together in a very musical way and adds punch. When it is not working, you would say it is muddying it up.

I almost never use the Sony, because it is not quite as full sounding as the Neve. The Sonic Solutions has a compressor that is good for one thing and that is certain kinds of classical music compression. Other than that, in my opinion, it is useless.

When working with digital tape, I feel that it is important to stick with digital dynamic signal processing because of the weakness in the A/D and D/A chain.

It is not a matter of choice. If the tape comes in the digital domain, I like to stay in the digital domain, because the A/D and D/A is the weakest link. In that case I will use whichever digital console, either the Harmonia Mundi or Neve console, that I feel sounds best for it.

Analog mastering still makes up about 60 percent of my mastering business. To tell you the truth, I like analog a lot. When I work in the analog domain, I normally use an old analog solid-state compressor that is very difficult to find, made by NTP in Denmark. It is the 179-120.

Concerning the application of dynamic signal processing in the mastering stage, I let the music inform me as to how I should work a signal.

It sounds like a cop-out, but I'm a fan of whatever sounds best. I really mean that. In the morning I might compress the hell out of something and in the afternoon I might not use any compressors at all. It is completely depending on what I'm presented with. My whole job is to get as much musicality out of it as possible. Also I must take into consideration if it is a single that is going to be on the radio, I should try and make it competitive so it will jump out at the program director when he is going through a stack of CDs.

It would take a book to cover all the angles on dynamic signal processing. There are loads of compressors, limiters and other related devices out there, but it really boils down to the ears and instinct of the user. Hopefully, some of these ideas and tips have been illuminating and will provoke some experimentation.

CHAPTER 8

Field Recording and Film Sound

The world around us is full of sounds that we take for granted. Those of us who spend huge blocks of our lives in studios and listening rooms—analyzing the soundstages and wet and dry properties of particular musical recordings at hand—rarely take the time to focus our awareness and appreciation of the natural sonic richness that surrounds us everyday.

Field recording for film and for ambient augmentation in musical settings requires much more than a mere documentary approach. An essential understanding of the gestalt of the cinematic or musical moment, in which the ambient recording is to be applied, is essential in conveying the proper tone. For example, if a scene is melancholy, then the audio environment around it should enhance that mood.

This chapter focuses on those who have spent a significant amount of time in the field capturing those sounds in every place imaginable. I enlisted Christopher Boyes, Ben Cheah, Dennis Hysom and Roger Pardee for this chapter. Each of these men has an enormous list of credits and has traveled the world in search of finding the exact sounds required for their projects.

CHRISTOPHER BOYES

Christopher Boyes started out in his teens wanting to be a part of movie making. For years, he thought that his calling was in camera work; that was until he realized the creative freedom one could have working in the realm of sound field recording, editing and mixing.

Wearing the various hats of sound designer, re-recording/sound/Foley/ADR and fx Mixer, Boyes has acquired an impressive run of credits, including all three Lord of the Rings *epics,* Pirates of the Caribbean: The Curse of the Black Pearl, Titanic, Million Dollar Baby, Mission Impossible, Jurassic Park, *and many more. Boyes won the 1995 Cinema Audio Society award for Best Re-recording Mixer for a Television 2-Hour Special—*Indiana Jones and His Hollywood Follies. *He also won the Motion Picture Society of Film Editors 1994 Best Field Recordist and Best Foley Mixer for* Jurassic Park.

Boyes' bonzai dedication to field recording and sound design inspired renowned sound designer and mentor Gary Rydstrom to call him "the Indiana Jones of effects recordists."

Jurassic Park II was a big challenge, only because I made it that way. Basically, we knew it was going to be more dinosaurs and more action, and it was going to take place, to a certain extent, in a tropical atmosphere. I flew down to Costa Rica, hired two guides for five days each, and went into jungles, both in the mountainous regions and down on the coastal areas. I recorded 25 DATs worth of tropical ambiance and everything that you can imagine, including volcanoes and alligators. It was a good trip.

Whenever I go off recording on that kind of scale, I like to capture every time of the day. Audio-wise, Costa Rica is really graphic. There is something different happening at every time of the day and night. In the morning, you get these incredible crickets that sound like a burst of a shower nozzle, but with articulation and brightness. They come in right as the sun is coming up. Sometimes, you get them at sunset. You only get a three or four minute period where this happens. It is the most incredible sound, and anybody hearing it would feel like they are in the most prehistoric place on Earth.

To get a really clean articulate ambiance is really difficult. It taxes you creatively and physically, because you have to find a place that can give you a beautiful natural ambiance, you have to get there at a time where you are not going to be adulterated by either motor sounds on the ground or planes in the air and you have to have absolutely superb equipment to get a clean ambiance. Everything comes to bear in that.

The second hardest thing would be animal vocalizations, because unlike humans, they do not perform well. Typically, if they see a microphone, they will think it is a gun. As a result, they clam up, so you have an amazing amount of patience. Tame animals are worse than wild ones. At one point, I wanted to record a hippopotamus, and I think I sat there for four hours, before it gave one vocalization, but it was worth the wait.

I have invested a lot of money in microphones and equipment. While I hate to slam a manufacturer, I bought a Neumann RSM-191. On the first night out in Costa Rica, we were trying to record owls, and we somehow managed to pull a little bit on the cable, going into the mic, and it came apart. We took it apart and it was like jewelry inside, and you breathed on the cables and it looked like they could come apart. Luckily, I was able to fix it with my Swiss army knife and gaffer's tape. I think it sounds great, but I think it's not robust enough for the kind of stuff that we do.

Granted, not everyone tromps into the jungle, like I do, but from my point of view, every film should have a significant amount of new fresh sounds that nobody has ever heard before. If someone is doing major sound effects for major films, and not doing things like that, then you have to wonder if they are recycling effects. I am a really strong advocate of recording effects for the purposes of sound design for each film that are fresh and new.

I don't really like the idea of a broad mic for some ambiances. In the jungle, if you point at one direction, you are going to get a different sound, than if you point the mic in another direction. I would rather get the ambiance in one location from two or three perspectives, as opposed to getting that whole ambiance from a 360 degree perspective. Then I can mix it as I like. For field recording the most durable mic that I have used is the sister or brother mic to that Neumann RSM-191, which is the KMR-81.

In the jungle, it is amazing. You move you a mic 180 degrees (especially if it is a slightly directional mic), the sound you hear is absolutely different than the sound you heard in the previous position.

This isn't to say that I wouldn't use a nice set of omni-directionals for some ambiances. Certainly, some ambiances aren't that directionally sensitive, in terms of the quality of the sound. But when you are deep in the jungle, there is all different sorts of wildlife.

By and large, 90 percent of the stuff we do is done with DAT. I would hesitate to use a Nagra for ambiances. That is an area where DAT really shines. DAT has totally revolutionized effects recording, because of its portability and also its economics.

On the other hand, the Nagra is a viable player, and I wouldn't want to work on a production where there wasn't access to one. I do love them.

For the movie *Volcano*, we recorded a lot of loud explosions. I had some guys out at a rock quarry, dumping dynamite down 30-foot holes, for base effects for lava bursting up through the Earth. We sent out a DAT and a Nagra and, without any doubt, the Nagra was much better, in terms of low end response and dynamic range and in terms of forgiveness, if there was any sort of apparent distortion. It was sort of sucked up in the analog medium, whereas the DAT would have a problem.

Some sounds don't go down well with digital like, for instance, a 1950s Cam Siren. Those are like the old fifties wind-up fire engine sirens. When you try to record that close up, and you are going to find the digital medium doing something very strange. I was working on the movie *Quiz Show,* at the time, and I discovered that I couldn't get Cam Sirens to read on DAT. I couldn't figure out why. We ran up to the tech building here at Skywalker and grabbed a Nagra, and the result was beautiful.

Field recording always seems to have its surprises that end up expanding the sound library with fresh elements.

At one point in Costa Rica, while I was waiting around to record any given ambiance, I noticed that the mud I was standing in, which was around six to twelve inches deep, made a very powerful sound. I started recording that. That turned out great, and the sound I captured made its way into *The Lost World* and *Volcano* in separate entities, for things like dinosaurs eating and for lava glops. You can be anywhere in the world, and you can be looking for one thing out in the field and you can stumble across something else, of which you will never know what you use it for.

Even though I love capturing great recordings of sounds out in the field, I also feel that mere documentary sound recording isn't good enough when you are trying to assist in the capturing the impact or tenor of a specific scene in a film.

If you and the effects editor and sound designer were hired to work on a scene, like taking a situation where someone is swimming, you would say, "What is happening in this scene? What is happening in the film?" That would affect how you would address the sound. You wouldn't just say, "Okay, this is what she is doing. She is moving water." Your sounds would reflect some emotional content that would read on their own, to some extent, to anybody, what was the mood of that part of the story. If it is a melancholy moment, you might find that the water moves heavily and more slowly than you would expect it to, in real life. A good sound person automatically applies that sort of principle, and it comes out in their work.

Often, a number of these sounds that I capture get compiled with other sounds to create some of the unique memorable sonic statements in movies.

Fire is a very difficult thing to capture in any film. I believe that it is one of the more difficult things. I find fire to be very difficult to be anything other than a snap, crackle and pop. It takes a lot of work and a lot of patience and a lot of recording to create anything other than a rumble or high end. For *Backdraft*, the approach on that

was to make the fire live and breath. and talk. We actually used a lot of human and animal vocalizations as well.

I have to say that every film has a very challenging element. For the film *Volcano*, the biggest challenge on that were these lava bombs, where the director (Mick Jackson) asked for the lava bombs to be a cross between a screaming banshee, a Dopplered train whistle and a Stuka Siren. Of course, I immediately started working with those very elements, but it was a little hard to define what the screaming banshee was [laughs].

BEN CHEAH

A graduate of the National Film School, Ben Cheah serves as a sound supervisor and editor for New York-based C5, Inc, one of the film industry's top post houses. Ben's recent projects include films such as Hedwig & The Angry Inch, Camp, Home at the End of the World *and* The Ballad of Bettie Page. *Cheah's sound effects and field recording work has also graced films like* Fargo, The Royal Tenenbaums, The Man Who Wasn't There, Frida *and* Get Shorty.

Part of making quality sound effects is recording the live organic elements of those sounds. Without good original sounds, it is difficult to make original sound effects. It doesn't matter how simple or complex the sound is going to be, it all relies on the source sound that you have.

It is important to have original source material in every soundtrack and make things sound like they don't just come from the (sound library) CD. Otherwise, you find different sound editors from every sound house, using the same sets of CDs, and that really limits the amount of fresh material that is coming in.

Sometimes, when you are seeing a movie, it gets to the point to where you know which disc a sound effect comes from and the track number from which that certain sound originates. Believe me, it takes away from the movie [laughs]. It happens all of the time.

When you are doing on-location recording, you are able to fine-tune perspectives, whereas the people who are limited to just using CD sound libraries are usually stuck to the one perspective that has been offered.

Our job is highlighting drama in a scene, be it a very subtle moment or a very violent moment. We are trying to create more interesting elements and dimension through the use of sound. You are often over-acting the drama with sound, but that is the way that you can translate things into telling the story. It adds a whole extra dimension to the scene. The emphasis is on drama, and recording it in the correct situation.

For instance, when you are recording vehicles, the real thing usually doesn't sound big enough. If you find the right vehicle, and you drive it in and follow the action, it doesn't sound dramatic enough, so you have got to screech the car in and out to make it sound right. Otherwise, the difference between reality and filmmaking falls apart.

DENNIS HYSOM

Dennis Hysom has enjoyed substantial success wearing the hats of producer, composer, musician and field recordist for numerous environmentally inspired audio CDs that feature his extensive field recording work and evocative compositions.

Of particular note is his series of releases for the Nature Company, inspired by the Nature Conservancy's Last Great Places program to protect wilderness habitats of rare and endangered species. The titles include Cloud Forest, Glacier Bay, Caribbean, Bayou *and* Badlands.

Hysom has also recorded numerous children's albums, including the Parent's Choice Gold Award-winning Song Play Hooray!

For environmental recordings, I have traveled from Alaska to Costa Rica, and points in between, to capture the desired ambiances. Most of the problems that you find in field recording can be solved if you are patient and persistent, and if you plan carefully enough. If you have done your research, and know where your species are, and have talked to all of the various park rangers involved in managing the wilderness areas, then you can pretty much locate what you want to record. So most of the problems can be avoided.

For my very first Nature Company project, the one that I did in the Costa Rican rain forest, I took a Nagra. You get these little reels that will last a total of about seven minutes, which in the field is just nothing. It is also very heavy. After I got back, I bought a Sony TCD-D10 Pro portable field recorder. I also bought a Sanken CMS-7. It has got a front microphone, as well as two side microphones that are configured in a figure eight pattern, so that you can move the stereo sound around to be as wide as you want. It is a really a wonderfully versatile and durable microphone. I have had it in rainstorms, steamy hot weather, and I've never had it fail.

I also have a back-up machine, which is a Tascam DA-P1. It is a nice quiet machine, but I don't think it is built as durably as the Sony. The Sony is a real solid workhorse.

It is getting to be a very crowded world and it is very difficult to get truly natural sounds for any length of time at all. The sensitivity of the gear can pick up a lot of human sounds like machines, boats, saws, and airplane noises, as well. Consequently, I have to do a lot of editing. For every hour I record, I may hopefully come up with a minute of sound that is, not only quiet, but also interesting. You can sit out there in the field for eight hours at a time, and not get anything, until something special takes place. In North Dakota, for example, I sat out most of the night, trying to record coyotes. Then, finally, there may be two or three cries right near you.

An extreme example of how a recording expedition can be interrupted, concerned a recording trip I made in North Louisiana in a place called Kisatchie National Park. It happens to be near Fort Polk, I believe it is. The Conservancy land, where I was recording, was nearby. I was trying to record this endangered species of woodpecker, called the Red-Cockaded Woodpecker. This is a real fragile sound that this bird makes. All the trees are marked where the Red-Cockaded Woodpecker has its nest.

The best times to record are very early in the morning or late at night. So I got there before dawn and I was down in this culvert, and I was waiting for the woodpeckers to start vocalizing. I heard this rumble and it got louder and louder. I turned around and there was this big tank from the fort, and there was a guy pounding on the top of the tank, and screaming and yelling to the guy inside the tank, "Left, I said, damn it!! Left!" I was over in the culvert, and I had my earphones on, and I had this microphone that had a windsock on it. It sort of looked like a gun. It had a pistol grip and everything. I was sitting there aiming it at this tree. The guys in the tank were fifteen to twenty feet away, and they were oblivious to me. The gruff sound of the tank and the very quiet fragile sounds of the woodpecker was a funny juxtaposition of sounds. I could probably use it, if I ever get to do a war movie, or something like that [laughs]. It was a very funny situation.

Sometimes what it takes to really capture a sound can place you in some pretty harrowing situations. While we were in Alaska, we went out for a couple of days to record Stellar sea lions. There were these small little islands all over the area where they gathered. The boat captain actually took me out on the bow of the boat, and he pulled up fairly close to the two colonies. Each colony of sea lions is looked after by an alpha bull and both of them were warning me away with these really low belching sounds. I had this really great stereo recording of a bull on the right and a bull on the left warning me away from their harems.

We were floating in a rough sea, and the waves were making us move up and down extremely in the boat. I was up on the bow, trying to balance myself, holding the microphone, and it was frightening, because the rail of the boat wasn't very high. It would've been very easy to lose equipment or fall over into the freezing water. It would've also been all over for me, because of the rocks, which were everywhere. We were within twelve to fifteen feet from the rock outcroppings. The boat Captain was constantly having to back pedal, because the water was pushing the boat towards hitting the rocks. It was pretty wild.

My favorite part of an entire production, from the concept planning stage to the final duplication mastering process, is scouting out a location and going in recording. Even though it can get a little hairy once in a while, most of the time there is something very peaceful and serene about doing this.

ROGER PARDEE

Roger Pardee grew up in the Midwest with a desire to get into the movie making business. Getting into the industry, via the academic route seemed to make the most sense, so Pardee studied film in grad school at the University of Southern California and discovered that recording sound held the greatest appeal.

Pardee hooked up with Supervising Sound Editors Jay Wilkinson and John Larsen to work at John Glascock's Location Sound Services in the early eighties. It was the beginning of what has been a successful ongoing relationship.

Pardee's film credits include Flight of the Phoenix, Apt Pupil, The X Files, Waterworld, Last Action Hero, Trespass, Raising Cain, *and* To Live and Die in L.A., *among others.*

When he isn't working on productions, Pardee teaches courses in film sound recording at the University of Southern California.

I have recorded an awful lot of vehicles. It seems to be a kind of specialty. The first time I had to record cars was for *To Live and Die in L.A.* (1985). I filled up tape after tape, teaching myself how to do it [laughs].

There is no big trick to recording a car starting and driving away, or a car driving by. The trick is for the shots where you are tracking along side the car. It is not an interior sound. It is more of a mixture of the sound that comes from the engine compartment, and also the exhaust, and a little bit of tire work. That kind of sound doesn't always play well in a movie.

Basically, what I ended up doing was putting a mic under the engine compartment and another mic back by the tailpipe and mix the two together. I used the term "onboard" to distinguish that from an "interior" sound.

An "interior" sound is distinctive, too, but it is not real exciting, in terms of drama, if you are just driving along in a car, with the windows rolled up. You don't really hear a lot of engine, yet that is an element that you would like to have, when you have got a shot of the good guy driving along inside the car.

So what I do is record a simultaneous onboard track, and a stereo interior track, using two synced DATs. That way, when you are inside of the car, you could play the interior, and sweeten it, with the onboard engine sound. Now we have used that technique with quite a bit of success.

For onboards, I tend to use stuff like dynamic mics, like RE-15's, because they are very sturdy, and can take a little bit of heat. You could put a condenser mic in the engine compartment, but it is not the best treatment for an expensive condenser mic.

Miking the engine compartment isn't hard, but miking the tailpipe gets tricky, because of the wind noise, when the car is in motion. After some extensive R&D, we designed some special wind noise attenuators. It's true that they look like old coffee cans, lined with carpet, but that is only because we never got around to painting them [laughs]. I tend to use an Electro Voice RE-15 or a Shure dynamic back by the tailpipe. We tend to have those pretty rigged.

I use a Sony TCD-D10 Pro DAT recorder with Schoeps hyper-cardioid mics. For more rugged stuff we have some E/V RE-15's that go back many years; they're practically indestructible. And I have some other mics I've accumulated, but rattling off equipment lists isn't that revealing. More important are decent mic placement and a sound source with character.

I've recorded some really nice effects using analog cassette decks and forty-dollar mics; I just happened to be standing in a good spot during a good sound. You don't have to be an audiophile connoisseur. After all, you can take Madonna's voice and run it through some Art Deco pre-amp the size of a cinder block but it's still going to come out sounding like Madonna. Personally, I'd rather hear some lo-fi recording of Billie Holiday.

There are guys waxing enthusiastic over certain mic pre-amps now, like they are some kind of fine wine. The gimmick is to have huge knobs and dials on everything. It is like a fad. I am sure they sound fine, but it sometimes strikes me as absurd and trendy. It is like "Here is my Rack-O-Gear." Yeah, I've got a rack-o-gear, but how interesting is it to rattle on and on what is in the rack. If having a rack full of the latest shiny gear gives you goosebumps, then go ahead. It's harmless fun. But I'm not sure it's that important. I'd rather hear sophisticated dialog out of a crude sound system than the reverse.

When I teach intro film sound classes, I like to reassure the students that they do not have to be engineering or computer wizards to do creative sound work. In a sense, you need to become just comfortable enough with the technology so that you can ignore it, because if you're busy thinking about SCSI drives and file management, then you're not thinking about the story and the feel of the sounds.

I like to start by playing a series of sound effects and getting people to discuss the feelings they evoke. Then you can start to analyze the causes of the feelings. Some sounds have subjective memories and associations linked to them: the clickety whir of a Lionel train set can trigger intense nostalgia in some baby boomers. Or you can look at the objective character of the sound—maybe one reason that gentle surf is so soothing is because it's analogous to the heavy regular breathing of someone sound asleep.

Once you start thinking in those terms you begin to appreciate how even fairly mundane sounds like air conditioning can have character. In the end you ask yourself: Is the sound interesting? Is it involving? Does it do any good?

CHAPTER 9

Film Music

A movie might always be something that you go "see," but if you took away the composed musical elements that help drive the emotional thrust of the storyline, you might become very aware that a large element of what carries the viewer for two hours has to do with what is heard in the music.

Some of the greatest themes in movie music, like "Lara's Theme" from *Dr. Zhivago* or "Also Sprach Zarathustra" from *2001: A Space Odyssey*, have helped indelibly cement key cinematic scenes in viewers' minds, helping elevate the films to classic status.

Over the last few years, a number of labels have begun seriously using the "soundtrack" album as a vehicle to push the latest priority acts in the world of popular music. While this has ensured a glut of flavor-of-the-month mediocrity, it has also helped foster a growing awareness and market for releases that feature music by the film composer. Many labels have begun aggressively restoring and repackaging classic scores.

These days, the creation of memorable soundtrack music has been aided with the evolution of digital recording technologies and project studios. Nevertheless, it still takes the raw talent, vision and extraordinary self-discipline. Those have always been the key ingredients needed to have the music truly work in a fashion that makes "seeing" a good movie a transcendent time-stopping experience.

For this chapter, I enlisted four composers who have each enjoyed substantial success and years of credits: Danny Elfman, John Ottman, Trevor Rabin and Michael Kamen. (Kamen has since passed away, but his several hours, generously sharing his passion for this subject, on a long distance call from London will always be remembered.) As can be expected, these composers have had years of formal training, but it is interesting to note that three of our contributors also came from notable rock careers.

DANNY ELFMAN

Before Danny Elfman entered the world of scoring for film, he was the leader and front person for the quirky California pop sensation Oingo Boingo. In the mid-eighties Elfman began what has been an ongoing body of soundtrack work with director Tim Burton, beginning with Pee Wee's Big Adventure *(1985),* Beetlejuice, Batman, *and* Edward Scissorhands, *through to more recent Burton pictures including* Corpse's Bride, Planet of the Apes, Big Fish *and* Charlie and the Chocolate Factory *Other Elfman compositions include the scores for upcoming film version of* The Simpsons, *both* Spider-Man *and* Men in Black *pictures, and* Chicago *as well as the TV themes for* The Simpsons *and HBO's* Tales from the Crypt.

I found that trying to come up with ideas from the script has always backfired on me [laughs]. The score, for me, is dictated by the way the images are laid out. The movement, the pacing, the timing and how the cameras are positioned help dictate this. Other than the common denominator of whether it is going to be a romance, an action film, or a fantasy, you can take the same script and make twenty different movies out of it, and that for me would require twenty different scores.

What works best for me is to look at my first rough cut of the movie with absolutely no preconceptions of what I'm going to do. In other words, the more blank I can make my head, the better it is going to be for the project.

When I read the script to *Beetlejuice*, I came up with this series of ideas in my head of what I thought was going to work for it. But when I started watching the movie, there was this sad process of slowly abandoning all of the things that I had been thinking of, and I finally began realizing that this was just a different movie. What I was hearing in my head, just wasn't working. So I had to step back and kind of re-approach it fresh and then I came up with the *Beetlejuice* theme.

So the first level of my process is the initial impression of a musical piece. Now I've got something, a theme, or motif, or rhythmic feel, that I think is going to work towards a feel that is probably going to be part of a main title or some thematic piece throughout the movie. The next part is really hard, because it is about really applying it to the film and coming up with some piece, and that involves watching it a lot.

I will take half-inch viewing cassettes to my bedroom, in my studio and watch it in my den. I literally watch it in different rooms over and over, until I start coming up with lots of ideas and recording them and trying them out and moving them around and coming up with more variations. It is kind of a maddening process, because then I get to a point to where I have too many ideas and I have to see how this idea will fit next to that idea and can they go together. That is the part of the process that becomes the big jigsaw puzzle.

I can't start actually writing the score until I'm very confident that I have all of the pieces to the puzzle laid out. Now I don't know how they are going to fit together exactly, but getting those components all ready and laid out and knowing that "A" fits next to "B" and that fits next to "C" … if I need to "C" can fit next to "A", is like the hardest part of scoring to me.

This is what I call laying out "the platter." I always think about it like doing a painting, and I can't start the "painting" until all of my "colors" are completely worked out. It is setting all of the melodic pieces out. I'll work up lots of stuff and mock up maybe a half a dozen scenes and play them for the director.

I have to say that working out stuff with a director, in one's home studio, before you get in front of an orchestra is usually a very positive thing. Because whatever differences you have, you try to get through as many of them as possible, without a big orchestra there. This way, you can duke it out on your own time, so to speak.

It is good to know that the technical stuff doesn't make the score. It helps with the presentation, and directors really want that nowadays, but it still hasn't changed the fact that the art is still the art, and it is still about capturing tone. And capturing the tone is probably the most important thing you are going to give the film.

I'm real adamant about not hearing the temp score more than once. If I start hearing it too much, it is going to start pulling me in a certain direction and there is always a little bit of a struggle there, because the director will want you to hear that temp score and pull you into that direction.

If I'm arrogant, I'm only arrogant in that one regard. Because then what it comes down to is the working relationship with the director. I really want to please the director, but I also want them to know that I will not be shoved into a temp score.

As composers, there is this little bit of lap dog quality of wanting to please, and that is the part of the job that I detest in my own nature the most, because I honestly get to a point where I go, "I really do want you to be excited about this." So there is a line in the sand, where I can be very tough about it and the other is jumping up on the hind legs, with my tongue hanging out going "How's it boss? How's it boss? Do you like it like it like it?" [laughs].

In a way, writing a good score is the easy part of scoring. Convincing a director to let you write a good score, and to actually use it, is almost more work than writing it.

I would say that it helps these days to be equal parts composer and psychologist. The reason why

I'm so loyal to people like Tim Burton and Gus Van Sant is simple. They just let me do my work. It always amazes me. I'll do some work with Tim Burton and then I'll work for another director and this director might be getting very frustrated and referring to some work I did with Tim, and I finally have to say, "You know the only difference between us is you won't let me do a fucking thing, and Tim lets me do my work." Therein lies the difference. I have done some wonderful work with Tim. Why? Because he lets me. If you try and micro-manage every bar of music, you don't get a brilliant score. Period. If you make the composer spend all of his time trying to mimic what you are hearing in your head, you don't get a brilliant score.

Dubbing is getting worse every year in Hollywood films. If you take a really good 45- or 50-minute score and add 25 more minutes of music that the movie doesn't need and then put that together with sound effects in every scene sharing the moment, you won't remember a note of it. It is really only through the director's ear that everything can come to life. The director is everything. My model of the perfect dub is still David Lean and how he did his films. On some sequences the music completely drove the film, and in other sequences, the sound effects completely drove the film. Steven Spielberg has much better ears than most directors. He manages to get some pretty dense mixes and still let the music really carry itself where it needs to. Where you don't lose it and the sound effects are still able to express what they need to.

Many directors have a tendency to look at their movies scene by scene, and not as a whole movie with a beginning, middle and end over the course of two hours. If you get too loud with this sound in this scene here and here, you have nowhere to go when you need it over here, at this other place. If you looked at the whole film, as opposed to every three minutes being a world unto itself, that you have to push to its maximum, the film would be better served, but it is hard for them to do that. I don't blame the sound design for creating too many loud effects, one after another after another, any more than I should be blamed for too many crescendos or big musical cues, one after another.

In any film, I'm trying stuff that occasionally goes beyond my ability. That is how I learn. Sometimes I succeed and sometimes, I'm stuck in a passage of music, and I'm so close, and I just can't quite make it happen, and it drives me insane. But if I don't keep pushing myself that way, I'm not going to improve as an orchestral composer. With every film, I'm trying to try something that is either new or something that I haven't quite mastered yet, and want to get better.

MICHAEL KAMEN

During the late sixties, popular music was rich with possibilities and flush with the spirit of experimentalism. Michael Kamen was part of the New York Rock & Roll Ensemble, a group that was pioneering the synthesis of rock with classical elements and could count people like Leonard Bernstein and Jimi Hendrix among its fans. Since the seventies, Kamen has enjoyed an incredibly successful film scoring career, ranging from unusual works like Terry Gilliam's Brazil *(1985) and* The Adventures of Baron Munchausen *(1989) to action blockbusters like all three installments of the* Die Hard *series and all four* Lethal Weapon *films and the TV mini-series* Band of Brothers. *Kamen also composed the scores and co-wrote the hit Bryan Adams songs from* Robin Hood: Prince of Thieves *(1991),* The Three Musketeers *(1993), and* Don Juan DeMarco *(1995). Kamen's other film credits include* X-Men *(2000),* What Dreams May Come *(1998),* 101 Dalmatians *(1996),* Highlander *(1985), and* The Dead Zone *(1983).*

Mr. Holland's Opus (1995) was a special project for Kamen, as it resonated deeply with his own personal experience with a teacher mentor. As a result, Kamen founded the Mr. Holland's Opus Foundation, whose aim is to raise money and acquire instruments for school music programs in need of assistance. Michael Kamen passed away in London, England, on November 18, 2003.

So much of my process is influenced, curiously, by the teachers I've had in my life, which have become mentors for a lifetime, even though I may have only worked with them for a short time.

I had a teacher in my high school, the High School of Music and Art, that was my model for Mr. Holland, when we finally did *Mr. Holland's*

Opus. His name was Morris Lawner and he gave me one word that was the greatest music lesson of any, when you talk about composition. He said, "All great melodies share one feeling, and that is a sense of inevitability; the 'inevitable' result of the phrase that came before it." That word, inevitable, has never left me to describe unerring sense of correctness to brilliant pieces of music, and why a melody works. I apply that everyday, when I sit down with my Bach and my Brahms and try and be inevitable [laughs].

Another key lesson came from Mono Hadjidakis, who was the guy who wrote "Never on Sunday." This man was an uncommon musician. He had really stupendous talents of creating very elegant, ethereal and deeply beautiful melodies. He understood music. One time, he admonished me after listening to a composition that I was working on. He said, "You must never write on the piano." I was disappointed, because at that point, I was always writing on the piano. I said, "Why not?" And he said, "You'll become a prisoner of your technique." And that phrase has stuck with me every day. If you can only write what you can play, you're going to really be limited, if you are as bad a player as I am [laughs]. So I tend to write what I can hear in my mind. I try and let the music write itself, as much as I possibly can. I know it sounds rather grand, but it really makes me a passive part of the whole thing. It is all coming through me and I just want to keep my ears open, so I can hear the rest of the piece. If I have to, I'll figure out how to play it. The computer is, obviously, vastly helpful in that regard, because I can paint it in, and then it plays itself.

I do a lot of work on an Apple computers, and I love the new flat screen. I still use Performer, but in addition to being fantastically useful, Performer has some inherent bugs and it just crashes only when you have something really good waiting to be saved [laughs]. When I do a major work for an orchestra, I tend to do it with paper and pencil. I still believe that the brain is more comfortable manipulating that kind of data that way.

This is a very complicated commercial business, and if you are trying to make "art," you have to recognize that you're making art as commerce, and decide for yourself if you want people to pay attention to it, or just make "art." I'm certainly walking the line between art and commerce. I feel I'm an artist, and I love the result of the commerce [laughs].

I started out in *Robin Hood*, for example, insisting on using 12th century instruments. To me, that seemed to be a really imaginative idea; that we could be a wonderful noise that way. But the company's view of 12th century music was that it was probably too light to support a film like that. So they said, "If we see any crum horn players heading into the Warner Brothers lot, we are going to shoot them on sight" [laughs].

I've made some major tactical errors in my life, going to bat for a cue [laughs]. There are fifteen million different ways of solving a problem and I will always try and solve a problem by trying to make the music more potent, but that isn't how everybody feels, and it is not something that I can always do anything about.

Music, when it communicates anything at all, is communicating emotions. Very often, it appears that films allow music to become kind of a commodity, like a sound effect, and you watch sort of generic music for action adventure movies or even love stories, and you realize that the thing that is missing is the real heart of the score, the piece of music. I feel responsible to the overall legacy of music that I come from, to make music that's real and well-intentioned and is actually trying to express some little corner of a human being, if not the whole person.

JOHN OTTMAN

John Ottman is a composer in a unique position in film scoring. He is also a film editor, which allows him a lot of control in helping shape the musical elements. Ottman's scoring and editing credits include Fantastic Four, The Usual Suspects, Apt Pupil, *and all three* X Men *pictures). He is also doing the new version of* Logan's Run.

Film score, just like anything in a movie, is an illusion. However way you skin the cat, it doesn't matter, as long as that illusion is completed. If it means recording all of your instruments separately and using the music as sort of a sound design element, so be it. Whatever serves the film best.

The music is really the soul of the film. The best scores will tell a story on their own. With some exceptions, if you take a really good score

63

away from a film, you will actually hear a story being developed and themes being hinted upon and later coming into full fruition. That is a really well thought out score.

One of the most important things in story telling is making sure you have peaks and valleys. There are areas where there should not be music. The fear in many producers today is that, the moment there is any silence, the audience is going to leap up and run out of the theater. I think it just shows a lack of confidence in oneself. So the composers are often asked to score every moment, because there is a definite fear of silence. The tragedy is that the desire for a composer to do that in today's films is really going by the way side. So you have music now that is simply seen as an adrenaline pumping mechanism, as opposed to a storytelling device.

If you really study older films, you see that the score really carries them. Now everything but the kitchen sink is thrown in. Somewhere I read that the problem with filmmaking today is it is all about climax and no foreplay. That is really the crux of it. It is like we are creating a low attention span in the audience by never giving them a chance to experience peaks and valleys in the story. That is where creative sound design and scoring come in. I think we have lost sight of that a little bit.

I'm one of these guys who is barely on the threshold of understanding his equipment [laughs]. All I do is use it and I have some tech guy come and set it up for me. I've got an 8100 Power Mac that was basically out-dated the second I bought it. I use Performer, and I have four 760 Roland samplers. I have a Korg TR rack sound module, a Korg O1RW sound module, a Korg X3R, and old Proteus FX, and a Roland JB-1080. I've got a Roland R8M. My keyboard is a Roland D-70. Maybe I should do an ad for Roland. I have an old Ensoniq ASR10 sampler. I have Tascam DA-88 and a Mackie 32-8 mixing console, plus a couple of Lexicon reverb units and that is it.

I have this psychotic mission to try and do things differently. For instance, with *Halloween: H2O*, we had this huge score that we did with an orchestra. We mixed it in the back of someone's garage. You would never know that. It doesn't matter where you are and what you are doing. It just matters how you are doing it.

With *The Usual Suspects*, we recorded that score seven times with each section of the orchestra recorded separately. I'll stack the strings up and then it sounds like there is this massive sounding string section. The great thing about that approach is that it gives you complete control in the final mixing, because you have the groups of strings on separate tracks.

We also recorded the score with no picture on *The Usual Suspects*. Since I was the editor, I already knew the picture very well. It was a waste of time to try and interlock the picture and have people there complaining and saying, "Well, if you change this…" So we had no picture at all. We just recorded the score and plugged it in with the SMPTE, and it fit in like a glove [laughs].

You know you can break the rules. Everyone feels like they have hold allegiance to the rules of the game that it seems like they sometimes forget what it is like to be creative, when they started out.

TREVOR RABIN

At the outset of the eighties, English prog rock group Yes was suddenly enjoying a major comeback, thanks to hits like "Owner of a Lonely Heart," "Rhythm of Love" and "Leave It," among others. Trevor Rabin, a newcomer in this legendary band, was a key ingredient in these hits. After years of recording and touring with Yes, Rabin jumped into the world of film music and has enjoyed substantial success with films like Armageddon, National Treasure, Coach Carter, Con Air *and* Enemy of the State, *and he is working on* Glory Road.

Everyone has very clear ideas about what they would like to see or hear, but it is such a subjective thing. Obviously, what you can't do, if someone says, "I really want a big sounding orchestra here with choirs and make it sound like the biggest orchestra in the world," you can't go do something with a dobro and a double bass. You have to be a little more substantial than that.

On all stuff I've done with Jerry [Bruckheimer], and I've done the last three movies and a TV show for him, is I read the script and see some footage and go for a drive and think about it, and hum stuff to myself. I'll play the piano, go for a walk and come back and think more about it, and then I'll sit down and start writing themes, like a little suite, just to give an idea of how I see the movie—and this is without tying it to footage at this point. Once I've got that and the feeling is, "Yeah, that's the right feel," you've already won the battle of the "temp." Because your theme is now being accepted, and every time it comes up in the right place, it isn't a matter of "What is the 'temp' doing there?"

A temp score should be used to give you an idea of the best efforts of the music editor to show you where the director is hoping to go emotionally and rhythmically. When it gets to a point to where you are being a slave to the temp, it is a very dangerous place to be. That is why I really like to solidify what the themes are, so they can eclipse the temp score pretty easily.

Then my music editor will go and put down a comprehensive spotting list together of the cues, and then I'll start locking to picture. That only happens when I have established the themes.

I have a couple of dozen Emu 4's and about a dozen Roland 760's. As far as synthesizers go, I love the Korg stuff. It is pretty much all I use.

When I'm writing the stuff, I basically record it at home. I never record the MIDI stuff to tape. I just leave it and do everything in the computer, which is an Apple G3.

I use Digital Performer. It has a really great time stretching or tuning device which you can do weird things with. So everything goes down in the one format. With Digital Performer, it is pretty easy. You just crossfade one thing into another.

Jack Frost was a very interesting project. For the most part the score is a very Christmasy *Forrest Gump* kind of thing, with a lot of emotional things. In it, Michael Keaton is in a rock band that is about to break big. I wrote songs for them and created the sound of that band and what the band was. It was really fun trying to contrive everything.

When writing music, you sometimes need to take the keys of the source music songs into consideration. Quite often you will need to merge into what that song is and merge out. Sometimes it is a clean break.

With one of the *Jack Frost* tracks, the source was an old Cole Porter song called "Every Time I Smile." Since Michael Keaton was a blues player and singer in the movie and the song was a jazz standard, there were guitar fills that I thought it would be great if I introduced more of a blues feel, which was actually quite a challenge, because the chords don't lend themselves really to down and out twelve bar blues. Anyway, I had to re-do the song because it was really imperative for the movie, and there was no existing version of the song that was appropriate.

Sometimes I like to come up with things that play against the picture, rather than go with the picture. If you hit every sting, it becomes very predictable and you are telegraphing everything that is about to happen. Sometimes, it might be that I let the music try and tell people that things are going elsewhere, so that when things go to where they are suppose to go, it is a surprise. Those kinds of challenges are very interesting and very enjoyable.

CHAPTER 10

Horns

There is nothing in popular music that can elevate a track to a new level of excitement or richness like the addition of a well-placed horn arrangement or solo horn punctuation or lead ride. It would be hard to imagine many of the greatest pop, rock and R&B tracks of the last forty years with out the key horn parts that drove them. Even though this application's feature says horns, we are also including a woodwind instrument like sax, as it is crucial in the sonic chemistry of a typical section.

This time out, I sought out two legendary horn players (Tower of Power's Greg Adams and Memphis Horns' Wayne Jackson) and three engineer/producers (Ken Kessie, Jeff Powell and Shelly Yakus) to offer their pointers on the matter.

KEN KESSIE
Ken Kessie has made a name for himself as one of the finest and most in-demand engineers and remixers in the recording world, particularly in R&B and dance. His gold and platinum credits include En Vogue, Whitney Houston, Celine Dion, Tony Toni Toné, CeCe Peniston, Stacy Lattisaw, as well as mix projects for MC Lyte, Herbie Hancock, Jody Watley, All-4-One, Regina Belle and Tower of Power. Kessie's production credits include the million selling debut by Brownstone, as well as co-production of former Tower of Power arranger Greg Adams' acclaimed solo album Hidden Agenda.

Kessie has extensively worked with horns, particularly the world-renowned Tower of Power horn section. The following are Kessie's observations on

properly capturing the power and nuance of horn sections.

Most of the horn section work I've done in the last four years has been recording the infamous Tower of Power Horns. I've been lucky, because these guys are so good they make me sound great every time. Punchy, raw and somehow still sophisticated, this group calls for a simple, high quality recording method that just "gets out of the way," and lets the music speak for itself. This method was developed jointly with Maureen Droney, who actually recorded all the horns on *TOP*, their 1992 Epic release. (Besides being the Los Angeles editor of *Mix* magazine, she records a fat horn section.)

The whole philosophy behind the Tower of Power Horns is funk funk funk! This is accomplished by keeping the horns raw and live sounding. We record as quickly as possible, to keep the boredom factor down, and the excitement factor up. Only slight compression is used, and only on one instrument, to retain live dynamics. All the horns are close miked, to retain that in your face attitude. Separate room tracks would be nice, but we never seem to have enough open tracks. Ambiance can always be added later, but is impossible to remove. Feel free to try this at home (but without the cats themselves, and the impeccable arrangements of Greg Adams, you ain't gonna get the flavor).

The horns are always set up in a straight line, like they play on stage, and parallel to the con-

66

trol room window. The order from left to right is Lead Trumpet, Second Trumpet, Baritone Sax, Sax 1 and Sax 2. Any player who "flubs" during a take holds up his hand (or starts playing another song), and I can instantly back up and pick it up from before the mistake.

Mic choice is as follows: Trumpets/Neumann TLM-170, Baritone Sax/Electro Voice RE-20, Saxes/Neumann U-87's. I always kick in the mic pads, because these guys are way loud. (Years of live onstage and bad monitors) Mic pres are always Neve's. I will use any Neve console pre-amps, but on any other console, I'll rent 1073's. Neves seem to have the proper amount of musicality, richness and just enough edge to keep thing exciting. Using this combination, I'm able to cut without EQ. The only instrument that is compressed is the baritone sax. I only knock it down a couple of dB, just to keep it in place. A Summit tube compressor is my first choice.

Doubling horn sections is an oft-discussed issue. Usually, Tower of Power will double the trumpets and saxes on their own records. Sometimes inversion and notes are changed, sometimes not. The bari is never doubled, as that always subtracts from the "funk factor." However, on the blues, and other old school tracks, doubling sounds too slick and is avoided like the plague.

Solo horns are another story. Neumann U-67's sound great on the sax, what with the added "tube factor," although I've been known to use an 87, or even a 57, if I need a little more rock and roll. Solo trumpets, especially if muted, require a very dark mic. One really sweet combination is an RCA 77 with a Massenberg pre-amp. Other combinations that work well at my home studio use a Shure Beta 57 (!), and either a Neve, Mackie, or Aphex Tubessence pre-amp. Sometimes I'll throw a shirt (!!) over the mic to simulate a vintage RCA. I've never had to record a baritone sax "solo," but if I did I would stick with the RE-20. This mic adds the right funky mids to make all the bari notes stick out.

Remember to keep it simple. Keep the signal path short and get it on tape while the talent is fresh.

GREG ADAMS

Since 1970, Tower of Power has carved a name for itself as one of the most powerful and virtuoso horn sections in the world. From its inception, till 1994, Greg Adams served as the lead arranger and trumpet player. Adams and TOP's work has appeared on over a thousand recordings including work with Elton John, Santana, Eurythmics, Little Feat, Rod Stewart, The Grateful Dead, Luther Vandross, Bonnie Raitt, Terence Trent D'Arby, Huey Lewis and the News, Michael Bolton, Phish and Linda Ronstadt.

Since 1994, Adams has put out the solo Hidden Agenda *(co-produced with Ken Kessie), which stayed at the number one position on the R&R NAC charts for five weeks. Adams continues to enjoy high demand for his inventive horn and string arrangements, as evidenced on recent albums by singer/songwriter Lyle Lovett, Japanese superstars Dreams Come True and jazz/blues artist Diane Schuur. These days, Adams' horn section generally consists of Chuck Findley (who plays trumpet on* The Tonight Show*) Gery Herbig, Nick Lane, Brandon Fields and Adams.*

There are tried and true microphones that work well with horns. My favorite mic for trumpet is an RCA 44 … the big old behemoth. It is real warm, personal and it expresses well.

On my solo record, *Hidden Agenda*, I played a lot of Harmon mute. We used an Audio-Technica version of a 57 and it sounded great. Ken Kessie, who is my producer, didn't even use the room sound for those parts. With a wind screen or foam pad in front, it was like I was pushing against the mic, just to get all of that lip and the mouth noise. That was part of the whole performance. We are not talking about acoustics here. It was just about capturing the sensuality of the instrument itself.

I liked it because it sounded intimate like the way some of the old Miles Davis stuff sounded. I think that the way we did it, we took it a step further and put it right in your face. When you listen to my record, it comes across almost more like a voice than a trumpet.

If we are performing in a really dry room, we will say, "Wet it up and get some reverb going on in the phones." We want to sound like we are making a record. It is the role that we are playing and we are adding to the whole tapestry of the song.

Even if we are recording in a nice big live room and the engineer is using that room mic ten feet above you, you may not be hearing that room sound in the phones. You may only be hearing the direct signal from the individual mics, which are like a foot or two away and you are not getting much slap off of them. A little reverb goes a long way, if you are not getting that from the room.

We will always ask for stereo phones, but inevitably, everybody will have the left or right side of the phones off just a little bit to hear the room. It always seems to be that way.

You depend on the engineer to give you a good balance of the horn section in the stereo phones, along with the track. You should be hearing enough keyboards or guitar for the pitch and drums for the time. The vocal is always important, because that'll help you find a spot on the tape, if you have to stop and go back and punch in for a lyric cue, or something like that.

There are engineers who stand out in my mind as really taking time to make it all work for horns. Ken Kessie, Al Schmitt and George Massenburg are engineers who really take the time to do it right. Another engineer I like a lot is Russ Kunkel's son, Nathaniel. He has done the last two Lyle Lovett records, which I worked on. He is a brilliant up-and-coming engineer.

Probably my favorite room is Studio A at A&M in Hollywood. It is a big room and there is a lot of wood. It has a great vibe and I have worked there for years. It just seems to always be there. Capitol A, Skywalker and Conway are great rooms too.

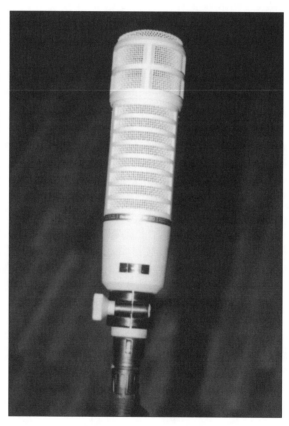

Electro Voice RE-20.

JEFF POWELL

B.B. King, Afghan Whigs, Jolene, Bob Dylan, Primal Scream, Stevie Ray Vaughan, and Sixteen Horsepower are among many artists who have benefited from Jeff Powell engineering expertise. Powell, who mainly bases himself out of Memphis' legendary Ardent Recording, has recorded over twenty albums with the Memphis Horns, as well as sessions with B.B. King's big band.

Overall, I generally don't like compressing horns to tape. I know a lot of people do that, but if you are not very careful, you can thin out the sound and squash the dynamics, which I try and bring out as much as possible. I like the little things that are swelling in and out, going from inaudible to the mighty sound that they can have. I think is very important to keep as much of that as possible, and you need to get as much of that to tape as you can.

I usually don't EQ the horns at all. I move the mics around until I get the right sound. I usually go straight to tape with them. I just keep my finger on the "Trigger," on the channel fader, as it is going down. If I compress anything, that is how I do it [laughs].

The Memphis Horns are a lot of fun to work with and they definitely have a formula on how they stack their parts. They usually do a pass with just the sax and the trumpet. Then they double that and either switch parts, do a harmony or double a part. They do all head arrangements on the spot. Then Wayne (Jackson) adds a trombone to it. He usually plays the bari sax line, or something similar to that. With the trombone, it is really the glue that holds it all together. It is really cool and it is an instantly recognizable sound.

Typically, I would use an Neumann M249 on Andrew Love's saxophone. It is an old tube mic and it is really warm sounding. It does a good job of capturing the air around it. I don't ever mic it directly coming out of the bell. I'll put it off the side a little bit, to the side where the keys are. It is also back a ways, about a foot and a half to two feet away.

On Wayne, I will use a Neumann U-87, or sometimes an AKG 414. I usually have to pad it with him, because he is really strong. I don't usually compress to tape. But I usually keep my finger on the channel faders, as it is going to tape and I ride it to tape a little, because they play very dynamically. I have worked with them so many times that I have a feeling when it is about to go up ... or when I need to pull it back a little bit. That is kind of how I keep it within the realm and get it to tape at the right level. I don't like compressing them, because it really squeezes the life out of the sound.

Sometimes, if I have the luxury of enough tracks, I will cut them each to their own track. If not, I will take the time to get the blend of the trumpet and the saxophone to one track, and then when we double, it is the same kind of thing, and listen and I go and I ride it to tape and try to blend it really well. They work very fast and you've got to be on your toes, because they will do head arrangements.

They will hum out a part as they are listening and it never takes them much more than a pass to come up with what they are going to do. They will get a lick going and they will vibe out. They will then go "Okay, every time that appears in the song, let's do that now. Now let's go back and ...."

They are really very good about vocalizing their opinions about whether or not something should go there or not. They will do whatever you ask them to do, but they are very helpful sometimes, like "I don't know if that part needs to be there. I don't really think that we need to play there."

They will go through the song, and say, "Let's do all of the choruses. Let's back up now and get all of the verses." You've got to make sure that you don't run into the other parts. It isn't like going from top to bottom with a song. You pretty much have to memorize the licks of the songs as they are playing them [laughs]. It always helps to have

a good assistant looking over your shoulder, saying "They want the third ba da bomp bomp." You've got to be able to get back there and punch that one place.

Generally, I've have the most success when I have just used three tracks. They sound very full and definitely have their own sound. Their instruments sound great, too. Like anything you record, the quality of the player and the instrument make a huge difference. Those two guys are some of the best in the world.

From working with them so much, I have learned that you have got to capture that energy out front. They really project. To just to stick something right on them, you don't capture the air and the blend of what is going on in the room. If you walk into a room and hear them playing together, it sounds amazing. Sometimes I will stick in an extra room mic further back and get some extra ambiance. I might use a Neumann 67 or a 249.

For the trombone, I usually use a Neumann U-47 FET. I have that mic set up to the side, so Wayne actually points at the trumpet mic, when he is playing trumpet, he sets it down and grabs the trombone and points at the trombone mic, off the side a bit. He actually turns around sideways in his seat, and plays pretty directly into the bell. Andrew and Wayne are very good at listening to each other and blending as well. They are among the very best at doing that. They know what is going on, and that helps a lot.

WAYNE JACKSON

Mention the legendary Memphis Horns to anyone who has avidly listened to and loved popular music of the last thirty years, and the raw sensual immediacy of classic Memphis recordings by Al Green, Sam & Dave, Otis Redding, Rufus and Carla Thomas readily come to mind. Wayne Jackson and Andrew Love, founders of this revered two-man ensemble, created a sound that has been the blueprint or template for what makes a great track greater with inspired horn charts. Since the Horns' classic mid-sixties dates, Jackson and Love have played on over 300 number one hits, including releases by Elvis Presley, Aretha Franklin, Rod Stewart, Sting, Jimmy Buffett, The Doobie Brothers, Fine Young Cannibals, Neil Diamond, Dionne Warwick, Willie Nelson and many others.

69

My philosophy is this: if it is not happening on the floor, it can't get on tape. If it is happening on the floor, then there is little you can do to screw it up.

The ambient room sound is important to me when we play. Andrew and I prefer to work in a live room that has a lot of ambiance or natural echo, so that to our ears, we sound wonderful.

A long time ago, there was one studio (not Stax, Ardent or American) in Memphis that was as dead as a Kleenex box. It was very painful to play in there. There were no ambient frequencies. I guess it was good pitch training, because all you heard were the core pitches, but there was nothing else coming back at us.

If an engineer deadens something behind us, that is okay. It is what bounces back from the wall in front of us and above us that is probably what we hear the most.

like, since back in the Stax Records days. It is a timeless microphone. For trombone, I like the old RCA ribbon mic. It gives it sort of a splatty sound, but not too much.

We have a technique that we have worked out for overlaying horns that involves overlaying three tracks in sequence … trumpet, tenor sax, then trumpet, tenor sax and finally slide trombone. We do that very quickly.

We have to have an engineer who is attuned to the process that we use, because we will listen to a song and at any moment, either one of us may hear a part that needs to be in the track; we stop the tape and we stack all three parts to that little section immediately. Then we go through the song and find all of the sections that are just like that and do all of the same parts, because we have the phrase fresh in our minds and we are hot on that phrase. So do all of them at the same time.

The Neumann U-87.

Andrew and I prefer the Neumann U-87 microphone for trumpet and sax. That is the microphone that has been giving us the sound we

We may come back and do the first one take again, because by the time we reach, let's say, the fourth chorus, we are hotter than we were when we did the first one; so we will go back and re-do the first one again.

Then we will go through the song and find another part that we like, whatever pops out of either one of our minds, and do the same process. The intros and the endings are usually spontaneous and inspired.

Andrew and I are big on unison parts, because unison is powerful. We do harmony parts, but normally, on the first track, we always do unison. On the second track, we put on harmony parts and then the final harmony comes with the trombone track. Still, it all just depends on the song.

SHELLY YAKUS

List the top engineers of the last 25 years, and Shelly Yakus will most certainly land in the Top Ten. Yakus learned under the great Phil Ramone and made a name for himself, from 1967 to 1978, at the renowned New York Record Plant. In 1978, Yakus went independent, working on Tom Petty and the Heartbreakers' classic commercial breakthrough album, Damn the Torpedos. *A few of Yakus' other credits also include John Lennon, Van Morrison, Don Henley, Edgar Winter, John Hiatt and U2.*

You have to make sure that it sounds right when you are recording the horns, or you won't get anything worthwhile.

Recently, when I did Edgar Winter and the White Trash Horns, Edgar played baritone sax, with two other players on tenor sax and a trumpet. Basically, what we did was record the horns in Edgar's house in a hallway that had a granite or marble floor. I went into the hallway and talked to Edgar and the guys and listened to my own voice. If my voice didn't sound right, I put a few small

The Neumann U-47 FET.

throw rugs on the floor in different places to try and make it sound like my voice sounded more natural, as well as the other people talking. The key to recording anything is to have the instruments sound like they are supposed to sound, and not altered so much by the room.

We weren't trying to deaden the room down, we were just trying to make it a little less wild sounding because of the hard floor and the hard walls in the hallway. It tended to make it a little too live and a little too ringing for the track.

We then positioned the guys in a North, South East/T-shape kind of position in this narrow hallway. The sax player and the trumpet player were facing each other about ten feet apart. Edgar was intersecting them in the middle, and he was back about five feet from the center.

We positioned that way, because you couldn't put two people side by side in the hallway, because there wasn't enough room, but it worked out great. The hallway filled up with sound when they played. The mics picked all of that stuff up and it translated into a good solid horn sound from bottom to top. It was one of the first times that I have recorded horns where it absolutely fit this raging track.

Usually you have to EQ them a little too much sometimes to get them through the track, and then they start sounding small.

We put a U-87 on the trumpet. Normally, once you put a pad on those mics, they are only good for banging nails in the wall. They are like blunt instruments. It kind of kills them, and they just aren't that great sounding with the pads. But for trumpet, it sounds very good, because they are loud instruments.

On a baritone sax, I will prefer to use a tube mic like an M-49 or a 47, but all we had to work with was the TLM-170, and it worked very well.

For trombone, I would use an 87. Trombones, even more than trumpet, tend to clip. They break up easy sound-wise. They seem to have overtones and, if you are not careful, the console will overload, or the console or tape machine will clip. So I find that I have to use a mic where I can put a pad on the mic when I'm doing a trombone.

Sometimes, if you get the mic far enough away, you can use a tube mic on it and they can sound really good. It just depends on what the player is playing.

If you were to put a bright mic on a bright horn, you are going to get a little sound. So I find that if I use an 87, it warms the horn up in the right way. I have tried other mics, and the 87 for me, and my style of recording seems to work the best on loud instruments—loud horns and stuff like that.

As far as positioning, I always pull the mics back quite a ways from the bell. I get it back as far as I can. I really believe that the sound doesn't become the sound until it is a few feet away. What I am looking for is the fullness. Typically, we were putting them all on one track.

When you pull that horn section down into the mix, if you don't get it right, all you are going to hear is the trumpet peaking through all the instruments and you lose anything else. Everything is sort of in there, but it isn't in there loud enough. So by getting a lot of body on the instrument, you are more assured that when you pull the horns down into the track, you are going to hear everything that they are playing.

What I would do is limit the low horn, like the bari sax. Typically, when you drop the horns into the track, you are going to lose the lowest horn first. The brightest horn, in pitch and frequency, is the one that is going to stick out. So if you limit the low horn a little bit, or the low two horns, like the bari or the tenor, it holds those horns in a place on the track, so that you are not going to lose them in the final mixdown.

I don't limit the trumpet, because it just doesn't sound right to me. You also lose a lot of the dynamics. The trumpet being unlimited seems to make the other horns sound not limited, even though they really are.

Another reason why I leave limiting off the top horn is that it appears to give the whole horn section life. It is sort of an audio trick.

If you put the mic too close into the bell of the horn, it may appear, when you are listening loud to the horn solo in the speakers, it may seem exciting sounding, but when you drop it back into the track, it is going to be this little farty sound.

I find that if I take the mic and move it around to get what I am looking for on the horn, there are enough places you can face that microphone and get what you want.

CHAPTER 11

Keyboards

From Charles Earland and Jimmy Smith funking up jazz on the B-3, to The Moody Blues' Mike Pinder with his densely orchestrated Mellotron atmospherics, to E. Power Biggs' grand pipe organ performances of Bach, or the amazingly subtle and musical application of analog synth on the Beatles' masterpiece *Abbey Road*, keyboards have always provided music with an almost endless array of colors and nuance.

It would take a book to adequately cover all the elements of recording keyboards. For this chapter, I enlisted Christopher Greenleaf, Cookie Marenco, Leanne Ungar, and Tony Visconti to offers their thoughts on recordings everything from pipe organ and Fender Rhodes to accordion, synths and Mellotron.

TONY VISCONTI

Over the last three decades, Tony Visconti has produced, engineered, mixed and arranged orchestral parts for some of the most innovative artists in pop and rock music. Among those he has worked with are David Bowie, T-Rex, The Moody Blues, The Move, Iggy Pop, Wings, Sparks, Strawbs, Badfinger, Gentle Giant, The Radiators, Boomtown Rats and many others.

One of the most exotic keyboards to record is the Mellotron, and its first cousin the Chamberlin. They are not dissimilar in concept; they are both keyboard samplers that play prerecorded analog tapes (Mr. Chamberlin left the Mellotron organization to start up his eponymous keyboard company).

I started recording Mellotrons as early as 1968, after hearing that haunting flute intro to "Strawberry Fields Forever." In London, in 1968, you could actually hire that very same Mellotron The Beatles hired to play that very same flute sound and also that flamenco guitar run used at the beginning of "Bungalow Bill" (by pressing one key). One could also request the sound effects library rack of tapes that the Beatles also used for the jet airliner wheels squealing at touchdown at the beginning of "Back in the USSR." Even before hot string sounds were available on early ARP synthesizers, the Mellotron afforded the average Brit pop band a sleazy opportunity to have a string section on their record and it wasn't synthesized, it was the real deal, real strings.

It isn't so strange to learn that the Mellotron was intended to be a home keyboard, an alternative to an electric organ. The infernal mechanism that played a seven second piece of tape at the touch of a key was not meant for heavy studio or road use. I have witnessed many times the contents of a Mellotron tape rack spewing all over the control room floor. It was a gifted roadie who knew how to wind the tapes back onto their rack.

There are special ways to record a Mellotron. The Moody Blues were one of the first groups to get a reasonable quality sound from this instrument. Justin Hayward confirmed to me that Mike Pinder used to smooth out the erratic wobble of the tapes and the limited seven second playback by recording the same parts triple-tracked and playing slightly ahead and behind the beat so that the wobbles would smooth out a little by subsequent overdubs. In my early use of the Mellotron I did this too, with session players Rick Wakeman and others.

The only way to record a Mellotron was from its direct output, to get cleaner access to those tapes. It had built-in speakers, but they made the sound even more intolerably low-fi. The tapes were divided into three discrete tracks, so you had a violin, a cello and a flute available on one tape rack. It was soon discovered that you could have a violin and flute sound simultaneously by jamming the tape playback head between settings. This is a physical procedure, not electronic switching. One can only assume that tape head azimuth was never a strong point of Mellotrons.

In recent years, the Mellotron has had a renaissance and many of these old beasts have been resurrected from scrap heaps. In the late sixties it was apparent that the tapes were not getting any younger or fresher with constant use. I've heard that now there are enthusiastic Mellotron users who've found the original master tapes and are making copies for current use. This may be all well and good, but then there are the tape heads themselves, which are rutted almost beyond use on some units. In the eighties I realized that there will come a point when the last Mellotron (or Chamberlin) will fall sideways into the dust so I decided to record and sample as many Mellotrons as I came across.

I first did this when recording with the Moody Blues in recent years. I produced the albums *The Other Side of Life* (featuring the single "Your Wildest Dreams"), *Sur La Mer* (featuring the single "I Know You're Out There Somewhere") and *Keys of the Kingdom* (seven tracks). The Moodies were reluctant to use their old Mellotron, kept in storage for over a decade, because of its inherent unreliability. I coaxed their road manager to dust it off and fire it up and I found the most exquisite string sample. Justin told me that they commissioned the string sounds themselves because they didn't like the original batch that came with it. I had my assistant engineer run a DAT as I played and identified each note of the chromatic scale. I then sampled only the best

The ARP 2600.

notes based on clarity and the least amount of "wow" and "flutter." Then I spanned them along the keyboard as Akai S1000 samples (a good, clear G# would also have to substitute for a wobbly G and A). The results sounded better than any Mellotron on the planet. We used the results on tracks of *Keys of the Kingdom*, and of course I retained the samples for my personal sample library. The Moodies are using my sampled string patch on their live dates to this day. What is even more special about my samples is that I looped the notes very carefully so that I am not limited to the seven-second length restriction.

I was also fortunate to have a friend in Los Angeles who has an excellent Mellotron in his possession, Jan Paulshus,

Mellotron 400SM #1671, owned by David Cilia.

a salesman for Roland. He kindly allowed me to stick his instrument's output into my portable DAT recorder and I played every note of every tape he possessed. Let's face it; these Mellotron tapes will never improve with age. They can't loop either. My philosophy is this: a good Mellotron is a sampled Mellotron. As for the wobble of the tapes (wow and flutter), I intend to start resampling from my DAT originals and run these samples through my Pro Tools rig to even out some of the more vicious wobbles with my Antares Autotune plug-in.

Here is my Mellotron credo:
A good Mellotron is a sampled Mellotron.
A good Mellotron sample is looped.
A good Mellotron loop is Autotuned.

An obvious bonus to having a looped, optimum keyboard-scaled Mellotron patch is that it is MIDI-addressable—you can pitch-bend, play dynamically, use a sustain pedal and add chorus effects, etc. These enviable features are lacking in the standard, vintage Mellotron. The original,

first generation Mellotron players clamored for these features.

About other units, an electronic keyboard is a musical instrument, not just a playback machine. An engineer thinks nothing of reaching for outboard equipment, compressors, equalizers, effects boxes, etc., when recording guitars, drums or vocals. With modern synths, sound designers give you their versions of onboard effects added to their patches and, in most cases, they are not what you would want. I try to take the effects off by accessing them in the synths menu and then process the dry patch according to what the song demands. For lead sounds a fat tube compressor really toughens the sound. The best way is to actually play the synth through a hot guitar amp, mic it and maybe blend it with the direct signal. A brass patch can benefit from being made punchier by putting a gate across the output and a compressor after the gate.

I'm currently finishing an album for a group called Rustic Overtones, on Arista Records. Their keyboard player, Spencer Albee, uses vintage keyboards almost exclusively—a beat-up Hammond B-3, a Clavinet and a Wurlitzer electric piano. For a crunchier sound on the "Clav" and "Wurlie" we put them through a SansAmp, the Swiss Army knife of guitar amp simulators. Sometimes the Clav actually sounded like a shredder guitar. Other times we'd put these instruments through an actual Marshall or Soldano amp reserved for their guitarist. Of course, there is nothing like a dedicated guitar pedal to help spice up a keyboard. There are no rules that say you can't put a keyboard through a guitar pedal and that's what we did on many tracks.

Leslie organ cabinets can be recorded many different ways. The usual stereo mic placement, plus a third for the low-end speaker, quite often negates the Doppler effect and makes the B-3 unusually wide for a rock mix. In the sixties one mic was usually only used for the top of the cabinet and this actually pronounces the Doppler effect more. For the Rustic Overtones B-3 we often added ambient mics to capture the sound of the room we had the cabinet in, and we were fortunate enough to record the B-3 in two great sounding rooms, studio A at Avatar in Manhattan and studio A at Long View Farm in Massachusetts. This created a very warm, vibey sound on the quieter songs. For the loud songs Spencer simply cranked the cabinet amps to the max, which almost slices your head off.

In the earlier MIDI days, synths and samplers were more monophonic and lacked onboard effects. Virtual keyboard tracks were unheard of and a keyboard or sampler was recorded to tape. One way I made a monophonic source into a stereo spread was to double track the mono patch with either varispeed on the multitrack, slowing the tape down a few percents, or simply detuning the keyboard and playing back both tracks extreme left and right.

We did the tracking for David Bowie's *Scary Monsters* album at the old Power Station, now called Avatar. Studio A is virtually unchanged since the time we used it in 1979. We had the good fortune of having Bruce Springsteen and the E Street Band recording in studio B at the same time. We often met in the main reception area during meal breaks. Bowie drummer Dennis Davis casually leaned over to ask Springsteen what band he was in—that's how informal the atmosphere was then.

We borrowed Springsteen's keyboard player Roy Bitten for an overdub on a track that was later named "Ashes to Ashes." We adamantly decided that the intro of the song had to be played on a Fender Rhodes, with the vibrato on maximum. Unfortunately one side of the Rhodes output had blown and we were only getting on and off from one channel, no vibrato. We were too impatient to rent another Rhodes but we wanted that rapid vibrato, nevertheless. I had a bright idea, since the only other available keyboard that night was the grand piano. I sent the piano to an Eventide Instant Flanger and tweaked that thing until I was getting that long sought after vibrato. It was a better sound in the end than what we had hoped for.

That electronically flanged piano is what made the final cut. So radically different was it from a normal "steam" piano that to this day people are still asking me what that instrument was.

COOKIE MARENCO

Cookie Marenco is an independent engineer and producer living in the San Francisco Bay Area but working globally. She has worked with Max Roach, Charlie Haden, Mary Chapin Carpenter, Praxis (with Brain and Buckethead), Ladysmith Black Mambazo and Tony Furtado. Matt Rollings, Jon Carroll, Clara Ponty, Phil Aaberg, Liz Story, Rodney Franklin, Billy Childs, Carla Bley, Jon Jang, Dirk Powell, and Kevin Kern are among the keyboardists she has recorded. For the last few years, Cookie has been digging deep into creating compelling audiophile surround recordings. She has also launched a new label, Blue Coast.

I used to be a keyboard player in a past life and still have about a dozen instruments around. There's been a renaissance in the last few years of the older, classic instruments like the Fender Rhodes and Hammond B-3 organ. I still haven't found a synthesizer that can duplicate their sound, let alone the feel and touch. Many synths can come close—or at least close enough to save your back when schlepping it around is an issue. In fact, my Rhodes was packed up and hidden in storage for 10 years until Myron Dove (bassist—Santana, Robben Ford) came in one day, found all the pieces and put it together. I was shocked at how good it sounded.

There are two things that make my job of recording easier on keyboard. One is a great player who understands the nuances of these instruments, like the B-3, and the second is having an instrument in good shape. No easy feat. The B-3 can have problems like the percussion switch not working or the Leslie spinning at an odd speed—or not at all—and without a person who really uses those elements of the B-3, you'd never know there was a problem. But even a busted B-3 sounds better than any synth as long as it makes a sound.

For miking a B-3, I like to use 3 tracks whenever possible. A stereo pair on the spinning horns of the Leslie and one mic on the bottom. I've used 3 Neumann 87's a lot of times or 2 AKG C-12's as the pair and a Sennheiser 421 on the bottom. For Matt Rollings (on Jenna Mammina's record) I used two 414's and an RE-20. I placed the mics about 6 to 8 inches from the horns on opposite sides to make the most of the Leslie spin. Matt is a master with the Leslie toggle switch and the volume pedal, which certainly makes my job easier.

The B-3 can be tricky if the headphones aren't just right, because the player will make

pair of Genelecs up on the instrument and not using phones. Fortunately, with the Leslie, you can set it up to avoid bleed, but a lot of times, I'll record regardless of the bleed. No phones just makes for a better performance if your recording allows it.

A special aspect that few people know is that touch can really affect the sound of the B-3. If you pull out all the stops and slowly push a key up and

Hammond B-3 and Leslie cabinet.

adjustments with the volume pedal like it or not. It's one of the more difficult instruments to get just right in the phones. It will affect level to tape, how the other players are hearing and change the sound of the miking. It can ruin a whole session when it's not right. Even more difficult is when the B-3 player is using the bass pedals and functioning as the bass player. It takes real mastery of the instrument to not make a murky mess of the performance. Compression to the phones can help.

On rare occasions, I've been talked into doing a B-3 overdub and this headphone issue had plagued me so much, that I've taken to setting a

down, you can hear it go up the overtone series. A master musician will have the control to hit a key half way or less to get a certain affect.

Another thing about B-3 is that there's a volume pot on the Leslie, by the tubes, that can adjust the volume being output. That's the "grit" dial. It's like turning a 50-watt Marshall up to 10 for a natural distortion. I don't try to hide room noise of the Leslie spinning. You can disguise it a bit by making sure the volume is loud enough coming out of the Leslie. It can be REALLY noisy depending on the player, but with all the problems, there's nothing like that sound. You can amuse your friends and annoy your neighbors with that thing. I've done both.

And talk about annoying, one just assumes we're discussing the accordion! In the last month, I've recorded more accordion than piano. I keep one in the control room at all times now 'cause you never know when you need protection. Rob Berger (Tin Hat Trio) was just in playing on Tony Furtado's new record. We used two mics, an 87 about 12-18" from the keyboard and a 414 about 24" from the bellows side. Most of the sound is coming from the 87. I've used three mics for Dirk Powell (Cajun multi-instrumentalist on Rounder). Stereo 414's about 12-24" back, over the keys and an 87 catching the bellows. There can be a lot of key clicking and air moving, but it's part of the sound so you just accept it.

The most fun I had recording the accordion was on an indie rock record for Terese Taylor. I was producing and decided to surprise her with an accordion part. So I dragged an 87 into the control room, ran it into a Princeton amp with the tremolo all the way up and put a 57 on the Princeton. I turned up the speakers in the control room so I got lots of room bleed and proceeded to play the part myself. Okay, punching in was a problem, but I didn't really care. What I discovered was how good the drums sounded through the Princeton and the tremolo, which eventually became the basis of the song. That's the power of the accordion. It makes you do crazy things. Next is the stack o' Marshalls.

For synthesizers and electric piano, 95 percent of the time you're not going to go much farther than taking a direct out, use some tube direct boxes, go into some good pre-amps and you're done. But I will share an experience I learned early on: If you have a big synth session you can blow up a console. Some small studios may not have all the DI's you need to separate all the tracks out and you might find yourself using the mic ins instead of the lines. Make sure you have a 10 pad in or you could cause serious problems. I have seen the light and smelled the smoke.

At a session with Wayne Horvitz and John Adams a few years ago the SSL at Fantasy blew up twice on the same channel. We were running about 21 keyboard tracks live to tape (and 100 tracks internally sequenced), running the synths through amps and miking speakers, the works.

To this day, I'm not sure how it happened, but I was told that the assistant plugged an amp and speaker into the wall that caused some kind of voodoo to the channel. At some point, we noticed a funny smell. Electrical smoke can be a very bad thing in the studio.

Aside from the smoke, we had a great time running the synthesizers through various Marshall, Roland and Fender amps and miking those speakers rather than taking the direct sound. Gives some "air" to the sound, some life, some character.

One thing I have discovered is how important great sounding effects can make even the most mundane stock patch sound good. I rarely use onboard synth effects. Most of the time I head right to the 480L or 224XL or PCM 60, Lexicon Superprimetime or 42 delays, Eventide Harmonizers and AMS whatevers. Doctor it up with multiple effects, create the sound in the mix or print it to tape. I have a vintage Minimoog and Prophet 5, which I still love. I own some digital synths like the M-1 and Proteus, but they are pretty plain sounding in comparison. Unfortunately, they are so easy when you just need to get a job done, they get used often.

For myself, I think I'm heading towards using more and more outlandish recording techniques, hands on effects that you can create loops live, miking speakers in odd places, etc. And I'm finding that many of the young artists are not only willing, but encouraging about it all. The bottom line is the song and the performance. If you've got that, even the most stock M-1 patch can't destroy it (but it might come close).

LEANNE UNGAR

Producer and engineer Leanne Ungar's credits include Laurie Anderson, Carlene Carter, Leonard Cohen, Holly Cole, Janis Ian, Ray Charles, The Temptations, Willie Nelson, Billy Joel, Elton John, Luther Vandross, Natalie Cole, Peter Gabriel and the Paul Winter Consort.

When I started working in the studio in New York City in 1973, the Fender Rhodes was at the height of its popularity. It's still my favorite keyboard. It was standard equipment in every studio, along with a grand piano and a B-3.

When my client, keyboardist and producer John Lissauer (who did Leonard Cohen's "New Skin for the Old Ceremony"), would come in to record, he would call S.I.R. and rent a certain Rhodes by the serial number. He liked the distortion and harmonics of the low end on that particular keyboard. (Something not easily replaced by a sample!)

If I were using Rhodes on a basic track, I would take it direct and cit the speakers with a dummy plug. But when possible, I preferred miking the amp. It's a more aggressive sound. To bring out the attack and clean up the midrange, I generally cut at 400 Hz and boosted 1.5 kHz on an API EQ.

There is no "art" to recording sampling keyboards, but some sound better than others. I always like the sound of the Synclavier. It had a richer, more lush sound. A sample is only as good as the sampler.

I was working with Laurie Anderson when she first got hers in 1982 or 1983. We were waiting one day for Phoebe Snow to come sing backing vocals. We were listening to her record to get in the mood. She called at the last minute to say she had a cold and wanted to postpone. We took the beautiful a cappella vocal stack from "Two Fisted Love" (recorded by Glen Berger, to give credit where credit is due) into the Synclavier and tuned it down considerably, until the key was right. Phoebe was thrilled that she didn't have to travel with a cold, and she got credit and was paid as if she sang.

I was on the phone last week with the owner of a home studio, talking him through how to mic a B-3. I like to use a kick drum mic for the low end, like an RE-20, D112 or 421, especially if I'm lucky enough to work with a great rhythm organ player like Jim Cox. Those mics can give low stabs a good punch. I'll usually use one or two large diaphragm condensers on the high end, like 414's, for instance.

Don't give in to the temptation to mic the open back of the Leslie cabinet. The wind from the rotors can pop the mic capsules. Place the mics at the vents on either side (or just one vent works fine, too). If you are fresh out of expensive microphones, no problem. The drawbars on the organ are so expressive and so precise you should be able to compensate and achieve any sound with the player's help.

For recording B-3, make sure that the sound isn't eating up the space in the midrange in your mix. If you are recording quiet passages, make sure you have enough signal to mask the rotor noise. And if things get loud, be alert for distortion, unless, of course, you want some. Don't forget to use the line in on the Leslie pre-amp for possible guitar, vocal, etc. effects.

CHRISTOPHER GREENLEAF

Christopher Greenleaf has extensively recorded work acoustic instruments under "classical" conditions. He is respected in audiophile circles as an engineer of exceptional recordings.

People always ask for formulas, but there's nothing less useful than an imperfectly understood rote method. If I do have a rule, it is that each instrument and each acoustic setting and each performer determines my miking. While anyone who's been around the block approaches a given situation with possible miking approaches in mind, very few engineers or producers have an inalterable laundry list of set-ups.

Here's an example. I was recording two solo harpsichords built a year apart, after the same plan, and by the same maker. I ended up using different mics at slightly different distances from the instruments and each other to achieve a comparable sound. For one harpsichord, I used fairly widely spaced (1.7 m) KM-130's axially; for the other, I placed a pair of upward-angled KM-131's closer in and slightly closer together. The direct sound was virtually a match. There was no apparent disparity between the two instruments, though the very lively room came through slightly different with each array. Listening and experimentation, not formula, produced this result. I should add that, as with all my recordings, the performer and session producer had as much say in miking as I did. It'd be sheer arrogance to think I can do it all on my own, especially when a performer's ears can help me dial in aspects of the instrument I may not even suspect exist!

In approaching miking, I strive to establish a deeply musical balance between attack and warmth, clarity and richness, the performer's intentions and the eventual listener's enjoyment.

79

I like the distance between main mics to be less than their distance from an instrument or ensemble; otherwise, the soundstage becomes disconcertingly broad. This is one of the two formulas I'm willing to pass on, the other being that there is always a dominant microphone pair (or, more rarely, a three some of mics), whether I'm doing minimal miking or working with more involved arrays.

While I do go for sufficient proximity to perceive attack and the small beginnings of normal mechanical noise (because that's part of the true sound) I never rely solely upon the instrument's sound. This invariably brings the project into a room whose acoustic is more reverberant—sometimes startlingly more so—than a hall in which a musician typically would want to perform the same repertoire before his/her public. Needless to say, artists inexperienced in recording must be gently but firmly awakened to the fact that mics and the human ear perceive sound vastly differently, and that the aims of the recording process rarely duplicate those of live sound production.

Miking a harpsichord or piano extremely closely robs the instrument of its chance to interact with the air, to acquire the special coloration the lid imparts, to develop true power and breadth. You're left with white-hot attack. That may be very sexy, jazzy, and exciting, but such an approach makes it impossible to evoke the magic of acoustic bass or the singing vocal quality of middle registers. Virtually all the subtleties the instrument and room have to offer escape the recording process... allora, ciao bellezza [bye-bye, beauty].

With any other long-keyed keyboard instrument, there are three basic zones of sound production. There are also a number of areas relative to the instrument and room where the disparate elements that make up the sound come together.

What are these zones? One sound source is obviously piano hammers or harpsichord plectra (the two to three little tongues that pluck harpsichord strings for each note played). While these make a certain pitchless sound on their own, most of the tone production comes from the second sound-generating zone, the bridges and soundboard. The most interesting tone originates here, where the strings cross the soundboard and where the vibrating soundboard reacts most strongly to the bridge's movement; this may not be right at the bridge, but inches or feet away. One example of this is the justified popularity of miking a piano frame's open holes, which often have an amazing timbral character. The third source of direct sound is the reflection and refraction off the lid (and from the underside of an open-bottom acoustic instrument). This last direct source helps establish the overall context and blend that make for interesting keyboard sound. The instrument's maker spent a lot of time matching the lid's shape and angle to the rest of the instrument. Removing the lid or altering its angle is a common way of pulling a "different" sound out of the hat, but be wary of the sometimes-drastic effect on the sound this approach can have.

For me, then, effective miking derives from finding the beauty of resonance and sustain, from unlocking the innate power and beauty of an instrument, from marrying the instrument's magic to the vibrant air of a world-class room. This is one way of describing the "classical" approach, as contrasted with the many others. To this end, I listen for and analyze the tone-producing elements of each instrument in the context of the room chosen for the recording. My aim is to achieve a sound that can be edited and released. Period. I happily reach for the many technical fixes now cheerfully lined up on the cyber-shelf when noise or odd acoustics require massaging, but I just do not record with the intent of relying on them to salvage a challenged project. That's not recording purism—it's just common sense for music in which beauty, clarity, and visceral realism are at stake.

I happily resort to gentle EQ and occasional dabs of assisting reverb when DSP will supply what the room and mics could not. A noisier than hoped for session will require less ambient miking, so you 'verb it afterward. Persistent over-support of certain pitches in the instrument or room make a little EQ taming a logical part of post. But the best feeling in the world is to release exactly the sound we recorded, unchanged and vibrant.

I recently recorded Elaine Funaro, a fire-eyed harpsichordist in North Carolina, using the Earthworks omnis, Millennia tube pre-amps, and a Troisi A/DC. Just as important as the impact of the two very different harpsichords she used was the supportive, responsive acoustic of an all-stone, uncarpeted chapel on the Duke University campus. The resulting recording is a sizzler ... it's almost scarily alive. I had also brought my Schoeps and Neumann omnis along, but once we'd heard the Earthworks QTC-1's in this room and with these instruments, all the other mics stayed in their cases. I think the QTC-1 is one of the major achievements in miking. It doesn't sound like any other mic I have ever heard. It is so unbelievably neutral that I don't hear a lot of the effects I normally think of as "audio." I merely hear good or bad miking, and that is what I want. It is strikingly transparent. In appropriate applications, it is as close to a perfect transducer as you can get. Needless to say, there are situations in which my Schoeps MK-2 has the edge, or rooms that fully respond only when the KM-130 or KM-131 listens in. While the B&K 4006 has its moments of glory, I find it sitting there in shockmounts for a session noticeably less than the others I've mentioned.

A microphone is in part a truth-sayer. But it is a coloring tool, like tinted glass. Its placement determines flavor and perspective. Some people will deem the Earthworks omni to be inappropriate because it lacks the coloration they're after. My cherished Neumanns and veteran Schoeps (including an original tube model) have their own beautiful take on things, and they often sound breathtakingly visceral, but for an amazing number of projects, this Earthworks omni is as close to the real thing as I've ever heard. In a very real sense, discovering how to use this new mic sound has been a private revolution. Because they are so transparent, truly fine mics help you punch through to things that you wouldn't be able to reach for with other mics. You learn to hear detailed, clearly defined sounds in your head and go for 'em. It's also loads of fun.

Music recorded with a superior microphone through radically good electronics has a different dynamic signature. That means that it has more life and air, more integration of vanishing, ephemeral details that add up to ... being there. It can acquire a different kind of "life" when you put it through an exciter, but that's not same thing as experiencing that startling moment when mere speakers and living room disappear and the performer is there. It is because more of the acoustic cues from musician, instrument, and gorgeous room come through, and that is an unforgettable experience.

Let's get away from movable keyboard instruments. I've also used all these mics on pipe organs of all sizes. Bach once said that "the room is the most important stop on the organ." So it is sort of a no-brainer to state that a pipe organ in a bad room is utterly beside the point. The deep 16-foot and profound 32-foot bass don't come together unless the room is sizable and resonant. What you can get out of a top-flight, two-channel recording of a pipe organ in a good room simply of defies belief. Most people would be stunned to experience the extent to which two (damned good) speakers can reproduce what we has been marketed to us as "surround sound." A properly made two channel recording will survive surround processing well, but you lose both awesomely deep bass (produced largely by phasing differences between a pair of transducers) and the amazingly fragile timbral cues that communicate beauty and presence.

The chapel at Holy Cross College in Worcester, Massachusetts, is a favorite miking challenge of mine. The four-manual Taylor and Boody organ there, a stupendous modern realization of Dutch and North German Baroque tonal schemes, embodies all of the unbelievable sounds that these instruments are capable of. The room, though beautiful, is a challenge, since it is ferociously difficult to accurately reproduce on tape what the ear tells you is there.

There are countless delicate, finely shaded registers in this instrument, yet the gathered might of full organ is breathtaking. Marrying the instrument to its room is the great challenge, and it is here that each flavor of microphone becomes crucial. No post-production can cure miking inadequacy under these conditions, so one learns to be inventive and to write down every positioning, when it's all working. In this room, I have variously used Schoeps, Earthworks, and Neumann mics, and each has captured a different splendor, a different credible soundstage. That's humbling.

For pipe organ, I often start with a pair of omnis two and a half meters apart and maybe ten meters from the organ (substantially closer in a smaller room). If you become aware of the cancellation and reinforcement of certain frequencies in the room, which results in over- and under-emphasized fundamentals, you allow for them by repositioning relative to the center line, to each other, and to floor-to-ceiling height.

One invariable phenomenon with spaced omnis, even in the case of a modest organ, is the great ease and authority of even very quiet low frequencies. Shoddily done, the sound is vague and soundstage-less. When nicely judged, such miking pulls in bass of great depth and power. Full organ, needless to say, is exciting as hell. When room, instrument, and repertoire want more upper voice clarity and location, I may add an ORTF or vertically spaced (20-30 cm) pair of Neumann cardioids or the same firm's amazing sub-cardioids, placed just forward of a line between the omnis. I have no qualms about getting more room sound with an ambient pair of fairly widely separated omnis, provided the main mics have the principal say in the mix.

The sheer power of organ sound in a big room is nicely comple mented by the gigantic dynamic range … no wonder the recording world has long been fascinated with this special challenge.

As I said above, I like to use three clearly differing main mics, depending upon the application: the Earthworks QTC-1, the Neumann KM-130, or the Schoeps MK-2.

The Schoeps pre-amp and capsule test better than almost any mic in the world. They were a bold design when they debuted decades ago, and they remain a standard to this day. They and the Earthworks QTC-1 are about as uncolored as you can get. To them I add the challenging-to-use but very beautiful KM-131 omni and the KM-143 sub-cardioid. This latter boasts the useful virtues of a directional mic and the timbral honesty of an omni, as well as an omni's unparalleled ability to define room ambience.

The more transparent the transducer is, in a sense, the harder it is to use, because the less it is capable of "lying." You are hearing everything. You have to be more careful than with lesser designs. Conversely, the more colored a mic is, the more you can get away with odd placement or mixing approaches, because the ear's built-in litmus test for verisimilitude doesn't apply to the same degree. We all use colored mics, like the stunning Neumann TLM-193 card, for very special purposes and revel in their versatility, their

relatively bulletproof resistance to strange positioning.

The QTC-1 does have a few idiosyncratic characteristic colorations, such as a tendency to make strings and reeds recorded too closely sound breathily insubstantial. It also hardens or dries up rooms that have a small or harsh acoustic. This is not coloration in the standard sense, but it does mean that this microphone is inappropriate for overall ensemble pick-up in an ungenerous room. It is a very alive sounding mic as a main mic. As a spot mic (percussion, low brass and winds, piano tail), it blends into the main mix with absolutely amazing ease.

All omnis are proximity-sensitive. Moving twice the distance away is effectively moving four times the acoustic distance away, so they are not indiscriminate in what they pick up. For this reason, they make killer spot mics on loudspeakers and various keyboard instruments. Good mic placement obviates a lot of post. The old, proven saying in the classical music industry is "record well and long, post-produce cheaply and briefly."

For recording an electronic keyboard, I like to record the instrument directly (stereo only) and with two sets of speakers. I position two or three mics per speaker—one at a relative distance, even if there's risk of cross-bleed. Consider a just-off-axis mic as well as a standard off-axis mic. The two will pick up very different things. The options available from multiple miking of speakers are many. Mixing them together or in stereo opposition is an amazing tool for effects even before you're into post, thanks to the natural workings of phasing and mic proximity. It involves committing a greater number of channels, but your post-production time can be somewhat or significantly reduced, since there are so many options nicely synced up already. I'm prepared to be anally fussy about the quality of speakers and electronics I record. I would record dirty electronics for that specific effect, but only through top speakers.

In recording amplified instruments, I use absolutely audiophile amps and crossovers with extremely beautiful speakers. They don't have to be going very loudly to sound like heaven, but they do need to be away from coloring surfaces. I would naturally consider the color of the electronics and the speakers to be part of the instrument's recorded character. The most advanced home speakers are often better for miking than professional speakers, because they are more fine-grained. They will stand the close scrutiny that modern audio permits. The old Celestion SL-600, the stunning little ProAc One

and for the middle range of the piano. I like solid-state mics and a tube pre-amp for organ, string orchestra, French horn, deep bass winds, and low percussion. All-solid-state chains work superbly for the top and bottom of the piano—but so do all-tube systems. Each just sounds different.

The Millennia mic pre-amp.

SC, and the world-standard Revel Salon are my picks. As a session and post monitor, I always opt for the ProAc One SC, if available.

I would certainly urge performers and engineers who have a high-resolution sound source to experiment with omnidirectional mics for loud-speaker pick-up. Omnis have the sweetest sound and the best dynamics.

I adore my Millennia vacuum tube mic pres, but I also am happy with my custom-configured API pre/mixer. When they've been available, I have often used tube mics and thoroughly enjoyed the result, but I am equally convinced of the musicality of the best non-tube contemporary circuit design. If you work in the real world, it is pointless (and impractical) to step firmly into one or the other camp. I greatly prefer an all-tube mic-amp chain for strings and woodwinds, reverberant rooms, banjo, guitar, lute, the oboe,

Which approach you opt for is a matter for you, your client, and your (I hope) stunningly competent session producer. The relevant commercial and aesthetic concerns may have gratifyingly more in common than you anticipate—if you mic well.

CHAPTER 12

Mastering

Mastering is the final refinement that helps give a finished recording the best sound that it can have. A good mastering job can make a well-engineered recording sound perfect on the radio and audiophile systems. Listen to Dire Straits, Steely Dan, Sting, U2 or any number of classic releases to underscore that point. Mastering also helps restore and present very old recordings in the best light. Since the arrival of compact disc, re-issues of back catalog items have dramatically improved, largely thanks to the advances in digital mastering and restoration techniques. For this chapter, I have invited some of the industry's best: Andrew Mendelson, Kris Solem and Denny Purcell to offer their insights to mastering, from technical issues to interpersonal client perspectives.

ANDREW MENDELSON

Currently the owner and Chief Engineer of the renowned Georgetown Masters in Nashville, Andrew has worked on multiple Grammy-winning and gold and platinum projects. Previous to that, Mendelson worked at Sony Music Studios and Telarc Records, where he helped create some of the company's and the world's earliest SACD and DVD-A recordings. In 2001 Andrew was united with legendary mastering engineer Denny Purcell at Georgetown Masters. Upon Purcell's untimely death in late 2002, Andrew took on the duties of Chief Engineer at Georgetown and then purchased the company's assets in early 2004. Andrew's list of credits include Kenny Chesney, Johnny Cash,
Neil Young, Ricky Skaggs, Emmylou Harris, Dave Brubeck, Big & Rich, Gretchen Peters, Reba McEntire, Los Tigres Del Norte, Adrian Belew and Duane Eddy.

For this chapter, Andrew offers a number of thoughts on mastering for stereo and surround.

Today's recording industry is rapidly changing, and the role of the mastering engineer is changing with it. The decentralization of the recording business as well as new techniques and production standards have made the role of the mastering engineer more difficult to define than it once was.

The first step I take when approaching a new project is to determine the most effective role I can play. Many projects I work on have teams of producers and engineers who have spent countless hours working with the artist, picking apart every detail of the music. Through their efforts they often come very close to completely realizing their vision. Other projects come from musicians who have done their own recording and feel apprehensive about the results they were able to achieve. These two situations will often require different sets of skills and tools. Additionally, there are many desirable sonic possibilities for any given piece of music. Understanding what is appropriate in a given style and what your client wants, even when they are unable to express it, is a necessary skill set to develop. Accurately determining the role your client wants you to play and the role the source material requires you to play is fundamental to successful results.

The mastering stage is essentially a bridge between the studio world and the consumer world. My primary goal is to make sure the vision of the artist and the producer will translate as intended outside the production world. This is one reason my mastering room at Georgetown Masters is set up to feel like a listening room you can work in rather than a work room you can listen in. The room consists of two sides. When facing one side you have the mastering console in front of you along with a pair of nearfield monitors. When you turn around you face an audiophile quality listening chain with nothing between the listener and the speakers—the ultimate environment for listening with minimum sonic and mental distractions. In addition to its sonic benefits, this type of set-up promotes a different way of listening from that of a typical studio—one more conducive to someone enjoying a song rather than creating one. I listen in a different way than my recording and mix engineer counterparts. I can listen to songs as entities in and of themselves, never having been intimately involved in their creation. This provides me with an important vantage point to find flaws missed by the tunnel vision that can be created by being too close to a project.

To become a successful mastering engineer, remember that you are collaborating with people, even if you never meet face to face. In my experience, people tend to want to work with somebody they feel they can relate to. Building strong relationships with your clients will lead to not only repeat business, but also more successful sessions. The first thing I do prior to starting a session is to ask the client about their recording philosophies, their desires for dynamic range verses apparent volume, and any other subjective opinions they may have. Although these opinions may change over time or from project to project, working with somebody with whom you have a strong, long-term relationship can give you greater insight into their beliefs, and may greatly enhance everyone's ability to achieve their goals.

Mastering is among the most exciting yet misunderstood processes in music production. Mastering is both an art and a science, drawing upon musicality and emotion, technique and methodology. The creative stage of mastering, in its simplest form, involves taking what are essentially completed songs, then, primarily utilizing elaborate but similar controls to those used daily by music listeners on their own playback systems, extracting the full potential of each song's musicality. The difference is that the tweaks I make are allowed to become a part of the music's identity, rather than simply a personal playback preference. If my concept of musicality translates and resonates with those who created this music and those for whom this music was created, I am successful in my job. For all intents and purposes I am a professional music listener (pretty good work if you can get it).

Mastering for surround requires different tools and a modified approach from traditional stereo mastering. While my general philosophies for stereo and surround mastering are similar, additional considerations include: release format, dealing with a variety of speaker configurations and calibration techniques, alternate compression and EQ techniques, and how the surround program relates to other programs on the disc.

There are many potential formats on which a surround program can be released, each with their own set of standards and encoding processes. The mastering engineer needs to be intimately familiar with these constantly evolving formats and techniques.

Many release formats that can provide a surround sound program can also contain multiple other programs on the same disc. DVD-Audio and DVD-Video releases will allow you to put multiple surround and stereo programs in different menus on the same side of the disc. The Dual Disc and Hybrid SACD formats allow you to put a standard CD program on one side of the disc while putting stereo and surround programs on the other side.

These possibilities bring up the issue of how to ascertain the appropriate apparent level for each program. One philosophy would dictate that all of the programs should be level matched to each other. Another philosophy would dictate that the CD layer of a Dual Disc should be made competitive with other CDs while the DVD content is matched to an appropriate level for DVDs. Yet another philosophy would dictate that all content on a DVD or SACD should be optimized in apparent volume with little regard to other content on the disc. These are decisions that need to be made through discussions with the artist, engineer and/or producer.

To date, I have mastered surround projects for DTS-CD, DVD-Video, DVD-Audio, and SACD. The latter three of these are currently the most popular surround release formats, and each requires its own set of tools. For SACD projects I use SADiE and Sony Sonoma workstations. For DVD-Video and DVD-Audio projects I use SADiE and Sonic Solutions workstations. I really like the surround processing tools in the TC-Electronic System 6000, especially the MDW 5.1 EQ. The small remote interface allows me to sit in the center of my full-range monitoring set-up and have nothing between the speakers and my ears.

There are a few different speaker configurations that are popular for 5.1 surround. I like to check my work using both 110 degree and 130 to 135 degree angles on my rear speakers both with and without bass management. This way you can work in an optimum listening environment while ensuring that the final release will translate well to a variety of listening conditions. Additionally, I'll often check the final program on a small speaker system with bass management, which models the set-up of most consumer surround systems. As a final quality control measure, all final masters are monitored two channels at a time on headphones to be sure no noises or dropouts are present that might be hard to hear while all six channels are playing simultaneously.

In my experience, surround music recordings react differently to signal processing than stereo recordings. Changes in frequency or dynamics that have a pleasing effect on a stereo program can easily pull apart the image of a surround mix and leave it feeling disjointed.

Compression will often react differently on the front left and right speakers than it will on the center channel, which may be less dense musically, possibly containing only the lead vocal. Special attention must be given to the interaction between the speakers, and this applies not only to changes you make but also to the way you evaluate the mix you receive. I've had multiple experiences where the mix engineer had misaligned their monitor system and I needed to correct the unbalanced mix in the mastering stage.

On most surround sound music releases, I recommend that the mix engineer avoid using the LFE (Low Frequency Effect) channel. The content of most musical programs has nothing that can be achieved through the use of an LFE channel that can't be achieved on the full range channels. Conversely, a lot of damage can be caused by the LFE, including conflicts between the LFE and the low-end from the main channels, issues caused by data compression used for the delivery format or a myriad of other problems that are an unnecessary risk. Even when small satellite speakers are used, the bass management on the playback system will send the appropriate low-end information to the subwoofer. Nevertheless, a mix engineer may choose to use the LFE channel, and it is the mastering engineer's job to ensure these potential problems are minimized.

Surround sound mastering brings into the equation a host of new responsibilities including encoding and authoring stages that are not necessary for traditional CD release. Mastering engineers need to educate themselves on these additional stages to the same extent that one would for traditional stages of the mastering process. These encoding processes, used to fit the large amounts of data required for surround sound and possibly simultaneous video onto the release media and through the playback buffer will often have a significant effect on the sound. Additionally, with mastering no longer being the final creative stage (as you may not be doing the authoring as well), it is fruitful to understand the stages that follow. It is advantageous to be able to have an educated conversation with your client (who may not understand some of these processes) and with the people providing those services.

Music reproduced in surround sound can have an emotion, reality and musicality far beyond what can be achieved by even the best stereo recordings. While at its heart, making music for surround is simply an extension of making music for stereo, the traditional techniques you use must be reevaluated for their merit in this different listening environment.

KRIS SOLEM

Kris Solem has worked as an engineer in Los Angeles since 1981 and as a mastering engineer at Future Disc Systems since 1996.

His experience includes mastering projects for a variety of artists including Bette Midler, Coolio, Enrique Iglesias, Sascha, Motley Crue and Yes. Solem also teaches a UCLA Extension course called "The Mastering Process: Preparing Your Recordings for Release."

In the business of making sound recordings for release, mastering is both the final creative step in the production process and the first step in the manufacturing of commercial product. What comes into the mastering room are the finished (or not so finished) mixes from the recording studio. What comes out is the music industry's equivalent to a proof coin, which, if it passes scrutiny, will become the first of many replicas.

Each of the commercial formats, from vinyl record to compact disc to DVD-A and even MP3, has its own unique quality. To make the transfer from the studio tapes to the release format successfully, the mastering engineer must understand the limitations of the destination format, the character and nuance of the music, and the market in which the finished product must compete. Despite the many compromises which will be made between the fantasy world of the recording studio and the requirements of manufacturing, a good mastering engineer will try to find every way to enhance the quality of the recordings he or she is given to work with.

If I have a basic philosophy, it is to not get stuck in my ways. The demands made on a mastering engineer today are quite different than even a few years ago. Pretty much any day at work, someone will ask me to do something I've never thought of trying before. While the basic skill of a good mastering engineer is still to know when the finished product really sounds its best, everything else is changing. We work in an industry that loves technology, and today technology is advancing at an accelerated pace. I am convinced that those of us who want to be useful to our clients in the future will stay on the cutting edge, learning, feeding our curiosity, and adapting to change.

When I'm in the studio, working with sound, I try to approach the work from the point of view of a purist. If I do nothing to this mix, how will it sound in the end? Identifying what will be deficient, what will be less than competitive in this market, tells me where to take the material I am working with. I try to remember that in many cases less is more, but don't be afraid to get out the hammer if the hammer is the tool you need.

Every mastering session starts by playing back the mixes to be mastered. Therefore, the choice of format used for mixdown will determine how the mastering session begins and progresses.

A wise producer will give serious thought to this important choice, and mastering engineers are often consulted on this subject.

"What would you like me to bring the mixes in on?" or "What is your favorite new digital format?" are typical questions I'll get from a producer who is thinking ahead.

Mastering at Future Disc, all roads lead to our networked hard disk systems. This makes sense now that most current and all new future release formats are digital (even the holdout analog cassette and specialty vinyl record are normally made from digital masters).

I still hear from mastering engineers who are suspicious of using computers as audio tools. In my opinion, there is no better way to handle digital audio than with a properly set up and maintained hard disk system. The audio data is rendered more accurately and quickly than any tape-based system can hope to achieve and it can be moved around on our facility network without degradation. In addition, the capabilities of non-destructive and non-linear editing have changed the mastering environment profoundly.

My sessions tend to proceed in three basic steps. First, we play back the studio recordings, decide the best way to transfer them to the hard disk system, and make the transfers.

Analog masters (as of this writing we still see a lot of analog tape) need to be processed through an analog to digital converter, maybe with some analog compression or EQ along the way. I like to use the Pacific Microsonics HDCD converter, sending hi-res 24-bit audio to the hard drives.

When the mixes come in on a digital source, I face a fork in the road. One path, often preferable, is to stay in the digital domain, since the critical step of A to D conversion has, for better or worse, already been made. The other path, which can pay off mightily in certain situations, is to convert back to analog to take advantage of the unique qualities of one or another pieces of gear, and again back to the hard disks via an A to D converter.

Step two is to do all of the sequencing, editing, fades and so forth to create a finished album. Little things like the end of a fade, or time before the next track, can have a profound effect on the continuity of the finished album. All of this work is done using the digital audio workstation to direct the playback of the original sound files on hard disk.

Step three is called "rundown," a term held over from the vinyl days. The edited hi-res files are played back through the digital console. The Studio 1 desk at Future Disc includes a Weiss 102 console with EQ, compression, limiting, de-essing, and reverb (rarely used in mastering), an additional Weiss 7-band parametric EQ, and the HDCD processor or Apogee UV22 for dithering to 16 bits for CD release. This versatile chain of gear can be used for anything from subtle hi-fi to hardcore slam, and can be programmed to change as the album plays through. The console output is passed directly back to hard disk, and becomes the new master sound file from which reference copies and master parts are made.

DENNY PURCELL

Up to the time he passed away in 2002, Denny Purcell was one of the world's pre-eminent mastering engineers. For almost 30 years, he mastered thousands of albums, many of which have gone on to become gold and platinum successes, as well as many Grammy-winning classics. In his contribution on mastering, Purcell shares advice that is not only good for mastering engineers to remember, but for anyone working in any recording industry field. That advice has to do with the human component. After all, this is a service industry.

For 28 years I've held these secrets close to my chest. At age 50 I've decided to share them with anyone interested in this fine craft. I feel sort of like you're watching the TV programs about magicians' secrets and tricks once and for all revealed. You've noticed I'm not wearing a mask though; I've identified who I am, and here are the secrets to mastering delivered to you as promised: The emperor has no clothes! Just kidding!

The real secrets to what I've done to become this successful are these: all humans are from the same seed and are equal as humans. Vocations, money, social class, etc. do not make us more or less equal. We begin equal, but cannot elevate above equal.

I have some of the best artists, producers, and engineers as clients. I get some of the best tapes in the world. I try not to ruin them. I try only to help them if they need it.

Usually, what I hear on the first listen is the key. One can only do a thing for the first time once. Remembering this is imperative to success. As with most things of importance, in any vocation, what one needs is already there. One has but to peel away whatever is hiding it.

I love songs. I use some of the best, most specialized proprietary technology in the world to capture the sonic "picture" of where I stop work. Technology, the best available from inventors and company designers, is extremely important but never more important than the song, performance, and production. If we follow the electrons, we miss the song, performance, production and sonic integrity of the piece.

As I said, I love songs. What I do with knobs allows me to help others (consumers, etc.) hear songs better. It is that simple. It is extremely important to hear a piece, get your impression and act on it. One must stay fresh. I actually leave the room while my client is checking out what I've suggested sonically.

Here's a big secret: anyone can EQ, anyone can edit, anyone can do production parts! So what makes my mastering facility superior to any other? It is this: People make companies, companies don't make people. You must have a real relationship with your clients. I said real; they'll know if it's not. You must treat your clients like you'd want to be treated at their house. If they like you and your house, they'll be back. You've given them what they wanted and they feel good. Everyone likes to feel good.

My son, Weston, asked me years ago, "Dad with all these home studios, computers, mastering, etc., what are you going to do?" That's a good question. I answered Weston this way: "Worst case—mastering has been, is, always will be, another place to listen with a person who listens daily in that room." Though simply stated, this is significant.

Each album is important to me. I've worked on over 7,000 thus far. Each album is sort of like birthing a child to those involved. They want their child best looking, best dressed, and best educated in order to have a fighting chance out there. Amen.

I am convinced after all these years, though, if it weren't for budgets and release dates, artists might never be finished. After all this is their baby!

As far as home mastering, some is good, some is bad understandably. I look at it this way: if I were to have some serious heart problems, God forbid, I wouldn't try home care, home surgery, or let a friend try on the kitchen table. I wouldn't phone a friend to ask for current home surgery techniques.

I would and will pull all the stops, call in all my favors, call friends at Vanderbilt University, St. Thomas Hospital, Baptist Hospital, etc. I would ask my doctor of 25 years, Roy O. Elam, who's the best heart surgeon in the world and try to get him to see me (and try to figure out how to afford this). After all it's my heart we're talking about here.

Is an artist's music not the "heart" of his or her artistic passion? Why should it deserve less?

In closing, here's my last secret: it's never the guitar, it's always the player. Keep it simple, never overlook the obvious, keep your perspective at all costs. Fly carefully. Keep it on the road.

CHAPTER 13

Mixing

If you ask most consumers what drives them to purchase certain albums, chances are the way an album "sounds" figures in as almost as much as the artist's elements of songwriting, playing and singing. If you ask most any mixer to state a mixing "philosophy," he or she will probably tell you that it is to be as transparent as possible, allowing the artist's vision to shine through.

The average music listener might be content with the idea that the artist naturally "sounds" the way he or she does on record, but what would the Beatles have sounded like without George Martin? Would the Righteous Brothers' "You've Lost That Lovin' Feeling" or "Unchained Melody" have the same transcendent power had Phil Spector not imbued them with his Wall of Sound? Surely, some of the most appealing qualities of Sting's music come from the sonic detailing, impact and space revealed in Hugh Padgham's mixes.

None of this is meant to discount the very real talents and artistic statements made by those artists, but even the most "transparent" mixing by a great engineer has a way of enhancing the magical elements of a performance, elements that might otherwise have been hidden in less capable hands.

Those who obsessively check out album credits will often find the same names appearing on many of their favorite albums. It's a great argument for the value of the right mixer with the right project, and many reading this book will

certainly recognize names like Tom Dowd, Chris Thomas, "Mutt" Lange, Tom Lord-Alge, Creed Taylor, John Potoker, Don Was, Eddie Kramer, Bruce Swedien, Brian Eno, Daniel Lanois, Steve Lillywhite, Glyn Johns, and Eddie Offord.

Mixing might merely be a matter of, as one producer put it, "turning up the good stuff and taking out the bad," but it takes great ears and a sure command of the tools of the studio to know what to enhance and what needs eliminating to create the most emotional impact.

BOB CLEARMOUNTAIN

In the world of mixing, Bob Clearmountain is a superstar. Among his extensive credits are Bruce Springsteen, the Rolling Stones, Chic, Bryan Adams, Roxy Music, Robbie Robertson, and the Pretenders.

Since the mid-seventies, when he first made his name at New York's Media Sound and the Power Station, Clearmountain's mixes have expanded the possibilities of dimensionality and nuance on the popular music musical soundstage.

For example, check out Clearmountain's mixes of "Tougher Than the Rest," from Bruce Springsteen's Tunnel of Love, "Hymn to Her," off the Pretenders' Get Close, or the title track from Roxy Music's Avalon. His mix of Chic's dance classic "Good Times" blended the song's visceral R&B bass and drum punch with an almost otherworldly atmospheric string and vocal sound; it perfectly suited the heady spirit of disco escapism. Clearmountain could also get incredibly raw, as evidenced on his mixes of the Rolling Stones' Tattoo You. The track "Neighbors" benefits from possibly one of the trashiest snare sounds ever committed to tape. For those wanting to hear fine examples of Clearmountain's earlier work, get a hold of David Werner's self-titled 1979 Epic album or Can't Stand the Rezillos *by the Rezillos.*

Also among Clearmountain's favorite projects are Aimee Mann's first solo album (particularly the track "Jacob Marley's Chains"), Willy DeVille's Miracle *(especially "Assassin of Love"), "Satisfied," the opening track on Squeeze's* Play, *and "Floating World," off of the second King Swamp album,* Wise Blood.

Mostly everything I do these days deals with music that I haven't heard prior to the mixing session. It doesn't matter what kind of music I have before me, if I'm unfamiliar with the music, I might listen to the lyrics as I'm putting together a real quick rough mix. Of course, in the case of something I have produced, I don't have to listen to the lyrics. I know it inside and out.

There is no systematic way that I go about putting this rough mix together. I don't automatically start with drums and go on to bass and guitars or anything like that. I put up all the faders and begin working on the first element that grabs my interest.

Usually, I will work out the pans first. I may go into the guitars and try to figure out what should be panned to the left and what should be panned right. I'll start to set up the soundstage and try to picture everything visually and see where everybody is standing. Once I kind of get a visual thing happening, I will start going into individual sounds. I often work on the vocal sound pretty early in the mixing process. At this point, I will usually figure out what effect I want on the vocal in the context of this sort of rough mix that I have going. Sometimes I won't put on any effects.

Once I have a perspective on the vocal, I will start basing the rest of the mix around it. To me, the vocal is the most important thing in pop or rock music. After I have the vocal approximately where I want it, I start working on the drum sounds and do whatever has to happen with the drums and bass. After that, I usually begin to work on the individual guitar and keyboard sounds. I really don't have a systematic way of doing this, I just go back and forth between each musical component. I might work on keyboards a little bit and then work on the drums a little bit more and then go work on some guitar sounds or

Ocean Way's Neve 8078 console.

background vocals. It is almost random, but very instinctual.

When I am monitoring, I listen at an average level, usually quietly. For my monitoring set-up, I use Yamaha NS-10M's, KRK-E7's and a pair of Apple powered computer speakers. The NS-10's are a bit ugly sounding, but for some reason, they make me do a certain thing that seems to translate on to other systems. Unfortunately, they kind of roll off very quickly on the bottom end, so it is really hard to tell about anything happening on the bottom. The KRK's are quite a bit more hi-fi sounding and a lot more fun to listen to. I usually set the mix up on the Yamahas, and at some point switch to the KRK's. I will switch back and forth and make sure that everything is translating between the two. I also use the KRK's for surround mixing.

I was mixing the Pretenders with Chrissie Hynde and she said, "Hey, do you have some little mono speaker we can listen on, just like a car radio?" I said that I had these Apple self-powered speakers that I got free as part of a promotion at Comp USA. I plugged one of them in and put the mono mix through it and it was fantastic. I could hear everything so clearly. It is just one of those speakers that hangs off the side of your computer monitor. It's got two speakers in it so it has got enough bottom end that I can tell exactly what is going on with the mix. I use them in stereo, although they sit on top of a rack off to my left and they are about a foot and a half apart. They really offer an objective perspective. Too bad Apple stopped making them!

One of the common problems I encounter, concerning mixing vocals, is harshness on the track. It may be a case where the engineer chose the wrong mic for the singer. Sometimes I find people will go through great pains to be esoteric, just for the sake of being esoteric. It's like job protection. They will put a vocal through some really bizarre, very expensive pre-amp, and use a very expensive old tube mic, and some very exotic compressor, when really they could've ended up with a better vocal sound by using a newer mic that is in better shape, through an SSL pre-amp, which actually sounds pretty good. I've gotten some amazing vocal sounds from a nice new U-87 through an SSL pre-amp and an LA-2A or an LA-3A, or something like that.

Some singers think they have all this mic technique. They think that if they sing really loud, they should move away from the mic. It is something that many vocal coaches teach. Moving back from the mic might work well live on a stage, but the more the singer moves around, the more the tones are going to change. When a singer moves away from the mic, the voice gets real thin and harsh. If he or she moves in too close, it gets warm and wooly sounding. When there are these loud notes and that get all harsh and shrill, and quiet notes that are all warm and muddy, getting a pleasing vocal sound becomes difficult. If the singer had just stayed in one place, it would have been great. There's a great gadget that can help with this problem – it's the DPR-901 by BSS. It's a dynamic equalizer. You find the offending frequency, as you would on an EQ and it attenuates just that frequency as it hits a threshold, like a limiter.

I know a lot of mixers who end up with all of the faders pushed to the top. Don't keep pushing stuff up. Turn stuff down. Figure out what is in the way. If you are not hearing a guitar part, figure out why you are not hearing it. What is covering it up? The same is true with the bass. It is all about getting the right balance. If you are not hearing the bass, ask yourself, why not? Is there something getting in the way? Sometimes it is an EQ dip on some instrument that will clear another instrument. It also might free up more room for the voice.

Proper balance with EQ is often what it takes to create the right space around the voice. A lot of people don't realize that EQ isn't just adding top and bottom. It is actually balancing the frequencies in the overall mix. Sometimes it is a matter of dipping some frequencies out of the guitar to make room for something else.

Sometimes you go nuts trying to EQ the bass and you just can't get it right. Really what is happening is something else in the mix is clouding it. I will solo the bass with various instruments, like the keyboards and the guitars, and listen to what it sounds like. If the sound gets muddy when I put in another instrument with the bass, I'll start rolling out bottom on that instrument to make the bass guitar clearer. You might have this big warm [keyboard] pad and if you thin that out a bit, suddenly the bass comes shooting out and it sounds real clear.

Generally, I find that the bottom end affects the compression more than anything in a mix. First of all, I usually compress the bass guitar if it needs it. I won't compress the bass if it has already been done.

I really get particular about the way the bass drum sound blends with the bass. It should become part of the bass, rather than have a sound on its own. The bass and the bass drum should ideally sound like one thing. Hopefully, the players are playing tight enough to where that is possible. If they are not, then that is a whole other problem [laughs]. If I put a sample on the bass drum, the intention is to make the kick work with the bass more effectively.

Again, I must emphasize that I believe the most important element is the vocal in a song and all the music has to complement and work with the song. I don't dissect the drums and work on a big bass drum sound first and then go work on a big snare drum sound. I have found that if I just sit and work on the drums by themselves, I will get what I think are pretty cool sounds, but the end result may be out of proportion when put in context of the song. Everything has to be in the context of the song. I suppose part of it is that listening to soloed instruments all day gets kinda boring!

The most important thought that I like to get across to aspiring mixers and producers is to always keep the song in mind. At every stage try to step back, listen to the song and ask yourself, "Is this actually helping the song? Is this something that makes the overall thing better?"

Think of it from the point of view of a listener who isn't paying attention to all of those little tricks and doesn't care about that fancy flange you put on the hi-hat, or whatever. The average listener is listening to the vocals, and possibly the lyric, and hopefully the performance. All those little extra things that you are doing may be fun

and interesting, but are they distracting from the song? Are they taking anything away?

If one of your fancy sound tricks is distracting, then forget it or bury it or do something with it to make it work with the song. I think that people get carried away with their drum sounds and this sound and that sound and their tricky things. Sometimes the best thing to do is nothing. That is why on some of my favorite mixes that I have done, the vocal is totally dry. I have done absolutely nothing and there are very few effects in the mix. Those are the ones where you know, first of all, that the song and the performance are strong enough to carry it.

One mix that I used to judge my own work by was "Refugee" by Tom Petty. Shelly Yakus mixed it. There is something very special about that mix. There is nothing fancy happening, but everything is so incredibly clear and perfectly well

The Yamaha NS-10M Studio monitor.

balanced and it all works with the song. Every element is complementary to every other element. It is fantastic. In contrast, "Killer Queen" by Queen (which was produced in the seventies) is one of the trickiest mixes ever, but it serves the thrust of the song too—in a different way. Another song I'd love to mention is "Tempted" by Squeeze. It is one of those records that I think is absolutely perfect. There is nothing tricky happening in the mix—the song gets the full emphasis. Roger Bechirian and Elvis Costello produced it.

Having just made a case for simplicity, I'd like to add that I'd rather receive a cluttered multi-track than one that doesn't have the necessary ingredients. I have had more frustration with tapes that were under-produced, where you get to the outro and there is this rhythm section where nobody is singing and there is no melody or solo. Where's the rest of it? That's frustrating. I would rather have something cluttered and have to weed through a bunch of junk and find something that works and have to take things out. You can always take stuff out.

In the end, my favorite records I've mixed are usually because of the music, more than what I did in the mix. I can't do a good mix of something that is garbage. To me, the reason a mix turns out well has to do with what's in the recording. Even though I did the mix, I have trouble separating what is the mix and what is the overall record. If I did a good job, it is because of the music.

RICHARD DODD

Richard Dodd's mixes vibrate raw organic musical energy, like molecules blasting off the walls of the aural soundstage. Preferring analog and manual mixing over digital and automated mixes, Dodd revels in the challenge of making something special happen in settings that would cause many engineers and mixers to pack up and go home.

Artists like George Harrison, Tom Petty, Roy Orbison, Jeff Lynne, Joe Cocker, Boz Scaggs, The Traveling Wilburys, Clannad and Little Richard have benefited from Dodd's sonic touch. A number of these projects were recorded and mixed in home settings with the most basic and limited gear.

"With the exception of "Handle With Care," which I didn't mix, both Wilburys albums, George Harrison's Cloud Nine, *and at least 90 percent of Tom Petty's* Into the Great Wide Open *and Boz Scagg's* Some Change, *I used two more channels than I had tracks on the console," states Dodd, who usually used the spare channels for mono effects returns. "They were manual mixes, done without any computer whatsoever."*

When Dodd speaks affectionately about a mixing console, it is the old Soundcraft 1600, precisely the model on which he mixed Tom Petty's hit "Mary Jane's Last Dance." Incidentally, that was Dodd's rough mix.

Recently, Dodd finished MCA country artist Marty Brown's third and best album, Cryin' Lovin', Leavin', *a masterfully imaginative piece of engineering and mixing work that captures the raw energy of great country and roots rock.*

There are no wrongs and, if there are, I make sure that I don't know them. I have one thing that I take with me whenever I mix, and it is not a piece of equipment. It is an attitude of "I'm going to make this thing work. I don't carry monitors and I don't have a favorite room. I'm looking for something that I haven't done yet."

When Dodd does bring along a complement of outboard gear, the set-up often consists of a Urei 1176, an AMX DMX, a pair of Drawmer gates, a D-76 Telefunken mic pre and a Groove Tube for changing guitar sounds.

I like Urei 1176's, especially the black faced ones with the little transformers in them. People go for the silver ones, without transformers, because they have a cleaner signal path. I like the distortion. Distortion and noise have never bothered me.

The Drawmer 201 gates have got great high-pass and low-pass filters that will actually overlap. Very few consoles have got that.

Basically, if you put your mix up and it sounds a bit dull, why go through 24 equalizers, when you can put the whole thing through one stereo one, brighten them all up in one go and all in phase with each other. I hope that you could play any of my things in mono and still enjoy the balance. That is a criterion that I have.

The most important thing to me is understanding and knowing the song and knowing what is wanted. Generally, I like to start the mix with something that represents the song, something with the chord structure, like a couple of acoustic guitars, if any are there. You've also got to get a clue from something other than the drums about what the drums are going to sound like, in my opinion. I very often attempt to balance the whole song, before I consider what things will sound like.

It really makes me feel sad when I see an engineer about to commence a mix and he lifts up the mikes closest to the kick drum and snare and reaches for every piece of equipment he's got on his hands, to try and make it sound like a drum with a mic two or three feet away. A few faders off are the overheads, and that is where his drum sound is. If he listened to that, he would know what he's got. Very often, all he would need those close ones for is to give the feeling that is where the beat is, and where they are in the stereo picture.

I also encourage mixers to consider the unintended colors that mic bleed presents as an asset. Throwing various mics in and out of phase is a favorite way I expand my sonic palette.

Just because a fader says "kick" doesn't mean it is just a kick mic. There is a little bit of hi-hat there as well, unless it came out of a machine. The drums all interact and they are all miked for each other.

Today, however, mixing manually is more the exception than the rule. It's the exception, because it requires a very strong artist/producer/engineer relationship and an understanding that the dreaded recalls are just not going to happen in the way that fully automated and documented mixes operate.

A manual mix has a feel and rough edges, whereas a computerized mix often has all of the edges smoothed out, and that isn't always a good thing. Manual mixing still has the facility of analog or digital editing to change a section or part of the mix.

I mixed George Harrison's *Cloud Nine* album manually in his home, as I did for both of the Traveling Wilburys' albums. They were done on a console without any computer whatsoever. It even had Quadrant faders, the kind that went up and over. All of Boz Scaggs' *Some Change* album, Clannad's *Magical Ring*, Tom Petty's *Into the Great Wide Open* and 17 out of 22 tracks on *Wildflowers* were done manually. In fact, "Mary Jane's Last Dance," which appeared on Tom Petty and the Heartbreakers' *Greatest Hits*, was my rough mix that was done on an old Soundcraft 1600. It's funny: The faders feel more alive.

When we started mixing *The Last DJ* (Tom Petty and the Heartbreakers), we started with the intention of using automation. The majority of the board, which was a classic old Neve at Cello Studios in Los Angeles, had automation, while the monitor section didn't. Three of the songs on the album used significantly more than 24 tracks, because they involved orchestra. So I set up the console to leave the orchestra on the monitor section and had it submixed onto the automated side of the console. George Drakoulias, the producer, was very busy with the monitor faders during playback and eventually said, "I wish we could mix on the monitor side," so we did for the rest of the album. Only the overflow of the 24 tracks and effects returns went through the automated side of the console. As a result, the mixing went a lot faster [laughs]. It made the process immediately a lot less tiring for those involved.

When you are doing manual mixes, [engineers] go, "That felt great," or, "Oh, I don't know.

Did the voice feel loud enough?" They refer to feeling. When you're working on a computer, they refer to tenths of a dB, which really annoys me. It doesn't annoy me to the extent that I won't do it. It doesn't make any difference to me. If someone could tell the difference as to whether something was up or down a tenth of a dB in a mix, then they are a better listener than I am.

I spend more and more time on digital. It is the way things are going. Instead of saying, "No, I won't work on SSL's or a Sony 48-track," I now say, "Okay, I'll have to do this to make it sound right."

To help put the right amount of attitude in a final digital mix, I use some Telefunken tube mic pre-amps, and I run the whole output buss through them, before the signal gets anywhere else.

I always vary the chain according to the song. Somewhere in there is a stereo limiter, I guarantee you. It is not always before, not always after the limiter or the Telefunken. The output bus will invariably have an equalizer, a limiter and a tonal device, whether that be an analog mastering machine or my tubes, both or whatever.

I'm fascinated with the idea of the physicality of music etched on acetate. For "Too Blue to Crow," off of Marty Brown's *Cryin', Lovin', Leavin',* we pressed an acetate off of the two-track and dubbed the master off of it.

One day, I want to do a whole album like that. You could master tracks individually, using good quality twelve-inch acetates, if you could find them. Every track could be that great perfect vinyl thing for one moment in its life. It is like giving it its final meal before it gets executed. At least I'd be giving it a good time before it goes.

I've strived to not be pigeonholed and I'm satisfied that, to a large degree, I've succeeded. However, the successful stuff I've been fortunate to be associated with does probably fit into a narrow bandwidth. But the stuff I've done overall in my career is a lot wider, so I'm personally satisfied. I can listen to my body of work and there are very few things that sound the same. I'd like to think that I consider everybody's product to be a unique work and do my best to try and find something fresh each time. I have to consider what I do and how I do it on a daily basis because I'd like to be better than I am.

I have a picture of The Beatles in my mixing room and I use it as a little ego-squasher for myself. When I think that I have done something "new," I'll look up there and mentally scan through their body of work and think, "Yeah, they've probably already done it."

KEN SCOTT

Since his first dates as an assistant engineer during The Beatles' sessions for A Hard Day's Night *at London's Abbey Road Studios (then known as EMI Studios), Ken Scott has been at the forefront of many key developments in the history of popular music, which includes work with David Bowie, Mahavishnu Orchestra, Dixie Dregs, Lou Reed, Supertramp, Devo, Happy the Man, The Tubes, Missing Persons and Level 42 and Dada, among many others. Scott has also done the 5.1 re-mix of Bowie's* Ziggy Stardust, *which he originally produced, and worked with the George Harrison estate on the re-release of* All Things Must Pass *and other Harrison projects.*

The way I worked for many years, when I worked in analog, was to do a short section at a time. For instance, I'd get the intro right and then go onto the first verse, get that section right, splice it onto the intro and move on to the next section. I used to piece everything together like that and it enabled me to make some drastic changes between sections.

This process evolved from the Bowie sessions. Up to that point, there'd be the producer, myself, a second and quite often an artist, and if we needed to make changes, there would be hands everywhere on the console as we'd go through an entire mix. When it came to mixing *Ziggy Stardust* and *Hunky Dory*, it was just me, and quite often there wasn't even a second. The only way I could do what I wanted was to do it in sections. The knack was having it so the edit didn't sound like an edit. You had to have the very beginning there, and there had to be enough "hang-over" from the section before to make it sound right so it would all fit together. I would mark everything on the desk and then change it to the way I wanted it to sound. Then I would go back and put it where it had been and quickly I did it—bits and pieces.

I still think that my best work was done that way. These days, with computerized boards—and

not necessarily going on to analog—I don't like it as much.

[I asked Scott if the physicality of printing to analog tape and splicing together sections allowed him to mentally and emotionally change gears and get "outside of the box" more; to which he had the following reply.]

"Yes, absolutely. I know you can do things in sections with automation, but it just doesn't feel quite the same way. Mentally, I'm into it in a different way now and I don't know if I like it.

When mixing in short sections, I found I could really focus and keep my attention on a specific thing—for instance, the bass—through the section and make sure it's exactly where I want it at all times. I'm afraid that with automation, because one is dealing with much longer sections—normally, the entire song—I seem to suffer with a short attention span and drift around between instruments more. And along with this, I tend to think more in the long—the whole piece—than the short: the intro, verse or whatever. Just a little, but certainly more than I used to.

I've always liked dynamics. I hate the compression that's used these days. It bores me to tears. How has it evolved? I feel that it has devolved. It's not something that I'm particularly happy about, but it's just the way it's gone with technology.

KEN KESSIE

R&B dance mixes are an art form unto themselves, and it takes a special kind of engineer to understand what constitutes a mix that gets people moving, while tapping into the lyrical heart of the material.

Ken Kessie has successfully done that for the likes of Whitney Houston, Celine Dion, Tony Toni Toné, En Vogue, Stacy Lattisaw, Bell Biv DeVoe, Sister Sledge and a host of others. Since the late seventies, when he started working at San Francisco's Automatt, Kessie has amassed a string of Top-Ten pop, dance and R&B singles and albums, including En Vogue's platinum Funky Divas.

Unlike the glossier side of Urban R&B, Kessie prefers to keep his mixes slightly raw sounding, because he feels that the rough edges make for a more interesting listening experience.

The foundation of R&B and hip-hop are kick and bass. The Holy Grail is a fat low end that shakes a club or Jeep system, while at the same time sounds clear and punchy on a small radio or TV speaker.

To help accomplish that, I sometimes use a lot of fader multing, which is a twist on bi-amping.

What I do is mult the kick onto two different faders. The first fader gets the low end and without too much punch. I usually add some slight compression (SSL or DBX 160X) and lots of Pultec boosted at 100 or 60 dB.

The other fader is set for maximum punch, heavy compression (again using SSL or DBX 160X), harder EQ (SSL, API Graphics, Massenberg), boosting upper mids and cutting speaker distorting low mids. I then mix the two faders till I get a kick drum that booms on big systems, but doesn't distort the NS-10s.

Another trick for removing those pesky low-mids is a BSS DP904, set to remove 200-400 Hz on kick impact only, restoring them after the attack has passed. I use a similar multing process to achieve the ideal bass tone.

I go for the lows on one fader, using Pultecs or my pet Moog parametric. On the other fader, I use SSL filters to take out a lot of the bottom and a bit of the high end, until the bass pops out of an Auratone speaker at low volume. For bass compression, I will use either the DBX 160X, SSL, LA-2A, LA-3A, Dynamite, Summit or Tube Tech. I often chorus the bass slightly with a TC 2290 (preset 85) to fill out the sides of the mix.

I don't hesitate to employ snare samples, particularly from the Alesis D4. In dealing with the flams, muddy bottom, hiss and completely filled in midrange found in the obligatory sample loops, I often use an API 560 graphic to boost or cut desired frequencies.

Sometimes I spread a loop using a short delay (14 milliseconds), then pan the original to the left and the delay right. This can prevent clog up in the center of the mix.

For vocals, I'm a firm believer in a clear, bright, more personality than effects, Motown-style vocal.

The vocals are the most important element in a mix, so they get as much attention as other key elements. Vocal and groove combined get about 70 percent of my mixing time.

For male lead singers, Urei 1176's seem to work best for compression, while I prefer to use API or Massenberg EQs to address the top end with a Pultec or Focusrite for warmth. I use a DBX 902 De-esser if necessary.

Female singers generally require a more complex outboard chain. On the last En Vogue album, a typical lead vocal went through an 1176, Massenberg EQ, a DBX 902, and a DBX 165.

To give a lead vocal some ambiance and help it punch through the mix, I may use a couple of delays and some reverb. Delay number one might be very short, usually a 32nd or 16th note, and EQ'd very brightly to make the esses and other consonants bounce slightly. Delay number two would probably be set for an eighth or dotted eighth, and EQ'd to give a subtle trail to the singer. For reverb, I use AMS Ambience (480 Warm Plate, Zoom 9300 Clear Plate) set for pre-delay to keep the singer up front.

If your lead vocal isn't bright enough, you don't necessarily EQ the vocal itself, because you might start thinning it out. Add an effect to the vocal that is very bright, and that way you get to keep the body and tone of the original vocal, but you have added the high end that you need. That works great on background vocals, too.

Unlike many mixers, I start loud on the mains and then switch to NS-10s, with only occasional moments back on the mains.

Many pop mixers remove bottom from a mix until they can crank up the NS-10s without distortion. This would be too thin for a good R&B mix. I leave in a little bit of low end break-up when the NS-10s are loud. As the mix goes on, the volume gets quieter. Just before printing, I am switching between nearfields, a mono Auratone and headphones. I use the headphones to check for any left-right imbalances, unwanted noises, and to insure seamless transitions between all sections.

For the transfer from console to 2-track, I like using an Apogee A/D, before going to DAT (for rock) and I use the A/D converters of the Panasonic on R&B/hip-hop. I usually print a variety of mixes to cover any possible situation—vocals up and down, no lead vocal for TV, an instrumental for single and editing purposes, a cappella lead and background for sampling and digital editing and any other variations that might be desired.

PHIL RAMONE

Phil Ramone has always associated himself with great artistry. Certainly the artistry of his production and engineering skills have gone a long way towards attracting great talents like Paul Simon, Billy Joel, and Frank Sinatra, among many others.

Over the years, Ramone has worked hard on fine-tuning his methods of storing mix information for easy recall. Ramone was eager to share his ideas on storing digitally sub-grouped mixes.

Traditionally, I don't mix quite the same for an album any more than we used to years ago. Once I worked in film, I realized that the subtleties one goes through to recall mixes and make subtle changes required that the music be stored in a different medium than the standard 2-track format. It was then I began to use a multi-track format in stereo pairs for storage.

Once I finish a mix, or am close to finishing it, I will store the rhythm track onto two tracks. Then I'll put the horns and/or whatever sweeteners there are on two tracks, the keyboards and guitars on two tracks. The vocal, with its effects, and any background vocals, go on a couple more tracks. I also commit specific effects in the master that I feel are available in a certain studio, in case I'm unable to use them again.

Some places, like Capitol A, have access to eight live room chambers. You are not going to get that when you leave that place and come back. So you should store the material, with its chamber effects, separately.

It was about eight or nine years ago, when I first did this. It was for a movie for Disney, where we used Billy Joel's voice. As we added or subtracted from the piece, I realized that I didn't have to keep remixing it, but just keep reservicing the same six or eight tracks with additions or subtractions.

With increasing demands for multiple mixes by record companies and others, my sub-group mix storage method was a logical evolution.

What does happen between label, producer and artist, is that on reflecting upon a mix or the album mix, two weeks later you hear the little things you might have missed and felt could be slightly better. It is not always about redoing something. It is also about refining it. If I went back to recall a mix, it can be quite expensive.

When we get a call five or ten days later, or you look at it yourself and say, "Hm, I could fix this in twenty minutes. I know exactly what is needed." This way, I have got all the tools at hand.

You can make your tracks in the world's greatest studios and do your vocals and guitars in the project studio and go back there and mix, if you wish. Any re-mixes don't have to go back. I'm happy to pay top dollar for the best studio for re-mixes, but once you leave, the storage method is what is going to save you money and give you variety.

I have two monitoring levels that I set in the room and I don't veer away from them. I'll mix extremely soft, almost to the point that people can hardly hear it. Once I've got a reasonable soft mix that I am comfortable with, I'll mark that on the fader. I'll then do the hype playback, which is playing it back big. For that, I go to the big speakers to see where I am, just to make sure that I haven't veered off.

You have to start with something for a reference. You should bring a pack of CDs that you love and you should play them at two different levels. Maybe one level would be putting out at 80 or 90 dB on nearfields, which is plenty loud. The other setting might be at 65 or 70 dB. That would be a level that would stress your brain and ears to have to hear little nuances that you can't hear in a normal world. If you want that little bell to cut through lightly with a shaker, you will never know this, if you are listening too loud all the time. I can work much longer hours, because I am not forcing myself to burn my eardrums. I take ear breaks, because I have worked for two or three hours.

I tend to print mixes very quickly. I don't leave them in the computer for someone to say, "Ah, what was take 2 like? You never played take 2."

Within the hour that I start, I have put a mix on tape. I will then go to a couple of other rooms, or I will set up a pair of self-powered monitors with a DAT machine out in the lounge, which is another way to listen. This way, you can get yourself a picture of where you are going. I'll then go back to that original monitor level setting and I don't change.

I beg all my assistants, if I am physically doing the mix, that wherever I walk into the room, that the level is set where I left it. When I say, "Now play it at the other level," it comes back exactly at that level.

By the way, when I go to master, I don't have levels that go all over the place, because I've been consistent in maintaining a set listening level during the mixdown.

Sometimes, if the artist is in the room, I might hand him a pair of headphones so that he can hear it with all of the subtleties he wants to hear. Some artists, however, like to crank it up and that can cause problems and interrupt your creative flow in a mix. If you are going to do surgery, and it is microsurgery that you are dealing with, you have got to concentrate. If you are there to make a great record, you shouldn't be interrupted.

I generally have an open mind about what the mix process is. I tend not to come to the table with the same thing every time. I've been in situations where I didn't have much equipment and I still made it work. I think it is in the hands of the mixer. Putting all the right tools in front of a monkey might get you a mix, but it may not be the one you want [laughs].

It is nice to have a couple of pieces of equipment that you feel secure about. I know there are guys who really feel strong about having an old Fairchild limiter in the chain somewhere. That's fine. Old tube equipment keeps coming back like antiques. Some of us who remember that equipment don't always fall in love with it, because it was painful when it made noise or was crumbling, or it was sounding like bacon and eggs.

I do think that tubes bring you warmth, but I think that it is your ears that bring warmth. The so-called cold sound of digital is purely something that is poorly recorded and not thinking about where to place the mics, as well as how to use your tonal controls. In this day and age, it is inexcusable to not make good sounds.

We have forgotten how spoiled we have become. We can get all kinds of bottom and tremendous amounts of power on recordings now that you couldn't do on a record. You never could do that twenty years ago. It is much more fun for me to mix now, than it was then. I also know that, with CD, the average home reproduction system is better. There are no stylus problems.

I still listen to my mixes in the car. Roy Halee taught me that a long time ago when I went to watch him make a mix. He used to transmit it from the mix room down to his car, on a little cheap transmitter. When he put his own compressor on it, he got a true feeling of what the record mix was about. I always thought that was a cool idea. We use to do that between our cutting room and our mix room at A&R Recording when I worked there. We could broadcast from two rooms and see what was going on. You listened on your favorite little portable radio. Overall, I think you have to test your music on about four different systems to know whether the mix really works.

BRIAN AHERN
Brian Ahern has produced most of Emmylou Harris' albums since the beginning of her career.

I could tell you what I do that's really sneaky that really helps create an interesting sense of sonic space in a recording. It's kind of a mix kind of thing. I use tape speed to alter the delay time of rooms. I've done this with EMT's.

I've got a great sounding recording space now, but the pitch of it and decay time doesn't suit every song. So I might record a drum track, or vocal or whatever and I'll speed it up or slow it down. For instance, if you speed it up and run it back through the room and record that sound in the room, when you play the tape back at normal speed, the room is bigger. You can do the opposite too.

What I'll sometimes do is, I'll also record something at normal speed, and I'll pan the normal speed in a bit, and I'll spread the larger room, the larger version of the same room, out wide. The sound will seem to zoom out, through the small room into the big room. These are time shifted versions of the same room. As a result, I've then got two spaces I've recorded in stereo, one space recorded in normal speed, and another space recorded at high speed. When I play it back at normal speed, it's much bigger. I'll have them panned at like 3 and 9 o'clock. Since it's true stereo, it works up in mono and it's great. It creates a different illusion of dimensionality. It's been time warped, like *Star Trek: The Next Generation* [laughs]. The effect sometimes puts you on the edge of your chair.

There's a track on a Terry Radigan record I produced, where I had some mics about 60 feet from the drums. With the microphones set that far back, you should use some kind of a slap or delayed sound to them right? Well I used ADAT,s to change their position. With the ADAT,s, I could move them backward or forward, however I wanted to look at it, not 60 feet away. For this recording, I moved them forward to where they were not delayed sounding. They were right in your face.

When I mixed it, I had the sound of the far away drums but without the delay. It does a strange thing to your head, because you have the immediacy and the distance simultaneously. The catch is, what your brain hears is something from a distance that has no delay. It's very spooky sounding.

BILL SCHNEE

Bill Schnee is one of the recording world's most legendary engineers. Since his start, working on Three Dog Night's classic Suitable for Framing, *under the tutelage of Richard Polodor, Schnee has gone on to enjoy a hugely successful career that has included over 55 gold records, 33 platinum projects and 50 Top Twenty singles. Schnee has worked with Barbra Streisand, Carly Simon, The Pointer Sisters, Chicago, Whitney Houston, Dire Straits, Amy Grant and Neil Diamond. Schnee is also an accomplished producer. Artists who have benefited from Schnee's production touch include Boz Scaggs, Huey Lewis and the News and Pablo Cruise. Schnee has been nominated eight times for the Grammy Best Engineered Recording category, and has won two for Steely Dan's* Aja *and* Gaucho.

When I get a tape to mix, I usually ask for a rough mix to "see" where the producer and artist think the song belongs. Unless they want a completely fresh approach, this helps me save time in getting the mix going.

People usually hire a "mixing engineer" for the specific talent he brings to the mix, and therefore I never feel shy in offering my ideas—musical and otherwise. The amount of "creative input" I personally feel I should give to a mix varies with the type of music being mixed. With a jazz record, I start with the basic assumption that what is on tape is the record they want—not a lot of effects, etc. But with a pop or R&B record, I feel I have a lot more freedom to try different effects,

"rearrangement" ideas, or whatever—as long as whatever experimenting that takes place doesn't cause one to lose sight of the over-all picture. All too many times, in a complicated mix with a lot of experimentation, the musical "forest" is lost for a bunch of effect or idea driven "trees"!

Even though I've always felt engineers should have at least a basic knowledge of electronics, I truly feel mixing is a right-brain function. Like the musician doing a solo where he needs to forget all the technique he's spent years trying to develop, so he can give an inspired performance; so should an engineer "feel" and not "think" his way through a mix.

I love getting a tape where everything is organized and ready to go. I have never liked the concept of "fixing it in the mix." I would just as soon not have to "fix" things that could or should have been dealt with during the recording process and save my energy for more "creative efforts." Of course there are certain situations that are best left to be dealt with during the mix. My rule of thumb is: (1) If it ain't broke, don't fix it! (2) If it is broke, try to fix it before you mix it! Of course there are times when the kick or snare should be replaced or augmented, and I'm grateful for the Forat F16 at those times. Then there are times when I'll try running a track through a guitar amp or head to change the sound radically (e.g. bass or guitar). These kinds of "creative efforts" are where I would like to spend mixing time instead of fixing problems (or comping vocals for that matter!).

I "grew up" sonically in the world of hi-fi … tubes and such. As a result, I've always gravitated towards consoles that are more transparent ("open, natural" top end), and have good "punchy" bottom. I suppose in this category you find old Neves, API, and Focusrite—although I constantly found myself going for studios with "one-off" custom-made consoles with minimal electronics in them.

When I committed to opening my own studio (16½ years ago), I decided a console of this type was a must. I designed the console with Toby Foster and Steve Haselton. It uses discrete amplifiers and tube mic pre-amps and bus amps. Since every amplifier (even resistor or capacitor) in the audio chain acts like a piece of gauze through which you listen, my philosophy is "less gives more"! I would rather have to make extra patches or find a more creative way of accomplishing a certain signal flow for events that take place 10 percent of the time in exchange for less electronics that you listen through 100 percent of the time. What does any of this "sonic purity" have to do with getting great mixes? Very little, to be sure. But since this kind of fidelity is so hard to capture and so easy to lose, I would rather not have to "fight" the console to get it. Note that in many types of music or various situations you might not want extended fidelity but it's much easier to "throw it away" when unwanted than to get it, when desired, if it's not there.

My console has GML automation, which, for me, is a necessary evil! I say necessary because with 48 tracks (or more) of music and only two hands, there's a need. I say evil because I much prefer to do all the mixing myself—in real time. In fact, one of my favorite things to do is live-to-2-track (or direct-to-disc in the old days) where you have to mix or "perform" on the spot. I don't like having to need to use automation, but in most cases, I'm afraid I do. The good news of automation is how it allows you to perfect subtleties in a mix. The bad news is there's not as many last minute "right brain" moves or accidents in a mix (a.k.a. spontaneity!). As a result, I usually get the mix to a reasonable state before I even turn the automation on (most of the EQ, effect and reverbs set). Then I fine tune with the computer. When mixing, I love to find or create dynamics in various parts of the song for added impact. The automation definitely lets me do more of these more precisely, but hopefully not at the expense of spontaneity!

The big monitors in my room are the same ones at The Mastering Lab—a custom system with an EV tweeter, Altec midrange horn, and Utah woofers. However, what I use mostly for mixing are modified (by Steve Haselton and Doug Sax) Tannoy Golds (10"). I don't like mixing on speakers that sound "too good" (like Genelecs), even though I love listening to music on them. I find I don't work as hard on those types of speakers because everything tends to sound so good. I use a modified Yamaha 2200 power amp which Doug Sax found to match up great with the Tannoys. I don't mix at any fixed level. Rather, I vary the level throughout the day, and never very high. I decided years ago to insure longevity in my career by not "blowing" my ears out! Besides, if I monitor at reasonable levels, then there's someplace to go if I want a "hyped" playback.

TOM TUCKER

Since 1990, Tom Tucker has engineered and mixed five Prince albums, including Emancipation, The Gold Experience, *and the hit singles "The Most Beautiful Girl in the World" and "Betcha By Golly Wow." Other artist credits include George Benson, Brand New Heavies, Kid Jonny Lang, Mavis Staples, Nona Gaye, Boz Scaggs, Sergio Mendes, Phil Upchurch, Joe Sample, Ricky Peterson, Mayte, Big Head Todd and the Monsters, Trip Shakespeare, and the Rainmakers. His tracking and mixing work can also be heard on the 1993 film* Hoop Dreams.

It is important to stay in the tune, when you are mixing, and never kid yourself, "Is this magic? Do I have goose bumps, yet?" If I am not getting goose bumps, then I should ask, "What is wrong?" I try to keep it exciting, and sometimes that means starting over or re-grouping.

I guess the biggest lesson I have learned is not to get carried away on any one thing. If the snare drum is driving me nuts, and I find that is all I can think about then I may blow the whole mix.

I very much like to put in a long day, like twelve hours, and then leave the mix up and come in with a real fresh head in the morning. I want to make sure that I am not kidding myself about there being magic there.

You can't make a performance be magical, if it isn't there in the tracks. That is something that all young engineers should know. I quit trying to do that years ago. You can enhance things in a mix, but I learned that you have to work with quality people, or you may just be kidding yourself.

Particularly in R&B, the groove itself should be magical. By that, I mean that the groove should be hooky, before you even hear a single note of the song. I look to put all of that together, so that it is all meshing together very well.

Paul Peterson (Prince's bassist) plays a five string that really growls around 40 Hz, which is really nice. Prince became fond of that, so between the Moog basses and the five string basses being able to get the real deep thing going on, I don't think there is a record that

I have done in the last five to six years that doesn't have a lot of 40 Hz on it, for example. In the old days, we couldn't do that, because they couldn't cut it on vinyl. Now with CDs, we don't have to be afraid of bottom end, and I really like to pound that on. I limit it pretty heavily going in with tube limiters, like the Summit, and then, in the mixing process, I like to use the Neve 33609, which I hit pretty hard. I am also very fond of Avalon EQ. It is very common for me to use Pultec or GML on the program, but the Avalon stuff is just unbelievable. It is 50 volt bi-polar and it goes down to 18 Hz and it has the high frequencies up to 25 kHz, so you can put a lot of air on the top and really get the bottom to be big, too.

My technique of equalization is normally subtractive. I begin my mixing with subtractive EQ. It is less phasey to do that as well, versus additive EQ. It is a little more difficult technique, but once you learn it, you can build holes in the musical spectrum, all the way from 1.5 kHz down to 150 Hz, opening those areas for the other instruments to speak through. I think it very typical that the lower midrange is the "mud" area. Often times, keyboards, like Rhodes sounds, are all lower midrange. By opening the window in the other instruments, the vocals can speak through there.

I love the really great sounding EQs, for additive EQs, like the API, the old Neves and Pultecs. If I use any additive EQs, it is usually that. If I want something to be crunchy, I use SSL EQs, like for drums. However, I use a couple of different EQs for the bottom. I will use the SSL EQ in the 80 to 150 Hz range, because it is kind of punchy, and then for the deeper stuff, where I really want the subs to be pure, I will go to an Avalon or Pultec.

The API is very clean and pristine. It can get harsh, though. If something is already a little harsh, I might opt to add the Neve for the additive EQ or a Pultec, which has a very soft top.

I don't gate anything, while I record it. You can really screw things up. It really bothers me when anybody does that. There is really no reason to gate something, while you are recording. I pretty much always use Drawmer gates, like on the toms and snare, kick, when I am mixing, because they are frequency selective. If I am in a studio that doesn't have Drawmers, I will use Kepex, but I will key them off of an EQ, so that they are frequency selective. That is very critical.

Toms will ring and put a rumble through everything. It is like a big low-grade cloud, so the gating process is real important in the mixdown situation.

If I have any say over the mastering, and I know that it is going to go to radio, I probably will ask that some of the real deep low end get knifed off, just because it isn't going to translate, and so that it won't grab it too hard. I think for radio, if it sounds a little crunchy, it's better.

I naturally go for a very even natural sonic spectrum. The kick drum, the snare and the bass, and the lead vocal are probably all at equal levels. Those particular instruments won't get in the way of a lead vocal either. The lead vocal can feel really loud, and those things will not clobber the vocal, in terms of hearing the lyrics.

MATT WALLACE

In the world of Modern or Alternative pop and rock, Matt Wallace has scored significant success with artists like School of Fish, Paul Westerberg, Dimestore Hood, Red Five, Satchel, Dog's Eye View and Suncatcher, as well as the Replacements' Don't Tell a Soul, *which featured the band's biggest hit, "I'll Be You." Wallace's biggest success, however, came with Faith No More, whose 1989 album* The Real Thing *struck platinum sales.*

For me, when the concept of building a mix is mentioned, my approach tends to be backwards from some of the folks I know who do a lot of mixing. I tend to start from the vocal and the guitar and kind of build down to the drums, instead of starting from the drums and building up. For me, most songs tend to "live" between the voice and an acoustic or electric guitar, or some kind of keyboard. As I build the voice, guitars and keyboards, or whatever, I will get the balances set and then I will mute the lead vocal and listen to the play between the instruments make sure that the EQs are right, and that sort of thing.

To me, it has been easy to get the drums to sound good or big. In the past, if I got things sounding good and massive from the drums up, it might be like, "Where does the voice fit?"

The problem I had, building a mix up from the drums, was that you'd find yourself EQ'ing the voice to be heard in the mix, instead of EQ'ing the voice to sound wonderful. I think that is slightly backwards. The voice is really the reason we listen to most songs. I try and get it to sound really great, and then build around it.

I've had a lot of success in the past mixing with a lot of compression, but over the years, I've learned to use less and less stereo bus compression. Stereo bus compression can be like an instant shot of heroin. You can push it on, and all of a sudden, it is like, "Wow, this mix sounds like the radio." The problem with that is that it tends to not force me to focus on what is or is not working in a mix. If you put enough compression on it, you can pretty much make anything kind of stand up and work.

You can actually start fighting compression in a mix, because you get to a point where you've got to turn up your voice a little louder, and you push the voice up, and suddenly the compression from the kick or the entire mix will start to suck it down. It really opened my eyes when I was mixing. One day, while I was mixing, I went, "What the hell. I'll turn the compression off." My mix sounded horrendous. It was like, "Oh my God! What is going on here?" It was really unbalanced.

Now, I may mix for six or eight hours, and once I really feel that the mix is in its place, I will go, "Okay, now with the addition of minimal compression, it should actually help and give things that extra sheen or gloss that kind of glues everything together." It has certainly made me work a lot harder as a mixer, and try and make things work on a more organic level. At that point, compression is kind of the icing on the cake, instead of the main spice or ingredients.

Conceptually, the major questions in starting a mix are "What am I going for? Am I going for something that is loose and slightly sloppy, or am I going for something really polished and hi-fi, or do I want lo-fi? What kind of feeling do I want the listener to have at the end of the day? Should it be very together and tight and well performed and mixed, or should it be a little more organic sounding? Should the listener be impressed with the technical prowess of the musicians, or should people be moved to tears by the feeling of the performance?" All those things are in the forefront of my mind. You can mix a song any number of ways. You can bring things to the forefront that will draw you in, or things to the forefront that

are really aggressive and impressive. It really depends on where you are going with it.

I also have a theory that a good mix really isn't necessarily the same as a perfectly balanced or EQ'ed mix. It is really all about the emotion and feeling. For the most part, I think that perfect mixes can be boring. I like it when things are slightly odd or interesting or flawed. When it gets down to it, with all of the equipment that we have these days; with automated mixes and delays, to put things in time; harmonizers and putting things in Pro Tools; you can actually create a technically perfect recording and mix pretty much anyone off the street. But does it actually move someone, and is it something that is a little unique? When you listen to some of those Jimi Hendrix mixes, there are phase anomalies, where you can barely hear the drums at all. Everything is swimming in the mix, and occasionally the tom toms will jump out of no where. From a rhythmic technical perspective, they are horrible, but from an emotional spiritual place, they are outstanding. You listen to that stuff and go, "Oh God, I must be on some awesome drug here. What this guy is putting across, has got me in his sway."

An emotional mix can enable me to remove myself as a professional and go, "Oh my God!" Maybe for five minutes, I have forgotten about my bills and life and everything. When I actually get an emotional response, I want to go jump in my car and go buy that record and listen to it a million times. It is just wonderful and that is what it is all about, whether I am speaking as a fan, or as a professional.

CHAPTER 14

Percussion

When most people think of drums, they think of the traditional trap set that contains the usual snare, toms, kick drum, hi-hat and cymbals. Rock and roll, country and rhythm and blues may be great American musical forms that express many rich sides of our rhythmic sensibilities, but most records in those genres offer little more than a drum kit, tambourine and shaker of some type in the mix.

There is a world of countless exotic percussion instruments that subdivide time and define the rhythmic "pocket" with subtlety, amazing complexity and earthy directness. This chapter attempts to touch on recording and mixing a very small part of all those things that add richness to our music.

For this chapter, I have enlisted four highly regarded engineers, Mike Couzzi, Rik Pekkonen, Eric Schilling and Allen Sides, who have certainly done their share of accurately capturing the spirit of great percussion performances.

MIKE COUZZI

Mike Couzzi is one of South Florida's most successful independent engineers, working at Miami's legendary Criteria Recording, as well as other facilities like Crescent Moon, New River and South Beach. A native of Los Angeles, Couzzi worked at Wally Heider's studio in the seventies before deciding to relocate in Florida in 1980. Besides working with artists like Jaco Pastorius, Herbie Hancock, Rod Stewart and Jermaine Jackson, Couzzi has done extensive work recording Latin and African influenced music. Couzzi's work can be found on many award winning albums, including Paraguayan harpist Roberto Perera (Latin Jazz Album 1993—Billboard), Arturo Sandoval (nominated for six Grammys) and Vikki Carr. Other Latin credits include Julio Iglesias, Gloria Estefan, Jose Feliciano, Chayanne, Roberto Carlos and Jon Secada.

In dealing with recording most Latin music, I have the challenge of recording obscure and exotic percussion instruments from around the world. A lot of the percussionists I work with travel all over the world and bring in some really bizarre instruments. A lot of this stuff is so primitive, it's like pre-historic recording. It isn't just bringing in a shaker and a conga.

With some of these instruments, you don't know where the sound is going to come out. You hear it in the room, but you can't just stick a mic anywhere. The most important thing with recording percussion is listening to the sound in the room. You've got walk around and put your ear close to the instrument and far away and see where you really hear most of the sound and the harmonics taking place. The sound of the room, of course, is very critical. I look for a live neutral sounding room usually, and I will always use an ambient microphone, and vary the distance for effect. A very dead room will work also, providing it adds no ugly coloration or standing waves.

Most of the time the artist wants a fairly acoustic natural sound, without a lot of processing. For miking a large drum, like congas, I might use one mic close and one ambient overhead. If there are three congas, I use an X-Y set-up, usually three feet directly over the drums. Congas sound best placed on a wooden floor. I usually use Neumann TLM 193's or AKG 414 TLII's, which is also my favorite mic for small handheld percussion. Both of these new design mics sound great and have a wide dynamic range and frequency response. If I know the instrument is to be the primary percussion holding "the groove" together, I'll use some compression with a DBX 160 to add slap or attack. With congas, that is what most percussionists want to hear. Sometimes on small hand drums I'll use a Sennheiser 421, boosting between 4 kHz and 10 kHz.

Recently, I recorded some Udu drums and Moroccan hand drums and an instrument called the Box (also known as a Cajon), which the percussionist sits on and hits with his hands like congas. It looks like a big speaker cabinet with a hole in it. I miked it in the back, outside the box hole to get all the bottom end, but I put the mic close enough to the hole to get a lot of punch out of it, too. I put the front mic about two feet away to catch the slap of the hands. Both mics were Sennheiser 421's. On the Udu drum, I placed a 421 in the hole and used an AKG 414 overhead. You can get a very deep sound, almost like a huge drum, just by changing the mic blend.

A Bata drum is a two-headed drum that is worn around the neck and played with sticks. One side of the drum is bigger than the other and the player hits both sides all of the time, making a rhythm. The larger head gives you more of a low impact and the high one will give you more of like a flap sound. You can't really put a mic in the middle and get all of that. I found that for the most impact, it is better to mic both sounds,

The Sennheiser MD-421.

because it is kind of like two drums. You put one mic on each side, but when you do that, you usually get some low frequency cancellation, so you have to flip one of the mics out of phase to put it back in phase, so you can get all of the low end out of it. If you don't, it will sound really small.

The same is true with the Bombo, which is like a huge Andean bass drum that is played with a muffled rawhide mallet. You have to mic both sides, because they are hitting it with a mallet on one side and you are getting that big thud on one side, and on the other side, you are getting a boom coming out the back side, like a double-headed kick drum. In order to get the "boom," it is good to mic it from the back. It just gives you a big low-end sound.

A Berimbau is like a tree branch with a gourd attached it with steel strings coming out of it. You play it by striking the strings with this other tree branch that looks like a bow with steel wire wrapped around it. You tune it by sliding this other pre-historic looking piece of wood up and down the neck. It sounds like a huge Jew's harp and it's really loud.

For that, I use a really good tube condenser microphone overhead, like a Neumann U-47, between where the musician was striking the instrument and the gourd, about three or four feet away. You are catching the room and you are trying to get the whole instrument. If you close mic, all you will get is this weird stringy noise. You've got to get an overall picture.

When I close mic an instrument, I'm prepared for a percussionist to start wailing on his drums, so a mic with a huge dynamic range and some compression is essential for analog tape. I don't really like to overload transients on analog tape, because I find, that with a lot of percussion, the sound starts to get dull, even with the new formulation tape.

As far as mixing goes, sometimes the percussion should be in your face, so I'll EQ it and compress it a lot. Sometime I'll auto pan a shaker or other single instruments that are really thin or bright. Panning is very important, and I usually try to keep percussion as far left and right as possible. The reason being that if there is a singer or lead instrument, the percussion isn't going to fight with it.

For more ambient sounds, I'll use an AMS "room" program, which is very natural, or I'll use the newest software for the Lexicon 480 Ambiance programs. Sometimes I'll use heavily gated reverbs for impact and blend in a room or bright plate.

RIK PEKKONEN

Ever since 1965, when he started as an engineer in Los Angeles, Rik Pekkonen has carved out an impressive track record that ranges from jazz and fusion (fifteen Crusaders albums, Dixie Dregs, Freddie Hubbard, Jeff Lorber), R&B and blues (Booker T. and the MG's, B.B. King, Peabo Bryson, Sly and the Family Stone), country (Willie Nelson, Waylon Jennings, Nitty Gritty Dirt Band), rock/pop (Brian Wilson, Ringo Star, Was Not Was, Guns 'N' Roses, Joe Jackson, The B-52's, Roy Orbison, Jackson Browne), and more undefinable artists like Bob Dylan, Leo Kottke, Ladysmith Black Mambazo, and T-Bone Burnett. From T-Rex's Electric Warrior *to Joe Cocker and Jennifer Warnes' Grammy winning "Up Where We Belong," Pekkonen has done hundreds of albums and dozens of film soundtracks like* Backbeat, An Officer and a Gentleman *and* Brewster's Millions.

A percussionist used to always be a guy who could play vibes and marimbas, as well as all the toys. Victor Feldman was a percussionist, in the old sense of the word, who was not only a great piano player, but played vibes and all the percussion instruments. My favorite microphones for marimbas and vibes would be KM-54's. They are very smooth sounding old tube mics with these wonderful highs.

Schoeps mics will work well, too. They would probably be brighter, but the KM-54 has this really nice smoothness to it, but with lots of highs and presence. Vibes can be very percussive. You can literally get too much percussion on them and be in your face too much. That is why you should move the mics away, maybe three feet above the instrument, and use a smoother sounding mic on them. That way you can get a much more even sound out of the instrument. In fact, for all the instruments that "speak" and have all this super clarity to them, the Neumann KM-54 smoothes those guys out and gives you a much more usable signal.

Also, unless you are going for a special effect on vibes or marimbas, I wouldn't record with compression or limiting. I have a rule of thumb that I never compress it, because the producer might change his mind about the direction of the song or arrangement, and if you had compressed it originally, you might be in trouble, because you can't undo it.

I just used tympani on a Bonnie Raitt track that is a version of the Traveling Wilburys song "You Got It." It was for a Whoopi Goldberg movie called *Boys on the Side*. Jim Keltner played the tympani on it. I used a Neumann M-50, at least six or eight feet up above the kit. That was an omni pattern. The tympani has so much sound, that to capture the entire instrument, you have to get the room "working" for you.

Andy Narell, a steel drum artist on the Windham Hill label, is someone I recently worked with. He likes to use two KM-54's, and a transformerless AKG 414. The mics were maybe three feet above the drums. He got the stereo from the two KM-54's and he filled the middle with the 414. It worked very well.

The KM-54 is also good for instruments like chimes, timbales and glockenspiel. For tambourines, a Neumann M-50 is an ideal omni mic for capturing the instrument in a room. The Shure SM-57 is one solid choice for a closer in-your-face recording.

Bongos are so bright and percussive sounding that they will cut through anything. You can put on almost any mic and you can get a decent bongo sound.

For gongs, a Neumann U-47 FET, which is a cardioid mic, would probably be my first choice. It has a nice clear midrange with a lot of bottom to it. It also has pads, so you can pad it down. A U-67 is also a good alternate choice. I would probably put the mic a little bit to the side, instead of putting it directly at the instrument.

I think what is interesting about this whole thing, is that there are no rules, no clear-cut way. Even if you started every rhythm base the same way, you will find that you will have to change up here and there, because of what is going on in the song.

ERIC SCHILLING

One of the most successful artists to synthesize Latin American musical sensibilities to mainstream American pop is Gloria Estefan. As a solo artist, and with the Miami Sound Machine, Estefan and her husband Emilio have created an impressive string of hits, including "Rhythm Is Gonna Get You," "1-2-3," "Get on Your Feet" and their first hit, "Conga." The man who has recorded and mixed thirteen of their albums and runs the Estefan's Crescent Moon Studios in Miami is Eric Schilling. Schilling, a late seventies Los Angeles transplant and former engineer for Bill Szymczyk, has also recently worked with artists like Jon Secada and critically acclaimed Latin music legend Cachao.

When I started to work with Gloria, I was exposed to a lot of beats and instruments I hadn't heard before. I came from a place where I did a lot of rock, so there was a certain period of time where I had to re-think my approach, because there were no drums (trap sets) in some of this music. I also had to learn that you don't balance them the same way that you would a drum kit.

With dance and rock stuff, the kick drum tends to be very up front. Whereas in the real Latin music, you tend to put it way back, because that part of the beat is not something they want you to hear a lot. It isn't emphasized.

Only one song on the [Grammy-winning *Mi Terra* by Gloria Estefan] album had a trap set on it, and it was used in a very background way. Normally, you would build your mix around the drums and bass and then piano and so on. In this case, I started with congas and timbales being the main part of the song. That is where you start your mix. Then I will start working on the bass and then the piano. After that, I may start to work on all the hand percussion. It takes a while for you to re-think your approach.

Timbales are a special recording challenge, due to an extremely wide range of dynamics and sounds. You have to think about how you are going to cover the whole drum, because it is going to go from some fairly soft stuff, with the drummer playing on the side, to playing extremely loud fills, or cow bell. You've got to capture this all at the same time. What I tend to do is put a Sennheiser 421 in the middle of the bottom side of the two drums about a foot away from the rim of the shells.

That way I capture the ambiance of the wood coming through the bottom of the shells and the tapping on the sides. I feel that dynamic mics are preferable to condensers, when recording that close to the drums.

I will then put one tube mic, probably a Sony 800 set in a cardioid pattern, four to five feet above the kit, facing straight down at the cowbell, so I will get a lot of the top skin and get a more even sound. If I get too close, I won't get a good blend, between the two side shells and the cowbell and, say, a crash. Sometimes, if the mic is up six and a half feet or so, I might move it out two or three feet in front of the kit. It is just something you have to play around with, because each guy's kit has a certain sound and he will play it a certain way.

I really like to use compression on timbales. Generally, I would use an Urei 1176. It has the attack and release time, so you can fine-tune it and get what you want. I might set it for a medium attack and a fairly fast release time. You don't want something that is too fast, because if the attack is too fast, then you hear it too much. It sounds very stepped on.

I normally use an API "lunchbox" for EQ. I would tend to mix the two mics, compress them and then EQ the whole thing, so I work on the sound more as a group, as opposed to one EQ on the low mic and another EQ on the top mic.

For congas, most players come in with three drums, a high tuned one in the middle and two lower drums to the side. I will tend to catch a lot of it with one microphone. If a large part of what he is playing is on the high drum, I will put the mic so that it is facing the high drum, but it has got a wide enough field so that it can get the low drum that tends to be quite loud, as well as the medium drum. If one of those drums feels too far away, I will throw in a 421. I will use that to fill in the blend.

If they want to have a stereo sound, especially if it is for part of a song that is sparse with only that, a shaker and a timbale, then I will use two mics of a matched pair. I generally use the same mic that I use for timbales, the Sony 800. In some cases, I will use a Neumann U-67, two cardioids at 90 degrees. I will just move them around until I get a good spread.

For congas, you can't be as drastic with compression. I tend to use a different kind of compressor on them. I will use a Compex, which was manufactured by Audio Design. The Compex was the stereo version of the Vocal Stresser. It is a compressor that you can tune a lot, in terms of the ratios, attack time and gain.

The Urei has got more pumping to it and it tends to make the drum feel, when you hit it hard, more exciting to hear. It's great for timbale, but on a conga drum, the Urei would tend to pull down the attack a little too much for me and make the sound seem a little too small.

I really like to get warmth from congas and I will work a long time to achieve that. I don't tend to like those drums sounding real bright. Congas are probably the most work for me to record. I am always trying to find a balance. I want to hear some nice "air" on them, and I want to hear some nice snap and attack, but I don't want them to sound thin. It is a matter of finding a balance of trying to make the drums feel fat, but still have some attack up at the top. If you dial in a lot of 5 kHz and 10 kHz and all of that, then it will sound thin. On congas, I tend to do from 12 kHz and above for "air." I might just do a notch of 3 to 5 kHz, just to give a little snap to the attack. I probably wouldn't do more than +4 dB on any of those settings. At that point, if it still isn't sounding good, I would be saying that probably isn't miked right, or I didn't use the right mic.

In the case of the Cachao album, I had one piece where we didn't use congas and timbales. We totally abandoned that and went for a more street level instrumentation. There was one guy who played a hoe, the same thing that you use in your garden. He had a steel rod, and was playing the subdivision part of the beat, so I had to mic a hoe. You might say, "How do you mic a hoe?" Well, basically you take an AKG 414 and get about two feet away and point it at the hoe. He held it in a way that didn't dampen the steel part of it. He was hitting the metal part, so that the hoe had a really live sound. It was great.

For mixing Latin music, I have found that where the percussion tends to be very dense, you kind of have to pick what is going to be wet and what is going to be dry. It can't all be one thing. You have to create a contrast. The toughest part, especially if you have ten things, like congas, timbales, guiros and shakers and cowbells and so on, is to create a space for all of this stuff. You kind of have to pick what is going to have a long reverb and what is going to have a short one. It is really a question of contrast. Typically, the stuff that is playing a lot of fast time is going to tend to be drier. Stuff that is a lot sparser I will make more wet.

You have to look at Latin percussion in a very different context than you would philosophically approach a trap set in a mix or production. See, you really can't say that it is just one part. You have to look at all of them. You can't really say that a certain drum is the equivalent to a snare. That would be simplifying things too much. In an orchestra you might have crashes and tympani and, maybe someone playing a glockenspiel, but you have all of these guys making the whole piece, and that is the way it is with Latin percussion.

ALLEN SIDES

Allen Sides is one of the recording industry's most respected engineers. His album credits run into the hundreds. Some of the artists Sides has worked with include Frank Sinatra, Count Basie, Ry Cooder, Sarah Vaughn, James Ingram, Nancy Wilson, Barry Manilow, Little Village, Ray Charles, David Benoit, Fleetwood Mac, Sinead O'Connor, Neil Diamond, Irene Cara and a Miles Davis Tribute with Herbie Hancock. He is currently doing a Brian Setzer project.

Sides also started (in 1975) and continues to run the legendary Ocean Way/Record One Studios, a seven-studio complex in Los Angeles.

I am very big on stereo with percussion, particularly things like shakers. They sound so cool when you have a shaker in a space with a pair of great microphones. It can create such a presence, where a mono recording would not. It makes such a difference in size and space. If I want to position something, I will basically move the mics to the left or right of the instrument. That way I can have a true perspective.

Usually I want the mics close enough to get an even stereo symmetry between the two. Obviously, if you get them too far apart, then you have got a hold in the middle. With shakers, I would probably put the mics about eight inches to a foot away right where the player is shaking it. The microphones would probably be about eight inches apart.

My microphone of choice for cutting most percussion is the Neumann KM-54. The KM-54 has tremendous punch and presence. It doesn't matter if you are using bells, congas, vibes, anything you can think of, KM-54's are stunning. It sounds big, and in the dialogue of recording, the one thing I always listen for is size. It is easy to make something small, but it is real hard to make something bigger sounding.

If I can't get some KM-54's for recording percussion, then I will use a pair of Schoeps cardioids, which are among the most impressive phantom powered mics I have ever heard. If you have never heard a pair, they have an effortless top end that is very present and clear. It isn't harsh. The KM-54 is similar, but it is silkier sounding. There is a certain richness to it that goes beyond the Schoeps.

Another mic that I like, particularly on timbales, is the AKG C-12A. Sometimes, in a busy thick track, you can hit a timbale and all you hear is the sound of the stick and the top, and not the tone of the drum itself. The AKG C-12A helps, because it has a lot of low-end proximity and it tends to make things sound fuller.

I feel that the highly transient elements of most percussion instruments require special considerations that differ between analog and digital.

In digital, if you keep the signal out of the red, you are recording too low, because the dynamic range of a loud timbale hit is so staggering, it is like you are in the bad area of resolution. You are probably only getting about nine bits of resolution in the average program, because you are down so low in the spectrum. Usually, I think nothing of hitting a couple of reds, if I can't hear it, in order to bring the overall program level up. If you have a couple of great limiters on timbales, it is not unreasonable to limit the peaks. My

favorite limiter is probably the DBX 160. It is a very musical, good sounding limiter.

If you record analog at a normal level, it does a wonderful job of limiting the peaks. Say you have a very good sample kick, and you listen to Repro and experiment with different levels. There is a certain level, which is the *optimum level* of tape compression versus noise versus keeping as much punch as you possibly can. Let's say we are using Scotch 250 and set up for +3, and recording a kick. If you were listening in Repro and changing the levels and the peaks were hitting zero on Scotch 250 at +3, it would come back sounding very muddy. You would begin to drop the level and come down to −3 or −4 on the meter, and then all of a sudden, the kick would sound as clear as can be. Now the shelf noise on 250 is 2½dB lower than Ampex 456. On 456, the self noise is higher. You could record at −1 to −2 and the kick will sound about right, in reference to noise. If you are recording on 3M 996 at +3 dB, you could actually hit zeros and the level of tape compression would be acceptable, so you end up getting a certain level of tape compression, but you want the absolute maximum impact you can get, and that goes right back to the timbales. There is a big plus in analog, because you have got some natural limiting.

CHAPTER 15

Recording Piano

Piano is one of the most amazing creations in the universe of musical instruments. It is capable of some of the most delicate melodic expressions, as well as delivering brute percussive attacks that are startling in their immediacy. It has been a vehicle for timeless classics like Beethoven's haunting "Moonlight Sonata," the playfulness of Chick Corea's "Spain," and Count Basie's swinging minimalism. Rock and roll, blues, and R&B's finest moments have been served well by the piano, thanks to Jerry Lee Lewis, Charles Brown, Fats Domino, Allen Toussaint and many others.

Capturing piano on tape is an undertaking that requires a good understanding of the instrument at hand and its effect on the room in which it is being recorded. We rounded up four experts on the matter of recording piano, two of which are professional pianists. The points of view range from classical to rock and roll, and from philosophically seeing mono as the best way to present the instrument, to the virtues of dead strings. I would like to thank Jim Dickinson, John Hampton, Richard King and Cookie Marenco for their insight and enthusiastic participation in this piece. Ellen Fitton and Michael Omartian also deserve thanks for their input.

RICHARD KING

Richard King has traveled all over the world, from La Scala in Italy and Abbey Road in London to China, recording serious symphonic, small chamber group and solo piano music. As a senior recording engineer for Sony Music Studios in New York, King has worked with Yo-Yo Ma, Riccardo Muti and the Filarmonica della Scala, the Los Angeles Philharmonic, the Philadelphia Orchestra and many classical pianists, such as Yefim Bronfman, Emanuel Ax, Murray Perahia, as well as other renowned artists and ensembles.

Two main elements needed are a good piano and a good hall. After agreeing on a recording venue, the producer and artist will choose a piano, out of many pianos, so they are really deciding on what piano sound they want, based on the instrument. I only use two omni-directional microphones, and I really rely on the piano sounding exactly the way the artist and everyone is expecting it to sound. From that, I try to duplicate exactly what we are getting in the hall. Very rarely will I add any additional mics to enhance the hall sound.

For mics, the B&K 4009 is my choice, which is a high-powered 130-volt input mic that has been matched at the factory. People would probably be more familiar with the 4003, which is a powered omni. The 4009 is a matched pair of those. They match them throughout production, choosing pairs of caps and other elements, to build them. They are a true stereo pair. The serial numbers are an A and a B. B&K 4006's are good, too.

On a number of occasions, I have also used the Schoeps MK2S, which is again an omni with a high frequency shelf. The B&K has a peak way up high, around 18 kHz. So it has more of a sparkle on the top end, rather than the brightness characterized by the Shoeps. The B&K is a little tighter on the low end, than the Shoeps.

I will use outboard pre-amps and go straight to tape, so there is no console involved. I have used with great success, fully discrete Swiss-made pre-amps made by Sonosax. They are solid state, and they are very fast. The extension to the low and high end is very good. Like the B&K mics, it is incredibly quick, which is a sound that I like.

I've also used the Millennia pre-amp, which is very good. It has a 130-volt input on it, so I can use the high-powered B&K's without their own power supply, which I think is inferior. I can go straight into the Millenia, with a 130-volt line, which is kind of nice.

We have customized the input gain stage to one and a half dB steps, on the Millennias, in order to optimize level to tape. Millennia did the mods for us.

The other thing that I've done on occasion, is put my A/D out on the stage with the piano, and then just run an AES snake back to the control room to the tape machine, so that I am converting digital on stage, so the analog line is getting pretty short.

We record two tracks. We've use the Nagra Digital tape machine with great success. It is a four-track machine, but I just put stereo down on it twice, for redundancy. Lately, we've been experimenting with 96 kHz/24-bit stereo, which we also store across four tracks of the Nagra.

We've also used the Sony PCM-9000, which is a magneto-optical recorder, and also the Prism set-up with the PCM-800, which is the same as the Tascam DA-88. It'll do four tracks at 24-bit, but I'm just printing two mics again. So I just put the two mics down twice for redundancy.

I tend to prefer a more live hall. For my mic positioning, I could be anywhere from four feet to eight feet away from the piano. The mics are set, from the audience's perspective, somewhere around the middle of the longest string on the piano, halfway down the instrument. The mics will be pointed, however, towards the hammers and are normally set up parallel to one another.

For spacing the mics, I sometimes tend to go as tight as eighteen inches apart, and I've been as wide as four or five feet. The mic spacing directly correlates to the desired image of the piano recording. The deciding factor depends on the repertoire and the sound that the producer and the artist want. It is always subjective.

I just did a record with Arcadi Volodos in England of all piano transcriptions, which means that orchestral scores were reduced to being played on a piano by one player. For that, it seemed right that we had a much larger piano image, so there was a much wider spread on the microphones. Prior to that, I did a record of Prokofiev piano sonatas, where I really wanted a good solid center image, so I went with a tighter mic spread.

Obviously, with omnis, you can't pan them in at all, because there will be phase cancellation, so I always leave them hard left and right. In fact, I'm not even going through a console most of the time, so it really is just left and right. If I want more of a mono image, I'll place the mics closer together.

If the hall isn't so great, then I will also go a little tighter with the mics, and add a little reverb. But generally, it is all natural recording, if I can get away with that.

When I need to apply reverb, I like the "Random Hall" setting found on the Lexicon 480L. I also like the "Small Random Church." Between the two of those, I usually can find something that I can work with. I always change the parameters and customize the settings. They are just the settings usually I start with.

I tend to pull down the "Random Hall" in size to around 31 or 34 meters, depending on the recording. Again, I am trying to bring in something that matches the existing hall sound, because these recordings are never dry. I try and sneak in something where you can't actually tell that I've added additional reverb to, so I am very careful to match the characteristics of the existing room reverb.

On a 480, I find that the Shape and the Spread controls offer a lot of flexibility. There is also a high frequency cutoff that actually enables you to change the basic overall sound of the reverb, without actually running an additional EQ stage.

I only do this if the hall isn't so adequate. Most piano records that I have done have just been two mics and that is it, no EQ and no additional reverb.

Sometimes, if a grand piano sounds a little "covered," I'll extend the stick (the prop that holds up the lid). I'm always on a full stick (the piano lid prop fully extended) anyway, but if I want the piano to sound a little more open, I'll bring a piece of wood that is maybe another four inches longer than the regular stick, and put the lid up slightly higher. I've used a pool cue with great success, because of the rubber base of the stick and the felt tip. It doesn't damage the piano, and it gets the lid open a little bit more.

Concerning panning, I always go with the image of the lower notes to the right side and the high notes coming out of the left, so it is always audience perspective for me. There are usually some tell-tale extreme low notes usually come from the right, and extreme high comes from the left, but the main sound of the piano comes from the middle. I think that most people in jazz and pop do the opposite panning, which is from the player's perspective.

My absolute favorite hall to record in is on the east coast of England. It is called Snape Maltings. It used to be the malting place, where they created the malt that then would get shipped out to the brewery. It is an old brick building with a wooden roof, and it has a really great reverb. Even the higher notes of the piano ring into the room with a great sustain, but it is still a very warm sound.

My favorite pianos are Hamburg Steinways. I think they record the best. For classical, the Hamburg Steinway has a better balance of low and high notes. The Hamburg Steinways also seem to be a little better for me than the New York Steinways. I find that Bosendorfers sound great, but for some reason, I've had real trouble recording them. It is kind of a wild instrument. The Steinway sounds the most even over microphones. I've used Yamahas for pop and jazz, and they are really great for that, but for classical, I find they are a little too bright.

COOKIE MARENCO

Before Cookie Marenco entered the wonderful world of engineering and producing, she was a professional jazz keyboardist who had been classically trained since the age of four. Since 1981, Marenco has owned and run a Bay Area studio called OTR, and also worked as an A&R person during Windham Hill's 1980s glory years. Her credits as an engineer include Mary Chapin Carpenter, Charlie Hayden Quartet West, Ladysmith Black Mambazo, Brain and Buckethead, Mark Isham, Turtle Island String Quartet, Philip Aaberg, Steve Swallow, Carla Bley, Glen Moore, Ralph Towner, Oregon and Clara Ponty.

One of the hardest things to find is a good piano in a good studio. At my studio, I have a seven-foot Steinway that was built in 1885. A lot of people from all over come to play on it. As a player, I like the Steinway for the touch, and because there is a roundness to the sound that I prefer.

We keep the piano brighter than most Steinways. We don't voice it down as much as a classical instrument for a concert, but it wouldn't be as bright as a Yamaha, which tends to be a brighter sounding instrument. Personally, I'm not a big fan of Yamaha.

You can hear the difference between the various pianos, once you get familiar with all of them. You can hear a recording and tell if it is a Yamaha, Steinway or Bosendorfer.

Sometimes, Steinways get a little muddy in the midrange, between the octave below middle C and the octave above it. That is the only thing you have to watch for in a Steinway.

Usually, when I record a piano, I'll use two B&K's (the 4011's or the 4012's), placed in sort of a "V" position, about 8 or 9 inches apart, with one mic pointed towards the keyboard and one pointed towards the back end of the piano. They'll be placed at more of a 45-degree angle, somewhere in the center of the instrument, where the midrange is, about halfway up, between the piano lid and where the strings sit. If I do that, I get a lot of clarity in the middle.

If I am doing more of a classical session, the mics may be backed off more—not even inside the piano—to get more of the room. It depends more on the sound that the artist is looking for.

If I were in a situation where I didn't have B&K's, then KM-84's would be another choice. The Schoeps mics work well, too.

You really have to listen, because every player attacks the piano differently. Even slightly different positionings, or placements in a room can change the phase relationships.

On a lot of the 9-foot pianos, I'll even put up a couple of other floor mics, as sort of "insurance" mics, to capture the range of the instrument.

I'm a big fan of stereo piano. Mono piano drives me crazy. I know a lot of classical engineers will record with one mic, but if there aren't two tracks of piano, then what's the point? [laughs.]

You know what drives me nuts is that whole low-high issue, with the bass of the piano on the left side and the treble end of the piano on the right. When I get that in reverse, my whole world goes bananas.

Sometimes, when you do this miking in the center like this, it is actually tough to tell. A lot of other engineers don't seem to care, so I will have to make the record and the stereo image will be reversed. Something will be wrong, and I won't know what it is. It almost always turns out to be the piano in reverse. There is nothing wrong with it, it is just me psychologically. I just can't handle it.

Unless it is a solo piano record, I rarely hard-pan left and right. It depends on the instrument and the instrumentation, because I don't necessarily pan at 10 and 2. If I have a lot of guitars going on, I might do an 11 and 5.

When I am laying down tracks, I try not to EQ anything. I try to go flat. Almost always, I am using Dolby SR.

I prefer everything analog. With digital, I find that the transients are compromised. I don't like the sound of what digital does to an instrument like a piano, or any kind of plucked or attacked instrument. Every generation of digital gives you more unpleasantness on the top end.

JIM DICKINSON

Memphis-based producer and session keyboardist Jim Dickinson has produced critically acclaimed albums for Ry Cooder, Big Star, the Replacements, Mojo Nixon, Toots Hibbert, Jason and the Scorchers, Claw Hammer, and most recently blues legend Mose Vinson. Dickinson has enjoyed a successful piano and keyboard sideman career on notable releases by the Rolling Stones, Dr. John, Eric Clapton, the Cramps, Arlo Guthrie, Los Lobos, Aretha Franklin, Carmen McRae and most recently Bob Dylan. Dickinson engineered Phineas Newborn's Grammy nominated jazz piano album Solo, and has also worked with Ry Cooder on eleven movie soundtracks.

First off, I want to dispel some mythology, which is you should mic the piano from the inside. I've gone back to recording piano mono. I did record stereo piano for years, which I now think is incorrect, because you simply don't listen to the piano with your head inside it.

The whole idea of stereo piano, which is a seventies idea, is totally incorrect. You can create a kind of false stereo, if you are interested in the horrible idea of separating the left hand from the right hand, which of course, no piano player would want to do. You are trying to create the illusion of one big hand anyway.

When you sit behind the piano, you do hear the treble in your right ear, and the bass in your left ear, but no one else does. It really depends where you think the piano image goes in the stereo spectrum. If you see the stereo spectrum as 9 o'clock to 3 o'clock, I think the piano goes at 1:30, for instance.

The lid of the grand piano is designed to project the sound out horizontally to an opera or concert hall, and the sound of that piano actually focuses about ten or twelve feet in front (meaning the audience side of the piano that the lid is open to) of the instrument, towards the audience, which is why it is idiotic to put the mic inside it.

The best textbook example of concert hall grand piano recording that you could ever want is found in a documentary from the late fifties of the Glenn Gould Columbia sessions. There are microphones all over the room, but they are recording in mono. There isn't a microphone any closer than eight feet. There are some microphones considerably further away. They are recording with no EQ and no compression and when they wanted more top end, they simply turned up the microphones that were close to the top end. It was just a beautiful thing to watch. They were recording with a mono unit and a stereo unit, which was really a safety, because the needles were moving in unison on both tracks.

Even with the multi-microphone approach, these old-school Columbia recording engineers were making a blending of the different mics. That is what a grand piano sounds like.

Much of vintage rock and roll is an upright or a spinet piano, which is, of course, a vertical harp, rather than a horizontal harp, in a whole different miking technique. The Jerry Lee Lewis records were cut on a spinet piano, with a microphone placed behind it, because on an upright or spinet, the sound comes from the back of the soundboard. There is a place between the struts there, to the treble end of the keyboard, behind the third brace, where there is a sweet spot on any upright or spinet piano. That is where I mic it.

The Jerry Lee Lewis piano recordings were interesting in that part of the piano sound was coming through the back of the vocal mic, as well.

On my recordings of old blues musicians, I like to mic the front of an upright piano, so I can get the sound of the fingernails on the keys. That is a subtle thing, but to a piano player, it makes a big difference. Some guys click louder than others. It adds personality. It is a question of what you think you are recording from a keyboard player.

On the movie soundtrack for *The Border* we had an old piano that came out of Amigo Studios, and it had a sticker on it that said "This is the property of the Los Angeles County School System." It had been painted white with house paint. Nobody used it, except for us. Nobody cared what I did to it, so I could cover the strings with duct tape and tinfoil, and whatever else I wanted to use. The strings were all really dead, so there weren't any overtones, which is what I wanted it for. I wanted the piano that way to insure that its sound would not interfere with the guitar's tonalities.

Someone might wonder why I would choose dead strings. Why not just EQ out the clashing frequencies on the piano? Well, I would rather listen to signal than EQ.

The overtone series of a piano is very complex. The longer the strings, the more dominant the overtones are going to be. With dead strings, the first thing that goes are the overtones. The deader the strings, you primarily end up with the principal frequencies. With Ry, the guitar is a dominant instrument, so it is imperative that the piano is out of the way. Conversely, if was I making just a piano record, I would want a strong representation of overtones from a piano.

My personal favorite piano is an old white Bush & Gerts that was made in Chicago before World War II, that I took out of Stax Recording. The best piano that I ever put my hands on is Willie Nelson's sister's full-sized grand piano at Arlyn Studios in Austin, Texas. I can never remember the name of it. It was just this fabulous instrument that made a Bosendorfer sound like a Kimball. It is exactly the kind of instrument I normally don't like, but this one is wonderful. I have known that piano for twenty years, and it has gotten better. Steinways are really best suited for classical players.

There is a piano down on Beale Street in Memphis that is absolutely whipped; but yet every time I sit down and play it, I enjoy the experience. Here is this old piano that Mose Vinson and God knows who else has played since Year One, and you can feel the humanity through the ivory keys, which is something that plastic can never convey.

You can be "Save the Elephants," and all that, but I'm sorry, man, give me ivory keys [laughs]. I like elephants as much as anybody, but I hate to put my fingers on plastic keys. It feels like a synthesizer [laughs]. Ivory feels so much better. You can feel the ivory, the wood and the felt on the hammer and the metal on the string. It is all part of what is in your hand, and it is a wonderful feeling. Now that is a piano, and there is not a real piano player on Earth who won't understand what I'm saying.

JOHN HAMPTON

Since the late seventies, John Hampton has worked with wide range of artists, including B.B. King, Travis Tritt, the Replacements, the Vaughan Brothers, Lynyrd Skynyrd, Robert Cray, Alex Chilton, Little Texas, the Bar-Kays and Afghan Whigs. Hampton's productions of the Gin Blossoms have gone multi-platinum, and for a number of years, many of Nashville's most successful country artists have come to his home base studio, Ardent Recording, in Memphis for his engineering and mixing expertise.

A piano was meant to be heard phase coherently. When you listen to a piano, you're hearing the piano hammers hitting the strings, and the sound reflecting off the lid, and coming to your ear. It's all pretty phase coherent, out there where you're standing, because it's all hitting your ears at the same time.

Now there are a lot of people who'll put one mic on the bass strings, and then about three and a half feet away, place another mic on the top strings. Now you've got your low end happening in one speaker and you've got your top end happening in one speaker, but what about the strings in between, which is the main part of the piano where most people play? You've got the sound meeting these microphones at all these different timing intervals and it's totally not coherent. In a mix, if you pan it left and right, it sounds like it's coming from behind your head. That's not correct.

There are several ways to obtain a phase-coherent piano recording. If you want the low end of the piano on one side and you want the high end of the piano on the other side, that's fine; but there are a lot of ways to obtain that and still have phase coherency to where the strings in between don't sound like they're coming from behind your head. One of them is M-S stereo, or mid-side stereo. I love mid-side stereo. An M-S recording of a piano can give you a truly phase coherent, left to right picture of the piano without all the weird phase distortion on the keys in between the low and the high.

The best microphone I have found for that application is the Shure VP-88. Put the mic over the hammers, but not too close, because you don't want the mid-strings to be louder than the low strings and the high strings. Pull it back a foot from the hammers or so and put it on the "M" setting, which is a medium M-S picture. If you do that, then you will have a phase coherent picture of the piano. You also don't need to EQ the VP-88, because it is such a natural sounding microphone.

There is a French method of miking a piano, which is called ORTF. It was developed back in the seventies. That is where you take a couple of mics, like KM-84's, and put them in an X-Y set-up with the capsules seven centimeters apart. That's the magic number. Its actually not phase coherent on the frequencies that are seven centimeters long, but it gives a fairly phase coherent picture of a piano low to high.

My favorite method, believe it or not, is to put two PZM's back to back. Just tape them together. I will put them 12 to 15 inches above where the hammers hit the strings. They need to be the kind of PZM's with the high frequency boost. With those, you never need to EQ the piano.

Those are the three ways that I have recorded piano that I have consistently experienced the most satisfying results.

CHAPTER 16

Production Philosophy

This is probably the most open-ended chapter in the book. The subject at hand isn't so much how one captures instruments on tape or builds a great mix, and yet this is the heart and soul of this whole undertaking.

In the world of recording and producing music, it is easy for some to get caught up with the latest gear and what it does, or focus too much on cleaning up extraneous noise on tracks and achieving some kind of idealized sonic clarity. In other words, focusing on the details so much that one can't see the forest for the trees.

We are trying to capture magic in those fleeting moments where brilliance happens—not sand it out of existence.

I really believe that art generally happens in spite of artists, and the function of great producers and engineers (and really everyone on the staff of a good studio) is to assist the artist to be in the self-actualized moment of creating and being. That is where truth happens.

It is important for producers and engineers to remember that they too are equally susceptible to letting too much "thinking" get in the way of paying attention to the intention of the flow. A true pro knows his or her craft enough to be here now.

Over the years, I've been blessed with many wonderful ponderings from many amazing talents in the recording industry. The following excerpts are from some of my very favorite interviews, with special thanks to Tim Palmer, Cookie Marenco, Jack Clement, Tony Brown, Roy Thomas Baker, David Briggs, Norbert Putnam, David Kahne, Gail Davies, Jim Dickinson, and Denny Purcell. I also have included some thoughts from the irrepressible and incredibly talented Dolly Parton. She might not be a producer, engineer, mixer or masterer, but what she says about taking ownership of one's uniqueness is worth pondering.

Among the longer contributions is the section from the late great David Briggs, who produced Neil Young's greatest rock albums. This might be the only place you'll get to read any extended comments from one of rock's production legends.

Basically, the ruminations in this chapter run the gamut on everything, from what is a producer, to tricks to get something extra out of performers, to the state of the industry and a few war stories and a lot of attitude thrown in for fun.

In the spirit of what I just shared, this chapter is intentionally fluid, so just go with the ride. Something might shoot sparks in between the words and notes that you'll carry with you for a long time.

TIM PALMER

Tim Palmer has enjoyed a lengthy career that has covered a wide range of rock and pop. His credits include Pearl Jam, James, Live, Tears for Fears, Robert Plant, Ozzy Osbourne, U2, Rancid, the Cure and many others.

What really defines producing a record? Who the hell knows? The only thing we do know for sure is that it is an ever-changing scenario. If it had a job description, it would be very hard to pin down.

Sometimes when working with an extremely creative and proficient group, producing is quite an easy occupation and very enjoyable; other times it is a pain in the ass from beginning to end.

There are many psychological aspects to producing a record. Aside from making the record you want to make, you have to be best friend and confidant to the artist, and of course the record company. This you may think is a conflict of interests, and you would be right. Your job is to sort through the chaff, listen to both sides of the argument and hopefully come to the right conclusions. There is no point in pissing off the record company to keep the artist happy and in the end have no push from the label in the marketplace. Conversely if you tow the company line and don't have any feeling for the artistic vision, you wont last more than a couple of days in the studio. Don't forget to be proud of your work. If you don't have any confidence in what you do, it will be hard to convince others.

It is probably worth being careful in your choice of reference points. This can be explosive to your artists. If you are trying to get them to like an idea, telling them it reminds you of Kajagoogoo will not help if you are producing Motorhead. Firing a musician is a very touchy subject. Choose your words extremely carefully. In the past I have actually received death threats from thwarted musicians who took their dismissal very badly. As it happened, this wasn't even my decision, but the producer gets the flack.

Being a technical wizard in the studio or at the computer is obviously a plus, but if you are going to create a piece of work that has no emotion or feel, then you are wasting your time. We have all heard too many wonderfully engineered, yet terribly drab albums. If you have a crap song then you are off to an extremely bad start. I was always told that you cannot "polish a turd" and "you can't shine shit." Pro Tools has created an amazing aid to recording and as a creative tool it is phenomenal, but don't forget that the "listening public" never demanded records that were more in time or more in tune. Don't waste countless hours making dull lifeless recordings. Leave

some mistakes in, they may turn out to be your favorite bits.

Pre-production is a great opportunity to find out some of the parameters of how you will make your project work. You are looking for ways to create the most comfortable and creative environment in which the project can proceed. Sometimes it is just making it work any way you can. If a band like to record underwater, eating bananas, then that's probably your best plan. Don't forget that being a producer is a bit like being a juggler.

Your basic overview is to ultimately create a valid piece of work that has something credible to offer. You should aim for at least one redeeming quality. This can come from many directions: maybe the artist writes great lyrics, maybe the music is aggressive, maybe the band writes great pop songs. Decide this early on so that when you are burnt out trying new ideas you don't lose sight of your original plan.

Accept the fact that you will sometimes have to be a father to your groups. Many times I have had to actually go in, wake a band up, make sure they have eaten and drive them to the studio. In one instance I had to carry a singer out of a Los Angeles bar over my shoulder to stop him from drinking any more vodka. Of course, I hadn't drunk anything!

You may have times when you haven't worked for 6 weeks and you will feel you are over. Don't let your crushed ego get the better of you. Overall don't forget, "if you can't take a joke, stay out of the music industry!"

ROY THOMAS BAKER

Roy Thomas Baker has produced some of rock's most audaciously distinctive recordings of the last thirty years, and the world has bought millions upon millions of albums bearing his production credits. The utterly unique "Bohemian Rhapsody" by Queen, or The Cars debut album are just a couple of examples. Other credits include Journey, Foreigner, T-Rex, Free and T'Pau.

Baker's musings on being unique are something that every person in the music industry would do well to remember.

My whole thing is this: The more unique you can sound from anything else around and still be commercially successful is great! I hark back to that philosophy over the years. Back when I did "Bohemian Rhapsody," who would've ever thought of having a single with an opera section in the middle?

The first Cars record was totally unique. Even stuff I did when I was going from second engineer to engineer, like T-Rex's "Get It On (Bang a Gong)" or Free's "All Right Now," they all had a different twist on what was basically the same thing. Now nobody wants that different twist. They all want to sound like each other. It is very odd.

Now I have all these bands all come in with their little CDs and say, "I want that snare sound" and "I want that bass sound" and "I want that guitar sound."

I'll go, "Hello! These guys you are playing to me have already done this. Why do you want to do it?" It has totally gone backwards.

They want to look like each other and this might be a throwback to the late eighties, where everybody had to look like each other, and they all had to wear the same leather bracelets and they had to have the same haircuts. We ended up with every record sounding the same. It was so generic and I hated it. I drove away from the business in the States for a little bit and went to Europe and worked with people like T'Pau, and people like that.

Over here, it was getting silly. Everyone was going to the same mix engineers to get the same drum sound, which used the same snare that everyone was using with the same echo on it, with that horrible sound. Every record was interchangeable. It didn't matter who the band was. They might've thought they were different; Pepsi and Coke are different, but who gives a damn? The shit is still cola. It's not champagne [laughs].

I stay clear of that. It is funny how many people put down the eighties, but the early eighties were great. You had the Cars, and the Pretenders and Joe Jackson and Elvis Costello.

To sell records, you don't have to be the people who are also selling records on the charts. In fact, if you can sell records by doing something different, then you have found a little niche for yourself and you can be around for years. It is the ones who sound like each other who are the one-hit wonder bands that come and go. When that scene is over, it goes like it went from horrible glam heavy metal to alternative overnight.

Where did all of those bands go overnight? They were all okay bands, as far as being able to play their instruments. They just vanished! Nirvana and Pearl Jam came along and what happened to all of those other bands? They were all carbon copies of each other. They said they were alternative bands, and yet there was a time that if I saw another pair of checked shorts and everyone walking around saying they were from Seattle … It was very weird. Luckily, that has gone too. Alternative became generic as well, because everyone was copying that thing.

Then it goes on to the next thing, which now it seems to be pop. I have no problems with pop. I'm not too cool to admit that I liked Abba in the seventies. I thought they were a really good band. I do like pop songs, but I do like a different type of pop song. I don't like generic pop songs.

Selling yourself as something different is the root of where everyone should go.

In one respect, most bands don't want to sound like each other. I agree with that, but I don't believe that selling records is selling out. Communicating with the most people you want to communicate your message to is the whole point. Anyone can sit around in their bedroom and twiddle around with their guitar and not communicate with anyone. Duh! Everyone who is sitting in front of a video game is doing that!

If you want to communicate with the most people, you have to go out there and communicate. Communicating, in a sense, is selling records, and what is wrong with making money? There is nothing wrong with making money as long as you don't sound like the next band along. A lot of these bands that say, "I don't want to sell out," sound like some other band who did sell out [laughs].

When it actually comes down to it—and this is going by what people are willing to accept—a great song recorded on a 4-track Portastudio stands a better chance than a lousy song recorded in a real recording studio. That is because people will communicate with that. That has been proven time and time again. There have been far more hits out of lousy sounding good songs than there have been with great sounding bad songs.

Every time a band either raises the money or gets a contract with a major label (or even with an independent with some means), the first thing they do is look at the back cover of all of the favorite producers they want to work with based on what they like. They do that whole guilt by association thing, which is "I don't want to work with that, because of that artist. I want to work with him, because he worked with this artist." Using these criteria is very strange. They get into a situation where they expect perfection from everyone around them, except themselves.

So what happens is, if they think they can surround themselves with the right producer in the right studio with the right technical abilities, it will make them sound a million times better. But the old proverb about "you can't polish a turd" still applies. Somewhere you've got to turn that turd into a piece of gold and then it can be polished.

It all ends up in this situation where there are thousands and thousands of bands out there with these really smooth great generic sounding records that nobody gives a toss about. Then somebody like Beck comes along and he hits a can and sings about being a "loser" and he gets a number one, and who knows what that was recorded on? [laughs] And who cares? I loved it! So that is all that matters to me. For all I know, Beck might've spent a year trying to make that sound like it was really crappy. I doubt it.

The other thing that keeps coming out, and it has to do with (A) the artist and (B) the record companies. Every band would like to produce its own records. That to me is a bit like someone wanting to be their own lawyer in court. It doesn't matter that, even if you are a lawyer, you shouldn't represent yourself in court. I think even if you are a great producer who happens to be an artist, and you are great at working with other artists, you should never produce yourself. I think you still need the element of somebody else kicking you up the ass to make sure you get the best out of yourself, because you can't be in two places at once. You need that extra brain on that.

A lot of artists will often go to an engineer, who is probably a great engineer, but as of that stage, has not produced anything. But you know there is more to a production than getting a nice polished sound, and people will still not go out and buy a nice drum sound, if the song isn't there.

I came up with an engineering background, and some of my favorite producers have come up with an engineering background. But engineers have got to realize that producing is totally different from engineering. The first thing I did when I took up producing was to give up engineering. I can still engineer and it is a great tool for me. I can still talk to whomever I have as my engineer and talk to them on a technical level, but I don't actually physically engineer myself anymore. I might go over the shoulder and twiddle a little bit, and on mixing I do some of the rides, but I too abandon that.

I think that a lot of people confuse the role of the producer and the role of the engineer.

If an engineer decides to get into producing, I would hope that he would automatically have an engineer working for him. Producing has its own difficulties and twiddling knobs is only a means to an end. It isn't an end in itself. Get another engineer and train that engineer so they can become producers.

I haven't seen a single band that can work out a budget and stick to it. The first role of a producer is to get the budget together [laughs]. Most bands are totally useless at that. Even if I was to become an artist tomorrow, I wouldn't produce myself [laughs]. I have to be out there being creative. Meanwhile, the producer is trying to kick me up the ass to make me stay on track and make sure that I go to the level beyond the level I thought I could go to.

When the first Cars record was number one on the charts, I was driving on Sunset in Hollywood with Ric Ocasek. We drove past the billboard for the Cars record and he said, "If someone had told me a year ago that I would be driving along Sunset Boulevard with Roy Thomas Baker looking up at a billboard of my record that is number one, I wouldn't believe him."

That is a classic example. When Ric Ocasek does his own records, he doesn't always produce himself. He lets other people produce him. Yet, Ric is a very good producer and he has produced some hits himself like Weezer. Ric is a classic example of somebody using his brain. "Hold on! I need someone to kick me up the ass in the same way I kicked that other artist up the ass!" [laughs].

The thing is, everyone thinks "It's in the mix. It's in the mix!" But that is like saying, "A movie is in the editing." It is not strictly in the editing. Yes, a bad editing job can screw up a good movie. Yes, a great editor can enhance a great movie. If it is a lousy movie, you can't get anyone to edit that to be great. It just can't be done. The same thing applies to music. Yes, a bad mix can mess up a great song. And yes, a great mix can enhance a great song. But a great mix can't make a bad song a hit or make it sound great for the radio otherwise.

People need an identifiable sound. They want to know that when that song is being played on the radio, people can hear who that is, even without the DJ mentioning who it is.

All the great bands have that quality. When a Stones song comes on the radio, even though they have had a lot different changes of sound, you can hear instantly who they are, regardless of the period of music they are in. You can hear exactly who it is and you don't need a DJ to tell you, "That was the Stones." You can hear it. That rule applies for every great band of the last 30 years. That is the thing that people are missing. If you don't have that identifiable sound, you are getting merged in. If the DJ isn't mentioning who it is, then nobody will know who it is. It will just be another band, and nothing is worse than being anonymous. That is exactly what you don't want.

NORBERT PUTNAM

Since the early sixties, Norbert Putnam's career has taken him from being one of Nashville's most in-demand session bassists to multi-platinum producer. His studio player credits range from Elvis Presley to Henry Mancini to Linda Ronstadt. As a producer, Putnam credits include Dan Fogelberg's and Jimmy Buffett's biggest records, as well as New Riders of Purple Sage, Joan Baez, Dobie Gray, Jerry Butler and Eric Anderson.

There is an emotional aspect to the arts that many people seem to lose sight of. Rick Hall, with his four-channel Shure mixer and Fender bassman monitor system, was completely adequate for the emotional brilliance of the legendary Arthur Alexander. Willie Mitchell didn't need the latest console or the microphone for those records he did with Al Green. Al Green could sing the phone book and people would love it.

When I lived in Nashville, they used to always talk about the songs. Of course, Nashville is run by publishers; but, to me, it has never been "the song." A great song is a wonderful thing, but you take an artist like Al Green or Elvis Presley and you can give them a very trite lyric and they can sing it with such emotion and power that will give you chill bumps. It's not the lines. It's the artist. So I totally disagree with all those people who pedal the idea that the song is the thing. If you take those songs and put them on a sheet of paper and read them, you'll know that the song is not the thing. Elvis Presley definitely proved that me.

What we sell in this business is emotion. When you have a purveyor of emotion, like Al Green or Elvis Presley, then you have magic. That is the beginning and end of it. It is never the equipment. It is not the SSL, Neve, Mackie or Trident console. It is not the snare drum or the reverb. And I would've argued this point years ago, but it is not the bass line [laughs]. It really is the artist. People hear the artist and they hear the emotion. They either buy it or they won't. I think it is a quick study.

I had a friend who was president of Elizabeth Arden cosmetics. He said, "Norbert, we just sell boxes. We sell these beautiful decorated boxes and when a lady walks by the perfume counter, she glances at the boxes and the one that catches her eye, she buys. And we probably have a five to ten second window to capture her imagination."

When you and I are listening to the radio, we may not even give it five or ten seconds. We lock on a station and we may hear three or four seconds and then we pass on to another station. So it is a magical thing that a good artist does with his or her voice that attracts us or sends us away. That is really what this industry is all about. Anything else is disposable art. It is like a piece of candy that is good for a few moments and it's gone.

DAVID KAHNE

I can tell when something is right when I am kind of scared of the person I'm considering signing or producing. I'm always looking for that little fear in myself when I try and decide. I think that is where the greatness is going to come from. If I know what they are going to do, it is not going to be good enough [laughs]. I'm not the artist.

When people are really good, you've got to know what you are doing and what you are talking about. You've got to be able to hear and listen, because you are going to be challenged. If you don't, you are just going to be ignored.

It is very important to understand that A&R is more than just signing someone who can make a great record. I mean I've made records that I thought were really great, but I found out that the artist couldn't really follow through on being a recording star. I'm not just talking about looking good for the video. I'm talking about having the energy and the kind of thing to go out and be somebody that is going to be an image for a lot of people.

In the last few years, it has become so easy for someone to make a record. A lot of people get record deals and put out albums way before they should. They might have a good song, but you can feel the boundary very quickly on what is going on.

In the sixties, the best bands had the best drummers and there weren't that many good drummers around. If you had a good drummer in your band, and you sucked, eventually he would be quitting and joining a better band. Nobody has to go through that gauntlet anymore. You can just get loops or machines. (Even though I love using loops, I love more than anything making loops with a great drummer.)

That whole thing of being able to make a pretty good sounding record with less rehearsal and less performing and weight and depth in your experience is a pretty weird thing. It not only affects the bands, it also affects the A&R people. There are a lot of A&R people who don't know how vast it is. If they did, they would run screaming from music. Once you sign somebody and make the record, it is like "Whoa! What is going on?" It just gets wider and wider and wider. You push on music and it is completely malleable. You are building something out of nothing.

Bands go in and they'll have something that feels pretty engaging, but then you go in to record and try to blow it up into the space of a real record, and there isn't enough to become a real record ... a full album. I think a lot of people are

disappointed in buying albums and not finding whole albums there.

At my apartment in New York, I can look out and see the CBS building and the Time Warner building, where Elecktra and Atlantic and all that stuff is. One day I was listening to tapes that people had sent me thinking about me producing a record. I was into about my tenth tape and every one was "This is really not good, not good, not good, not good." Then I was playing this song back, and it had this chorus and there was this really cool thing going on, and I was thinking, "God, this is really great."

I started thinking how music is so private and it is so perverse and when you are in recording, you might've been working for three weeks and nothing is coming together and in a split second, there is something there that has meaning and it has tone. My feeling from that is that the artist always lets a secret out and that secret and that moment always shows up on tape. It is this invisible thing that you can't really pinpoint in time and space. You just happen to be recording and you set this whole track up, and someone may be out there singing. All of a sudden there is shape to the music and a center to the song.

Anyway, I was listening to this song and I thought that when I hear something that really works, it is kind of a miracle, because it kind of defies gravity. It is like, "Why does this sound mean something and all of these other sounds don't mean very much?" While I was listening to this, I turned around and looked out the window and I looked up at these buildings and I saw this inverted pyramid of this giant corporation and this little teeny song with this big corporation on its back [laughs]. And I was thinking, "These songs are struggling to save these giant companies. That is really what it is about." It has gotten more and more that way, I think. "Is music really made to support this whole thing?" Well in a certain way, I don't think it was.

A hundred years ago, a guy would've been sitting in a village with his guitar playing at a local wedding, and it was probably what was popular music at the time. Now it's been amplified and the whole distribution of it is huge. Nevertheless, it still begins with somebody with this little secret that slips out. That is the part of it that I love. I love being there and hearing it come together and going, "A second ago, this wasn't music and now this is music." From that point outward, it is all kind of a mess [laughs].

I think that trying to save these huge worldwide companies with these little songs is sometimes humorous and sometimes I really despair over it. Because it affects the people playing the music, and it just changes the values of it.

I'm not a purist by any means. I'm not saying that music shouldn't sell. But I think that it is harder to operate in that environment and I didn't think that it used to be so much that way.

The companies are bigger and they are worldwide and it takes more and more energy to keep them going, and they need music faster and it is just a kind of an odd relationship between the two things. Still, you know a record is not going to be good, unless a guy sits in a room and that weird little thing happens.

As a producer, I take everybody individually, but I think my one sort of guiding principle is that I don't like to make an album without at least one single on it. By "single," I mean not necessarily something for the radio. I just mean that I always have to have a place to start from and it is usually based around a song where I feel I really can get the essence of everything about the band or artist into that one song.

I've noticed that whenever I can leave an album, and I have a track like that on the record, the record tends to do well and take the band to another level. That was true with the Bangles, Sublime and Sugar Ray.

When I listen to someone like Cream or R.E.M or anyone that has ever had a career, and you listen to their first record, you always hear a song that has that thing on it. On R.E.M's first album, it was "Radio Free Europe." It wasn't a hit, but it was definitely a single. It got airplay on certain formats and it kind of coalesced the energy around the band. They had that one song on that record that got on the radio and it had that great melody and release on it.

It is something that I have to hear from the artist. That has really been the thing that I have followed in my whole career. I'll do whatever it takes to get a song to be the point at the end of the spear.

When I was working with Sugar Ray, I heard "Fly" in the rehearsal room. It was just barely started, but I heard Mark singing in a lower register and I thought, "I know I could make a great record out of this song."

It is important to build up a song and create a tone so that you can hold somebody's interest for three or four minutes without one single tiny glitch. Somebody has got to know, from that first measure, where they are and you've got to keep them there until you are ready to let go. I still do that today.

The thing about A&R versus production, there are some people that have this A&R philosophy of just signing stars. I think that is great, but there has to be some sound on the record has to be a start, too.

TONY BROWN

If you are producing a session and there is one person in the room that is holding things up, you've got to move them out of there. How you do it is as important as deciding to do it. It can be done. You can either completely close down a session or you can deal with it in a smooth kind of way where nobody knows it happened, but it happened.

I've seen one person completely start shutting down a tracking session. I just know it, and everybody in the room knows it. That's when it becomes the producer's responsibility to take care of that problem. It is not the artist's responsibility. That's a hard job to take care of and an artist shouldn't have to deal with that. He needs to be creative. He shouldn't have to worry about that. I think that is when a lot of musicians look at a producer and they see you do that, and they respect you for doing it.

You have to do it just right. You can't make a scene. If it is a scene, then you have blown everything. It may take you 30 minutes to get the nerve to do it, but you can figure it out. There are all kinds of ways. You can pull them out of the room, or have them sit in the control room. You have to give them a reason. Nine times out of ten, depending on their ego control, they will usually say, "Have I got time to run an errand?" [laughs]. That means, "I'm embarrassed. I'm out of here." They might say, "I'll be at this place. Call me if you need me."

At the time that it happens, artists will look at me with fear in their eyes. I just would say,

"Listen, this is business. No problem." Then two hours later, I realized that they had already forgotten about the incident. Maybe they would ask me about it later on, but at the time, I think they thought it couldn't be done.

I find that great musicians even know when they are not cutting it. That's one thing I learned years ago with Rodney Crowell. Rodney would have no quarrels saying to me, "Hey, Tony. Your part is sort of messing up the groove. Let's overdub you." I was fine with that, because I just wanted to be a part of this record making process, even if I didn't play a note. That's the way I felt. Rodney picked up on that. I figured that whenever it was right, it was right. You need to learn how to deal with the record making process and learn that you've just got to be in control of your ego.

For Rosanne Cash's "Seven Year Ache," I played that for seven hours, but then Emory Gordy ended up playing the piano part on the record. He ended up playing all the staccato eighth notes. The only place that I exist on "Seven Year Ache" is somewhere in echo return, if I bled into somebody's earphones [laughs]. Otherwise I'm not on that record.

Emory was sweating it, saying, "Ah Tony. You can do it." Meanwhile, Rodney would say, "Emory, I like the way you do it. You play those eighths better than anybody." He did and Rodney was right. When Emory played them, it was just different.

I learned from all that to just suck it up and learn. It is crucial to learn that when you have the access of anybody's talent in a room that maybe even the engineer could play that part. Whatever! Who cares! You've just got to learn how to make records. If you are there, then you are part of it.

JIM DICKINSON

Somebody once asked me down at South by Southwest whether I felt my obligation as a producer was to the company or the artist. I replied that I felt my primary obligation was to the project itself. That said, I tend to be more sympathetic to the artist than the company, but that's just a personality flaw. It keeps me from getting work [laughs]. I do think that the vision belongs to the artist even though he or she may not be aware of it. Huey Meux once said, "You gotta keep the artist in the dark, that way his star shines more

brighter." You know? [laughs]. It may not always be, you know, to the advantage of the outcome of the project for the artist to know what's going on.

I do think that the record kind of pre-exists in the collective unconscious. I try to hear what's in the artist's head and figure out how to get that space between the notes on the tape. If you think about what you do visually, there's a big difference between high contrast production and what you could call earthtone production. I think that contrast is at the basis of all art. It is the contrast between motion and stillness, sound and silence and light and darkness where the sparks of artistic realization are born. I want to show the artist how to use the studio rather than be abused by it, and that's what I try to do with any artist that's interested in that. If they're not interested in that, I try to eliminate the problems that are between them and a successful recording.

Back before I produced the Replacements' *Pleased to Meet Me*, I literally never talked to A&R people. I was always hired by managers or groups to protect the artists from the company. Then after the Replacements' record, I started getting hired by A&R people who had "problem" bands. So I sort of inherited the so-called problem groups [laughs]. Yeah, I think I've had my share of them.

I think that, in the case of many young bands who can remain nameless, the more they compromise, the more they eliminate the very thing that they might have had that could have gotten them across more meaningfully to an audience.

I have a reputation with companies, they'll say: "Oh yeah, well Dickinson, he goes for the quirks." That's right, I do go for the quirks. And they say that as if that's bad. I think the quirks need to be magnified, because music—good music—shoots sparks. And I try to catch those sparks. I try to turn 'em up to where they're in your face, maybe a little more obvious than normal, because I think a record has to be bigger than life. I'm not a documentary producer. I try to capture the moment and enlarge it to where it's more obvious.

I look for the overtones, the squeaks and squawks on the strings and the human element that many engineers and some producers try to eliminate. I know engineers and producers who go back with the computer and systematically remove the breath from the vocal performance. Well, when you take away the breath it seems to me obvious that you are destroying the life. Obviously, that's what's alive is the breathing. When I record horn players, I'm very aware that there's always that breath before they play and I always try to get it because I think it sounds alive. No musician that I've ever heard breathes out of meter, you know.

I do try to consider why it is specifically that people come to me. I mean, I think that it's hard to get in touch with me, so they have to really want to seek me out and that's part of it because I think some of 'em should be eliminated, you know. As I told one A&R person in a situation that didn't turn out well for anybody, "Be sure you want it. Don't ask me for it if you don't want it, 'cause I'm gonna give it to you, I'm gonna put it on ya and it's not for everybody."

Some labels who approach me aren't interested in integrity as much as they are interested in manipulation. There are producers who do that, you know, but it's just not my long suit to go in heavy-handedly and fire members of the band and reconstruct things musically. That's just not what I'm good at, and I do try to make sure that whomever it is that I'm working with understands that.

I used to hear that if you are coming into a new job as an executive, the first thing you should do is fire somebody and then promote somebody to prove you can. There are producers who do this as a rule of thumb. They fire the drummer, because it is easier to bring in another drummer. They also set out to make someone feel important. I know that I tend to "produce" certain members of a group more than others. There are always members that require more production.

When you lose a band member, that is a casualty. I've had band members quit and that can be devastating too. It's like the run of a play. A chance camaraderie develops that is part of the production process. There is enough of a trance bond that happens in the studio from playing the songs over and over and listening to them back, that it really becomes a little sub-family unit. Tensions and casualties are very serious to me in a recording project.

I grew up watching and learning from these old blues men—Fred McDowell, Bukka White, Furry and John Woods, Nathan Beauregard and Reverend Robert Wilkins—who provided a different understanding of the realities of the music business. I learned some very important life lessons about survival and how not to take things personally.

In this business rejection and humiliation are literally a daily occurrence. You can't ask an artist not to be sensitive. It just doesn't make sense. At the same time, if you do take it too personally, it will kill you and your art.

I had this coach in high school who told me and a friend of mine (when we were considering joining the Marines as an alternative to being drafted), "If you do this thing, you've got to remember that they're not doing it to you … they're just doing it." I didn't apply that to the Marines, but I have applied it to the record business and it has true meaning for me. They are just doing it. They're not doing it to you. It's happening, you know. It's falling on you, and it's falling on your art, but you can't take it personally.

GAIL DAVIES

When Gail Davies came to Nashville in the seventies, the production world there was pretty much a boy's club. In fact, it still is to a degree. Davies has enjoyed a lengthy successful career as a singer and songwriter. Unlike many artists, Davies produced her own albums and enlisted the cream of the A-list session players from Los Angeles and Nashville. To this day, she is one of finest singers in Nashville. All this is to say that Davies brings a wide diversity of experience to the picture.

Having been in the music industry all my life, I sometimes take it for granted that people understand what it means to produce an album, but I'm finding more often these days that they don't have a clue.

A producer's primary function should be one of oversight. To hire the right people, maintain a focus on the project from conception to pressing and end up with the final results you and the artist are after. In the simplest terms, producing an album is similar to building a house. The producer is the contractor who's been hired by the homeowner to oversee every step of the building process. She/he is responsible for hiring specialists to come in and add their talents to the project in the same way a contractor would use carpenters, plumbers, roofers, etc. The producer has to make sure the finished product sounds great, is on budget and ready for delivery on time.

Finding the right studio, engineer and rhythm section is like pouring the foundation for the building. The musicians who lay down the basic rhythm tracks are that foundation and it has to be solid for everyone who comes in to overdub parts later on. This is one of the most important aspects of production. You can move walls and other things around but once you've set that foundation, you're pretty much locked in. The producer has to know how to get these tracks down and at what point they've got them.

An engineer with the right personality has always been my first concern. I've found this is very important if you're a female producer because you're often being tested as to your expertise. It was much harder when I started back in 1978, but I don't have as much trouble these days as I'm older and don't put up with much nonsense. The bottom line is that you need to be able to trust your engineer and he/she needs to trust you as well. It's good to know as much as you can about the studio and the recording equipment but, unless you're planning to be an engineer yourself, it isn't necessary to try and know more than your engineer any more than you need to know how to play everybody's instrument.

In trying to help aspiring female producers, I've found this is a point at which they often get into trouble. You don't have to be an expert on every aspect of the project, what you have to know is who to hire and how to get them to perform at their best. On the other hand, if you've got an engineer who "acts" like he/she knows more than the producer or is constantly challenging you in front of your team, then you have the wrong engineer.

Putting together a great rhythm section is not as simple as some people think. You can't just stick your favorite musicians in a room together and assume they'll cook because they're all good. You have to know the musicians' personalities and styles and who works well with whom, especially under stress. Sometimes the drummer, who may be great, doesn't feel the beat in the same way as the bass player, who also may be great, but they might not jell together so you have to know that

before you put them on the same team. If it isn't working and you've put incompatible musicians together, then the responsibility falls on you, not the musicians.

One of the biggest problems I've seen with women in the studio is their fear of making a mistake or being wrong on a call, subsequently exercising more control in the studio than is needed. Men aren't exempt from making mistakes so I suggest dealing with each moment as it comes and not being too dogmatic or overbearing. There's a fine line between being a dictator and presenting yourself in a way that makes people feel comfortable about your competence. If things are going smoothly, let it go. It isn't necessary to say something every minute or fix it if it isn't broken. If you've done all the ground work, booked the studio, found the right engineer, great songs, a good artist, musicians in place and well written charts then you should be able to enjoy the process.

DAVID BRIGGS

Look on any number of Neil Young's finest albums (including Everybody Knows This Is Nowhere, After the Goldrush, Tonight's the Night, Rust Never Sleeps, Zuma *and Young's self-titled debut) and you will see David Briggs listed as a producer. Not only that, Briggs produced Spirit's remarkable* Twelve Dreams of Dr. Sardonicus, *which featured "Nature's Way." Up until his death, Briggs brought a special passion to his work. The following are excerpts from many conversations with Briggs during a production in Memphis of a band called Royal Trux.*

Production is an art form, or it is the world's highest paying babysitting job. It is kind of like coaching sports. You've got to know when to kiss ass and you've got to know when to kick ass. You can't do them both at the same time and you can't do the wrong one at the wrong time, or you will just ruin everything.

As a producer, the one thing I always remember is I am not making David Briggs records. I am making other people's records. Even though everybody leaves a little piece of themselves behind, I try and stay as invisible as possible on my record. No matter what genre of song it is, it is all the same music to me. You listen to the songs and there is a performance and I just try to lay out the context as clearly as possible so that no side roads present themselves to the artists as they go towards their art. If you can do that, then their art will stick through and it will stick on tape.

I actually don't like to work in studios very much. Most studios are so sterile. If you give me a chance, I'll take a remote truck and record in this hotel room and get a better sound than most people get in a studio. I would rather record in a house or a barn, a high school gym, or any place, other than a studio.

If I have got to work in a studio, I want to work in a giant room or soundstage. There are a few good studios, like Criteria in Miami or Bearsville in New York. Bearsville has a really great room. Criteria has got a huge playing room and they've got a great old Neve 80 Series console.

The reason I like to use the big rooms is because I prefer live recording. You can't do it in a little room, at least not with the bands I work with. They all play at such big levels, and to work the way I work, I need a huge room. I don't use any baffles and I use a full P.A. in the room. It is enormously loud when I work, so I have to have a big room to be able to keep the sound from coming back in on me. Basically, that is it. Most people use baffles to keep it in. I use baffles and hang things to keep it from coming back.

On the last record I did with Neil [Young], I used a soundstage. I rented lights and set them up. I set the band up like they were onstage and put a full P.A. in there and let it rip.

I mic the amps. I mic the drums. Of course, I mic all the vocals, because they are all live vocals as well. Then I also mic the room and I use that as well. It is in the Swims where the Spook lives. That is exactly what it is. It is like everything sounds like records, until you start to bring that room up and then it is just like who the hell knows what it is. It sounds like something different [laughs]. It doesn't sound like you are in a studio anymore. That is for sure.

I look for the spook in the swim. The swim is what happens when you've recorded the space in the room and all the instruments you put into any volume of space (whether it is Madison Square Garden or House of Blues in Memphis) get dumped into the mix. That is the swim.

The spook is the weirdness, the strange unpredictable shit that you'd never know, if you just tight miked everything. If you haven't done this, then you ain't living [laughs]. You might be living, but you are living safe. You are not skating out on the edge. When you start using rooms and things like that, and the big sound, strange things happen. They really do. If you know how to control it, and you know how to focus your tight miking and how to make your tight miking work with you, instead of against you, you can do some great stuff. Otherwise, it will sound like a mush. Obviously, great mic technique is a key.

One of my aims is to take the "studio" out of the sound. With the Neil Young stuff, a lot of his records (like *Rust Never Sleeps*, for instance) were all recorded live. The only difference between *Rust Never Sleeps* and *Live Rust*, is *Live Rust* has the crowd in the mix and *Rust Never Sleeps* has the crowd stripped. That is the only difference.

All of the electric stuff was cut at the Forum and Madison Square Garden and you name it. It was all over the place. I took the truck with me. I did *Rust Never Sleeps* and *Live Rust* at the same time. I used all the same performances and I just stripped the crowd. When you listen to the record again, you know what you are hearing is a performance in front of fifteen thousand people. When I digitally stripped the crowd out, it sounded like the studio stuff, except that it had the performance energy of playing in front of fifteen thousand people. That is a big difference.

The reason I personally like to record like this is that I am lucky, or unlucky enough—I don't know which one it is—to have been making records for a really long time. I can remember when Little Richard or Ray Charles made records. They made them by everyone going into the studio and they all played at once. They would all get their tones on the spot and they would all play at 75 percent of their abilities all together and it would make a 100 percent record. It would sound really fucking great. There was no introspection or nit-picking and pulling things apart, like wings on a fly.

When you work like that, the most critical part of it is that, instead of the vocal coming in later and shoehorning itself into what a bunch of other people have decided is the dynamic of the song, you have a band playing to the vocal's dynamic. That is where the magic is.

You would be amazed at how little bleed I get in my recordings. I use what everybody else uses. When people come in and iso up my tapes, everyone is always shocked. They go, "Jesus Christ, there is no leakage. Why is it so clean?" Well, you just have to know where to place the mics.

When I did [Neil Young's] *Ragged Glory*, we cut it in a barn. I had mics six and eight feet away from Neil's guitar, as well as up close. I had four or five microphones on the amplifiers, including ones that were five, six and seven feet away. I also had a full P.A. in the room, plus everything blasting and we put them (the mics) all in the right spots and got it. If you don't put them in the right spots, you get this big fucking wash of shit. It is the same with drums.

When you are live recording drums, for instance, if you focus the mics back at the snare drum, then you don't get phase cancellations, and the ones that you do, cancel out leakage and shit like that, as opposed to loading up all the leakage on the drums. I will tell you that even in the cases of where I have to re-do the vocals, for instance, I don't ever have to compromise the room for it, because of leakage, because it is not there. You never hear the leakage.

I like *Ragged Glory* a lot. I got seven of the songs on that album all in one pass, all in one night. We just went straight through song after song after song. We just doubled the background vocals and that's what we did. It was the night of an earthquake and nobody felt it. We just played right through it. The ground was shaking and we thought it was us [laughs]. Any time you can get even finished masters in one night, you know you are doing something right.

Producing the Royal Trux was five days, from the day I walked into the studio door, until the day I walked out with the rough mixes. It took a day and a half to cut all the songs. I spent a day overdubbing and three days mixing. It was all there right from the start. That is the kind of thing I like. You walk in the door. Nobody is working. It is not hard. There is no effort. You walk out the door and seven songs are done, and you go, "How did I do that?" The first blush is, "They can't be any good. Anything that easy, can't be that good." It is a philosophy I see repeated in the bands and

record companies and everybody. "It can't be any good. It's too easy. Anything that you can do in two days can't be any good." Not! Two years is when it is not any good. I love things that just get up and go and have their own life to it.

When I did Neil Young's *Tonight's the Night*, we started that record off in L.A. in the studio and then, one day I fired the studio and tore it all down and went to some studio rentals and a rehearsal room and kicked a hole in the wall and put a truck outside and started recording. They would come in and play and bash around and have fun every night and I would just take notes. Every time when something happened that I thought was extraordinary, I would walk to the truck and mix it on the spot. Then I would walk back in. Five minutes would go by and they would be out having a cup of coffee and they wouldn't even know I was out doing mixes. When we finished the record all up, I remixed the entire record three times in every studio known to mankind and remixed it and remixed it and remixed it and finally I got so bored with it and said, "Fuck it, I don't want to work on this record anymore." I totally lost interest in it and Neil totally lost interest in it.

Two years later, he played it for the band and they played my original rough mixes and they went, "What record is this?" He had just played them *Homegrown*, a record he was going to put out. They said, "Oh, *Homegrown* is great, but what record was that you just played?? That is the shit!" So three years after I did it, it came alive again and was released.

I like *Tonight's the Night*. It has got the edge, balls, and attitude. There is no fear in those takes. "Tired Eyes" is one of Neil's most underrated performances, with that talking voice. It is so fucking spooky. The spook was in the swim on that night. There is no doubt about it.

It was like one of those things where it was so easy and everyone just played and had fun. Nobody ever said, "Let's work music." They all said, "Let's play music." A lot of people do work music, but I like to play music. Anything that comes like that is almost always, inevitably good.

I think when you are looking too much at what you are doing, all you see are the "blue" spots. You don't see the shine and the magic. When you do it layer by layer by layer, you never have a chance of seeing the magic of the whole picture, until you are somewhere on down the road. This way you see it immediately. Immediately! If the band delivers something that is great, they walk in the door and they listen to what is close to a finished record. It is a big difference.

I couldn't tell you the year I met Neil (Young), if it was on the calendar, but I know how I met him. I was driving my Army Personnel Carrier down the road and Neil was just walking down the road. I just thought I would give the hippie a break and pick him up. Give the hippie a lift, you know [laughs]. It was the beginning of a long relationship. "Nice truck!" [imitating Neil]. Neil and I have a lot in common. We both like cars a lot. Cars and guitars. We don't do it so much anymore, but we used to drive a lot. We used to love getting in the car and fucking just go. It didn't matter where. I still love to do that.

Every time when we finish a project, and we have got a four or five day jump, I always drive home. Anytime I can drive somewhere, I'm happy. I like to sit there and smoke a joint and blast the fucking tape as loud as you can with the windows down and the air rushing by. It's great. Anybody that doesn't do that, doesn't have a musical soul. People that really love music, love to get in their cars and drive.

When I am done at night, even at three in the morning, I get in my car, with my tape from the day and drive until I hear it all, even if I have got thirty minutes of work on it and I live eight minutes away from the hotel. I have been that way, since I have been a kid and I still feel that way. That is where I hear music.

For my rent-a-car, I found out about four years ago that the Cadillac Seville had a sound system that I fell in love with. The graphic equalizer and how the speakers are placed are great. In all honesty, it has been my ghetto blaster ever since. I rent that Cadillac Seville. I have spent thousands and thousands of dollars renting this ghetto blaster. If I had just gone out and found this ghetto blaster that had a good tone, I probably could've saved myself ten grand or something in the last four years. I like the sound of that car. I just get in that thing and go.

COOKIE MARENCO

Marenco is no stranger to audiophile-level production and engineering, having worked with some of the music world's most creative talents and consulted for a number of innovative manufacturers. She also worked in A&R at Windham Hill, where five albums she produced earned Grammy nominations. Her production credits include Winter's Solstice Vol. 2 *(which went gold),* Oregon, Ladysmith Black Mambazo, Paul McCandless *(of the band Oregon),* Turtle Island String Quartet, Tony Furtado and Alex De Grassi, *among others. As an engineer, she has recorded many artists, including Mary Chapin Carpenter, Ladysmith Black Mambazo, Praxis, Charlie Haden's* Quartet West *and Max Roach.*

I am often asked by those wanting a career in the recording industry what classes they should take to become a producer and engineer. Take a look at where you'll find some of the finest musicians and engineers when they've passed the age of 35. Look at their financial status and their home life. Ask yourself if that's what you want. Take classes for a back-up plan or that might enhance your career in any field—basic business, accounting, sales, marketing, Web design, graphics, and computer skills for Word documents, spreadsheets, and databases. Most successful studio owners are involved in real estate. With unpredictable cash flow, it's common to dip into the equity of the real estate during harder times. It's hard to think about making enough money to ever buy a home, but somehow people find thousands to build studios on rental properties and purchase digital recorders that devalue to nothing in two years. Protect yourself and your career with property.

For day-to-day operations, communication and a great attitude are key to working with clients and staff. Learn how to communicate clearly and quickly. Maintain relationships and enjoy the people you're with. Make friends with your competitors; they might be your employer someday. Network constantly and offer your services to help. Be active in the community.

The studio is really a great venue for an actor's workshop. There is a cast system that needs to be learned and heeded. Know who you are directly responsible to answer to and attend to their needs first. Sports, traveling, and reading in general can be handy to fall back on when a session grinds to a halt and you need to keep spirits lifted.

Some of the most talented people I know chose to leave the business early to have a more normal lifestyle with a family. The industry is portrayed as glamorous and financially rewarding, but in reality it is a much different picture. Many people find the job of studio engineer to be too difficult a lifestyle. It requires religious devotion to one's craft for little money, long hours, and limited social life, if any.

You will be judged on your reliability to accomplish your tasks. Do what you say you're going to do. It's better to say no if you're in doubt. Turn down failure and accept responsibility for errors. One bad decision can put you out of business. Your reputation is all you have.

If all this seems too hard to accomplish, then perhaps it's time to look for another career. You've got to love your job and the people around you. Compassion and respect will get you farther than a Pro Tools certification.

Practice the art of listening. Listen to what's being said. You might have to learn to translate. That's part of the job; get used to it. If you're an assistant, never talk, just listen. Listen to the artist, engineer and producer. Don't act unless asked, but make sure no one has to repeat what's already been said. Listen for the phone, and if it's your job to get it, then *get it!*

Listen to the instruments' sound in the room. This is the greatest compliment you can make to a musician. Appreciate what they do for a living and how they spend their money. Fifteen seconds won't kill you. Make sure you know how to get the sound in the room through mic placement without EQ. Walk around the room, stand close and stand far away to see how the tone changes. Move the mics to capture the best tone. Later, you can do whatever you like. It's not hard, and you won't be to blame for a crummy drum sound if the drummer brings in a crummy kit. By the way, how do you get a great drum sound? Get a great drummer.

Listen to the vocalist's intonation. The vocalist may not really be able to hear well and may not realize that it's because the headphones aren't right. Make simple adjustments of vocals using headphones, give the artist their guitar to hold, or do whatever you can to change the intonation other than suggesting 600 vocal lessons. Use your imagination to figure it out.

Listen to the timing. If the drummer and bass player's grooves are off, it's probably a headphone issue. Here's a trick and the reason why I like not giving headphone control to the players: If the timing is off, I'll add a little more kick to the bass player's headphones—gradually. If it gets better, I leave it—no need to discuss. If it gets worse, try adding a little more bass to the drummer's headphones. If it gets better, great; if it gets worse, fire both of them (just joking!). Even great players are often fooled by their ego and think they have a good enough headphone mix to work. They don't want to hold up a session and move on before getting it right. Bad mistake. People are usually paying a lot of money for the sessions, and if you can't hear and interact with the musicians, the money being spent will have mediocre results.

Listen for stray sounds on tape, subtle changes, low-pitched hums, and buzzes and noises that shouldn't be there. You can make a career out of this. Listen to the hard drives and tape machines as they engage. Learn what normal sounds like and know when it's going bad. Listen for air conditioners turning on and off in a room, power brown outs, and bad punches. You might decide not to fix these problems, but you should know when they are present.

Listen to the effects of repositioning or placing a mic at a different angle. Listen to what compression and over-compression does. Listen to what happens to a song when you use Beat Detective or Auto ruin—I mean Autotune. Be in control of these effects and be conscious of what you do.

Listen at low levels when mixing, and know how the room affects your mixing balances. Your room needs to be adjusted and tuned each time you mix. Don't assume that it's the same as you left it or that the studio has set the left and right balance correctly in the room. Check all stages for signal path; at least get the right and left correct. Listen for the hiss or noise floor of a room or of the speakers and make adjustments to push your mix over that. Make sure to listen for the noise floor of all effects and faders so that you don't introduce unneeded noise.

Listen for when people are getting cranky and need a break. Listen for the sound of "low blood sugar" when an artist is continually pushing to finish something but is getting nowhere. Listen for the time when people are tired even if they do not admit it. Listen for when you're wasting time.

Listen to the lyrics of a song. As a producer, ask the drummer if he knows the lyrics—although, not if he's paying for the session; I got fired once for that. The vocalist was thrilled, but the money guy didn't want to be tested. They made a bad record elsewhere and saved me the headache of asking that my name be removed from the record credits. Bottom line: stop talking, start listening.

JACK CLEMENT

Not too many people can claim to have worked with a range of artists that includes legendary Sun Records artists Jerry Lee Lewis and Carl Perkins, as well as singer/songwriter Townes Van Zandt, jazz icon Louis Armstrong, country music hall-of-famers Johnny Cash, Waylon Jennings and Charley Pride, polka king Frank Yankovic, and socially conscious Irish rockers U2, but producer, songwriter, artist and all-round character Jack Clement can.

As a songwriter, Clement's compositions have been covered by artists such as Garth Brooks, Ray Charles, Johnny Cash, Hasil Adkins, John Prine, Cliff Richard, Richard Thompson, Roy Orbison, Gerry & The Pacemakers, Foghat, Chicken Shack, The Move, and too many more to list here.

Clement was there at the beginning of rock and roll in the 1950s, working at the Sun Recording Company in Memphis, TN, which was owned by the iconoclastic visionary Sam Phillips, one of rock's greatest production talents.

Clement's insights and humor concerning capturing the magic are as relevant now as they were 50 years ago.

Sam Phillips was always saying that he was looking for something different. He wasn't necessarily going for correctness or any of that stuff. He wasn't trying to compete with Nashville. He knew that, by being in Memphis, he was in a place that was sort of isolated in a way from Nashville and all of the slick stuff. He knew that he had to come up with his own thing, and that was always the theme.

Sam liked to work with musicians before they got too good, like while they were learning, because [that's when] they're experimenting and

he'd get that benefit of the experimentation. You don't get that sort of freedom from super-polished musicians. He favored working with people who weren't too seasoned. That's what recording is about: When you do it right and let it all hang out, you get lucky. You stay in the studio until you get what you want.

Many records sound like there is too much thinking, too much tuning, and too much trying to make things absolutely slick and perfect. There is a big difference between being smooth and being slick. Smooth is cool; slick is like shit. Have you listened to the radio recently? There is nothing smooth about it.

There are a lot of people in the record industry now who don't seem to understand anything about capturing the moment and that "semi-translux" state you have to go into when you record. When it comes time to record, you've got to throw it away.

Louis Armstrong demonstrated that to me when I was producing an album with him in 1970. The first time he went to the microphone, he sat at the piano next to Larry Butler, and they ran over the songs a little bit. He kind of learned them halfway and went to the microphone and started singing. The first time I heard him, it sounded awful. I thought, "Oh Lord, what have I gotten myself into?" The next time he ran it through, he nailed it. I realized that he had done something that I had always done, which is to play around and do it all wrong and get it out of your system, and then you can do it right.

Jerry Lee Lewis always amazed me at how he would go into any room and throw it away. If there was a piano and an audience of one or more people, he would give you a whole show and not hold anything back.

The first one I did with Jerry Lee was a song called "Crazy Arms," which had been a big hit for both Ray Price and the Andrews Sisters. What we did was kind of an audition tape, really. Sam [Phillips] was in Nashville at a disc jockeys' convention that day, which was a Thursday. I was in there with Jerry Lee, Roland Janes and Billy Lee Riley, and we cut two or three things and I asked Jerry Lee if he knew "Crazy Arms." He said he knew a little of it, so we cut it. Billy Lee [Riley] was in the bathroom and he thought we were just messin' around, and he was supposed to have been playing the bass. The only thing the record had on it were piano and drums. At the very end, Riley strolled in, thinking that we were goofing off and picked up an electric guitar and hit a little off-chord at the very end and that stayed on the track. When Sam came back the next Monday, I played it for him and he flipped and did the lacquer right there in the studio control room. Dewey Phillips added it on the air that night on his radio show, and by that Thursday, we had records. Those were the fun days. You could cut a record on Thursday and have it in stores the very next week.

"Whole Lotta Shakin'" was a one-take deal. We had cut a whole bunch of other stuff that day, and we were working on a song I wrote called "It'll Be Me." I got tired of it and walked out of the studio and said, "Let's get off this for a while and get back to it later." Jerry Lee's bass player, J.W. Brown, said, "Why don't we do something else? Hey Jerry! Why don't we do that song we've been doing on the road that everybody likes so much?" He said, "Okay." So I said, "Let me go turn the machine on." I hit Play and Record, turned around and sat at the desk, and they did ["Whole Lotta Shakin'"] in one take without a dry run—nothing. Blam! There it was! We didn't overdub or do anything to it. In fact, we didn't even play it back for a while [laughs]. We started getting back into "It'll Be Me" or something. Later on that evening, we started playing it back and we just played it all night. It's fun to be able to cut a record and just hear it after one take.

I don't see how you can have a good production without a certain amount of freedom. You should try to go in there and get it right and throw it away. Remember, we are in the fun business, and if we're not having fun, then we are not doing our jobs. Here are my three universal truths. Number One: All people from Memphis speak in parables. Number Two: Women don't like steel guitars. Number Three: If you throw enough shit against the wall, somebody will see a picture in it [laughs]. Somebody will see a picture in anything.

DOLLY PARTON

There are only a handful of artists who are seemingly larger than life to the point that all one needs to say is a first or last name, like Dylan, Lennon, Jagger or Elton, and people know who is being addressed. In that spirit, when someone is talking music and says "Dolly," it can only mean Dolly Parton, one of the most critically and commercially successful country music artists of all time.

Her flamboyantly exaggerated country girl-meets-Hollywood look is one of the most identifiable in American culture. A less talented or less savvy artist would ultimately have his or her artistic achievements overwhelmed by such an audacious visual statement, but Parton is so incredibly gifted as a singer and songwriter that everything she brings to the picture only supports her understandable inner grounding and confidence.

If you don't take some chances, what are you going to do that's of any quality? I've made a lot of mistakes in the minds of some people, but I've made few, if any, in my own mind. If I make five mistakes and do one great thing, well, I'm not going to worry about the five mistakes I made. I'm going to just wallow in the glory of the one great thing I did in hopes that it brought some joy to somebody else. What some would call a mistake is just me trying. If it works, fine. If it don't, what are they going to do? Kill me? Then, if they kill me, are they going to eat me?! [Laughs.] You can't really go about your life like that and be productive. That's why I think I've been at it for so long.

I've been doing this since I was a little kid. I was nervous, but my desire to do things was always greater than my fear of it. I just always kind of drug from that God thing. Everybody thinks of God as a different thing. To me, God is that greater, higher energy—that greater, wiser wisdom. It's that thing in all of us that we all have to draw from. I've always trusted God and trusted myself, which to me are intertwined. I'm a creative person, and what gifts I have come from that divine place that I try to tap into. So who have I got to be afraid of?

I am so much inside to just have a plain surface. I feel so many things and my heart is so real and my soul is so real. And that's important and intact but there's so much stuff inside that to be a plain old person on the outside just don't get it for me. Like Minnie Pearl used to say, "Any old barn looks better with a little red paint on it." That's sort of like how I feel. People always say "Less is more" but I say, "Oh, that's bullshit! More is more! And I can't get enough of more!"

People say, "Do you wear that makeup all the time? Do you wear those shoes around all the time?" I say, "Yeah, I do most of this even when I'm by myself. I can't stand to walk around slouchy all day. When I'm alone writing songs, sometimes I'll go for a couple of days and I won't put on makeup and stuff, but I don't look at myself. Sometimes I look in the mirror and I'll say, "Oh good Lord, go clean up!" Everybody's comfort level is their own and that all depends. But to me I'm more comfortable when I got on makeup and look the way I want to look.

Everybody's different and I understand what they're saying, but I just love stuff. I love playing in paints and crayons and I love the way things feel on my body.

A lot of my look came out of a little country girl's idea of what glamour should be. But then it got to be really comfortable and I liked it just like how people like to dress up. Like I've always said that if I hadn't have been a woman then I'd have damn sure been a drag queen. That might be a funny line and people get a kick out of it, but I mean that in all sincerity. I just love it.

I always wanted to be pretty and look good … but just poor ragged-ass looking kids … you just look the way you look. You do with what you do and you always think, "Well, when I get money I'll have this and I'll have that," but it didn't buy me any class. I like looking like trash, but I know in my heart that I'm not.

Thank God that early on I understood who I was. I understood that, being from a family of 12, I was in a spot where nobody was going to pay that much attention to me, so I had to get to know myself through God and through the birds and the bees and the stuff outside and my imagination. Thank God I had talent. But most of my family had talent. I took it and channeled it and the better I got and the more I wanted to do good and the more I realized that this is important stuff.

Ain't that awful how people have crippled so many wonderful people that would have been so many good things, but they had to spend all their time worrying about how to get by because of somebody else's perception of them. I just think that's terrible.

Those people who aren't willing to open their heart or minds to anything other than what they understand are missing out on everything really. They're the ones that are truly unhappy, because I think they live in a real shaded world. I think you should be free. God gave us that freedom and those really free, true, good-hearted spirits should be left alone because they would do greater things for the greater purpose.

And no matter how phony I look to some people or how much shit I've done that people criticize, I know that when I get into that God place … where my music is … when I start to sing a certain kind of song, whether it's a gospel or a mountain song, there are just certain things that I mean to tell you does everything inside of me. That's why it comes out like that. I just open my mouth and thank God I can deliver. When I get one of those songs that's got all that heart and guts and souls and tears—whether it's a happy song or not—there's a certain kind of a song and my soul just dances. It's in that real place, and as long as it comes from my gut and from my heart in a very real place, I think people will accept it.

I'm proud of all the business stuff that I've been at least smart enough to be wise to where I could make my money doing other things. But, to me, all that other stuff just affords my habit, which is music. First and foremost, above everything else, I'm a singer, a musician and a writer. I never got so busy I didn't write songs. I write all the time and I love it. I pay for my own sessions, then I lease them to whatever label, and then my masters go back to me. After a certain amount of time, I'll want my masters throughout the years to go to my family. That's the way I'm doing it. I'd be singing if I had to sell it out the trunk of my car. I will be doing my singing and my writing no matter what.

DENNY PURCELL

Denny Purcell is one of the top mastering engineers in the world. His state-of-the-art Nashville-based facility, Georgetown Mastering, has refined the sound of thousands of albums over the years, including hundreds of platinum, gold and Grammy-winning releases.

"Fish don't hold sacred liquid in cups. They swim the huge fluid freedom." —Rumi

I always have a difficult time writing the words "music" and "business" in the same paragraph, let alone the same sentence. "Music business" is an oxymoron just like government intelligence and marijuana memory.

Music business only occurs at the intersection of two very broad streets: Art and commerce. Music is art at its purist. It is not a business. I believe people communicated with art, including with music, before any spoken word. Look at cave drawings out West. Look at drawings and sculptures of the Mayans, Aztecs, Incas, and Toltecs. Look at the glyphs and drawings of the Egyptians. Look at the drawings by small children. Almost all of them picture some type of musical instrument.

Art is art, without being perceived by anyone or anything. Art is. As engineers, we each have the opportunity to perceive art in the form of recorded music and preserve it forever. This fact has always excited me and still radiates through me. What a time we are blessed to live in! We get to come to work and play with art, and in a sense, never really have to grow up as some do. We must never take this opportunity for granted. The recorded music that all of us take some part in is, after all, in some way or another, preserved forever. Forever may be hard to fathom, but I said forever.

For at least the last three years, there isn't a day that goes by where my clients and I, or someone I know doesn't expound on just what has happened to put us where we are right now in this "music business." I believe I've heard most of the popular theories on this subject. I am fortunate in my job as a mastering engineer for the past twenty-eight years, for I am allowed to spend one to three days one-on-one with some of the most interesting and insightful people in the recorded art world; artists, producers, and engineers. What a great gig this is!

What I'd like to do now, if you would indulge me, is to reach over and open the passenger door for you and ask you to take a ride with me and see some of the scenery I've seen and am seeing on "the road down," as my good friend Jim Rooney would say.

As we travel together on these roads today, we'll converse freely, but I won't actually hear you until you've read this and get back to me after your ride. You, of course, can do this via phone, fax, or email. If you must know, I currently own thirteen computers, but also know that I drive them; they don't drive me.

Simply as a preference to this ride we're taking, I believe we're all from the same seed and equal as human beings. Our vocations do not our status as humans reflect. For years I thought I was a human being on a spiritual quest. Later, I realized I was a spiritual being on a human quest.

So now that you're in the car as my passenger, let us take this ride and see what we shall see. Fasten your seat belt, for I drive as my friend Mike Ritter says, "like a computer on interrupt."

As we pull out of the parking lot, let me warn you, we'll take any side road that seems interesting. Before we make the turn out of the parking lot, it's important that you please know that I believe each of us has a "grid" (though not physical or literal), which every word from another must pass through for distilling one another's meaning from the same words. This grid is composed of inherited genes, things thought, the region one grows up in, what each of us tries to be mixed with whatever light that happens to be at our grasp. It is because of this grid that we each have a small circle of people that really do know what we mean when we say, "Do you know what I mean?"

I'm still very careful in this electronic age. Not afraid, just careful. I watch technology come and go. I have for 50 years. I work very closely with inventors and developers of new technologies daily. I work in this smaller-than-a-fly speck of a world called professional audio, specifically mastering, and have for over 28 years. I love songs, not technology. Daily in my work I turn literal knobs that, in the end, help other people (consumers) hear songs better. I love songs because they are the vehicle that allows thoughts and stories to be shared all around the physical globe.

An ancient Chinese philosopher once said, "You can tell the political state of a nation by its music." It is just this thought that led me to research where we are right now and just how we got here. Not a day goes by that some associate doesn't philosophize to me or I to him/her about this. It must be commonplace all over the music industry, especially right now.

My research led me to many books. Some on music, some on art in general, some on philosophy. It is these plus my latest reading and re-reading of Neil Postman's book, *Amusing Ourselves to Death*, given to me actually years ago by my wonderful artist/painter friend, Bill Logan, that have led me to the theories I now hold as truth. With all things in life, both timing and perception are critical.

Postman's book addresses so much that neither you nor I have the time to truly get into. Basically, with the preface of contrasting Orwell's dark vision, *1984*, with the slightly older *Brave New World* by Huxley, Postman shows what I have always known to be true, but never studied before. It is this:

Just how the medium itself in which we are presented discourse completely changes it. Neil Postman loosely defines the mediums as these:

1. Spoken Word

2. Written Word

3. Printed Word

4. Telegraph Word

5. Teletype Word

6. Radio Word

7. Television Word

I am also focusing here primarily on the effect on art, and more specifically, music, and how the medium of presentation itself changes the art. To quote Postman, "If we start from the assumption that in every tool we create, an idea is embedded that goes beyond the function of the thing itself." Or to quote Joni Mitchell, on the difference between the arts and the performing arts, "No one ever said to Vincent Van Gogh from the audience, 'Hey, Vincent, paint me another *Starry Night*.'"

Here, if you'll indulge me, is my version of "the list" he tackled above:

1. Spoken Word

2. Written Word

3. Printed Word

4. Telegraph Word

5. Teletype Word

6. 78 RPM Word

7. Radio Word

8. Wire Word

9. Tape Word

10. 45 RPM Word

11. Television Word

12. 33 1/3 LP Word

13. Audio Cassette Word

14. Video Cassette Word

15. Video Game Word

16. Computer Format Word

17. CD Word

18. Laserdisc Word

19. Virtual Word

20. DVD Word

21. MP3 Word

22. SACD word

23. DVD A Word

By now you're saying, "So what?!? Get to the point, Denny. I'm getting a little carsick!" Okay, here it is:

On Saturday night, February 17th, I found myself discussing Postman's book *Amusing Ourselves to Death* with my 24-year-old music aficionado, make that music lover, author of three novels, and retired editor of a national music magazine daughter, Sarah Beth Purcell. We discussed just how on target Postman's theories are. He writes that a person of 40 has seen over a million television commercials.

As Sarah Beth is digesting just what I'm presenting for her evaluation, I learn just how important again timing and perception are. Had I read Postman's book when Bill Logan gave it to me, Sarah and I probably wouldn't have had this discussion. Were I not 50 years old, I might not have seen the convergence of Postman's, Sarah Beth's, and my understanding of just where we are music-wise. After Sarah Beth had digested my version of Postman's point, some actually read aloud, she agreed with his points presented, but suggested that he was ignoring something important in his understanding. It is this: There are three kinds of people. Rather than have me go on about it, if you're still here, you will find the following... Sarah Beth's "Off the Top of My Head" explanation as a 24-year-old female consumer:

There are three kinds of people:

- **Visual**—that is, one stimulated, stirred, educated and affected mainly by what they see, what is presented as a visual image.

- **Auditory**—which concerns what is heard and understood through sounds, voices, words, music.

- **Emotional**—which is arguably most complex and advanced, one who takes what they see aurally, and what they hear, and then how they feel about both and how comfortable both make them, how they relate to it, and then forms a judgment, an opinion, a feeling, a reaction.

It is a fair assessment to say that most males are, by nature, visual. Emotionally, sexually, spiritually, physically, and artistically, males are inclined to react most effectively to what they see. This explains the high percentage of teenage boys playing video games, it explains the only Websites making money for the most part being porn sites with millions of pictures, it explains about 98 percent of commercials on television. It also explains the state of the music business right now. Britney Spears is the queen of all media right now because she is the image of what many of us either want to be, or want to bed. Music is mistrusted, minimized to a disposable form, belittled by media, on the verge of artistic bankruptcy because somehow, in the process of trying to sell the music, the vision of the music became more important than the sound. And you would think music was all about sound, wouldn't you? It's not little Britney's fault, of course. She didn't insist that her bosom take precedence over her voice. But our desires as listeners were translated and misconstrued into that message, and now we're feeding that beast, ultimately offering our own limbs up to keep him satisfied. Sex sells.

Sex sells because visual stimulation sells. The idea that a beautiful woman can make you feel like a more virile, effective, successful man, that a bright red Porsche can make a beautiful woman want you, that more hair on your head and less on your chest can make all of these things a possibility are visual thoughts sent to men by the car company, the pharmaceutical company, the mouthwash makers. And the message sent to women in commercials, magazines with scantily clad women, in movies where women wake up with lip gloss on, and by alternately, Madonna and her virtual reincarnation, Britney, is this simply: Be me. I will win your affection. I will win influence. Men will want you and women will want to be you. These are all visually motivated images sent to us by who else? Those in control, for the most part, visually motivated men in advertising companies and PR firms, record companies and even in the House of Representatives. And many of us have somehow bought into the idea that how something appears can be as good, or even far better than how it truly is. These visually stimulated consumers, unfortunately, are also the most fickle. They will turn on you faster than your own dog in a fight for a scrap of meat. One day, Britney rules, the next day, she is in the cutout bin along with Tiffany and C&C Music Factory. This is the consumer that music vendors, MTV and record companies have courted for so long, have raised on the idea that music can be as immediate and quickly digestible as a Gordita at Taco Bell, that this consumer has turned on its creator. Pardon the metaphor, but just as a Taco Bell Value Meal can tend to do, right now, music has given most consumers a serious case of the runs. And consumers are sitting in the auditory bathroom thinking, "I'll never eat (buy music) again."

Music was once founded on the idea that there were others out there. Auditory people. Men and women, boys and girls who closed their eyes and put on a record, sang the words that sang to their hearts. This was music in its purist form, before it became transportable, with a Walkman, a boom box, a car CD player. Before it became instantly accessible from any place on earth, and in the process, less and less devoted to the original sound of the recording. Distortion was a small price to pay for convenience. Many consumers still think this way. Once, the image was irrelevant. And for the most part, advances in music technology, better sounding music, more efficient forms of making music, and the mechanics of making and listening to music have been saved for those auditory people. Only people who know who Moog is really care what Moog did for music. Only people who buy three thousand dollar stereo systems for their cars really care about what appears in the latest music technology magazines. Only people in the business of making money by making better sounding music are supposed to care about things that make music better. That's why high tech music equipment is expensive. Only professionals whose job it is to perfect sound and people who can afford to care what something really sounds like are responding to the current advances in music technology.

The third type of person, the highest rung on the ladder, the emotional person, is the hardest to reach, but also the most devoted customer. If the sound of something can peel through the layers of this type's emotions, make them feel something simply by hearing or seeing something, you've got them for life. If you can prove to them that it's worth the journey once, they're in for the whole bumpy ride. The only way to do this, realistically, is to make the result so effective, so obviously more valuable that the emotional person has no alternative to responding and becoming a fan. An emotional type is driven, first and foremost, by the value of something. The effect it has on the way they conduct their life. If they hear something for the first time, especially in a recording they've heard a million times before, they realize the value in the new technology that makes it possible for them to hear it.

We have dumbed down so much of culture to make it visual, instant, disposable. But if we continue to strive to turn the wheels to the other fork in the road, the one that leads to the golden palace of new art, and making art worth more again, making music priceless again, more people will view music as not just a visually stimulated way of selling hair barrettes or an auditory way to sell hamburgers, but an emotional form of expressing life. If we show all these types why quality will always be more important than quantity, if an advance in technology can truly prove this idea, not only will music benefit, but the business of music will benefit.

Quality that's proven to have value and something we need is the only chance for survival of any new format to re-establish quality high-end audio on any consumer level. To be able to hear infinity in the form of high-resolution audio, including high-resolution surround sound, allows the artist and producer a palette to present his art as he wants the listener to perceive it: In front of the stage, behind the stage, in the middle of the stage, or even from the perspective of the artist himself. There are infinite possibilities of presentation now available for the artist and the producer. It is only by proving this proposition that quality and value and the need for it can exist along with the other "portable" formats. This will provide the listener with choices of MP3, etc. and high-resolution audio presented currently on DVD-A format.

We who have worked on DVD-A format for the past four years now need to make the consumer aware of what it is and why they need it. The value of quality will be decided by the consumer, whether or not it is needed. At the end of the day, this is the question that all of us involved in this new technology are asking the consumer.

We shall see what we shall see. You know what I mean? Hope your ride was pleasant.

CHAPTER 17

Production Sickness

Sometimes it is so easy to get in a rut and do what you know is going to produce predictable results. The elements of having too little time and the reliance on habitual recording methods, compounded with the ease of all manner of samplers, MIDI devices, digital workstations, and so on, have made it easy to work without ever really feeling like you need to make a journey into the land of fearless experimentation.

We've discussed compression, building mixes, and tuning rooms as well as miking bass and percussion. But this time out, we decided to let a few bold souls share their less-than-correct methodologies in achieving desired production results. Some of the folks we approached were amused. Some wouldn't dare share production sickness secrets, preferring to stay in the closet.

Some of you might ask why this silliness is included here at all. But where would we be without the creative recording leaps by the Beatles, Beach Boys, Pink Floyd and many others? They figured the music wasn't creatively "fixed" unless they took a chance breaking convention.

Regardless, we know there are enough of the afflicted out there who just love off-the-wall ideas, so this chapter is for you.

Some of you may already be well immersed in the advanced stages of this kind of thinking and may find some of these anecdotes to be old hat. Just remember the Mother of Invention is always looking for new victims.

What you'll find here are not only some great ideas, but also some outrageous stories that hope-fully will inspire you to never forget what it is like to be truly playful while you're recording. After all, humor and playfulness are at the root of creative magic.

We would like to thank John Agnello, Roy Thomas Baker, Jim Dickinson, Eddie Delena, Mark Freegard, Paul Grupp, John Hampton, Joe Hardy, Bob Kruzen and Jeff Powell for their gift of time and knowledge, as well as Greg Archilla, Brad Jones, and Eli Shaw for their fine input.

ROY THOMAS BAKER

Roy Thomas Baker is one of rock and roll's most audacious producers. Since the seventies, Roy Thomas Baker has done what are now regarded as classic projects with artists like Queen (including "Bohemian Rhapsody"), the Cars (their first four albums), Journey, Dusty Springfield, Nazareth, Foreigner, Alice Cooper, Reggie Knighton, Ian Hunter, Be Bop Deluxe and Ron Wood.

My experimental years begin with Queen. There is a song on *Sheer Heart Attack* called "Now I'm Here." We wanted a long delay, and an Echoplex wasn't long enough, and there weren't any digital delays in those days. So we got two Studer A80's and we ran a tape loop to the second Studer 2-track machine, which was about ten feet away from the first Studer 2-track machine. The distance was just far enough away for the delay to be in time with the music. To watch the tape go from one machine across a light fixture and down to a chair and over a table and then to the other machine was really funny. Because the Studers had double guides, and they wouldn't work unless they were both physically in action (otherwise the machines would just stop), we had to gaffer tape the rotary guides down.

So we had Freddie's voice going into one of the tracks on the Studer multi-track and we went out of that into the left hand channel of the first 2-track Studer machine and playing back off the left hand channel of the second Studer 2-track machine and that would go back to another channel of the multi-track as a delay. We would feed the left hand output of the second machine into the right hand input of the first Studer machine at the same time we were recording that on a separate track on the multi-track. Then we were playing back off the second Studer machine, on the right hand side, and that would go into the third track on a multi-track.

So whatever Freddie sang, there would be a delay coming from his vocal. He would sing something, like "Now I'm there," and then it would come out "Now I'm there," again, and it was all in time with the music. It was a really long delay and Freddie was actually singing harmonies with himself. When he heard the repeat coming out of his headphones, he automatically sang the third above, and when he heard the third above coming back, he was then singing the fifth above, so it was a three-part harmony.

I'm located on the Mojave Mountain Range, overlooking the Colorado River. Since we are on mountains that are half-volcanic and half-granite, there are loads and loads of volcanic rocks around. They are the rocks with the holes in them.

We've got these solar tubes called Burke Tubes. I've got one that is like six feet long and I stick it in front of the bass drum and seal the bass drum and the Burke Tube, which is the same width of the bass drum and we fill it with all of these volcanic rocks. Then we put in a couple of Shure flat mics inside. I think they are called the FM91's. That sounds really good. It livens up the sound, but deadens some frequencies more than others. We end up with this huge low end thud that comes from the bass drum. It is such a big, big sound, yet it is relatively short, because the weight of the rocks alone causes a lot of dampening. The sound doesn't go long like a normal bass drum. It

actually makes a [high impact dead sound] really loud.

Years ago, I did an album with Chris De Burgh over in Europe and he was always on tour and he has his own fleet of airplanes. So while I was mixing in Metropolis Studio in London, we hooked up the stereo mix going from ground to airplane control via satellite, on two separate radios in his private airplane. What he did was he had one set of headphones on one radio and one set of headphones on the other radio, and he put one headphone from each set on each ear, so he could hear the mix in stereo, as we were doing it, whilst he was flying from Ireland to Germany [laughs].

When the Cars first bought their studio in Boston and changed the name to Syncro Sound, we were doing the mixes of the fourth Cars record, and we weren't sure if the mixes were going to sound good over the radio, so we set up a link to the main rock radio station and we played the mix over the air at two o'clock in the morning, while we were still mixing. We had it on automation, so the faders were going up and down. The radio station was playing the mix live on the air, and we would drive around in the cars and wave at each other, listening to the mixes as they were going down on the radio [laughs]. That way we could hear exactly what it would sound like as it came over the radio, through their compression and through all of their EQs and stuff. We did that on the first mixes, just to see what it would sound like over those radio things.

EDDIE DELENA

Since 1979, Eddie Delena has earned a reputation as one of the industry's finest engineers. Delena (who has extensively worked out of the legendary L.A. studio the Record Plant), has worked with many of the world's top artists, including Stevie Wonder, Tom Petty, John Mellencamp, Mick Jagger, Black Sabbath, Kiss, and Devo. For his work with Michael Jackson, Delena and a couple of other engineers pushed the limits in the realm of radical mixing. He also discusses capturing Jackson's organic percussion methodology.

We've made entire drum and percussion kits out of Michael sort of beat boxing and stuff. Michael would sing on a wooden platform, because during his singing and sometimes without singing, he would stomp on the platform, which would basically be the kick drum and he would do all of the percussion with his hands and mouth. He'd clap and fingersnap and slap his thighs and make all of this beat boxing from his mouth. It was a cool sound effect. All of these sounds would be incorporated. At one point, we sampled every one of them and made a whole percussion kit out of that and he even wrote a song with that as the foundation of the song. One song was called "Stranger in Moscow," which was on *History*. He does that on a lot of his records anyway. Sometimes you are not sure if it was a percussion instrument or him. He is really tremendous to work with and that is a lot of fun to do.

During the mixing of *History*, we did something that was the height of overkill [laughs]. I don't know if it has been done before, but for mixing the song "History," we hooked up two control rooms with four 3348 digital multi-tracks DASH-locked and both SSL computers running sync at the same time from different rooms at Larrabee North Studios. That was 96 tracks in each room. This was for one song [laughs].

Basically, in Room A, we had an 80-channel SSL, so we were using both large and small faders. That essentially had the basic tracks, like all the music tracks and lead vocals, etc. and Room B had an orchestra spread out, a choir, background vocals, Boyz II Men and a bunch of other stuff [laughs].

The tracks in B Room, like the orchestra, were sent to the front bus and the vocals, like the choir, were sent to the rear bus, which came up on four faders in the A Room. Then the entire stereo mix bus, from the A Room was sent to an external monitor in the B Room, so you could actually adjust the levels in the B Room and listen to how everything sat in the entire mix. By changing which 3348 was master, you could run the mix in either room [laughs]. Between Steve Hodge, myself and a guy named Andrew Scheps, who kind of technically put it all together, we all worked on the ongoing song.

JOE HARDY

Joe Hardy is another producer/engineer renegade who relishes pushing the envelope whenever there is a chance. His credits include the Georgia Satellites,

Steve Earle, Colin James, Jeff Healey, Carl Perkins, Tom Cochrane ("Life Is a Highway"), Jimmy Barnes, Merchants of Venus, the Replacements, the Hooters and many others. Hardy is probably best known for his work with ZZ Top, with whom he worked for a number of years. Hardy's extensive knowledge of recording technique and sense of humor have made him a complementary partner in crime with ZZ in their steely synthesis of blues and roots music and high-tech. Aside from ZZ Top, his organic "Leslie" effect for acoustic guitar has inspired every person with whom we've shared this trick.

I just produced this female artist from Australia named Marie Wilson. For this one song, I wanted this acoustic guitar sound to sound sort of like a Leslie, but the problem is that when you run an acoustic guitar through a Leslie cabinet, it sort of destroys the acoustic-ness of it, because once you amplify the guitar, then it is no longer an acoustic instrument. It is an amplified instrument at that point. It may be a cool sound, but it is a different thing.

So to get a Leslie effect on the acoustic guitar, I miked the acoustic guitar by putting two wireless SM-58 microphones on a ceiling fan. That is how I miked the guitar. So instead of making the speakers spin, as in a Leslie, I was making the microphones spin. It really does the same thing, but this way it really sounds like an acoustic guitar. There is a lot of Doppler and phase shifting going on, except it is all acoustic and not electronic.

There are many of these boxes out now that try to simulate the Leslie sound, but real Leslies sound great because there are so many weird things going on at the same time, like the Doppler and phase stuff and amplitude changes. The sounds are getting louder and softer and louder and softer. It is crazy.

The stuff I did with ZZ Top stuff is the nuttiest, on the verge of being almost unbelievable, because they had money and time and Billy Gibbons, who is just insane. For example, on the song "Rough Boy," Gibbons had five different guitars tuned to the chords of the song and he played them with an airbrush, so there was no impact. He was just nuts and he could afford to have five guitars that were exactly the same.

On the song "Sleeping Bag," I bolted an EMT driver on to one of those gray metal utility shelves that you see in like anybody's garage, and we put that in the echo chamber at Ardent and that is on every snare sound on that song.

On the last ZZ Top record, which is the best album they did in many years, there is a song called "Loaded." Billy wanted a guitar effect on the end that sounds like a shortwave radio. Since he was a kid, he would listen to these crazy broadcasts from Mexico and he has always loved the way shortwave radios sounded.

The reason shortwave radios sound so oddball is because part of the signal gets there direct, but also part of the signal bounces off of the ionosphere, so it takes longer, because it has to go further. It phases with the original signal that was direct. Because the ionosphere changes so much, the frequency that it phases at changes really rapidly and in a really weird random fractal fashion.

We made a cassette of only the guitar part and sent it to a friend of his in Mexico who broadcast it over his shortwave radio to Houston, where Billy had this crazy shortwave radio that was made in South Africa and doesn't use batteries or plug in. It has some weird internal generator and you wind up the radio with the big wheel on the side and it works for like 30 minutes. Then you wind up the wheel again.

So we recorded it off of Billy's wind-up radio in Houston and then flew it back into the track. So it is just a nutty guitar sound. Since Billy wanted it to sound like a shortwave radio, the easiest way to do it was to broadcast it over a shortwave radio. You see instead of running it through a harmonizer that just happens to say "Shortwave Radio Effect" or something, we just did the real thing.

If you were across town, and tried it, it wouldn't work. You need to be far away, because if you are close, there is not enough phasing. Plus, Billy insisted that it come from Mexico [laughs].

MARK FREEGARD

If you listen to the Breeders' brilliant Last Splash *album, Madder Rose's* Panic On, *or the most recent Dillon Fence release,* Living Room Scene, *one name that pops up on each of them is Mark Freegard, a resourceful British producer/engineer who, in the realm of creatively treated sound, is to the nineties what Steve Lillywhite was to the early eighties world of production bizarreness.*

People are always a little surprised or concerned with the way I am using the equipment. There is a track on the Breeders' *Last Splash* called "Mad Lucas." There were times when Kim Deal would say, "How small can you make this sound?" She would keep saying, "That is still not small enough, Mark." Well, there is a guitar and a violin on that track that I managed to get pretty small.

At first, I would be winding out all of the bottom end, but finally, I ran it through a little Tandy speaker that I carry with me. It's a little mini-amplifier and speaker that is pretty hideous. It's not a personal computer speaker. It is worse than that. It is a tiny little plastic box that cost a couple of pounds in England and runs off a 9-volt battery. It works well for distortion or resizing a sound and sending it somewhere else. I put the guitar through that speaker, back through the board, and out through an Auratone, which I miked up in a toilet and recorded that and filtered that over again.

The ambient properties of the toilet at Coast Recorders were useful for other aspects of *Last Splash.*

We actually recorded quite a lot of the vocals in this toilet at Coast Recorders in San Francisco. Kim Deal really loved it in there. Anyway, it had a really good sound. I started recording more of the little speaker things in there, too.

I also use an Eventide 3500, which has a lot really cool distortion or Doppler effects that the 3000 doesn't have. Sometimes I find myself putting a signal through that and monitoring the return and not using very much source. I recently did that with a string section on an English band called Goya Dress. We had this one song where we put on strings, but we didn't think they were working very well. I just looked for a program on the 3500 that did something to the strings on the middle eight that took them to another place. The program made them become another instrument, certainly not strings.

I used the Roland Space Echo on the Goya Dress session. I changed the pitch of the tape loop, by pushing my finger up against the pinch roller. I controlled the pitch of the sustain spin like that.

For a more unique ambient touch on the vocals, I found Coast's grand piano a useful tool for vocals. On the Breeders album, on a track called "Do You Love Me Now," the vocal reverb on the intro is a piano. I had Kim sing into a grand piano. It is really quite useful, because there are all these resonances from the piano that make up the reverb. I just put a couple of mics on the soundboard. She was leaning over the front of the piano, singing into the soundboard. She got quite annoyed, because I had to set the gain really high, and if she moved, we couldn't use it. It ended up being quite a special moment.

PAUL GRUPP

Since 1972, one of Los Angeles' most in-demand engineer/producers has been Paul Grupp. Grupp has worked on many of the biggest sessions since then, including Roger McGuinn, Little River Band, Rick Nelson, REO Speedwagon, Sammy Hagar, Quarterflash, Charlie Daniels, Pure Prairie League, and Michael Murphy.

There are hundreds of things that I have done, but most of them are not worth mentioning. They are stupid things, like back in the old days, we used to dissect the old analog synthesizers and patch them into everywhere they weren't supposed to go. Everyone did it, so it wasn't that big of a deal.

Lowell George taught me the trick for getting his slide guitar sound, when I was working with him on a project. He told me to align this old 3M 79 tape machine at +20 dB. So I did, and it sounded really wonderful. There were tons of incredible tape saturation and compression, distortion and all of that stuff.

The next time I did a slide guitar, I did the same thing, and I burned up a head stack. As it turned out, when I did it the second time, I did it in stereo and used two adjacent tracks. I later found out that you had to put many tracks in between, because it heated the heads up so much.

I should have used track one and track twenty-four, or track one and track sixteen. What I did, was put the information on like tracks nine and ten. Since the two were right next to each other, there was nothing in between to dissipate heat.

I just basically melted down a $5,000 head stack, which the owner of the studio wasn't too

thrilled about. It was at Westlake Audio. When he came to me, I said, "Well it should take it." I went on about Agfa tape: "If you align it at plus ten, it should work out fine." Then I went on about the design of the machine and this and that, and he looked up at me and said, "I designed that machine when I was working at 3M, before I started this company! It is not designed to take that!" That was Glenn Phoenix.

For mono or stereo, if you do it carefully, you can definitely see how Lowell got this unique sound. You do everything else normally, like mic the amp and so forth. You just overdrive the machine well before you start hearing something. Normally, about +6 is about where you start noticing pretty good distortion. At +12, it is history.

A lot of the desired noise and impact gets lost in the normal signal path. This method got it straight to tape. See, you would distort the console and nothing in the whole recording chain would ever deliver it. It would clip the signal and prevent that level from ever from ever getting to tape. You might get +10, but you would have this distortion from all of the electronics, rather than the tape. This way, it was a matter of sending a normal signal to the tape machine and then cutting it onto the tape +20 dB hotter.

I can tell you of one thing that I witnessed, but I didn't do myself. Lee Kieffer was a producer and engineer of the first Tubes records. He had this brilliant idea that he wanted to take a tinny 2 or 3" transistor radio speaker and connect wires to it and hook it up to a microphone input. He took a couple of pieces of string and put in a couple of holes in the speaker and hung it from the tuning lugs of the kick drum. This speaker was hanging dead center in the back of the kick drum, where the head had been removed.

They used it as a microphone for the kick drum, and it recorded only the sounds that caused that speaker to really move. Where the speaker was efficient and moved, the sound would propagate down the line, and the ones that it couldn't reproduce or couldn't handle, it just didn't. When you did a final mix and played it back on one of those small radios, that kick drum really stood out. It practically ripped the speaker out that you were playing back on. On a big system, you didn't really notice any big deal. His whole idea was that

141

on small radios, the kick drum was always lost. He wanted to figure out a way to get around that. It worked great.

JOHN AGNELLO

Redd Kross, Dinosaur Jr., Screaming Trees, and Chainsaw Kittens are a few of producer/engineer John Agnello's credits. Inventiveness is something Agnello thrives on. Where Paul Grupp related his story about using a small speaker as a bass drum mic, Agnello went in the opposite direction for the Dish sessions.

A microphone and a speaker are the same thing. They are transducers. One sucks and the other blows, as I like to say. When you wire the sub-woofer as a microphone, it sucks. What it does is reproduce these signals out of the bass drum, which are sub-low frequencies. You can barely hear it, but you can feel it a ton.

My only real speaker of choice is like a 15" sub-woofer, as opposed to just a 15" speaker, which I've tried. It seems like the sub-woofer, for some odd reason, catches the frequencies in different ways. At least that is true with some of the ones I have had. Of course, I might just be insane, and I am just convincing myself of this. However, at the times I've not had actual sub-woofers, and just speakers, it seemed to me to be different.

If you have a guy with a small bass drum, it really helps to make it sound thicker or deeper. If you've got a guy with a big bass drum, you can hopefully make it sound even bigger. It is a matter of taste, but in optimum situations, it really works great. I use it all the time. People think I am crazy, but I do it.

BOB KRUZEN

Jerry Lee Lewis, G. Love & Special Sauce, Mojo Nixon, The Radiators and God Street Wine are a few of Bob Kruzen's credits, many of which he has done with producer Jim Dickinson. Kruzen, a lover all things with big tubes and vintage gear, has worked in Memphis, Nashville, Muscle Shoals and New Orleans, among other places. As a live recording engineer, he also recorded Live Aid, Hall & Oates and The Neville Brothers.

While recording the Panama album, which was produced by Dony Winn, we were looking for ideas to make a couple of songs a little more extreme. I had this Shure mic that is really old and it has this strange hollow sound to it that we liked. I mentioned to them that for a lot of the old time sessions, people would sing into a bucket for an effect. Dony found an big old steaming pot for crawfish, and we put mics in the bucket and had the singer sing into it. It was a really nice vocal effect with a tone we couldn't have gotten any other way.

I've got a couple of compressors that are great for weird things. One of them is an old Altec 438-A compressor. I've got it to where I have complete control over the attack and decay and compression. I can almost make it work backwards to where it is expanding, instead of compressing. It has also got a nice distortion element to it.

The great compressor for doing really strange stuff is an Eventide Omnipressor, and a lot of people don't know about it. It has a knob on it that will do anything from extreme compression to like reverse expansion with a gate, so it will actually make the transients louder and then cut off the low parts. It'll put dynamics into something, instead of taking things out.

I have used it to de-compress over-compressed things. It is also a great device for drums, because you can stick a point on a drum that isn't there. You can make it inside out, so when you hit a drum, it'll go away and then suck up in reverse.

I've got a Telefunken V-72, which I basically use to be a fuzz box. I know a lot of people use them for mic pre's, because they are usually looking for The Beatles "sound." I think it is a good mic pre, but when I overload it and use it as a distortion box, it really adds a special quality. I like it especially on the bass guitar or drums. If I want something clean and quiet, I've got some Universal Audio things that I use for actual pre-amps. I just use the Telefunken V-72 as an effect.

Another thing we have done is take a Rockman and patch it into the effects send of a console, like an SSL, and use it as a fuzz box. It isn't really made to run through a console, but when you patch it in, it really sounds pretty cool. The input/out works best, as opposed to using the cue send, because it has a really hot signal and it overdrives everything. I've run vocals, guitars and drums through it. In fact, a snare drum through a Rockman is quite a sound.

JOHN HAMPTON

John Hampton's credits range from The Cramps to Robert Cray and The Replacements to the Gin Blossoms, his most recent multi-platinum production credit. He has also enjoyed quite a bit of success engineering and mixing hit country acts like Travis Tritt, Little Texas, George Ducas, Marty Stuart, and Aaron Tippin.

Some of you may know about tapping into the atom smashing capabilities of the SSL Listen Mic compressor. For those that don't, Hampton freely shares his step-by-step technique, among other things

If you are looking for a total out-of-control effect, a lot of times you can go to the SSL Listen Mic compressor to achieve that. It is a total 100 percent ass-bashing trash compacting compressor. It takes any dynamic range and reduces it to one level. If you hit a drum and then stop, the compression lets go and the room tone gets as loud as the drum hit does.

Let's say we are doing this on mixdown. Generally, you use a regular echo send from a channel and send that to the Listen Mic input of the console. You kind of play with the echo send level and the Listen Mic input level to achieve the desired effect. This is done while in Listen Mic Mode. Once you've done that, the only way you can get that to tape is to hit the Listen Mic To Tape button and put a track into Record. The reader should be warned that you cannot control the level to your monitors, because the monitor volume pot is out of the loop now, as is the Cut button. In other words, you can't turn it off. The only thing you can do is unplug the speakers, or turn the monitor amps off. The end result is fucked up and great. You record it onto another track and add it into the mix when you need it. A lot of The Replacements *Pleased To Meet Me* album was run through the Listen Mic compressor. I've used it a bunch.

Many things have been said about where the paths of excess lead, and I'm more than happy to relate one such experience.

Joe Hardy (ZZ Top, Tom Cochrane, Jeff Healey) and I used to do lots of stupid things. We once had an old Les Paul, and we were looking for an odd sound, for a band called Photons on Line Records in Germany. The song was

called "Idle Jets." For the hell of it, we ran the guitar through every piece of equipment in the room that we could get our hands on. The guitar ended up sounding exactly like an elephant charging. It was totally completely fucked up.

I know for a fact that we started off going through an Orban 2-channel parametric equalizer." "We went in one channel, maxed it out and took the output of that channel into the input of the other channel of the equalizer. We maxed that out, too, and took that through an EMT 140 plate and took the output of the plate to a Langevin Passive Graphic. We took the output of that to a Lexicon Prime Time digital delay and went from that to a Pultec MEQ-5 and took the output of that through another Pultec MEQ-5 and went into a rack-mounted MXR flanger and then into an MXR phaser. We took the output of that into a Dolby unit on encode and took that into Pandora's Time line. We recorded that onto tape at +17 over 185 nW.

On the same song, we took the mix and ran the left channel and right channels through separate Fender Twins, out of the board onto a separate piece of tape. The Fender sound was very distorted.

As the song was ending, we would cut to the Fender amp recordings every four bars of the mix, and then to the normal signal came straight out of the board, and went back and forth every four bars. The desired effect was hi-fi/lo-fi. The end result was indeed very sick. Too bad I did all that stuff when I was younger, because nobody will let me fuck up their records like that anymore.

JEFF POWELL

Jeff Powell, who works out of Ardent Recording in Memphis, thrives on afflicted production and engineering. His credits include Afghan Whigs, Primal Scream, Alex Chilton, Lynyrd Skynyrd, The Allman Brothers, and most recently The Lemons and 16 Horsepower.

One time, when I was working with a band on the Ardent label called Neighborhood Texture Jam, we basically needed a big disastrous noise on a track called "The Brucification Before Pilate." It was on an album called *Don't Bury Me in Haiti.* The song was in the key of E and we borrowed a cheap old Fender Strat copy from a friend who didn't care what we did with it and strung it up with nothing but big low E strings. The band was so broke that it took all of the band's money to afford all of the E strings.

We put the guitar on a stand and ran it through a Marshall head with all the knobs turned up as far as they would go and, at this one point in the song, where we wanted this big noise, we cranked up a weed eater and ran the it over the guitar strings above the pick-up. The weed eater played the guitar for a few seconds, and before we really dug into it blew it up. It took about eight seconds before the strings totally snapped and went everywhere. It was a really wonderful noise that was perfect for what we needed.

It took about thirty minutes to buy all those big E strings and string the guitar up, and it took about eight seconds to record it. It was definitely a one-take kind of thing. We added a little reverb to the sound and I added a bit of EQ. It all came across on tape really well.

JIM DICKINSON

Producer/musician/songwriter Jim Dickinson thrives on the murky mystery and history of the American mid-south, particularly its music. Orchestrating the voodoo the region offers is one of Dickinson's (an avowed fan of studio wrestling and vintage detective novels) special gifts.

From his production work with artists like The Klitz, Big Star, Ry Cooder, the Replacements, Toots Hibbert, Sleepy John Estes, Jason and the Scorchers, Mudhoney, Billy Lee Riley, Mojo Nixon and True Believers, to his soundtrack work on movies like Crossroads, Gimme Shelter, The Border, Streets of Fire, *and session work for the Rolling Stones, Arlo Guthrie, Flamin' Groovies, John Hiatt, Aretha Franklin, Primal Scream and many others, Jim Dickinson synthesizes earthy instinct and a love for the theater of the moment to capture the wild moments of creativity.*

One Dickinson production that slipped through the cracks and never got released was Dan Penn's second solo album, Emmett the Singing Ranger Live in the Woods.

I quit Ry Cooder in 1972 or early '73 to produce Dan Penn. Dan and I were going back and forth to Muscle Shoals a lot at the time. I was helping him get his first record, *Nobody's Fool*, mastered.

I didn't have anything to do with that album, but on one of those trips to Muscle Shoals, he said, "Jimmy, why don't you produce me. I needs to make another record. I think you ought to produce me." I said, "Dan! Right on!" So I started producing Dan's second record, which was called *Emmett the Singing Ranger Live in the Woods*. It's my greatest unreleased record!

We recorded quite a few songs for this project at Sam Phillips Recording (in Memphis) with Knox Phillips as the engineer. This is where we cut the session for this album with the two live Harleys. It was a song called "Tiny Hinnys and Hogs." Yeah. "Tiny hinnys and hogs, funky ladies love outlaws." It contains one of the greatest Dan Penn lines that I know of. "This chrome hog is a rollin' rocket. A two-wheeled Caddie with a highway sprocket" [laughs]. No one yet has written a motorcycle song at the level of a hot rod song, like "Little GTO." There is no motorcycle song that comes to that level. This song did, had we been able to finish the project.

Dan is the master of cutting a screwed-up demo and he had this demo of "Tiny Hinnys and Hogs," where he was slapping on his leg like this (imitates rhythm) and making the sound of a Harley-Davidson. Japanese motorcycles scream, but there is a rhythm to a Harley-Davidson engine. It goes ba-da-bump ba-da-bump ba-da-bump and that was the rhythm of his hands. Not to be outdone, because Dan can come up with some crazy shit, Dan had Gene Christman, a brilliant drummer, go in on the drum set and played this screwed-up hambone rhythm that Dan was doing.

I thought what we need now is some Harleys to play the percussion part, like bongos. So I got Campbell Kensinger and one of his other cronies from the family nomads to bring their bikes into the studio. Campbell was an artist anyway. Campbell was in the center of the studio playing lead Harley. He had his buddy, who didn't really "get it," off in the corner playing rhythm Harley. Well the rhythm Harley was just playing. He just started the motor and let it run. Campbell was actually trying to get the motor on the beat. He was retarding the spark with his screwdriver, to slow the engine down, and giving it gas with the throttle to keep it from dying, so it was sort of choking out. Every time it would choke out, he would rev it up and he was shooting like three feet of blue fire out of the exhaust. The whole studio was filling up with carbon monoxide. It was great! Eventually, Campbell got to the point to where he was really playing the fucking bike. Not only was he keeping this beat going, but when we got to this solo part, he was doing this saxophone thing. Dan was playing acoustic 12-string and playing on the floor, where he insisted on singing with the Harleys live in the vocal microphones.

Knox Phillips was engineering these sessions, and he was crazy as a shit house rat at that point, and willing to let me do anything. Knox is tight buddies with Mike Post, the Hollywood guy who does all the TV music, like *Hill Street Blues* and all that stuff. I had met Mike a couple of times, but we weren't what you would call "friends." Post had a session that was starting the next day at Phillips. There was another person from L.A. that was also with Mike who was a "somebody," too.

Anyway, they came in during the session, just as we were starting the bikes and all that shit. Post was horrified by the whole thing and he had to leave. The guy who was with him said, "No way in the world am I leaving. You go on. Just come back and get me later. I am going to stay here and watch this shit" [laughs]. Post was basically saying, "This is crazy. I know who these people are and they should know better than this."

So Post returns a few hours later and we are playing it back and he says, "That's incredible. The motorcycle is playing the beat. It sounds like a saxophone." He just went crazy. I'm going, "Yeah. Sure." I sort of had the attitude like the time to appreciate my genius is before I do it. You better believe I can do it. Of course the motorcycle is playing with the beat. Where did you think I was going to put it? Did you think I was going to bring them in here and have them play off the beat? I'm not going to bring some amateur to come in here and play the motorcycle! [laughs]. These men are professionals!

Everybody, when they hear the tape, thinks the bike is playing along with the instruments. Well of course, what is happening is the instruments are playing with the bike. The bike is so hypnotic and Gene Christman is such a brilliant drummer, that you hear Dan say on the tape "Start your bikes. Campbell! [Dickinson makes motorcycle sound]" Then you hear the rhythm of

the engine. Christman just played with the bike. It is so obvious, but nobody ever sees it.

CHAPTER 18

Radio and TV Mixes

Y ou've worked seemingly endless hours in the studio trying the produce the ultimate single that you think has a real shot to make a dent at the top of the charts. You are thinking that this is the pop music shot in the arm that will cause a zillion listeners to go into an appreciative trance and head over to the nearest music store.

It all comes crashing down that first time you hear your local nationally consulted radio outlet squash the life out of your pop opus, right as the first chorus makes its big entrance. Even that magical moment where the singer delivered the heartbreaking hook was lost in a sea of swimmy effects. What happened?

While it is a good bet that many of the most formative musical moments in our lives arrived courtesy of tiny transistor boxes, single dashboard speaker car radios, and other less than ideal audio set-ups, none of us as kids realized the degree of processed sonic mangling stations employed to deliver those magical sounds.

I knew I hit a hot topic when producers, engineers and mastering engineers lined up to speak their minds. The following are a number of those very folks—names most of you know quite well—taking their turns with solid advice, horror stories and the occasional dig, towards those broadcast mediums that have caused us as professionals to pull out hair out with frustration, while having to admit that our lives would be very different without them.

I would like to thank John Agnello, Michael Brauer, Greg Calbi, Richard Dodd, Don Gehman, Brian Lee, Gavin MacKillop and Benny Quinn for their generous gift of time and insight for this piece.

JOHN AGNELLO

Over the years, John Agnello has earned a reputation as a producer and engineer with extensive credits in the modern rock and alternative music world, including The Breeders, Dinosaur Jr., Redd Kross, Screaming Trees, Grither, Dish, Buffalo Tom, Triple Fast Action, Bivouac, Lemonheads, Tad, Gigolo Aunts and more.

Obviously, before music television, a lot of people mixed for radio, and a lot of those records were mixed for radio compression. There are a couple of different schools of thought. One is that you make it sound slamming on the radio, and when people buy it and bring it home, they get what they get. Another school of thought is to not really concern yourself with the radio. Then there is the guy in the middle, which is what I think I try and do. At least back when I was really concerned with radio, I tried to make a record sound kind of punchy on the radio, but not like a whole different record when you brought it home and listened to it on a regular system without the heavy radio compression.

For me, I just like the sound of bus compression on the mix anyway. I am a big fan of that stuff. When I was mixing more for radio, I would have the whole mix up and basically sit there with this really hard line compressor that was cranked at 20 to 1. I would check vocals and work on the mix, so I could tell what the radio might do, while monitoring through the compressor. This would help you tell how much of the "suck" you would get from the radio.

In fact, I would go to tape with the compressor, but not at twenty to one, but I would go back to more of a normal setting. MTV is here, but most people still listen to TV on a little mono speaker. Phasing is a main concern. If your snare drum is out of phase and it comes out on MTV, there is not going to be any snare in that mix. *Phase cancellation* is the correct term for what has taken place.

I use the phase button more than I use the EQ button, especially on drums and things like that. Also check the phase if you have a bass DI and a microphone, or if you are running a bunch of different mics on a guitar amp. You should always check the phase on those. If you are really careful about that kind of stuff, you can actually mix for maximum rock, as opposed to constantly EQ'ing something that is screwed up on a different level.

I think that it is really important to regularly reference your mix in mono, if you are really concerned that your records really slam on MTV or any kind of music television. You can really tell how well your vocals are going to come out if you work in mono at lower volumes, and referencing on different speakers is also a good way to get a sense of your mix.

MICHAEL BRAUER

Michael Brauer is truly one of popular music's greatest mix masters, having created hit soundscapes for Bruce Springsteen, Aerosmith, the Rolling Stones, Sade, Eric Clapton, Tony Bennett, Luther Vandross, James Brown and many others. Brauer, with the help of Nick Balsano at Sony Music Studios, designed and patented an audio processor called the MHB 850, which will be on the market within the year. When Brauer isn't mixing or inventing gear, he actively participates in bike racing throughout the world.

Over the past few years, the approaches to mixing for radio and for albums have become almost the same. This is because of the need for the recorded signal to be printed on tape or digital as loud as possible, with the possible exclusion of classical and jazz music, because those musical forms are so pure, and compression would be heard immediately. No compressors of any kind were used for my Tony Bennett *Unplugged* mixes.

The mixer accomplishes this task by using an array of compressors to keep the audio dynamic range down to 2 to 3 dBs. The mastering engineer takes over and has his own custom-made toys of A/D converters and secret weapons to make the CD as loud as those little 0's and 1's can stand.

Radio stations have their own limiters and EQs with which to process their own output signal, in order to make things as loud as possible. The less you do to activate those signal processors, the better your song will retain its original sound. The potential problem is that you can end up with a mix that has no dynamic excitement left to it. It's been squeezed to the point of being loud, but small.

Over the years, I've found ways to get the most dynamic breathing room possible within the 2 to 3 dB window. I break down my mix into two or three parts instead of putting my mix through one processor. The bottom part of the record (A) includes bass, drums, percussion. The top part of the record (B) includes guitars, keys, synth, vocals, etc. The third part (C) is sometimes used for vocals or solos only. I assign my reverbs to A or B depending on its source.

The dynamics of the bottom end (A) of the record are no longer affected by the dynamic of the top part (B) of the mix. Once this concept is understood and executed, you then experiment by getting A to affect B, B to A, or C, etc. When done properly, the bottom of the record pumps on its own, independent of the top end of the music.

The problems I used to have with just using a stereo compressor became a vicious cycle. If I wanted a lot more bottom, the compression would be triggered and work harder, causing the vocals to get quieter. If I wanted more vocals or more solo instrument, my drums and bass suffered. By the second or third chorus of a song, the dynamics need to be coming to a peak. You don't want the compressor holding you back. Ten years ago, the use of a stereo compressor was less of a problem, because the dynamic audio range was smaller. TR-808's and Aphex changed all that.

My mix of Dionne Farris' "I Know" is typical of this style of mixing. The bottom end just keeps pumping along as the vocals and guitars have their own dynamic breathing room, all within that small little dynamic window. The complete album, video and radio mixes are all the same.

GREG CALBI

Greg Calbi has mastered many of the greatest albums in the last twenty-five years, including releases by U2, Paul Simon, Talking Heads, Bruce Springsteen, David Bowie, Eric Clapton, John Lennon, Yes, Dire Straits, the Ramones, Lou Reed, Brian Eno, James Taylor, Rolling Stones, Van Morrison, R.E.M., Tom Petty and the Heartbreakers, Bob Dylan, Dr. John and many more.

In a very petty sense, people are very conscious of their records being louder than everybody else's records. Everyone wants their mastering to be louder. We are having a lot of problems with that, because people are cutting these CDs so hot, that they are not really playing back well on cheaper equipment, and a lot of people have cheaper equipment.

Many mastering guys have gotten disgusted, because it has really gotten to a point of diminishing returns. Why are we making them as loud as this? It is because musicians and producers all want a more muscular sound, but if they were all taken down a couple of dB, they might sound a little cleaner.

This is an example of almost like a lack of confidence. Everybody wants that little extra edge. If they feel volume is one of those edges, then that is something that I can give them, because all I do is turn the 0 to +1 and it is all of a sudden louder. The fact of the matter is, if you give radio something, and their compressors hit it the right way, and you have it tweaked up right, it is going to sound loud anyway. If your record is bright and clean, it will cut through a small speaker on a car. If it is real busy and dense, you will get that muffled quality.

Someone recently talked to a guy on radio who said that he likes to get stuff that is real low level off the CDs, so his compressors at the station can kind of do their thing. He felt it made stuff sound better than stuff that was real hot. We always thought that the hotter you cut it, the hotter it was going to sound on the radio. Well suddenly here was another twist on that debate. I thought, "Now this really takes the cake, because I've heard everything."

I have a feeling that things sound great on the radio, more on how the parts are played and the whole thing is thought out from the get-go. The other day, I heard a Springsteen song, "Tunnel of Love," on the radio. It sounded great and it was so simple. The bass was down there playing the part. Guys like Springsteen and Bryan Adams write and arrange songs that are in the range that are made for radio. They give you one thing to digest at a time. There aren't all these layered parts conflicting with each other. These are some basic tenets of arranging that kind of hold up on a little speaker. In my opinion, I think it comes more from the conceptual stage.

RICHARD DODD

Whether it is Tom Petty, with or without the Heartbreakers, or Wilco's gritty alterna-country/ rock, Boz Scaggs bluesy R&B-influenced pop, the Traveling Wilburys, George Harrison or the recent harmony-rich pop of Billy Pilgrim, producer/engineer/mixer Richard Dodd consistently creates exciting and unique radio-friendly records that still maintain a high level of sonic integrity. Currently, Dodd is wrapping up production on Atlantic artist Francis Dunnery's as-of-yet untitled second album. Dodd left us with the following parable to consider.

Here's a great analogy. We have a pint pot of beer and, with reference to mixing to radio, radio processing makes it a point to always keep that pint full. If we underfill it, their system will fill it. If you overfill it, or attempt to, it will chop it off and make sure that only a pint of beer is there. That only leaves us with control over the content of that pot. It can be a delicate light crystal clear liquid, or a thick dark and gooey liquid. Those are the parameters we have to work within. If you want it thick and dark and gooey, you can put a bunch of stuff in there and make it dense and sludgy. That is what it is going to sound like. If you leave it clear and open, it is going to have an apparent dynamic. It is going to be sparkling and have clarity and space. That is basically what we do. We make the decision.

The stronger the song, the stronger the performance, the clearer we can allow that liquid to be and get away with it. If the song or performance is perhaps lacking, we tend to go for the denser, thicker darker approach. That is the control we have, but basically, there is still only a pint pot. That is just the way it is.

Now some people will prefer Budweiser. You can also have a Guinness and fill it to where there is no head. You can chop the head off and you don't have a Guinness anymore. If you don't allow that half-inch for the head, then you haven't got the whole thing. You've got to extract in order to get it all. You can fill a Budweiser to the top, because there really isn't a head.

If you want a voice and guitar at the front of the song to be minus six, and when the band kicks in to be at least zero, you are never going to hear it like that on the radio. The nature of the compressor is to bring the quiet things up and the loud things down. But, if you use that facility correctly, then you can get the radio compression to re-mix the song for you.

I'm not going to make music for what type of processing radio thinks sounds right today, because tomorrow they are going to think something else is right. Then every piece of music that I made today is wrong. So I don't mix for the radio, but I do mix with the radio in mind. Sometimes, I strap on a couple of ridiculous limiters across the monitors and fake what an FM radio might do. I'm monitoring through them, so I can make the proper adjustments.

Even though you can't have the dynamic, there are ways to create that sense of dynamic on the radio. I take things out. I turn the band down. It is under-mixing. Otherwise, without witnessing what happens through a second set of limiters, you don't stand a chance.

A slower tempo song can be apparently louder than an up tempo song. If you have a drummer bashing away at a hundred miles an hour, it is going to eat up all the space and there won't be room for anything. Remember that whatever is bad about a mix, the radio is going to emphasize it and make it worse. If you have something that is really laid back, with all the space in the world, that allows time for the effects of radio to recover,

before they act again, that can also be an effective dynamic, which you otherwise wouldn't have gotten with the fast busy track.

By extracting from the content, you can compensate for the lack of dynamic in a song. Less is more basically and extraction is part of the trick. It is in taking away, even if it is just using the facility to bring what you took out back again. Basically, when Tom Petty is singing, not much else is going on. When he stops, something interesting happens.

Again, the texture and flavor is all we can mess with. We all want to fill the glass to the top, but the only facility we can effect is the flavor of pint, the texture, viscosity, color, and density, but basically a pint is still a pint.

DON GEHMAN

Over the last twenty years, producer/engineer Don Gehman has been associated with some of rock and pop's most significant artists, including John Mellencamp, R.E.M., The Bee Gees, Barbra Streisand, the Allman Brothers and most recently Hootie and the Blowfish.

I think the key to a great sounding radio mix is to get your balances correct. I'm not just referring to the correct balance of basic core elements, like snare, vocal, bass and guitar, but the frequencies within them are what have to be balanced as well. That way everything hits the compressor with equal power.

I used to always use bus limiting, like on an SSL or this little Neve stereo compressor I have. For many years, I just let that thing fly with 8 to 10 dB of compression, and just flatten everything out. When it went into mastering, I would have people sometimes complain that it was a little over-compressed, but they could work with it. They might say they couldn't bend it into the frequency ranges that they needed.

I have been working with Eddy Schreyer over at Future Disc Systems, and he has encouraged me to use less limiting and more individual limiting and get my balances right. It has taught me a valuable lesson.

What we are doing now is I'll try and contain that bus limiting to 2 to f4 dB, just enough to give me a hint of what things are hitting at. It is kind of a meter of which things are too dynamic. I'll then go back and individually limit things in a softer way, so that the bus limiter stops working. Then I can take it in and put it on this digital limiter, which is this Harmonium Mundi that Eddy's got, which is invisible. It doesn't make any sounds that are like bus limiters that I know. We just tighten it up just a little bit more to give it some more level to the disc. That results in something that doesn't sound compressed. It is very natural.

You can hit a radio limiter, and have something that is very wide open sounding, if the frequencies, like from 50 cycles to a thousand cycles are all balanced out, so that they hit the limiter equally and your relationships aren't going to move. They are all going to stay the same, but you've got to get that all sorted out before it goes into that broadcast limiter.

The way you do that is by using some example of it, to kind of test out. I use a bus limiter to kind of show me where I am hitting too hard and then I take it away and get rid of it and let the mix breathe. That is the trick that I am finding more and more in helping getting your balances just right.

With the whole practice of frequency balancing, I know you can have tracks that seem dynamic on radio. Green Day's "Longview" is a great example. That chorus slams in, but it is balanced out well enough, that when the chorus hits the limiter, it just adjusts the level and doesn't gulp anything else up.

If you have bass frequencies that come in too loud and aren't balanced in the midrange, the limiter "sees" whatever is loudest and puts that on top. If the low end is too loud, then everything will come out muddy when it hits. If all the frequencies are balanced, the limiter will equally turn down the balances, with them all staying intact and life goes on, just as you intended.

BRIAN LEE

For the last three years, Brian Lee has made quite name as Bob Ludwig's rising mastering star at his Gateway Mastering facility in Portland, Maine. Among Lee's credits are Janet Jackson, Pearl Jam, Ozzy Osbourne, Gypsy Kings, Lou Reed, Gloria Estefan, Charlie Daniels and Cachao.

It is very important to check for phase problems by referencing to mono regularly in the mix stage.

When you mix, you should definitely be listening in mono every now and then, so you know that when it goes to mono, it will still sound just as good and in phase. I believe that the fullness of the overall sound, when you are in stereo, can cause you to pay more attention to the instruments and effects than to the vocal.

Interestingly, a lot of people use phase for weird effects. We have done heavy metal albums that are really out of phase. They especially like to put a lot of effects on the vocal. Maybe they just didn't think it was going to get played on the radio, but some stuff was totally out of phase and if you pushed the mono button, everything just went away. We could've put everything back in phase, but I think they would think it would ruin the effect that they wanted.

It is important for producers and mixers to print mixes with vocals and other desired elements with higher and then lower settings, so as to allow the mastering engineer more flexibility in attaining the ideal presentation.

We do suggest that you get a mix the way you think it should sound and get a few different passes, like vocal up and vocal down. Mixing is very expensive and you should get as much out of it as you can. If you are going to the Hit Factory, or some studio like that, that is a lot of money a day. You don't want to have to go back and rebook time and re-mix the whole thing just to get the vocal right. When you are mixing, you should also do your instrumental TV track and versions with lead and background vocals up and down.

If you have the time and patience to do that, you will be in great shape, because when you get to this stage of mastering, you can actually sit back and reflect and say, "I need more vocal on this particular section," or, "I think this particular vocal is overshadowing this part of the song. I think it needs to be brought down." Then you can do edits at that point.

When you are traveling around from studio to studio, listening and mixing, you may think a mix sounds great, until you hear it on another system and for some reason things sound like crap. You may find yourself going, "What is going on here?" Usually, mastering is a third party's subjective opinion about the whole process. That is one thing that the whole mastering process is about. We know our speakers very well and when you bring your work in here, hopefully we will have some frame of reference for you to get it right.

BENNY QUINN

Benny Quinn is one of Nashville's most prominent mastering engineers, with mastering credits covering every genre from symphonic and rock, to country, gospel, R&B and jazz. His credits include Eric Clapton, Elvis Presley, Aaron Copeland, DC Talk, Johnny Cash, Isaac Hayes, Alabama, Dixie Dregs, Indigo Girls, Bela Fleck, Bob Seger, Cracker, Widespread Panic, Amy Grant, Boston Pops Orchestra, Willie Nelson, Nanci Griffith, Shirley Caesar, Lyle Lovett, Reba McEntire and many others. For the last 18 years, Quinn has worked at Masterphonics, one of the country's most highly regarded mastering facilities.

Mastering for radio is like a dog chasing its tail. It's really a losing proposition in that you'll never get there. Each radio station is different, and processes their station differently than the one next door in the same building that's playing the same music.

What most engineers (especially new mastering engineers) are not aware of is the fact that in FM broadcast, the FM standard requires an HF boost on the order of 15 dB at 15 kHz, and a complementary roll-off in the receiver at the other end. What does that mean? It means that as we push more high frequencies onto the discs, the more the broadcast processors limit and roll that off.

Also, as we push the levels harder, with more "clipping" and smash limiting, we end up with more distortion that the processors interpret as high-frequency energy, and roll it off even further.

The sequence is sort of like this: the processors measure the HF content and apply the "pre-emphasis" curve to see how far over 100 percent modulation the signal would be. Then, the overall level is turned *down* to allow that to fit in the station's allowed transmission bandwidth (100 percent is the legal limit).

So, let's say that the CD is mastered such that there needs to be a 5 dB level drop for everything to fit. Then the multi-band processing is added, then transmitted. At the radio end, there is no information that says "Oh by the way, this song has been turned down 5 dB." It just sounds duller, maybe smaller, and *not* like the record you mastered. The producer hears this on the radio and says "Hey, it's not bright enough, or loud enough. Next time I'm *really* going to pour on the highs, and limit and compress it." Guess what happens? The next record sounds even worse.

What's the answer? Well, if you listen to an oldies station that plays music from before the mastering level wars started, those songs sound great. If you listen at home to those same recordings, they have life, sound natural, have dynamic range, and are easy to listen to. Mastering for radio should be "Mastering for great sound." That's what works for me.

Here are some more specific pointers to consider. Everything has got to be very clear sounding. You have got to make sure that everything is distinguishable, as far as the instrumentation is concerned, and that can be done with a combination of EQ and limiting.

The low end is what will normally grab and kick a compressor or limiter at a station. If you have too much low end, and it is too cloudy and big, then all you will hear are the station's compressors grabbing the low end and moving everything up and down with it.

While I typically don't cut the bottom end off, I do try and make sure that the bottom end is clean and present. Normally, you will find frequencies in the low end that are rather cloudy. This changes from song to song and mix to mix.

You can often find one or two frequencies that may create more "cloud" than distinction. You may be rolling off at that frequency, using a real broad bandwidth and then possibly even adding back a very similar close frequency, maybe even the same one, using a very narrow band width. What you do is take that "cloud" and that "woof" out of the low end. That usually helps significantly, as far as radio processing is concerned. The top end doesn't seem to hit the station's signal processing as hard as the bottom end, and radio compression doesn't seem to hurt the top end as much as it does the bottom end.

Most rock stations compress more heavily than other station formats do. When something is out of phase, it causes very strange sounds in the reverbs. You will hear more reverb on the track, while played on the radio, if the phasing problem is with the original signal, and not with the reverbs on the tracks themselves. The original signal will want to cancel, and the reverbs won't, making things sound even more swimmy.

CHAPTER 19

Radio Processing

In the previous chapter, I enlisted some of the music industry's top producers and mixers (such as Michael Brauer and Richard Dodd) to discuss their feelings on what it took to create a recording that had a chance at sounding great on the airwaves, while hopefully maintaining enough sonic integrity to work well on good home systems.

While I'm very pleased with the advice in that chapter, it seems that it would also be helpful to have experts on the radio end of things offer some illuminating insights on the matter of increasing your chances of having a record truly sound great for radio.

The people I contacted were extremely generous in sharing information that may prove very helpful to many readers. While today's highly processed radio station signals understandably frustrate artists, mixers and producers by essentially "re-mixing" the records, many station engineers and broadcast signal processing designers share the same frustrations and (if allowed to follow their desires) would love to do what it took to subtly enhance the station's signal, while preserving the essential integrity of the music's production vision.

The following very articulate contributors are highly regarded in their respective fields and offer insight on why things are the way they are, what producers and mixers should watch out for, and finally some warnings on what is around the corner. I would like to thank Chuck Adams, Andy Laird, Stan Salek and Donn Werrbach for generously pitching in, and to Richard Faith, David Hodge, and Jack Otterson for further assistance.

DONN WERRBACH

When Mix *began hunting down recommendations for experts with hands-on knowledge of broadcast signal processing, one name that kept getting mentioned was Donn Werrbach, VP of Engineering for Aphex. Donn has overseen the development of classic Aphex items as the Compellor, the Dominator and Digicorder, each regarded as standard-setting processing devices for broadcasters. Before Werrbach worked for Aphex, he spent a number of years as a successful contract broadcast engineer for a number of radio stations in Hawaii.*

Absolute fidelity is not the most pressing concern for most broadcasters. A lot of the broadcast engineers would like to strive for the best fidelity and so on, but the station owners do not allow them to do that. The station owners will usually say, "Smash it and get it up in the face of the listener." This is especially true if you have drive-time car radio listeners being the bulk of your commercial audience. Since there is a lot of background noise in cars, the station just smashes the audio to keep things at the same level at all times, so that the listener doesn't have to fight with the volume.

Besides achieving a consistent signal loudness or presence, stations also desire a certain sonic consistency between songs. The multi-band processor is a device that stations use to create that evenness.

If you have one song that is real bright and punchy and has an extended high and low end, and you back it next to a song that is all mid-rangey, the listener gets irritated and feels that there is something wrong with the radio station. To combat that, most broadcasters re-equalize the music, in order to get them all to average around the same spectral or tonal balance of frequencies. That is done by what is called a multi-band audio processor. Almost every FM station has one of one sort or another. They will break up the audio frequency spectrum into three to five bands of frequencies and run them through individual compression, and then add it back together. So what it will do is, if you have a song that is really heavy on the bass and no high end and dark sounding, it will tend to bring up the high end and knock down the low end and balance it back out. If you are excessively bright and real tinny, with no bottom end, it will bring up the bottom end and throw some punch in it for you. This re-equalization is what most of the record producers are hearing on their music that either they like or don't like. A lot of times this multi-band compression actually enhances the song on the air, because it does something to the mix that just can't be done in a studio very easily with conventional audio equipment. It adds a kind of consistency and punch to the music that they (the artist, engineer, producer) might have tried to get, but couldn't get. The broadcasting processor might get it.

I have heard lots of people say that they wished that they could get that radio sound on tape. On the other hand, I have heard people say, "God, I wish I could hear it the way I made it!" Sometimes it is a good thing, and sometimes it is a bad thing, but it is there. You have got to expect it.

The wide variance of CD volume is another big problem. To me, one of the most annoying things about CDs is that there isn't a standard reference level for the loudness level, of where the average level of the signal should be. With digital, everybody records so that they don't go over the top on the peak, but that doesn't address how fat their recording is. That is, how loud it is below that peak reading. On an analog system, there is basically a reference level for the average, and the desire is to keep enough headroom to accommodate any peaks that come along. With digital, it is a whole different attitude. They don't use VU meters. So all of these records come out at different levels and the audio processors at radio stations are doing a lot of work to segue from one CD track to the next. There could be a 6 dB difference in the average level, because of a lack of standard on average record level.

The peak meter in digital recording doesn't show you what a VU meter would show. The VU doesn't show peaks. It only shows average, and that shows you what you are hearing more or less. If you record your VU meters so that it is hanging in there at about 0 VU then it is going to sound a certain level to everybody. With digital meters, you don't have that. You are looking at a peak meter and you really have no idea what it is telling you about the level. You only know if their peaks are within limits.

If you record really hot to digital, you are going to have to smash all of the peaks out of your signal. You may get a really fat sound, and it may be the sound that you want for your kind of music. But if you are doing it just to make the music louder, because you think it will play louder on the radio, you could be very wrong.

I think you are better off sticking with average ordinary standards. Don't try to make your record sound louder. I've heard some people say that, as hard as they have tried to punch up their stuff, it gets lower and lower and lower on the radio. I say, give the damn audio processor at the radio station some peaks. Let it see them, because it computes what it is doing based on the waveform that it sees. If it sees something that is all fat and topped off already, it may just push it down in the mud, because it already thinks it is too compressed. If it sees something that is real open and has lots of dynamic range, it will squeeze the heck out of it."

Usually, the broadcast processor on the air can do a fairly nice job of squeezing. You would almost rather let it do the job, rather than you do it. I have heard the opposite and some people would rather do it and not have the station have to do it. I have found that the best thing that you can do is be kind of moderate, go in there and do a little bit of peak control.

The last thing you want is to have most of your record, let's say on a peak meter, looking at like −20 dB, and then suddenly you have got some zeroes up there. Some really kickin' toms, or something that can bite your ear off might sound great on your home stereo, but on radio it will poke a hole in the loudness of the signal. This is because it is going to have to gain reduce on that sudden 20 dB peak and the whole level is going to be knocked down 20 dB for a few instances around that hole. So you want to keep those peaks down and under control.

I would say that the optimum thing for radio is to have the peaks ranging from a range of around 10 dB and then keep your average level as consistent as you can, but not using a lot of compression to do it. You just do it by doing a good mix.

There are a few other tricks to making a mix sound good on the air, like using general compression on some of the tracks. It is usually better to compress an individual track than to compress the whole mix, because most compressors will hear the artifacts of it on a whole mix. By doing that, it'll help to keep that track down a little bit more constant on the air.

ANDY LAIRD

Heritage Media Corp., based out of Dallas, is one of the broadcast industry's most successful and respected companies, with stations spread from New York to Oregon. As VP of Engineering, Andy Laird (one of the broadcasting industry's most respected experts on radio signal processing), fine-tunes the signals and sonic characteristic of the company's many formats, which run the gamut of formats from nostalgia, smooth jazz, modern rock, AOR, and AC to country.

There is a big push by several companies to change the way music is distributed to radio stations. The way this is getting started is that there is always a fight for a radio station to have the breaking songs ahead over your competitor, and it is a nightmare for record companies to avoid playing favoritism. Let's say that Garth Brooks has a new song, and program directors will assume that, "Hey, I've got to be the first one on my block to have it."

There is a new movement from certain people that is aggressively selling music distribution in real time at 128 kilobits per second. Now these people may think that 16-bit audio is a problem, but take 16-bit down to 128 kilobits.

The producer who thinks that his music is getting stepped on badly by broadcasters hasn't heard nothing till that stuff starts getting on the air. I understand the need to distribute product at the identical time to a bunch of radio stations, but don't stop there. If I could make any statement to the music industry, it is to make sure that the stations still get a high-quality disc.

I would also say that they should pressure the distributing company to have at least 256-kilobit distribution. Now the ISDN non-real time systems are 256. DG Systems and Digital Courier are bit-rate reduced systems, but they are at least 256 kilobits. The company that is fighting 256 and wants it at 128, which is half the bandwidth, is also the one that is aggressively trying to convert the music distribution to their system. They call themselves Musicam Express.

A number of broadcasters, directors of engineering and vice presidents, have really put the pressure on them, when they were not offering anything greater than 128 kilobits. We told them we wouldn't allow the hardware to be installed in our stations. We have gotten them to redesign the system so that it can be used at 256. Now the important thing is that the music distributor use it at 256.

The transcoding issue of digital bit rate reduction has become a big issue in the broadcasting. There really is no industry agreed upon standard. There are least three different forms of coding going on out there and it is not surprising to go into a station that has all three doing something here in this room and using a different one somewhere else. On top of that, sometimes it is required that you build some kind of coding scheme into your microwave, just by the nature of the path that requires it to be digitized.

You might have a Musicam-delivered piece of music that is stored in ATT-X and transmitted out to the transmitter, and then another coding at that stage.

Anything that keeps the CD un-bit rate reduced coming to the station is going to have a positive effect on the sound. Personally, I was thrilled that Sony Mini disc didn't take off [laughs].

If I could put on my editorial hat, it is to make people aware that this is happening. This is a third entity in the mix that affects the quality of music on the air. This isn't the broadcaster or the music producer. We should insist on a minimum of 256 kilobits.

Two hundred fifty-six kilobits is more rugged sounding (than linear 16-bit sound) and while that could be more acceptable on a more short-term basis of a few days, I would think that it would be a real loss to the music industry to not get the CDs out to the stations. In other words, the labels have to understand that the stations need the non-bit rate reduced CD. Sending it through a distribution service just isn't enough. The quality loss, after it goes through all the radio station stuff, is going to kill it.

Let's say we have three country stations in a city, and all three of them get Garth Brooks at the exact same time through the digital distribution service. They will all sound equally bad. Who loses in the long run? It's Garth Brooks who loses, and the broadcaster who continues to use that bit-rate reduced version also. Keeping quality in mind, labels need make sure that they get un-bit-rate reduced CD product out to the stations to replace it.

These distributing companies are going to pitch that you will never have to worry about sending out a CD. That's wrong! This is an issue that producers should be aware of and make sure that their labels don't stick it to the artists and producers by not getting the good product out to the stations quickly.

CHARLES ADAMS

Circuit Research Labs is one of the most respected names in designing and manufacturing signal processing gear. Charles Adams, another highly regarded designer of industry standard outboard gear, has worked at CRL for the last twenty years, and is the company's Engineering Manager.

The issue of the 75 micro-second pre-emphasis curve is one that the FM broadcaster has to deal with. If you have modern synthesized sounding music coming from the recording studio that has already been EQ'ed and is hyped-up on the CD, and then you put another boost of high frequencies on it that is required by the FCC for transmission, suddenly you find yourself exceeding your modulation limits in a big way.

The 75-micro-second pre-emphasis curve can easily add 17 dB of boost at 15 kHz. The job of the station's processing is to try and push that curve back down again, without sounding like it is doing it, and without the station sounding like it is over-modulating.

Let's say that someone really cranked up 8 kHz really high. The processor has to pull that back down again, to keep the station from over-modulating. Sometimes that is what you may hear. It is a kind of a pull back or ducking effect. If somebody has used the limiter at the studio to really increase the energy level in the high frequencies, it is just going to aggravate the situation at the radio station even more.

There are a number of issues, and high frequency is only one of them. I think that people at the studio should be concerned with this.

If they produce a track that has a lot of high-frequency energy, more than what is considered natural, then the processors have to work extra hard to reduce those back down to a level to where it can be transmitted.

There are other things that studios and producers pay no attention to whatsoever. They are not in a mindset to think about what the processing is trying to do. The signal processing is trying to build up the average RMS energy level to the greatest extent that it can. One of the things that can really bother an audio processor is having the signal coming into it as asymmetrical. For instance, there are some CDs that I have got that I play quite often, where the singing voice is extremely asymmetrical.

If there were some way that I could get to the voice without worrying about the music, if I could just get to the voice and make it more symmetrical, then there would be less destruction to the overall music later on in the audio processor.

I am talking about the symmetry of the voltage of the signal. Look at the signal on an oscilloscope and watch how far up the positives the voltage and how far down negative the voltage goes. In some recordings, it may go up two volts positive and down half a volt negative. When the processor sees this, it ends up working too hard on the positive side. As a result, all of the music suffers and the voice suffers. When the processor works hard on the voice, it tends to work hard on the music, too. You then end up with more distortion than you would have otherwise.

What we try and do on the processing end is we try to come up with some way of scrambling up the phase on the audio, so that no matter what you put into it, the voltage is fairly symmetrical. Keep in mind that we are trying to deviate the FM carrier. We are trying to swing that FM carrier to +100 percent and −100 percent modulation as much as we can and as much of the time as we can to optimize the signal-to-noise ratio of the station.

If you give us an asymmetrical signal that may go +100 percent on the positive side, but is only -20 percent on the minus side, the processor goes ahead and tries to push that on out. It does so at the expense of the positive side. It creates more distortion than you would have had, if you would of had some way of making the audio more symmetrical to begin with.

I am not sure that anybody anywhere pays any real attention to this at all in the studio. They probably have no meters or no instruments to tell them if something is asymmetrical or not. So it is pretty much left up to the broadcast audio processor guys, later on, to try and figure out how to fix it.

The only other thing would be to make the audio as natural and as dynamic as possible. Don't try to over-compress things in the studio. It is like garbage in and garbage out [laughs]. With audio processing, if it is garbage in, it is a lot more garbage out.

Most audio processing is multi-band audio processing for broadcast stations, so if there are distortions in the low frequencies, the processing tends to boost that even higher in gain because the bands get processed separately. They have a different amount of gain in each band, so what can happen, is you can increase the amount of perceived distortion in the audio, just from what was in the original source content. I find that the audio that our audio processor handles the best is the audio that has the least done to it. As dynamic as possible is good, and it will actually come out sounding pretty dynamic later on.

STAN SALEK

Stan Salek is Senior Engineer for Hammett & Edison Consulting Engineers, a firm that works in the radio and television broadcast industries. Salek has been at H&E for five years. Previous to that, he was a Director of Radio Engineering for the National Association of Broadcasters and also worked with Charles Adams at CRL.

Personally, I'm not completely sold that digital broadcasting is going to be a hit, with the bit rate reduction and the like. We still have more water to go under the bridge before we make a decision on that.

I think that the handwriting is on the wall and there is a lot of concern that not only will a lot of people employ this bit-rate reduced digital material, but they will also start mixing it with other digital systems of processing as well. So, it will be bit-reduced using one technique, and then it will be re-transmitted to the consumer using yet another technique. The techniques are generally not compatible with other, and what you will end up with on the listener's end is something that is fairly low quality.

I haven't seen a broadcast system yet that proposed to use linear (16- or 20-bit CD quality) audio, because of the bandwidth that it would take on the radio channel. This is really a form of data compression and what that compression really looks for are periods of silence or audio signals that are masked by other audio signals.

There is a system called Musicam, and part of the operation of that system is that it would look for quiet sounds that were masked by louder sounds. It would remove the quiet ones from the coding process. When you are all done, you end up with what they say is roughly equivalent to what the human ear hears.

For persons who have done A/B comparisons of linear and audio encoders, I think that some of them are quite convincing, but it really depends on the programming material.

CHAPTER 20

Room Tuning

Great recordings have been made in situations where mics were thrown up with little consideration other than capturing the magic of the performance moment. Great mixes have happened in environments that were designed for anything but mixing. However, these are exceptions to the rule. Anyone who is serious about creating a recording facility with a rep for putting out consistently good sounds needs to have the tracking spaces and control room set up to give the engineer and mixer the most control over the sound, and provide a level of security that what they are hearing is an accurate reflection of the actual sonic character of the final mix.

I enlisted four well-known leaders in the areas of room tuning and studio design to provide some thoughts and methodologies on what can make the difference between a facility that develops a waiting list of loyal clients jazzed on the great sound, or a place that finds itself struggling to keep the doors open, because word has gotten out that there are too many anomalies in the sonic profile of the room.

GEORGE AUGSPURGER

George Augspurger is one of the giants of studio room and speaker design. Past projects have included new mastering rooms for Sony Records in Mexico City, The Enterprise in Burbank, Criteria in Miami, and a hip-hop mastering room for Sony Studios in New York.

There are essentially two schools of thought concerning the art of tuning a room: one that believes the proper alignment of a room's sonic characteristic should be addressed purely from an acoustical design perspective, and one that is comfortable addressing the situation with electronic equalizers.

You will obviously get two camps of philosophy. There are some people that say, "No, you should never apply electric equalization to the speakers. Any problem should be taken care of with room acoustics." On the other hand, you will also find today, that those of us who still do very often use electronic equalization will still say that the best EQ is the least EQ. I would certainly say there are twice as many bad sounding rooms that have been ruined by too much EQ as the other way around.

The first thing I do, if it is a new room that I am setting up, is listen to the selected speakers on music. In setting up the speakers, I play with their location and probably with room surfaces, with no thought of electrical EQ as any part of that first go-around at all. The first thing you have to do is find out what it takes to make a given set of speakers sound right in a given room. Once you get them to sound pretty good, then you can come back and use EQ as frosting on the cake.

I happen to come out of loudspeaker design. I worked for JBL for 20 years. The reason people want custom monitors maybe is because of space limitations you can't really fit in a stock speaker that is the size you like. It may be because there was something that they heard at another studio. These days, it certainly may be that they are going to cater to rap and hip-hop and they have got to have something that will take four times as much power as any commercial monitor.

While I've designed many excellent large soffit-mounted control room speakers, I see the proliferation of good nearfields as a good thing.

We now have nearfield speakers of reasonable size that you can set on a console that really have a pretty wide range response. The NS-10 is probably the closest thing that comes to standard in the industry today. Some engineers absolutely hate it. The only really negative public comment that I would make about the NS-10 is that I get the strong impression that Yamaha keeps tinkering with it and not telling anybody. It is hard to get two pair of NS-10's that sound the same. They aren't far off; you can tell they are NS-10's, but still they aren't nearly identical pair after pair after pair. I think the NS-10M is a definite improvement over the earlier ones.

One of the secrets of the NS-10 is that there is a very slight rise right through the 1 kHz region. There is a very broad bump that is maybe a decibel and a half high. That does things for the vocals that you really can relate to what it is going to sound like on a TV set or an ordinary quality car radio. Whereas, to go to the opposite extreme, a classical music monitor like a B&W, is (if anything) slightly depressed through that region and is much more difficult to relate to on pop music.

The small Genelecs are pretty incredible. If you take to time to twiddle around long enough with all the switches on the back, you can make them sound like almost anything you want. They have done some very incredible things with those speakers.

CHRIS HUSTON

Over the last 30 years, Chris Huston has seen popular music, studios and the industry around them change dramatically. Huston (a fellow art school classmate in Liverpool with John Lennon) came stateside during the sixties and became an in-demand engineer and mixer. His credits include classic records by the Rascals, Led Zeppelin, War, The Who, James Brown, Mitch Ryder, Van Morrison, and The Nazz.

As a studio designer, Huston's credits include George Benson's Lahaina Sound (Maui), Baby'o Recorders (Hollywood), Mike Post Productions (Burbank), The Enterprise (Burbank), and most recently, the Sound Kitchen in Franklin, Tennessee.

In designing control rooms, the most important thing to remember is that this will be an environment for evaluating sound. When I design a room, I have to make sure that the basics are taken care of first of all, and that includes the bass building up in the back of the room. You have to confront that. If you put a jam box on a chair in an empty apartment and slowly turn it up, it will be fine, until the low end of blaster "finds" the wall. Then, very quickly, the sound is going to change in proportion of bass to highs. It is loading. At that point, what will happen is the low end will tend to be out of proportion to the mids and highs, because the physical boundaries have been met and the bass just jumps back. The bass has to find its physical boundaries, because that is the nature of the physics.

We have two ways we can deal with it. If we had the physical space, I would sometimes try to cheat and make the bass think it is traveling further than it really is to reach its physical potential. Instead of traveling 18 feet, you slow it down through the use of bass traps, so by the time it hits the mass of the back wall, its has theoretically traveled three more feet. When it comes back again, it is vastly weakened, if you can get it to be out of phase with itself, or in a waveform that isn't contradictory or building to each of the fundamentals. This way you have gone a long way towards smoothing the room out. I have done it this way in several rooms, but often you don't have that luxury.

What we are usually stuck with is a given space and maximizing it. Given that you cannot use the optimum situation, where you are actually slowing it down and reaching that physical boundary, I will then tend to use the ceiling areas for trapping bass.

I really don't like using an electronic Band-Aid for an acoustic problem. I would rather confront the problem in design, rather than in corrective measures later. Electronic EQ sometimes takes away more than it adds. It really takes the balls out of the performance, even with good White equalizers. Sure the sound is flat, but you have taken out so much of the excitement in order to achieve that.

You also have to work with the speakers you have decided on, or the ones your client has picked out, as far as making sure that the sound doesn't change too much, whether they are standing up or sitting down at the console. That is always a problem. You really want to try to make sure that the throw of the horns are not firing directly down into your face and right into your ears, because then you are evaluating the harshness of it, and nobody else is. The people who are standing up to begin with will be questioning what you are going to be hearing sitting down.

Basically, I try to place the horn about a foot or eighteen inches maximum above the head of somebody sitting down, so they are on-axis to the dispersion of the speaker, whether they are standing up or sitting down. You try to avoid being totally on axis with the high end or the midrange dispersion, depending on the kind of speaker. You then get the harshness, and that coloration exists in a certain form in one position only. With certain kinds of speakers, that is very important.

Control rooms are getting decidedly bigger, while the equipment is getting smaller. More is being done in the control room and it has become more than just a place to evaluate sound, it has become a place to create music. The equipment we have got today is so far superior, both in producing sound, evaluating it, and transferring it through all of its different phases to completion.

Nevertheless, I'm cautionary about losing sight of the roles of recording music and making music in an environment fine-tuned for such activity.

Twenty-five years ago, we were documenting a performance. Today, we are creating a performance. I think that is important to be aware of, both in studio design and control room design. Nowadays, it is sometimes like fighting to creating a performance. That emotion to chase is so elusive. I think that is a fault with many of the records that come out. They mistake technical superiority for the magic of performance.

BOB HODAS

Like many of the best room designers and tuners in the recording industry, Bob Hodas began as an engineer. It is said that necessity is the mother of invention. Upon realizing that many of his mixes sounded vastly different from room to room, Hodas began devising ways to compensate for control room anomalies.

Over the years, Hodas has tuned all the studios for studio bau:ton, as well as for John Storyk, Ted Rothstein, Studio 440 and FRMTS in New York, as well as Bad Animals (Seattle), Conway (Hollywood), Coast Recorders (San Francisco), DARP (Atlanta), Wonderland Studios (Los Angeles), Bosstown (Atlanta), Fantasy (Berkeley), Skip Sailor (Los Angeles), Platinum Island (New York), House of Sound (New York) and numerous private studios, like that of Mariah Carey producer Walter Afanasieff.

The first thing that I do when I go into a room is think, "How can we fix things acoustically? What can we do as far as baffling and trapping and diffusion or absorption?" Each situation is different. It depends on what is going on in the room. I really look at the acoustic problems first. As far as I am concerned, getting the room as close acoustically as possible is number one.

In the realm of sound diffusion material, I feel that crushed fiberglass or "spin glass" works just as well as many more pricey materials.

It may not look as cool, but if you want to compare absorption ratings, it is a heck of a lot cheaper for the same amount of absorption. That will get some manufacturers mad at me, but that is not unusual. I would encourage people to compare absorption coefficient and absorption ratings before they go blow a lot of dough on something that is pretty expensive.

The budget is a big consideration. I may go into a room and someone will have a weird low-end problem and the only way to solve it may be to rebuild the back wall. They may not have the budget for that. At that point, once we have worked within the budget to fix everything that we possibly can, then we'll say, "Now what can we do electro-acoustically through equalization to finish solving the problem, or to create a curve that is conducive to making records?"

A minimum phase parametric is really my equalizer of choice. That is a parametric that can address minimum phase problems, which are problems of corner loading. Any kind of boundary loading problems are minimum phase problems within rooms. By using a parametric, as opposed to a graphic equalizer, I can shape the equalization to perfectly fit the problem, as opposed to tuning around the problem, because I am restricted with fixed frequency centers and fixed cue. Room problems are not all third octave, and they are not all at these fixed frequency centers the third octave provides you with.

Nobody has got a flat room, or nobody really likes "flat," in my experience. Flat is not necessarily conducive to making records. Of all the rooms I have done, which are a good couple of hundred rooms, I have found that people tend not to like flat. If I was going to make a generalization to apply to the majority of the rooms, I would say flat from 80 cycles to 5 kHz, is generally the area people like to have flat; then with some kind of roll-off, from 5 kHz on out, with a slight low end boost somewhere around 50 Hz, just as a fun factor. It varies from room to room, system to system.

I feel that the general sonic profile I just laid out is more applicable for analog rooms than digital.

With analog tape, the particles re-align themselves, so you start to lose high end on the tape. Also contributing to that is, as you do overdubs, and the tape passes over the head for the overdubs, a little bit of the high gets lost through that process as well. The whole idea of that (creating this "analog" room tuning process) was developed to help compensate for some of that loss. It doesn't make any difference in digital, but it makes a big difference in analog. I usually encourage people to keep things a little flatter in digital studios, because they don't need that compensation. The only thing they are fighting against are the long hours and the high volumes.

Some speaker systems are not linear, in respect to amplitude. In other words, as you turn them up or down, the frequency response changes. So when I am tuning a room like that, I have to be careful to make sure that I tune it within the general volume that it is typically being used. Most

of the tuning that I am doing is for fixed soffit-mounted speakers.

For my own personal preference, I lean towards direct radiator speakers. At this very point in time, I have to say that the Dynaudio speakers have given me the best impression for a direct radiator speaker in several different rooms. They sound pretty darn good.

I have really gotten some great results from those Meyer nearfields. In fact, the first record I ever used them on, I took the tape down to Bernie Grundman for mastering, and he didn't do anything to it. That was when I had a speaker that I knew I could work with that was basically going to save my butt.

Recording studios spend more on coffee than on control-room monitor maintenance. It is true and that is the sad part of it. People have sort of let their monitor systems in their rooms fall by the wayside, which is a real scary thought to me, because that is what the recording studio is supposed to be all about. It isn't about the latest digital delay or effects box. It is about good sound. We, as an industry, have sort of ignored the sounds of our rooms and gone after the toys to make those sounds and that is the part that bothers me the most.

BRET THOENY

For the last fifteen years, Bret Thoeny (and his company Boto Design) has designed and tuned some of the finest facilities in the recording world. Among his accomplishments are electric Lady Studios (New York), Paisley Park Studios (Minneapolis), Britannia Row Studios (London), Westlake Audio (Los Angeles), The Complex—George Massenburg (Los Angeles), Pacific Ocean Post Sound (Santa Monica), CBS Todd-AO, Glen Glenn (Studio City), and private recording and mixing studios for Don Was, Bob Clearmountain, David Tickle, Jackson Browne, John Tesh, Giorgio Moroder, and many others.

People have even tried setting speakers up in meadows and mixing and it doesn't work. You have got to relate to how the music is going to sound being played back in your car or home, or wherever. That is why some people run out to their cars to hear something. That is why some studios have the portions of the back seats of cars with cassette players, so they can listen. You have got to look at it all in the same environment.

The (control) room size is determined by the function of the room and then by the criteria of the selected monitors that the client chooses, whether they are medium, high or super-high power. You can't put a small nearfield monitor in a huge control room. It is not going to load the room. You are not going to get the sound pressure.

Even speaker manufacturers, when they design a control room monitor, will say that this monitor works within 6,000 or 7,000 cubic feet to 10,000 cubic feet. They give you a parameter. All they are saying is that the type of drivers, the components and the speaker in that room can excite that volume of air, to get a 90/95 in optimum range of that speaker, so you are not overloading it. You are not pushing the speaker too far, so that it starts to go into distortion. That is what happens. You can put little speakers in a big room and crank it up, the speaker will be working beyond its optimum range and it starts going into clipping and distortion, which is bad. That is what they are telling the consumer and that is what the designer should take into account when they design a room.

I just ask, right off the bat, "What kind of speaker and what range are you going to be using this room?" Even if they don't know the model, even if it is going to be double fifteens. Is it going to be a nearfield? What's going on? How do you like to work? A lot of composers like to work in a very small space with nearfield speakers. They don't need soffit-mounted speakers.

Of the soffit-mounted speakers, I like Quested, ATC and Westlake Audio. For nearfields, KRKs and Genelec Golds.

The Genelecs are self-powering. That is a really good trend and I am glad to see that. You don't need to over-amp it or under-amp it, when you buy a package that is designed by the designer to be totally competent. It is great. JBL has done that for their industrial speakers.

We did a room for Bob Clearmountain, and I consider Bob probably the premier mixer in the world. He uses no soffit-mounted speakers. He goes back and forth between NS-10's and the smaller KRK, I think it is the 7000, which he puts up on the console.

While many people are primarily using nearfields, I definitely feel that good soffit-mounted speakers are ideally used for really hearing what is going down during tracking.

The reason for a soffit-mounted speaker is usually for a tracking situation. When are putting up the drums, you can hear the kick and get that energy punching right at you, as if you were sitting right in front of the drum kick. That is the reason for it.

If you can get away with it—if the low end can get out of the room, it is much better than trying to control it. Some of the rooms that sound good are sometimes rooms that are built very minimally, meaning that sound can actually go through the walls. That is a much better circumstance than containing it. The low end goes right through the wall, so it doesn't load in the room. It goes out into open space. Many old studios were great because they allowed the bass to escape.

If you build a block house like a vault, everything is going to stay in there. You have to dissipate it with elaborate traps and diffusers and all the elements, just to get the room back to sounding natural. Typical rooms that we are used to are usually ones where the low end sound can go right through the walls.

You can't always do that, however. In multi-studio complexes, you've got to use good detailing and good acoustical analysis, as well as walls and floors that work, and that is kind of what separates the boys from the men. You don't have a choice. In a nice free standing building, you still want to control environment.

In tracking areas, live sound is pretty much what people have been wanting. Ten years ago, things were so dead, because there was so much isolation and everything was individually miked. Now the engineers are back with much better tools and much better sophisticated knowledge of how to work a live room. Electronics have improved too, so they can work a live room and get a much more natural sound.

I believe that wood is the best material for recording space.

Wood has the most warmth to it. You can make it bright, but it doesn't get edgy or unnatural. Some studios will put in concrete block and the sound is much too harsh with the way they sound and the psychological aspects. If you make a room too high-tech, it kind of goes against the grain of musicians and what they like to be surrounded with.

Anything in large-scale acoustics, you need a lot of one element to make a difference. You need a lot of wood to really let the wood respond to the room. Throwing up some diagonal slats of redwood that you get at the lumberyard doesn't quite do it. If you dabble it here and there, and drywall everywhere else, the room is going to sound like the drywall and not like the sound of the wood.

It is really the percentage of the area that you cover with a particular material that gives it its character. If you have a hardwood floor and you have large splays and diffusers out of wood, you are going to be getting into that area. People say they have wood rooms and they have really put down carpet and a lot of drywall, and it is not going to sound the same.

CHAPTER 21

Recording Strings and Orchestras

There is nothing quite like the sound of a great string section or orchestra. A magic performance of a great symphony, concerto, or chamber piece is arguably every bit as powerful as any inspired rock, R&B, or jazz performance. Since the advent of popular recorded music, orchestras and string sections have been appropriated to elevate the emotional delivery of a recording or live performance. In some cases, the integration of symphonic or chamber elements to a band track has been nothing more than sweetening. In other cases, like the Beatles' "A Day in the Life," it has been an essential part of the composition's integrity.

For this chapter, I talked to experts who have recorded orchestras and chamber groups for "serious" classical music projects, as well as those who have primarily worked within the popular music contexts, and I have given them some space to share some important ideas on how to do it right. I'd like to thank Mylon Bogden, Richard Dodd, Ellen Fitton, Bud Graham, and Tony Visconti for their generous gift of time and insight for this subject.

MYLON BOGDEN

Mylon Bogden is one of Nashville's finest engineers. He is also owner of the Sound Emporium, one of Music City's premier recording facilities. Both of these statements are quite significant in a city loaded with hundreds of studios and engineers. Besides recording many TV and film orchestral dates, Bogden has done string sessions for many of country music's finest artists, as well as many great R&B dates for Motown artists like Marvin Gaye, Diana Ross, the Temptations and many others.

There is a lot to cutting strings. It isn't just setting up the microphones. If you want to do it right, it takes a lot of time, and the set-up is all-critical. You have to know the room you are in and what are its characteristics. Is it heavy at 400 cycles and should you turn that down? If so, then you don't want to put the lower strings in that area of the room, because it will muddy the whole thing up. It is the technique of listening to the whole room and then knowing where to stick the microphones and the instruments in that room.

Sometimes, we will dampen the room down. We might put carpet down on the floor, if it is too live. My preference, however, is for a liver kind of room.

Even though I like a live room, phasing can be more of a problem. You may encounter reflections coming back from a wall that may be almost as loud as the original source signal. You can get an echo effect that causes the strings to lose their presence. That now comes into the microphone technique of where and how far away it is from the instrument.

Omni microphones are always the flattest and the best sounding and more preferable than a cardioid pattern. In some instances, I would have to switch to a cardioid pattern to knock out some of the reflections in the back, if they get too loud.

To me, the high voltage mics always sound better than just the phantom powered mics. That is why I like the Neumanns, the 47's, 67's and 87's, and the high voltage B&K's and Schoeps mics with the power supply on the floor. The 4000 Series high voltage B&K's, especially for violins, are magnificent. They are mind-boggling. They are probably my favorite for miking the room and miking the strings.

For smaller sections, it obviously is a smaller more intimate sound right away. Usually, I will mic each instrument by itself and get a closer more up front present kind of sound. I will usually use a couple of B&K's in the room. I am playing more attention to each individual instrument, than I am with the overall room sound. When there is less of a phasing problem, then it is easier to make the whole thing work.

For solo cello, I like to use an Audio Technica 4041A. I would mic it fairly close, but that would depend on the room and how live it is. I would mic it fairly close to the large part of the body of the instrument, because that mic is so bright.

For bass fiddle, I would use a 47 tube and put it towards the body in front of the instrument, either slightly below, or slightly above where the bow is actually touching the strings.

For violin, I usually mic overhead, but here is also certain amount of sound that comes from under the instrument itself, too. It depends on what you are trying to get. You get a fuller sound underneath. If you are miking from both sides, the producer might say, "I don't like [the bow side sound]. That is too scratchy." A lot of times, it isn't that it is too scratchy. You are just getting too much of the bow. So I just turn that mic down and bring the other one up. All of a sudden the producer likes it, and I didn't change the EQ and I didn't have to change the mic.

I very seldom EQ strings as I record. There is no way to duplicate that. I would rather put some on later. I am so busy dealing with the mix and the blend and the phasing that I don't have time to screw with the EQ. That is why I pick good mics and just do it right that way.

RICHARD DODD

Richard Dodd's recording career reads like a who's who of greats. Since the early seventies, when he was recording hits like Carl Douglas' "Kung Fu Fighting,"

Dodd has worked with George Harrison, Roy Orbison, Boz Scaggs, Wilco, Robert Plant, Traveling Wilburys, Tom Petty and the Heartbreakers and Petty's solo album Wildflowers *(which earned Dodd a Grammy). Dodd has also earned extensive string date credits on both sides of the Atlantic. Dodd's favorite string recording environments are Lansdowne, CBS #1 and Abbey Road #2, all of which are in England. During the interview, Dodd shared many thoughts on mic selection and placement, but in the end he felt that his contribution to this feature should address the psychological aspects of string sessions.*

There are so many factors, other than the technical side, that make for a good string sound or recording. To focus on the method of recording strings and just to talk about microphones and that sort of stuff would be very remiss. If there's an art for me, it's in encouraging the people to be at their best, which gives me an opportunity to be at mine. That's the only art involved really. The rest of it is a series of choices, very few of them wrong. The microphone is almost irrelevant. In fact, if mics were invisible, it would be the best thing in the world.

Nevertheless, if you have a pretty good quality microphone, used in a pretty conventional orthodox manner, it is hard to mess things up, if all the other factors are right. Sometimes people can drop into a session while you are recording a big sixty piece orchestra, and it will sound amazing, and they think you are great; but truthfully it is sometimes easier to record that orchestra than recording a solo guitar and voice. It really is.

You have thirty odd string players out there and it doesn't matter if three of them don't play all of the time. The spectacle and what they produce can be quite amazing.

It really comes down to the caliber of musician (I can't emphasize that enough) and that musician having something worth playing and the person next to him doing his job too. If they respect the leader, and if they respect the arranger, and they don't mind the music (it's very rare they are going to like it in a pop commercial world), then you're on to a good thing. Give them some fun, and compliment them. Everybody likes that. After all, they're human and there's a lot of them in an orchestra.

Here's one little tip to make things better. I used to go around the studio, especially in the summer in England, when it was dry, and spray the room with a spray gun like the kind you use for plants, before the musicians would come in. I would go around and soak the cloth walls and the humidity would gradually leak into the room. It just made things better. I found that I preferred the sound of a wet humid environment to a dry environment. I think it makes the sound more sonorous. I learned that, from the fact that when it was raining, it sounded better than when it wasn't. It just obviously permeated the whole air conditioning system. Not having air conditioning helped, because it wasn't de-humidifying.

I also think it adds more of a psychological effect than anything. If you see someone taking care, it impresses you; just as much as if someone doesn't care, it impresses you in a negative fashion. There is a comfort factor as well. If someone isn't comfortable, then they aren't going to play well; so imposing the humidity was a good thing. It made people think that you cared and in turn would give you an edge.

You know, you can have the best players in the world, but if they don't like the arranger, or the engineer, or the studio, or the person sitting next to them, they are not going to play their best. Even though they might try, it just won't happen. Yet, if they have got a smile on their face, it comes through. You should try and make them comfortable, and try not to take advantage of them, and treat them with respect, it's the best thing you can do. They deserve your respect, because they have trained very hard to be where they are. If you do that, you can have some great days with them.

There are numerous recording strings tips, in terms of indoctrination, that I could share. My first session around string players happened when I had been assisting maybe about 2 weeks. Unbeknownst to me, the engineer had arranged for the lead violinist to teach me a lesson that I wouldn't forget. He told me that I must walk carefully when you walk around the players and the instruments. Make your presence felt. Speak firmly and clearly so people will know you are there; and don't creep up on anyone, because some of the instruments they are holding are worth thousands and thousands of dollars …

pounds in my case. You don't want to have an accident. So the engineer set me up to adjust a mic on the first fiddle, at the leader's desk and I had done everything he had told me to do. As I stepped back to make my final tweak on the microphone, he slipped an empty wooden matchbox under my foot. The sound of crushing wood under my foot is something you never forget [laughs]. It was very clever and a good education. You can tell people all you like about being careful, but there is nothing like that adrenaline rush of "Oh My God, there went my career, before it's started." You remember things like that.

ELLEN FITTON

Ellen Fitton's recording career has ranged from R&B (Chaka Khan, Dionne Warwick, Bee Gees), jazz (Wynton Marsalis) to rock (Firehouse), but her most extensive credits are in the classical world. Fitton has recorded the Chicago Symphony, the Philadelphia Orchestra, and the New York Philharmonic, as well as artists like Jessye Norman, Yo-Yo Ma, and Kathleen Battle. Among Fitton's favorite places to record strings are Royce Hall in L.A., Meyerhoff in Baltimore and Symphony Hall in Boston. For the last five years, Fitton has been working as an editing and recording engineer at Sony Studios in New York. On the day we interviewed Fitton, she was wrapping up editing work on a project with violinist Isaac Stern.

Classical music is all editing. It involves hundreds of takes and hundreds of splices. That's how classical records get made. You usually are talking about maybe 200 takes for the average record, but we just did fifteen Christmas songs for a Kathleen Battle record and there were 2,000 takes. When I say 'take,' it's not complete start to finish recordings of all of the material. It's little inserts and sections. There might only be several complete takes. Then they record a section at a time, or a movement at a time, or there might be a series of bars that they play 8 or 9 times till they get it right. It's that sort of thing.

The function of the producer in a classical record is kind of different than a pop record, because they're really sitting with the score, listening to each take and making sure that each bar is covered completely by the end of the session or series of sessions. They have to make sure they have all the right notes that they need and then they have to come up with an edit plan to put it all together. There's no drum machine or sequencers. So that's how classical gets it right.

The producer has to keep track of tempo, pitch, and how loudly or softly the orchestra played each section. The producer also has to know that if the orchestra plays the piece with a different intensity, then the hall reacts differently. When that happens, the takes don't match.

It is important to familiarize oneself with the piece of music being recorded, so you will know instrumentation-wise what you have, how much percussion there is, and are there any little solo bits by the principals in the orchestra. Then you start laying out microphones. We prepare a whole mic list before we go wherever it is we're going. We take specific microphones, specific mic pre-amps out with us when we go. All of the recording is done on location, in whatever hall we choose, and we take all of our own gear with us. Tape machines, patch bays, consoles, everything gets put in a case and packed up and taken with us.

For the most part, you want a fairly reverberant hall, but you don't want it so reverberant that it starts to become mush. A good hall should have at least a couple of seconds of reverb time.

Normally what we have is a main pick-up, which is usually what we call a tree. It contains 3 microphones set up in sort of in a triangular form and they are usually just behind the conductor, about 10 feet up in the air. Some are 8 feet, some are 12; it depends on the hall. We use B&K 4006's or 4009's because they're real nice omni's that are real clear and clean. They have a nice high end and give you a good blend.

The goal with classical recording is to try and get it with that main pick-up, and the input from all the other mics is just icing on the cake. If you end up in a really bad hall or a hall you don't know, then you end up using much more of the other mics.

Our primary machine is the Sony 3348. It is a great machine and it takes a lot of abuse. It is nice to have all of those tracks there if you need them. We also do a lot of 20-bit stuff that requires additional tracks. Twenty-bit material takes up more than a single channel. It takes two tracks, because of the way the bits are broken up.

We have also been using Sony PCM-800's, as of late, more for cost reasons than anything else. They are great for the small chamber dates, when we just need six or eight tracks. If we need twelve tracks, we will then take two machines and lock them up. It is easier cartage-wise and the tape stock is cheaper. They are nice alternatives to the 3348.

BUD GRAHAM

Over the last thirty years, one of the most highly regarded engineers for serious symphonic recording has been Bud "Buddy" Graham. Graham has recorded many renowned orchestras (Philadelphia, New York, Cleveland, Boston) in a number of the world's greatest concert halls. Graham, who is now retired, has earned six Grammys.

My feeling of string miking is quite different than normal "pop" miking. I like to mic from much more of a distance. It is question of taste. My feeling is that, if everything is miked close, the strings are kind of piercing and sharp. I prefer a mellower string sound and that is the way I like to do it. It is my style. Again, it is a classical sound, as opposed to a "pop" sound, where everything is close miked and people are desiring a more biting sound.

I like the natural room ambiance, but I am more constrained by a good or bad hall. If you are miking close, and it is not a good hall, you are not really hurt by it. If I am miking at a distance and it is a bad hall, it is going to sound bad. It has to be a good hall for my type of miking to work. It has to have ambiance and it has to have a high ceiling.

Some of the great halls, Carnegie, the Princeton University Hall, the Concertgebow in Holland, are hard to get, because they are booked well in advance. You have to book many months in advance to get a good hall.

I favor B&K 4006's for violins to cellos. For bass, tympani, French horns, tuba and other brass, I like Neumann TLM 170's, which are great mics for darker sounding instruments. For vocal choruses and harp, I choose Schoeps MK4's. Neumann KM-140's work well for percussion.

While I've done many projects that involved a combination of many close and distant mics, I feel that the proper application of a minimal number—like a couple of omni-directional mics placed out front—can achieve some of the most ideal results.

On occasion, it sometimes works very well to work with two microphones, usually placed at seven or eight feet behind the conductor with the two microphones placed at seven or eight feet apart. Depending on the hall though, it might be twelve to fifteen feet high.

The placement and focusing of the microphones is important. At one time, an engineer said to me, "What difference does it make, because you are using omni-directional microphones." I said, "Well yeah, but it may be only omni-directional at certain frequencies. The focusing is extremely important. It isn't just something that you put up and aim in the general direction of the orchestra. It has to be properly focused, or you will get too dark of a sound."

In order to focus, I would focus between where the first and second violins meet on the left side. I would try and aim it down so it was kind of cutting the strings in half, between the first and second violin. The one on the right side would be doing the same thing, aimed where the violas and cellos would come together. The leakage from the brass would come in and give it distance and provide a nice depth view. If I aimed too far back, then the strings would get dull and they would loose their clarity. It may also get more brass than you wanted. By focusing the mics at the strings, with the brass coming in, it gives the recording a lovely depth of field.

I found that when the two mics work, and you listened to it, you could hear the difference between where the first horn and the second and the third, with the first one being slightly left of center. The second one would be left of that, and the third one being left of the second. It gives a wonderful depth and spread.

I once heard a CD where the horns sounded like they were not playing together at all with the orchestra. It was a recording where all these multiple of microphones were used. Every one of them came at a different time factor, so that what actually happened was that it sounded like a badly performing orchestra. Actually, it was because of the lack of clarity that was created by all of this leakage. You were hearing the instruments coming to the picture all at different times.

The problem wasn't the orchestra. It is the miking process.

While many engineers still favor analog for recording, I feel that digital is more than fine and just requires a little re-thinking, as it concerns mic placement to achieve that warm sound.

Digital is a cleaner medium than analog and now that we are using 20-bit, there is a noticeable difference. Analog is like a window that has a little bit of haze on it. When you put it to digital, you clean up that window and it gets to be a little too crisp and sharp. We then learned that we had to change our techniques a little bit. What we had to do, when we started moving in from analog to digital, was to not mic as close. As a result, the air did some of the softening or mellowing that analog would do.

TONY VISCONTI

Since the late sixties, when he began working with the legendary Denny Cordell on artists like the Move and Joe Cocker, Tony Visconti has become one of the most notable producer/engineers in the world of rock and pop.

Recording strings is a huge subject. It must be looked at as both a recording technique and a writing technique. I've heard a string quintet sound enormous at Lansdowne Studios in London in the late sixties. I asked Harry the engineer how he managed to make them sound so big and he humbly replied, "It's in the writing, mate!" That was probably the biggest lesson I've ever learned about recording and writing for strings. I've also heard big budget string sections sound small and MIDI-like due to the unimaginative writing of the novice arranger. I also must stay with strings in the pop/rock context because there are certain things that apply here only and not in the classical world, of which I have very little experience.

The violin family is several hundred years old, more powerful descendants of the viol family which used gut strings and not the more powerful metal strings we're used to today. The violin family (that includes the viola, cello and bass) have a rich cluster of overtones that make them sound the way they do and there are many ways of enhancing these overtones in recording. When used in a pop context the huge hall and sparse mic technique of the classical world won't work with the tight precision of a rock track. Especially nowadays when we are getting fanatical if our MIDI strings are two ticks off center. The reverberation of a huge room is often anti-tightness. Recently I did some live recording in a large London room with a singer, also playing piano accompanied by a 40-piece scaled-down symphony orchestra. When I counted in I had to leave off the number 4 because the reverberation of my voice leaked onto the first beat of the song. I know it's every engineer's dream to record strings in a huge room but no matter how huge the room is artificial reverb is added in the mix anyway. Recording pop or rock is not reality! You could never record a loud rock band and a moderate size string section in the same room anyway.

Ideally I like to work with small section consisting of minimally twelve violins, four violas, three celli and one double bass. I like them to be in a room that would fit about double that amount of players with a ceiling no lower than 12 feet. I have worked with the same size ensemble in smaller rooms with great results too, because the reverb is always added in the mix anyway. But the dimensions of the room help round out the lower frequencies of the instruments. I like to close mic to get the sound of the bow on the string. If a string section is playing to a rock track you must hear that resin! So I will have one mic per two players for violins and violas, always top quality condenser mikes! For the celli and bass I prefer one mic each, and aimed at one "F" hole and where the bow touches the strings. Then I place a stereo pair above the entire ensemble to catch the warmth of the ensemble and I use these mics about 50 percent and the spot mics 50 percent in the mix. If I record a smaller group I use more or less the same mics. A string quartet gets one mic each, plus the stereo pair for the ensemble sound. If I had a larger section I'd use one mic per 4 violins, etc. Of course with lots of mics a phase check should be carefully made; it's the same problem as when you are miking a large drum kit.

In a perfect world I love to record each section on a separate track, dividing the violins into two sections, and the ambiance on separate tracks too. Often I have fewer tracks than that and sometimes only two tracks are left for the entire string section; then it's a careful balancing act with more lower strings in the balance than what appears to be normal. When using strings with a rock track, there is a lot of competition in the low end and the low strings seem to disappear.

I don't approach strings as something from another, more aesthetic world. If strings are to go over a tough rock track then they must be recorded tough. I've seen many a cool rock engineer intimidated by the sight of a room full of middle-aged players and $30,000,000 worth of Stradivari. If the track is loud and raucous then the strings should be recorded likewise. It's also quite appropriate to record with a fair amount of compression so that the energy matches that of the guitars and bass (also stringed instruments).

Headphones also changed the way strings are recorded. When I first started writing for strings in London, the players refused headphones. I had to wear them and conduct furiously to keep them in time. Often we had to play the backing track in the room through a speaker for them which would lead to leakage problems which was sometimes a blessing on the mix, but often not! In the early seventies the younger string players knew that their elders where always chronically behind the beat and so they "invented" the technique of listening to half a headphone, the right ear is listening to the track and the left ear to the fiddle. Remember, those things don't have frets!

As for writing, my Cecil Forsyth book *Orchestration* (my bible) has over 60 pages devoted to the violin alone. I won't go into this deeply here but the writing of some classical composers is worth examining when writing for a rock track. Beethoven comes to mind. Because the violin family doesn't have frets you must have the minimum of one or three players per part. Otherwise the tuning will be abominable! It is impossible for two players to play in tune for any length of time. One player can only be in tune with himself. But with three, according to the law of averages, one will be in tune, one will be sharp and the other one flat. This will "temper" the tuning of the part. With a small section I don't write in the very high registers; a few instruments will sound "squeaky" up there. With very high writing I almost always have half the violins playing the same part an octave lower.

There are so many ways of playing a violin. For more warmth they can clip a small lead weight on the bridge and this is called a mute, or *sordino* in Italian. This works well against acoustic guitar based tracks. For pizzicato (plucking the strings with a finger) the volume often drops considerably. This can be addressed two ways. Warn the engineer so that he can push the faders up on pizzicato passages, or ask the players to stand up and play putting them closer to the mikes. For 'col legno in a concert the players tap the strings with the wood side of the bow; in the studio a pencil sounds much better. Try col legno sometimes instead of pizzicato, you'll be surprised.

A final word on professionalism when recording strings: A room full of string players is very, very expensive. Each player is being paid hundreds for three hours of work. You should set up and test all mikes and headphones the night before or at least two hours before the session (string players start arriving an hour before the session time). You don't want to be setting up with twenty temperamental musicians underfoot (not to mention the odd violin, which is very easy to step on). With mic stands allow room for bowing (the right elbow). Give each two players one mic stand to share. Check for squeaky chairs and replace them! Because you have to get a sound very quickly on such an expensive section, ask every section to play the loudest section of the arrangement several times. In other words if you are using three mics for six first violins, have each pair of players play separately from the other four. When your mic levels and EQ are achieved (EQ the first mic and match the other two with the same settings) ask them all to play at once to check that the three mikes are truly capturing six musicians equally (these are mixed to one track so get it right, dude). Then do the same with the rest of the players. This should take about ten minutes tops, and then you can get on with the pleasures of recording twenty highly trained experts!

CHAPTER 22

Surround Sound Recording and Mixing

For decades, audio specialists have been trying to expand the sense of space and point of origin in recorded music. Reverbs and delays can only do so much sonic trickery in mono and stereo recordings to provide the listener with a sense of space. In the early seventies, the music industry launched quadraphonic sound to the consumer market. It was too early and, for various reasons, the format was a bust. Obviously, the motive behind quad was to place the listener in the middle of the audio experience. Almost thirty years later, the industry is ready to go after the consumer surround music experience. Much has changed since quad. The introduction of digital technology and the proliferation of home surround systems for television has sent an encouraging signal to the industry that the public might be ready and willing to buy into DVD-A. At the time of this writing, the major labels are in the midst of a major roll-out of back catalog classics.

While CDs hardly held a candle to a well recorded and pressed vinyl album on a good system, the average CD player and CD sounded better than most beat-up home turntables and scratchy records. The convenience of CD helped hasten the demise of the LP, along with the fact that the industry was determined to kill the vinyl record.

With DVD-A, it looks like we have arrived at a format that will allow listeners to hear typical CD quality surround, as well as serious hi-fi resolution stereo.

For this chapter, I have asked three very knowledgeable contributors to discuss surround. Elliot Scheiner and Chuck Ainlay have decades of platinum and award-winning credits, while Doug Mitchell has worked extensively in surround and is one of the country's most knowledgeable educators on the subject. Mitchell contributed a finished piece on surround, which included quotes from a number of pros in the surround field. Finally, I close out this chapter with some thoughts from Peter Gabriel on quality sound and surround.

ELLIOT SCHEINER

Elliot Scheiner is one of the recording industry's most esteemed producer/engineers and is at the forefront of surround mixing. Besides credits that include Steely Dan, Van Morrison, The Eagles, Fleetwood Mac, B.B. King, Aerosmith, Sting and many others, Scheiner has also done numerous surround mixes on classic albums by Queen, R.E.M., Sting, The Eagles, The Doobie Brothers and a slew of other titles. Scheiner has won five Grammys and has been nominated for twenty, and he received the Surround Pioneer Award in 2002.

I still remember how scared I was when I walked into Capitol Studios C to mix my first 5.1 surround. In this chapter, I'll give you the basic concept for creating your surround mix. I'll assume that your console can be configured for 5.1. You'll find that many studios and homes have totally different speaker set-ups. My recommendation is to use the DTS alignment for speaker positioning. You can probably get it from their Website. I've found this placement to be the most accurate. If you don't have a console or system configured for 5.1, you'll need to get a 5.1 monitoring system such as the Otari Pic Mix.

You'll be at a great advantage if you're mixing a project that you've already mixed in stereo. My recommendation, if this is true, would be to recall the original stereo mix and make that your starting point. When I proceed along these lines, I'll generally start with repositioning the bass and drums and any loops or percussion. Remember that there are no rules for this type of mixing. You can place them wherever you like.

I'm fairly old hat about this, so I would probably put the drums in the front left and right with a small amount of kick and snare in the center. I'm making use of the center for a bit more focus on those drums. I would also probably put the bass in the same place as the drums, including the center channel.

Once I've done this, I'm going to consider what of these elements I want to add to the sub channel. I don't use bass management. I just put elements that have low frequency characteristics into the sub. For example, I might place the kick, bass, toms, certain percussion instruments and (at times) low strings and low brass into the sub. I would recommend you being selective about this and don't allow there to be a sub channel that is derivative of the other five channels.

Now that you've gotten this far, it's time to start placing everything else into the mix. I couldn't possibly tell you how to go about this. This is all a matter of taste. All I can say is you should try to remain faithful to the original stereo mix in terms of balance. I think it's usually integral to the music. Too many cheap tricks in a 5.1 mix can become distracting. I'm talking about constant panning from speaker to speaker. Try to avoid the temptation to constant movement. It most definitely detracts from the music.

Now that you've created the mix, what are you going to record it to? There are many options at the present time, and most mastering and authoring facilities have most of the options. I will say that if you have a multi-track master that has been recorded digitally at either 44.1 or 48 k, don't waste your time trying to upsample. Even

going through an analog stage is not going to help. You'll never get your recording to be 96 k.

If you're mixing for DVD-A you can place a 44.1 or 48 k mix in a 96 k mix easily. At the present time, I don't feel that I should recommend a multi-channel mix, due to the unreliability of many of the machines available. Good luck on that one. However, the one format that you can trust is an analog 8-track machine. So, if you decide to do that, you'll be in good shape, especially in the future for any new formats that may arise.

In closing, remember that this is a new frontier and there are no rules for aesthetics. Just have a good time and allow the listener to have a good time.

DOUG MITCHELL

Doug Mitchell is an associate professor of recording industry. He received his B.A. degree in mass communication and his M.A. degree in communication, with an emphasis in recording arts and sciences, from the University of Wisconsin–Milwaukee. Doug worked as promotions director and production manager for Narada Records. After working as a sales consultant for AudioLine Inc., a professional audio sales and installation facility, he established his own company, Mitchell Audio Consulting, where he designed, built and supplied recording and production studios. He has worked as an independent recording and studio maintenance engineer with specializations in music and commercial production and live remote broadcast. Mitchell taught audio production courses at the University of Wisconsin–Milwaukee from 1984 to 1993.

Doug has a technical background and, in addition to maintaining and repairing professional audio equipment, he has worked as service manager for an audiophile retail salon. He continues to work as an independent recording and audio post-production engineer. His research interests are in multi-channel music and audio for film and video production, electronic music and audio for multimedia.

He is a member of the Audio Engineering Society (AES), the National Academy of Recording Arts and Sciences (NARAS), the Society of Motion Picture and Television Engineers (SMPTE), and the International Television Association (ITVA).

So, you want to get on the audio bandwagon and do some music mixing in surround? You'll be glad to know that you are in good company and you'll also be glad to know that there are many inventive possibilities with very few rules—in fact, many are being made up as we go along. Additionally, the tools and techniques for mixing in surround are improving at a radical pace to allow you the most creative freedom in your mix.

However, you must first be aware that there is some history to the world of surround music mixing. The first attempts in this arena occurred over 50 years ago. It was in 1940 that Disney Studios released the movie *Fantasia*. *Fantasia* utilized a sound reproduction process known as Fantasound. The Fantasound experiments included the placement of three horn loudspeakers placed across the stage and two horn loudspeakers placed in the rear corners of the auditorium. The panoramic potentiometer (now known as the pan pot) was developed as part of the Fantasound process allowing two optical tracks on the film: one to be delegated for the center loudspeaker and another to be divided among the four separate remaining loudspeakers. After experimentation, another pair of loudspeakers was added to the side walls of the theater and another loudspeaker added to the ceiling.

Following Disney's experiments, additional multi-channel formats were developed for widescreen format film in its competition for viewers with television. Then the debacle of quadraphonic sound occurred in the late sixties and early seventies. Mercifully, the quad era only lasted a few years. The market was unprepared for quadraphonic technology—especially in terms of technological delivery. The numerous and competing formats also helped to seal its demise. Multi-channel music delivery would have to wait another twenty years for an appropriate technological delivery medium to be in place.

Blockbuster movies in the late seventies, including *Star Wars*, *Apocalypse Now* and *Close Encounters of the Third Kind*, ushered multi-channel sound for picture into the public mindset. The soundtracks for these and most other films released throughout the late seventies and into the eighties relied on Dolby Cinema technology. Dolby Laboratories developed cinema sound

processors that borrowed from previous quadraphonic ideas so that the discrete left, center, right and monophonic surround channels could be matrixed onto a two-channel optical film soundtrack. In the theatre the two channels are decoded back to the four channel locations. It wouldn't take long for additional enhancements to bring this type of delivery into the home with Dolby ProLogic and THX home audio systems in the early 1980s.

Of course, the new delivery formats are in the digital domain—both at home and in the theatre. The Dolby AC-3 specification for digital film sound was introduced in 1992 with the release of *Batman Returns*. The data reduction technique developed by Dolby placed digital information between the sprocket holes on the film for each of the sound channels (left, center, right, rear left, rear right and LFE—Low Frequency Effects). The release of the DVD-Video specification in 1995 allowed for both an increase in the amount of data that could be stored on a CD-style disc and a specification that called for AC-3 coding of the discrete digital audio channels representing a full 5.1 channel listening environment. Two new formats: Super Audio Compact Disc (SACD) and DVD-Audio are intended to make high performance audio systems capable of playing back multi-channel audio mixes. Neither of these systems utilizes aural data compression. However, both are intended as primarily music-oriented release formats. Both formats are being developed to allow the inclusion of navigation systems and may include text, artwork and brief video material as well.

An appropriate place to begin with multi-channel music production may be at the recording end. Just how might you begin to record material that is intended for multi-channel release? As multi-channel music production matures, undoubtedly there will develop new sets of production standards—similar to the conventions presently utilized in two-channel stereo work. However, those who are currently engaging in multi-channel music production are developing their own standards and adapting previously proven techniques. There have been a number of microphone techniques proposed for recording up to 5.1 channels of information but these continue to be developed. I'll relate a few of the documented techniques here. However, keep in mind that in this arena there are few rules and if you think of an idea that might work, try it out!

To begin our discussion of microphone techniques for capturing a multi-channel soundfield it might be prudent to indicate that the conventions utilized for stereo two-channel microphone technique are applicable—if not more so. Obviously any technique utilized should minimize phase error to prevent phasing and comb filtering between two or more channels. It might also be a good idea to check the downmix performance of the technique being attempted. Keep in mind that not all consumers of your multi-channel mixes will have the capability of playing them back in full a 5.1 monitoring environment. We'll discuss more on the area of downmixing when we examine surround monitoring. Another item to keep in mind is that just as it is certainly appropriate to record certain instruments or amplifier cabinets with a single microphone for stereo mixes, it may also be appropriate to do the same for a multi-channel recording. In fact, monophonic sources in a surround mix are easier to pan to specific locations within the room. Jerry Bruck, of Posthorn Recordings, has proposed the use of a purpose-built multi-channel microphone technique utilizing Schoeps microphones. The system utilizes a Schoeps sphere microphone combined with two Schoeps CCM 8g bi-directional microphones mounted at the sides of the sphere. Schoeps now markets this arrangement as the KFM 360. The Schoeps sphere microphone is 18 centimeters in diameter. Its pick-up response simulates the natural pick-up of the human head (like a dummy head microphone) and also relies upon pressure zone response due to the positioning of the omnidirectional elements on the sides of the sphere. Two bi-directional microphones are mounted on the sides of the sphere in the same positions as the omni elements. A mid-side matrix of the resulting pick-up allows the engineer to derive both front and rear left/right outputs. The center channel is derived from a separately matrixed and filtered sum of the two front channels. Schoeps separately markets a pre-amplifier/matrix decoder called the DSP 4 Surround. This unit also allows for the alteration of the resulting front directional pattern from omni-directional to cardioid to figure eight. The

rear-facing directional outputs may exhibit the same pattern as the front, or a different pattern may be derived to suit the acoustical balance.

Another multi-channel microphone technique has been proposed by John Klepko. This microphone array is composed of three directional microphones representing left, center, and right channels. The surround channels are represented by pick-up from a dummy head microphone. Each of the three front microphones is spaced 17.5 centimeters apart. They are positioned 124 centimeters in front of the dummy head. Each of the five microphones employed utilizes the same transducer element (condenser/large or small diaphragm). The left and right microphones are configured for super-cardioid pick-up, while the center is configured for cardioid. The elements used in the ear molds of the dummy head are configured for omni-directional pressure response. Klepko's proposal indicated the use of a HATS microphone—a dummy head complete with a torso.

Curt Wittig and Neil Muncy developed the Double M-S microphone technique while they taught courses at the National Public Radio Music Recording Workshops in the 1980s along with David Moulton, Paul Blakemore and Skip Pizzi. It was developed for two-channel stereo as a solution to the problem of making stereo recordings that could be set up quickly with a minimum of fuss and visual clutter when making live and recorded classical music broadcasts for NPR.

The front M-S microphone pair is utilized primarily for direct sound pick-up. The rear M-S microphone pair is placed at or just beyond the critical distance of the room (the position where the power of direct sound equals the power of reverberant sound), facing away from the front pair and into the reverberant field.

The multi-channel application of this technique might be to place the output of the front pair in the front left and right, while the outputs of the reverberant field M-S pair are directed to the rear left and right. The matrix describes no center channel information, although it is easily derived by feeding the output of the front-facing cardioid microphone to the center speaker without the benefit of the mid-side matrix. Curt has successfully used this arrangement for a number of years. He also describes a variation of 5.1 stereo by modifying this set-up with a sixth captured overhead channel that creates a tangible, and very stable, three-dimensional stereo surround illusion.

Michael Bishop has developed a modified version of the Double M-S surround array technique. He uses both the Neumann KU 100 dummy head and laterally positioned M-S pairs. He describes the set-up as thus: "The M-S pairs are positioned three to eight feet behind the dummy head and are usually placed about six feet apart from one another on each side. For the M-S pairs I use the Sennheiser MKH50 and MKH30 microphones. When I matrix the M-S pairs I may have to pan the cardioid microphone to fill the sides. It's very touchy to get the panning and imaging correct, especially with panning across the sides. Prior to the recording, I'll have an assistant go out of the room and walk around the microphone array while I listen to the decoded M-S matrix. In order to get the surround microphones to breathe, I place them perhaps a few feet back or even further if the acoustics of the hall call for it."

The SoundField MKV microphone is uniquely suited to multi-channel recording. This microphone design consists of four separate microphone elements arranged in a tetrahedron (three-sided pyramid) in the capsule. The outputs of these four separate elements are matrixed in multiple M-S pairs in the SoundField MKV controller unit to form four discrete channels. These channels, called "B-Format" are termed "X" for depth, "Y" for width, "Z" for height, and omnidirectional pressure or "W".

The SoundField microphone, and the corresponding surround system called Ambisonics, was developed in the late 1960s by Michael Gerzon of the Mathematical Institute in Oxford, UK, Professor Peter Fellgett at the University of Reading, and others.

In 1992, Michael Gerzon, working with Geoff Barton of Trifield Productions, Limited in Britain, proposed a 5.1 version of the decoder. The resulting technique was presented at the 1992 AES Convention in Vienna, and is now referred to as G-Format.

SoundField Research now produces a 5.1 G-Format SoundField microphone decoder that allows users of SoundField microphones to produce 5.1 outputs from the microphone.

Two Tonmeister students from Germany, Volker Henkels and Ulf Herrmann, developed the ICA-5 multi-channel microphone technique following research they performed comparing various multi-channel microphone techniques. The design calls for five matched dual-diaphragm condenser capsules mounted on a star-shaped bracket assembly.

The front-facing microphones are positioned at 90 degrees to one another, mounted on spokes 17.5 centimeters from the center. The left and right surround microphones are positioned at 60 degrees to one another and are 59.5 centimeters from the center.

Two German Companies, Sound Performance Laboratories (SPL) and Brauner Microphones, collaborated to produce the Atmos 5.1—a commercial version of the ICA-5 system. Their Atmos 5.1 utilizes Brauner ASM 5 microphones developed by Dirk Brauner. The bracket allows for adjustable positioning of all microphones in the array. The second component of the Atmos 5.1 system is the controller/pre-amp produced by SPL. Although the ICA-5 defines the use of cardioid microphones, the Atmos 5.1 system allows for continuous polar variability to accommodate a variety of acoustical environments.

A recent development that has gained attention for recording in 5.1 is the Holophone microphone system developed by Mike Gottfried. This football-shaped microphone captures a full 5.1 surround soundfield and may be utilized with wireless transmitters to aid in the portability of the system. This technique has already been used with a high degree of success at major sporting events including the 34th Superbowl.

Another technique, described by surround recording engineer Bobby Owsinski, utilizes five small lavalier-style microphones mounted on a circular ring. This ring might be mounted over the head of a drummer to pick up the sound of the drums in a five-channel array.

Although most of the techniques described in this article might be most ideally suited for classical or jazz multi-channel recordings, there are certain situations where any engineer might try any one of these arrays. This "experimentation" is perhaps the most exciting aspect of the process of recording for multi-channel: there are few rules to go by, and we get to make them up as we go along.

CHUCK AINLAY

I got interested in the idea of doing surround sound production after hearing quad recordings in the seventies. They gave me my initial impressions, as well as hearing films in surround at movie theaters later on. I don't think I actually thought about doing a music mix in surround other than the work for film tracks that I had done, because at the time there wasn't any delivery format that I was aware of. When I was approached by Tony Brown, of MCA Records, about doing Vince Gill's "High Lonesome Sound" for DTS in 5.1, you can only imagine that I leapt at the chance.

When I started, the first roadblocks I encountered were primarily due to the fact that we were forging new ground and little was known. Speaker set-up, bass management, how to monitor in 5.1 on consoles not equipped to do so were some of the technical problems. There were also ideological questions as to what to do with the center channel and what to pan to the rears or how much to engage the listener with a music-only surround mix.

A lot of my concepts about mixing for surround had to do with how ultimately the casual listener might come into contact with a surround mix and I realized that most of the conditions would probably be less than perfect. Center channel speaker being a different voicing than the left and right speakers, rear channels intended only for ambience and being under-powered and of insufficient bandwidth, bass management levels and car systems were also some of the unknowns.

So far my experience is with 5.1 only and I haven't done anything for formats above that and really, I think that it is unlikely that the consumer will allow any more speakers in their home. Formats like 6.1, 7.1 and up are for the movie theaters and special venues. The formats of music I have done in 5.1 have been delivered on Dolby digital, DTS, DVD-video and DVD-audio.

Even before I started working with surround, I think the way I've always understood mixing was in a three dimensional environment. The picture I have always tried to create was three dimensional, but the tools that I had to create that environment only allowed for a three dimensional perception

within a two dimensional stereo space. So I had to create the perception that there was depth, but in reality, it was a flat space, with tricks to make the mind's eye to view depth.

Personally, I don't think the thought process I use for mixing 5.1 is really different than when I'm creating a stereo mix. The uninitiated mixer shouldn't get scared jumping into a 5.1 mix. You are probably already correctly thinking all the things that you need to think. The techniques of doing some things are different, but with experience, it'll become easier and quicker to do. You're just within the soundfield as oppose to looking at it.

With 5.1, we can now actually create a cubicle or create an expanse that surrounds the listener and the vision that was originally perceived for the stereo mix can now be actually expanded in a three dimensional realm around the listener.

It's the difference between looking at a canvas or looking at a holographic image. You can get a sense of depth when you are looking at a canvas, but that perception of depth happens only when you look at it one way. In a surround mix or a holographic image, you can walk around that image or you can be within and look at it from many different angles. Obviously, you can sit in the middle of it and be within that landscape or that painting and have it surrounding you. You can also move to the edges and look at each corner of it and see the picture from so many different angles. I think what's interesting about surround mixing is that it can take on so many different appreciative points of reference.

If you have a picture on the wall, you can look at it straight on or you can walk over to the side of it and look at it, but it doesn't really change all that much. You see what the painter had in mind by trying to fill your whole peripheral vision or create depth, but it's always going to be one landscape that never really changes no matter how you walk around it to get a different sense of the painting.

With a holographic image or 5.1 mix, you can actually walk around it and see the rear of it or the front of it. You can sit in the center of it, which is the reference perspective, but you can also move about within that landscape and you get a different mix of instruments. You appreciate the musical event in a completely different way. You may be able to concentrate more on one instrument than the whole if you're off to one corner.

As a mixer I think it's important to understand that the listener may be hearing this from more perspectives than that one central location and it is important to accommodate the variety of listening positions by making that mix compatible in many different listening situations. I think that will be the ongoing challenge for people trying this brave this new world of 5.1.

There is a real need to create tools that can fine tune signal placement of discrete elements better. I think the new Lexicon 960 or the TC 6000 offer that kind of power. That said, it's almost as if we need to be able to have one of those kind of units on every channel, so that you could take a discrete element and put it through a multi-channel processor that would create the space that you had in your mind. If you had that kind of set-up, you would be able to accurately put the discrete element where the sound would be initiated. That way you could create all the appropriate early reflections and reverberant fields around that within that 5.1 box, to accurately reproduce that locale, rather than take a dry element and just put it in the surround field.

Let's say for example, you place the signal to the left rear and then use lots of different reverbs and delays so forth, to kind of imitate what would happen in a real situation or even an artificial situation that you'd expect to hear.

Let's say I want a background vocalist to appear from behind me over my left shoulder. If I were to merely pan it, you would be feeding all the speakers the same thing in just slightly different proportions. The problem with that is, our ears have trouble with the phase relationship of those different point sources. It's actually coming from five different places, not one that's just over our shoulder. So if there is any movement by the listener there is a comb filter effect. It works fine in stereo, because our ears understand the two points where the sound is coming from, and create the appropriate phantom image. When you have more than two sound sources, the ear gets confused.

What I propose is to feed all speakers something slightly different. That way it tends to limit the comb filter effect at the listening position. It may be that I feed the front speakers a delay of

close proximity, like ten or maybe twenty milliseconds of a delay from the original source. That way, it's actually something slightly different. It might have some harmonizing to it or chorusing. That tends to pull the source off of the left rear speaker, but it's a unique element that's fed to the front speakers.

The way I actually go about doing it is that I set up delays and harmonizers for the front and the rear. Then I can feed those effects varying amounts to create the desired ambient space.

It would be great if each channel had something with the capabilities like the Lexicon 960 or the TC 6000. Right now, I'm experimenting with using the capabilities of my new Steinberg Nuendo hard disk system and mixing within it. This allows me to use surround plug-ins to achieve that capacity of dimensional controls per channel. The problem at present is having the horsepower to open up enough plug-ins to achieve this flexibility on every channel. I'm eagerly anticipating the release of things like the new TC Powercore that will provide external processing to the host computer.

When I'm doing surround re-mixes, things that may have worked in the stereo mix, maybe don't work when they're exposed in this new setting. An example may be a single delay on a guitar solo that may have created this sort of illusion of sustain and distance on a stereo field. Nevertheless, when the effect is exposed in the surround mix, you may actually hear that single delay in a different light and it sounds like a gimmick. In that situation, you may have to rethink the application of that single delay. Maybe it's a dual front back delay that bounces between front and back speakers, rather then the individual delay that was used in the stereo mix. In surround it's always more interesting to hear things with movement utilize this expanded soundstage.

If the album you are re-mixing to 5.1 is a classic that is held dear to many listeners in stereo, those listeners may feel cheated when they hear the surround, if the whole conceptualization has changed too dramatically.

Monitoring is definitely a huge issue in 5.1. It's important that the monitors be as full range as possible in 5.1. We can get away with small monitors, when working in stereo, because they're generally set on top of the console and have an increased bass response due to coupling from the proximity of the console surface.

Since the 5.1 set-up will be a mid-field speaker arrangement, you have to be careful about the way you handle the bass. There is a very real trap that many 5.1 mixers get caught in when trying to deal with low end. You may be just pumping a lot of low end into the sub-woofer channel which, when that's reproduced on a full range system, would create an exaggerated low end. It is therefore important to use bass management.

Bass management is a system where the feed to the five speakers is crossed over so that the low end of each channel is combined with the sub channel to feed the sub-woofer. As a result, the sub-woofer takes over the very low end frequency range of the entire speaker system.

When monitoring to see if the bass in the mix is properly balanced, I occasionally mute the sub feed to make sure that what I'm doing with the bass is necessary.

The most recent project that I have done is a re-mix of Mark Knopfler's *Sailing to Philadelphia*. The album was originally mixed at Air Studios in London, England, on their custom Air Neve that had no option for surround panning. In order to maintain the sonics of that desk and all of the automation and console recall parameters, we ended up busing out the 24 track bus and direct outs of a Neve to a Sony R-100 digital desk. The Sony was used for its automated surround panning and additional EQ, compression and fader moves. We monitored on KRK E8's with a Dynaudio 18" subwoofer. Most of the multi-tracks had ended up on a Sony 3348 by the time we originally got to mix so that's why the 48 kHz sampling rate was chosen and the mixes were then stored to Genex 8500 M.O. at 24 bit.

We actually did the mastering EQ and whatnot back at my studio in Nashville (Back Stage at Sound Stage Studios) where we loaded the mixes into a Steinberg Nuendo system. Monitoring was done on the new Nova powered monitors. We did a direct digital transfer to Georgetown Masters' Sonic Solutions system for authoring and MLP encoding.

I think artists and writers are beginning to think surround sound from the creation stage. I can't wait until Mark (Knopfler) and I make a record together where we're doing the sounds in surround and conceptualizing the music in surround from the very beginning of the project. One of the main reasons Mark wanted to do this 5.1 re-mix of *Sailing to Philadelphia* was to start understanding what 5.1 is.

When we did Dire Straits' *On Every Street*, that was back when Q Sound was available. Mark had been approached to do the album in Q Sound, but at the time, it was just a distraction to Mark because it wasn't discrete like 5.1. When he first heard 5.1, his comment was "well nobody's done it right yet, but I can see the potential." I think that was the same thing he felt when we did this surround re-mix of a stereo album. With the re-mix of *Sailing to Philadelphia*, I think Mark felt somewhat limited in that we were doing a recall. The effects had already been established in stereo and we were simply expanding everything into 5.1. I know he's really more intrigued by the idea of conceptualizing something in 5.1 and taking it from the beginning to the end. He's really pumped about the next album and doing it in surround.

Since we will be conceiving the next record as a surround release, I think we'll be approaching the re-mixes the other way around. By that I mean that the 5.1 product is what it is and the stereo will be a stereo reproduction of the 5.1. I think that's when 5.1 will be at its most interesting. You will not limited by the whole conceptualization of the original stereo event.

PETER GABRIEL

Since his role in the late sixties as a founding member and theatrical front man for the progressive art-rock group Genesis, through his over 25 years of critically acclaimed solo artistry and advocacy of human rights worldwide, Gabriel's conceptual and emotionally deep creative vision (as represented through his albums and other multimedia endeavors) has enabled him to achieve that rare balancing act of uncompromising artistry and worldwide multi-platinum success. Gabriel's fascination concerning the possibilities of technology, coupled with his altruistic consciousness-raising endeavors, has placed him in a position of high credibility as a voice for inspiring people to think outside the box for the good of art and humanity. The following are a few thoughts on quality audio and surround.

SACD and DVD-Audio are both worthwhile improvements over what we have at the moment. To an average listener, there may be small differences, but as you know, when you spend so much time in the studio trying to get things to sound right—anything that allows people in on all of that work and the effort that you put in, you appreciate.

Like most things in life, if you want to put love and attention into something, it will most likely have greater worth to people and mean more to them. That is certainly true with this 5.1 thing. I love 5.1. Sometimes you can't squeeze everything in comfortably into a stereo picture. There is a lot more space in a 5.1 environment.

Most record companies, I'm disappointed to say, are just throwing these albums out to mixers who sort of rush these through things without a lot of love and attention. It is a crying shame.

I really encourage people to take some time and effort and get people who really care [about doing] your 5.1's, and if you play with sound or enjoy sound as most of us do, then there are some wonderful things you can do with it and allow people inside the music in ways that they haven't been allowed before.

CHAPTER 23

Vocals

If you look at the classic popular vocal recordings that have endured over the decades, the primary element that has helped get the magic across was not a cleverly gated million-dollar drum sound, but rather a vocal performance that communicated something essential that touched countless listeners.

A great vocal performance often contains qualities that transcend mere technique. Great engineers and producers are those who are hip to the sometimes fleeting moments where art is happening—almost in spite of the artist—and genius is realized.

I enlisted five engineer and producers whose credits run the gamut from Gloria Estefan and the Rolling Stones to Metallica, Willie Nelson, and John Michael Montgomery. I also invited a highly regarded vocal coach and producer to offer extra input. I would also like to thank Lisa Roy and Susan Zekovsky for helping facilitate the realization of this chapter.

While this chapter addresses microphones, mic pre-amps and outboard gear techniques, each of these contributors underscores the essential importance of providing the right psychological support to the singer or singers. After all, great mic technique can salvage a bad recording climate, while some of the most powerfully immediate vocal performances have been caught in the most primitive of recording situations, where everyone felt in sync with the truth of the moment.

ED CHERNEY

Ed Cherney is one of the recording world's most highly regarded engineers, mixers and producers. Cherney's credits include Jann Arden, Bonnie Raitt, the Rolling Stones, and Richie Sambora, among many others.

To me, a vocal is the hardest thing to record. It is harder than a hundred-piece orchestra or a three-piece rock and roll band. That is probably because it is a very literal instrument. Typically, on a recording, a voice sounds like what a voice sounds like, unless you are filtering it or doing other things to it to make it fit into the music. It is also the most dynamic instrument there is, too. It goes from being really soft to being really loud and you need a microphone that can deal with that.

After about a dozen records, the Audio Technica 4050 is the first mic I put up for most singers. I used it on Jann Arden and Richie Sambora, as well as a lot of the Rolling Stones record I just did. The Audio Technica is smooth, very clear and open sounding and it has a lot of headroom. It is also a very consistent sounding mic.

That said, mic selection changes for every vocalist and situation, and sometimes I may get stuck with a microphone, not necessarily because of the way it sounds, but as a result of the way the music is tracked. I might have an artist who may like to be out in the room singing live vocals with the musicians playing for whatever spark of energy they can get out there and the groove. In that kind of situation, I have to consider the mic's rear rejection capabilities and how tight the mic is when you put the singer into the room. I also may not be familiar with the singer's voice and I'll put up a microphone and get a really great take and 75 percent of that vocal performance may be a keeper, and I'll have go back and match it up to punch in the lines in that I need. As a result, I'm stuck using that microphone and that particular set-up to get the vocal to match. Then later, in mixing, I will try and get it sounding the way it probably should.

I rarely use mic pre-amps that are on the newer consoles. I have a rack of old Neve 1073's that I carry around with me. I really love the way the old mic pre-amps sound. They have plenty of headroom and they are typically really rich and open at the same time.

To get singers to sing great is mostly psychological. A great performance will always transcend a less than great sound on a vocal. I think that everything that you do has to be designed around making the singer feel comfortable and for me that means getting it quick. The first time that singer is sitting in front of a microphone, I hit record and get everything they do.

Part of it, too, is letting them sing and staying off of the talkback. I let them sing the song five, six or seven times. That may entail building a slave reel, so you have plenty of tracks to comp and do your vocals.

It is all about creating that environment, making sure that the temperature is nice in the studio. If the lights are right and the headphone balance is perfect and that the singer feels that you are working with them, and you are not trying to bust their balls, then they sing better. I also always try to have the singer's principal instrument in their hand when they are singing.

Also as a producer, you have to understand that it may not be a great day for the singer, and you go on to something else.

Of course, you try and plan out the session, like you are going to have vocals recorded on this day, but "vocal" day is like putting all of your eggs in one basket. It is the added pressure of "Well I have to do it now. It is now or never." I never want to create that situation.

You should have the option of singing a song anytime you want. If you feel it now, well the mic is open so go get it. I even do that when we are mixing a song. If I feel there is maybe a phrase or a line or verse or something that can be phrased better and you are looking for that thing, I just want to be sure that everyone is free enough to go do it, when the moment happens. I want to make sure that I have tape on the machine and I have the tools ready to go in and get it. I want to be there to document these great moments that happen, because you never know when they are going to come and I want to be ready for them, as an engineer and as a producer.

RENE GRANT-WILLIAMS
Since the mid-seventies, Nashville-based vocal coach and producer Rene Grant-Williams has helped numerous singers develop artistically through her teaching methodology. Her clients over the years have included Huey Lewis, Bob Weir (of the Grateful Dead), Linda Ronstadt, Charlie Daniels, Tim McGraw, Lyle Lovett, Jill Sobule, Kim Wilson (of the Fabulous Thunderbirds), the Subdudes, Sonny Landreth, and Doug Stone.

One of the things that is important to keep in mind is that the singer is a living organism, and the quality of the vocal will depend on how healthy and resilient and well-prepared that organism is. One of the things to take into consideration is scheduling. Sometimes the singer will wear out the voice singing rough vocal with the tracks two or three days in a row, and then the next day final vocals may be scheduled and there is nothing left. It is important to remember that, while the voice is a very resilient thing, it can get too thin and lose its elasticity and resilience.

It is important to give the singer time to re-warm up and re-establish their technique and be aware that it is like a runner running short sprints. It is very important that runner limbers up and doesn't just run hard and then get cold and then run hard again. You always have to take waiting around time into consideration.

I very highly favor a microphone position that is fairly low. There is a tendency for some engineers to hang a microphone high, but if you have to stretch your head up or hold your chin up, it puts tremendous strain on the voice. The best position is right at lips level or slightly below, so you can kind of contract into your body support with your head tilted slightly forward. Think about the classic Elvis position; the way he cocked his head over the microphone that kind of looked up from underneath. That allowed all of that sound to resonate up in his head, instead of putting a strain on his neck and shoulders. Support, which is the way the body powers the sound, is very important.

Perfectly normal people, who wouldn't be caught dead running around town with their hands behind their backs, will do that when there is a microphone in front of them. Suddenly, it is like, "What am I going to be doing with these things at the end of my shoulders? Let's stick them behind the back." Well, that robs you of a lot of support.

The body language from people in the control room is very important. A lot of times, people don't realize that while they are having a laugh about something totally innocuous in the control room, someone singing out on the floor, who can't hear what is going on, can become sensitive and misconstrue things. Many singers, on some level, imagine that it must be about them. It is important to create an atmosphere that is helpful to the singer.

People tend to creep up on the mic as time goes by. That is why you need to put some kind of tape marker on the floor.

Give the singer a choice of headphones to listen through so they can find what helps them the most. If the vocal is too high in a headphone mix, the vocal will tend to go flat. If the vocal is too low in the headphone mix, then the singer will often tend to push things and go sharp.

I have a problem when I hear people telling a singer to "relax." It is the one statement that I find makes a singer uptight. Nobody wants to think that they are not relaxed. There was a studio in Canada that had a sign that stated, "Try to relax or we will find someone who can" [laughs]. The point of that being is that it is a terribly intimidating thing to tell someone to "relax." Everybody likes the kind of magic that doesn't exist anywhere else.

Oftentimes, singers have trouble figuring out what they did well during a vocal performance while they are out on the floor singing with their

headphones on. I think it is important for a production team to be specific. I've been in sessions where the production team is making a singer do something over and over again and only offering statements like, "That's not getting it. Let's do it again." If the singer doesn't specifically know what aspect of the performance it is that needs to be addressed, it can be very frustrating. Again, encouragement has more to do with getting a good performance than anything.

ERIC PAUL

Eric Paul has made a career out of recording country giants like Willie Nelson, Waylon Jennings, Johnny Cash, and many other too-real-for-modern-country-radio artists. While Paul loves working with great gear, he is quick to point out gear that he feels is exemplary and affordable for most studios.

We are taught to be purists in one sense when recording voices, but the right compression while recording is great. Compressors work better off of live signals than off of tape, because a reproduced signal is never as strong and pure and has the same kind of transients that it does when it is coming off of a live microphone pre-amp.

I am very careful not to over compress. I never use more than a couple of dB of compression when I am recording a vocal.

If I am in a studio where I don't have access to a good LA-2A, my favorite low-end compressor is the Composer by Behringer. The mass public has access to those and they are in a lot of demo studios across the country. The reason that I like it is that it is transparent and it will hold back the vocals from getting out of control, and you can't "hear" it.

While I prefer the LA-2A's, it depends upon the tubes. My favorite tubes are the old GE tubes, if you can find them. You take any piece of tube gear, compressors, microphones, and you put a good old GE tube in there and it will sound so much better than anything else. I've done many comparisons.

I have a Sony C-37A that is the sweetest vocal microphone on a female voice that you have ever heard. Daniel Lanois used my C-37A on Emmylou for the *Wrecking Ball* album. Again, the trick to the whole deal is old GE tubes, which greatly improved their performance.

For male voices, I generally like the U-47, but my favorite overall microphone for voices is the Shure SM-5B.

For mic pre-amps, the API 312 is my favorite bar none. Peavey makes a dual tube microphone pre-amp that sounds great. The combination of the Peavey microphone tube pre-amp and the Behringer Composer is an accessible affordable combination for most people that is great. If they can't get a Shure SM-5, they can get Shure SM-7's, which are still available.

With analog tape, you have to be really careful not to hit the tape too hard with the vocal, because it can really do terrible things to it. In the same manner, it is important not to get too low of a level. I usually like to have my vocal peaking out at zero on a VU meter. It depends on what tape you are using and how you have it set, but I am in this case referring to 499 set at +5 over 250, which is what most everyone uses now on 499 and the new BASF 900, which I personally like better because it is quieter and it has more energy to it. It sounds like old tape to me. There is something right that the old tape had that BASF has figured out and Ampex is not doing it.

CSABA PETOCZ

Csaba Petocz is one of Nashville's hottest producer/ engineers, most recently producing platinum artist John Michael Montgomery. That project generated three number one country hits. Petocz credits are also wide-ranging, including artists like Stevie Nicks, Metallica, and Concrete Blonde.

I don't think there is any such thing as the perfect vocal mic. It is just different mics for different people. You should just understand what each different mic sound like and how it changes the sound of the human voice, and obviously select the mic that enhances the sound of the voice.

You should go out on the floor and hear the person sing and hear what it is that they do and see what part of their voices are really special. Obviously, if the person is worth recording, there is a uniqueness there and you should really try and highlight that aspect of the vocal. Over the years, I have gotten to where I can hear a singer and know within one or two mics, which should work.

If you've tried out three very expensive tube mics and you aren't happy with any of them, then the next step should immediately be something at the other end of the scale, like an SM-7. I will almost always guarantee you that, if the expensive mic doesn't work, an SM-7 will. You have to screw with EQ a little bit, but for some reason, some people sound better on them.

I think that 80 percent of getting a good vocal is in giving the singer a good headphone mix. If you can make a singer enjoy singing and really hear what is going on with the small nuances in the voice, by giving them a great headphone mix, you can get the artist to do 90 percent of your work. This is especially true if you can get them to be attuned to what it is that you would really like to hear. Most singers get challenged by it. Artists really get into the fact that you care enough to make it that 2 percent better.

More than anything that you record, the human voice is the one that reacts most to small changes. You can really make a vocal sound significantly better by changing variables minutely.

I've been in country music for about five years, and the most hi-fi aspect of country music has to be the vocals. You can have a lot of liberties in country music, but taking liberties with the vocal isn't one of them. Country is not the genre to do that in. It just doesn't work.

I went through so many years of doing "alternative" rock records that it is kind of nice to record something really well. I know that may be un-hip to say that, but I get off on the purity of it. Also, without any disrespect to any of the other musical forms, I think country and R&B have some of the most accomplished singers, and it is a lot more fun recording with someone who is a great singer.

Most recordings get it 95 percent of the way there. The challenge is to get that last extra percentage and that is what separates great vocal sounds from everyone else's. It is more than just putting up an $8,000 microphone into a $2,000 pre-amp. That 95 percent is just meat and potatoes good recording, but the last 5 percent is about how to relate to this human being who is incredibly vulnerable in front of you singing and trusts you enough to go in there and work hard enough to get that last 5 percent of the vocal that makes them sound just that much different than every other artist that is out there.

ERIC SCHILLING

Miami-based engineer/producer Eric Schilling has worked with platinum recording artist Gloria Estefan throughout her long career. He has also recorded Jon Secada and Cachao.

When you work with someone who is singing, it tends to be a one on one process. The whole key to me is to keep a rhythm so the singer never looses the flow. If you are working and they say, 'Let's go back to the verse and do lines two and three,' you want to be fast enough so that it happens in a seamless way. The moment you start going, 'Oh no, I've got to figure out where I am and I've got to fix some EQ's, they start drifting. Recording voices is one of the most fun things for me to do and I love it when that "flow" is going.

When you are working with someone who has a really "pure" voice, it is harder for them when it comes to the issue of pitch, because there are less harmonics in their voice. You easily hear it when things fall from pitch. Just to make a crude example, Karen Carpenter had to be really in tune, because she had a very pure voice, but you take a Bob Dylan, who has a kind of gruff voice and he can move the pitch around a whole lot, because his voice has a very wide spread of overtones.

It is funny how you can find an album of someone like Dylan who has that kind of voice and though you hear some pitch stuff, you don't really mind it. On the other hand, if the voice is really "pure," it can be very grating if it isn't really in tune.

Concerning pitch correction tools, I think they have a use, but it is my preference that it gets used as the last thing that you do, and not the first thing that you do. I still like to see a person who is going to come in and work on the voice and not sing it through twice and say, "Well you can fix it." I don't believe in that. I'll use it to fix some minor things on a vocal performance that may have a great overall vibe, where the singer feels that he or she can't top that level of performance again. Utilizing pitch correction at that point is probably fine.

It is funny, but sometimes when you pull it too far in tune, it doesn't feel right and it takes away the character of the performance. I don't believe that music is meant to be a perfect thing. When you sing, you don't always sing exactly on the beat, or exactly in pitch all of the time, just like if you were playing a fretless bass or anything else where you have some room to move. You have to be careful when you tamper with the recorded performance.

Generally, I am a big fan of the John Hardy mic-pres, which I think are real neutral sounding. I also like the Millennium and API. My first choice of compressor is a good LA-2A, if I can get my hands one. Another compressor I really like a lot, which you don't find that much anymore, is a Compex. It is British made compressor that used to be called a Vocal Stressor.

I always cut flat, mainly because if they are going to come back and change a part or we recorded a month earlier and they want to re-cut some lines, I find that it isn't as hard to match the sound, if I cut it flat.

With many older mics, you have to be very careful about the room you are in, because if you are in too small of a booth, you will actually start to hear the sound of that booth, especially in the lower frequencies. They essentially behave like omni's in the lower range. So if I have somebody who is working on a tube mic and they are in a small room, I am going to have them about one hand wide or five inches away. I generally use a pop screen instead of a wind screen to keep the spit off of the microphone and it keeps people from getting too close. I can always tell when they can't hear enough in the phones, because they start to push the pop screen in closer to the mic.

Concerning singing with large groups, I guess I came from the school of putting up one microphone. When I came down to Florida, my old boss was doing the Eagles records. He would put up an omni and they would stand around it and work until they got the balance.

I am not a huge fan of flying vocals in and that kind of stuff, but some people I have worked with will say, "Great, I'll sing it once and you can fly it all in." Nevertheless, if I can get them to sing the whole song through, that is my preference. I like doing it this way because the emotion changes. I just think there is a kind of stride that you hit as a background singer that is also playing into the song from an emotional point of view. If you listen to a background track that is sung the whole way next to a sampled track with the vocals flown in, the sampled track will sound static. As a result, the music will tend to feel more static, too. I see why people fly vocals in, but there is an emotional side to this that they are missing.

GAIL DAVIES

A difficult aspect of producing can be the vocals. I've been asked by other producers to come in and help them get the vocals right as this is probably my strongest suit. I learned to produce from Henry Lewy, who recorded all the early Joni Mitchell albums. We were once listening to a playback of a song I'd recorded with him and he asked me if I was singing in my head while I was listening, which I was. That, he pointed out, was canceling out what I was listening to. Things like that may sound really simple but it helps to separate yourself, especially when you're producing your own music, so you can listen objectively.

Another point, if you're trying to move through a project quickly and don't have a lot of studio time or money, is to make sure you've got at least three good vocals that you can put together at the end. Sometimes producers will concentrate solely on the music, thinking they'll get the vocal later and then find they can't get the vocals. Then they're in vocal hell for the rest of the project. I was once called in to help a budding, young producer, who later became quite famous, on a project he was doing with a friend of mine. He had spent all his energy getting the band to sound great with wonderful guitar overdubs and so forth but ended up at the end of the night with his vocalist sitting on the bathroom floor crying because she was too tired to sing.

My suggestion for the future was, once you've decided on the track you're going to use, let the musicians take a short break and have the singer take two more passes straight through the song. Then, if you find yourself in a bind later, you'll have three vocal tracks where the vocalist has the same amount of phlegm in their throat, attitude, feeling and approach to the song. If I'm really under the gun, I'll do this while laying down another acoustic guitar track at well.

If I'm working with a good singer, I try to get the vocal in the first or second take as that's usually the best one. After a while, they tend to start doing what I call "over-intellectualizing" every note and then you're dead. I like spontaneity so I'll go on to another song and come back later if I can hear the singer thinking too much instead of just singing.

To me, emotional content is extremely important in the vocals. I don't want to hear music that's perfectly in tune, unless it's a symphony that has no feeling. I can live with a few dodgy notes if there emotional content, like with Janis Joplin. I try to get singers to think beyond the microphone in front of them to the lover or person they'd be talking to. That's what makes the vocal meaningful to the listener.

PHIL RAMONE

Some people create a track and then have the vocalist come in to sing afterwards. They make this enormously wonderful track and then the vocalist sometimes doesn't work. The best way to know what you are doing is have a pilot vocal that is there to build the arrangement around. By doing this, I have some place to go, even with the worst scratch vocal happening. With a pilot vocal, you can ascertain if the guitar player and the piano player's parts are going to stay in the correct range with the vocal.

If you have a double line going on in the background that is heavy, big and powerful, you've got to make its EQ work around the voice. You are kidding yourself if you don't, because in the end the band will hate you, because they couldn't hear what they played and the singer will hate you, because you downed him out.

I think that you make the singer sound great and then you take the singer out of the equation and listen to where the band is. If it is all nasal, somewhere in the making of the record, you either missed the boat by not expressing that or recording it properly.

Concerning EQ, you can be very tough with a vocal. There are a lot of things that you can do with a vocal that, if you listen to it solo, it may not please you, but you can really get it to sit in a track.

If you are making a vocal album, you have to remember who is paying the bill, in the sense that the front cover tells who the artist is. If you get the vocal to sound great, it will work in almost every track, if you are consistent in the way you record.

You should get the sound of the singer right early. It shouldn't be a last minute, wait-till-we-get-to-the-final-mix room logic. That is why I am happy to carry an equalizer, a pre-amp and a limiter in the recording process. I get it right from day one.

You know what? Half the time, what I put in my final vocal comps come from the rehearsals. Many times, when an artist is running it down, the vocal is incredible. I'm not going to sit there and say, "You know if I had used a compressor, I could've recovered this or fixed that." That is just stupid. If you come to the gig, and you are going to race the car, you better be ready.

Don't sit around and say, "Oh yeah. In an hour I'm going to have a sound. By the way, I'm switching mics." I switch mics before I am ready. If I am going to use an Audio Technica mic, I kind of know by looking at and hearing that person, that this is the right mic. I'm about being ready. If the singer loves their voice on the first playback and says, "This is the way I feel I sound," then you have done it. You and the engineer are then on an easygoing course.

You should record singers every time they sing, even when they are doing overdubs. I always keep a track for looseness while they are warming up. You might pick up six or eight lines that are just incredible, because they weren't over-analyzing what they were doing. They might go, "I'm not in voice yet, let me warm up. I can't hit those high notes." Suddenly these high notes come pouring out of them, because they are not thinking that you are recording. Without being ready with a good set-up, where do you go?

RICHARD DODD

Any vocal worthy of singing the lead in a song deserves to be recorded and mixed in a way that highlights all the personality the singer has to offer. For Richard Dodd, hiding a lead vocal in reverb and tons of effects is often counter-productive to delivering the emotional thrust of a song most meaningfully. One of Dodd's most unique abilities as an engineer and mixer concerns getting that vocal up front and rendered in a way that is very dry and present. Some of the best examples of that approach in Dodd's work can be found in The Traveling Wilburys and Tom Petty (with and without the Heartbreakers) recordings. When I asked Dodd about how he arrived at such an exceptionally dry sound, he started off by giving credit to producer Jeff Lynne, with whom he worked on platinum albums by former Beatle George Harrison, Roy Orbison, The Traveling Wilburys and Tom Petty.

I think it would be fair to say that I was given the confidence to present that [creation of an exceptionally dry sound] by having the privilege of working with Jeff Lynne so much. When I came into contact with Jeff Lynne, it was like I was able to breathe a sigh of relief. There was this kindred spirit. It was fantastic. Here was somebody asking me to do something that I wanted to do. We got into it, and we found that we could make things drier and drier and drier. We could actually make it sound like it was drier than it was [laughs]. We certainly developed a method between us of getting vocals.

Tom Petty takes charge of the track. He wouldn't suggest, I don't think, that he is perfectly in tune or anything like that, but he always performs perfectly. His vocal is interesting. If it is interesting, then it is worth listening to. If it is worth listening to, then there is no need to disguise it and cover it up and make excuses for it, which is what reverb can become.

I'm not against reverb; I'm against reverb used inappropriately. At its best, reverb can take you into an additional level of understanding. That is not meant to sound deep. It just can give you some of that element of fantasy when used correctly. In the wrong cases, it completely detracts from what is going on in the performance. The fantasy is already in there, and the story and the way the artist has cleverly constructed the lyric and the melody, the tone and phrasing. There are a million and one more important things than whether something has reverb on it, like are they going to spend any money and effort on promoting the record?

What I do is no surprise; it is all of the same things that anyone would do. I probably just do it a bit more extreme. While we were mixing Boz Scaggs' *Some Change* album, we had done a little vocal overdub. We had a lovely mic and all of this stuff. While we were listening to it on this track, Boz said, "The vocal sounds great, but I wish it sounded like it did on my headphones." He had these really hypey, wonderful Sony headphones that had this top end that never really exists anywhere in real life. So I went and got a microphone and I put the voice through those headphones and I miked them up and mixed that in with the track, and it worked! [laughs].

Distortion and noise have never bothered me. If someone can sing the tune, then you've got it right. If you haven't captured a compelling performance, nobody is going to listen to it anyway, no matter how clean or undistorted it is. If the listener hears an attractive performance, then you've played your part. Try not to screw up!

Technically, we can ruin everything. We can add reverbs and delays and sink the voice into a track and hide a perfectly good performance and kill a song: We can make it uninteresting. By the same token, when all you've got is a person with a good-sounding voice—not the greatest singer in the world, but an interesting voice—the more you put that up front and say, "Here I am. I mean this," the more credible it is. They're not hiding behind anything. It's just real.

Appendix

Expert Discography

The information in this book is the collected knowledge of many people who are among the best in the business. It makes sense that I would back up the assertion that you are reading the reflections of recording industry legends and experts by including some kind of discography to underscore the range of their experience. Trying to assemble a decent collection of album credits is quite a task; what I gathered is not meant to be a complete credits list for each of these contributors. Rather, it is meant to cover a blend of highlights and genres, as well as a few nuggets that might surprise readers. Obviously, not everyone in this book has a discography. There are equipment and room designers and other disciplines represented here, too. If there are any glaring omissions, I apologize in advance and will address this in the next edition.

Greg Adams . . . .

Michael Bolton

Timeless (The Classics) (1992)	Trumpet, Arranger, Horn Arrangements
One Thing (1993)	Trumpet

Ray Charles

Strong Love Affair (1996)	Trumpet, Arranger, Horn Arrangements

Chicago

Chicago 17 (1984)	Horn

Graham Central Station

Release Yourself (1974)	Horn
Ain't No 'bout-A-Doubt It (1975)	Arranger
Mirror (1976)	Horn

Heart

Heart Greatest Hits: Live (1980)	Horn
Bebe Le Strange (1980)	Horn, Horn Section

John Lee Hooker

Best of John Lee Hooker 1965-1974 (1992)	Trumpet

Elton John

Caribou (1974)	Trumpet, Horn
To Be Continued… (1990)	Brass Arrangement

Paul Kantner

Sunfighter (1971)	Trumpet

Dave Koz

Off the Beaten Path (1996)	Trumpet, Horn (Alto), Horn Arrangements

Huey Lewis & the News

Fore! (1986)	Trumpet, Arranger
Small World (1988)	Trumpet, Arranger
Original Gold (2001)	Trumpet, Arranger

Little Feat

Time Loves a Hero (1977)	Trumpet, Horn Arrangements

Waiting for Columbus (1978)	Trumpet
Lyle Lovett	
Road to Ensenada (1996)	Trumpet, Orchestration
Bobby McFerrin	
Bang! Zoom (1995)	Horn
Aaron Neville	
Warm Your Heart (1991)	Trumpet, Horn Arrangements
Phish	
Hoist (1994)	Flugelhorn, Horn Arrangements
Bonnie Raitt	
Nine Lives (1986)	Trumpet, Flugelhorn
Luck of the Draw (1991)	Arranger
Santana	
Welcome (1973)	Strings
Tony! Toni! Toné!	
House of Music (1996)	Trumpet
Toto	
Past to Present 1977-1990 (1990)	Horn, Horn Arrangements
Tower of Power	
East Bay Grease (1970)	Trumpet
Bump City (1972)	Piano, Trumpet, Arranger, Conductor, Flugelhorn, Horn, French Horn, Vocals
Tower of Power (1973)	Strings, Trumpet, Arranger, Conductor, Flugelhorn, Horn, Vocals, String Arrangements
Back to Oakland (1974)	Strings, Trumpet, Arranger, Conductor, Flugelhorn, Vocals (bckgr), Bells
Urban Renewal (1975)	Trumpet, Arranger, Conductor, Flugelhorn, String Arrangements
In the Slot (1975)	Trumpet, Conductor, Flugelhorn, Horn, String Arrangements
Ain't Nothin' Stoppin' Us Now (1976)	Trumpet, Conductor, Flugelhorn, Horn, Vocals, Producer, Horn Arrangements, String Arrangements
Live & In Living Color (1976)	Trumpet, Flugelhorn, Horn, Vocals
We Came to Play (1978)	Trumpet, Flugelhorn
Back on the Streets (1979)	Trumpet, Flugelhorn, Vocals (bckgr)
Direct (1988)	Trumpet, Arranger, Flugelhorn, Brass
Power (1988)	Trumpet, Flugelhorn, Horn (Alto), Vocals, Horn Arrangements, String Arrangements
Monster on a Leash (1991)	Trumpet, Flugelhorn, Vocals (bckgr), Horn Arrangements, String Arrangements
T.O.P. (1993)	Trumpet, Arranger, Flugelhorn
Direct Plus (1997)	Trumpet, Arranger, Flugelhorn, Brass
Soul Vaccination: Live (1999)	Horn Arrangements

John Agnello . . . .

Aerosmith	
Rock in a Hard Place (1982)	Engineer
Buffalo Tom	
Sleepy Eyed (1995)	Producer, Mixing
A-Sides from 1988-1999 (2000)	Producer
Rosanne Cash	
King's Record Shop (1988)	Engineer
Chainsaw Kittens	
Pop Heiress (1994)	Producer, Engineer, Mixing

Chainsaw Kittens (1996)	Mixing
Alice Cooper	
Last Temptation (1994)	Engineer
Dinosaur Jr.	
Without a Sound (1994)	Engineer, Mixing
Hand It Over (1997)	Mixing
Dish	
Boneyard Beach (1995)	Producer
Drive-By Truckers	
Dirty South (2004)	Mixing
Errortype: 11	
Amplified to Rock (2000)	Producer, Engineer, Mixing
Jay Farrar	
Sebastopol (2001)	Percussion, Guitar (Electric), Producer, Mixing
ThirdShiftGrottoSlack (2002)	Producer, Engineer, Mixing
Terroir Blues (2003)	Engineer, Mixing
Stone, Steel & Bright Lights (2004)	Mixing
Five for Fighting	
Battle for Everything (2004)	Engineer
Gigolo Aunts	
Flippin' Out (1994)	Producer, Engineer, Mixing
Miki Howard	
Very Best of Miki Howard (2001)	Engineer
Jawbox	
Jawbox (1996)	Producer, Engineer, Mixing
My Scrapbook of Fatal Accidents (1998)	Engineer
Jimmy Eat World	
Singles/Jebediah Split (2004)	Engineer, Mixing
Cyndi Lauper	
She's So Unusual (1984)	Engineer
The Murder City Devils	
In Name and Blood (2000)	Producer, Engineer, Mixing
Nebula	
Charged (2001)	Producer, Engineer, Mixing
Redd Kross	
Phaseshifter (1993)	Engineer, Mixing
Visionary (1995)	Engineer, Mixing
Skiptrace	
Skiptrace (2000)	Producer
Patti Smith	
Gone Again (1996)	Mixing
The Smithereens	
God Save the Smithereens (1999)	Engineer, Mixing
Son Volt	
Wide Swing Tremolo (1998)	Mixing
Steve Wynn	
Sweetness & Light (1997)	Producer, Engineer, Mixing
My Midnight (1999)	Producer, Engineer, Mixing
Here Comes the Miracles (2001)	Mixing

Brian Ahern ·

The Billygoats
Four (EP) (2000) — Producer, Guitar, Percussion
David Bromberg
Midnight on the Water (1975) — Guitar, Guitar (Rhythm), Producer, Engineer
Johnny Cash
Silver (1979) — Producer, Engineer, Gut String Guitar, Bass, Percussion
Johnny 99 (1983) — Tambourine, Producer, Engineer, Gut String Guitar, 6-String Bass, Percussion
Silver (SACD surround version—2002) — Producer
Rodney Crowell
Ain't Living Long Like This (1978) — Guitar, Percussion, Producer, Engineer
Emmylou Harris
Pieces of the Sky (1975) — Guitar (Acoustic), Bass, Guitar, Producer, Engineer
Elite Hotel (1975) — Guitar (Acoustic), Bass, Guitar, Producer, Engineer
Luxury Liner (1977) — Guitar (Acoustic), Bass, Guitar, Guitar (Electric), Producer, Engineer
Quarter Moon in a Ten Cent Town (1978) — Guitar (Acoustic), Bass, Guitar, Percussion, Guitar (12 String), Producer, Engineer, Gut String Guitar
Profile (The Best of Emmylou Harris) (1978) — Guitar (Acoustic), Guitar (12 String), Producer, Engineer, Gut String Guitar
Blue Kentucky Girl (1979) — Guitar (Acoustic), Banjo, Bass, Guitar, Percussion, Director, Producer, Engineer
Christmas Album (Light in the Stable) (1979) — Guitar (Acoustic), Guitar, Percussion, Arranger, Producer, Engineer, Gut String Guitar, Bass (Acoustic)
Roses in the Snow (1980) — Bass, Guitar, Percussion, Guitar (12 String), Producer, Engineer, Gut String Guitar
Cimarron (1981) — Bass, Guitar, Percussion, Arranger, Producer, Engineer, Remastering
Evangeline (1981) — Bass, Guitar, Percussion, Arranger, Producer, Engineer
Last Date (1982) — Arranger, Producer, Engineer, Remastering
White Shoes (1983) — Bass, Guitar, Percussion, Arranger, Tambourine, Vocals, Producer, Engineer, 6-String Bass
Profile 2: The Best of Emmylou Harris (1984) — Arranger, Producer, Engineer
Duets (1990) — Arranger, Producer
Songs of the West (1994) — Arranger, Producer
Portraits (1996) — Guitar (Acoustic), Bass, Percussion, Guitar (Electric), Tambourine, Guitar (12 String), Producer, Six String Banjo
Spyboy (1998) — Arranger
Anthology: The Warner/Reprise Years (2001) — Guitar (Acoustic), Banjo, Guitar (12 String), Gut String Guitar, 6-String Bass, Archguitar
Producer's Cut (DVD Audio surround—2002) — Guitar (Acoustic), Bass, Percussion, Arranger, Tambourine, Producer, Engineer, Gut String Guitar, Art Direction, Mixing, 6-String Bass, Package Design, Six String Banjo, Re-mix Producer, Guitar (12 String Acoustic), Re-mix Arrangement
Roses In The Snow (DVD Audio surround & expanded versions—2006/2002) — Bass, Guitar, Percussion, Arranger, Pipe, Guitar (12 String), Producer, Engineer, Fretless Bass, Mixing, 6-String Bass
George Jones
Bradley Barn Sessions (1994) — Guitar (Acoustic), Guitar (Electric), Producer, Liner Notes
Shane McAnally
Shane McAnally (2000) — Producer

Anne Murray

What About Me (1968)	Bass, Guitar, Percussion, Producer, Engineer, Arranger, Percussion
Snowbird (1970)	Bass, Guitar, Percussion, Producer, Engineer, Arranger, Percussion
Love Song (1974)	Bass, Guitar, Percussion, Ukulele, Producer, Engineer
Anne Murray/Glen Campbell (1972)	Producer, Engineer, Guitar
This Way Is My Way (1969)	Guitar (Acoustic), Producer, Engineer, Arranger, Percussion
Honey Wheat & Laughter (1969)	Guitar (Acoustic), Producer, Engineer, Arranger, Percussion
Straight Clean & Simple (1970)	Guitar (Acoustic), Producer, Engineer, Arranger, Percussion
Talk It Over In The Morning (1971)	Guitar (Acoustic), Producer, Engineer, Arranger, Percussion
Annie (1972)	Guitar (Acoustic), Producer, Engineer, Arranger, Percussion
Danny's Song (1973)	Guitar (Acoustic), Producer, Engineer, Arranger, Percussion
Highly Prized Possession (1974)	Guitar (Acoustic), Producer, Engineer, Arranger, Percussion
Best…So Far (1994)	Arranger, Producer

Linda Ronstadt

Get Closer (1982)	Producer

Seconds Flat

Seconds Flat (1997)	Producer

Billy Joe Shaver

Gypsy Boy (1977)	Guitar, Percussion, Producer
Honky Tonk Heroes (1994)	Guitar (Electric), Producer

Ricky Skaggs

My Father's Son (1991)	Producer
Solid Ground (1995)	Producer, Mixing

The Woodys

Woodys (1998)	Producer

Original Soundtrack

Horse Whisperer (1998)	Guitar (Acoustic), Vocals (bckgr), Producer

Chuck Ainlay . . . .

David Alan

David Alan (2001)	Producer, Engineer, Mastering, Mixing

John Anderson

Nobody's Got It All (2001)	Engineer, Mixing

John Berry

Wildest Dreams (1999)	Engineer, Mixing, Overdub Engineer

Tracy Byrd

Love Lessons (1995)	Mixing
It's About Time (1999)	Engineer

Beth Nielsen Chapman

Deeper Still (2002)	Mixing

Sheryl Crow

Very Best of Sheryl Crow (2003)	Mixing

Rodney Crowell

Let the Picture Paint Itself (1994)	Engineer

Dire Straits

On Every Street (1991)	Producer, Engineer

Dixie Chicks

Wide Open Spaces (1998)	Mixing

Steve Earle

Guitar Town (1986)	Engineer
Exit O (1987)	Engineer, Mastering, Mixing

Peter Frampton

Live in Detroit (2000)	Mixing
Frampton Comes Alive: 25th Anniversary (2001)	Mixing
Now (2003)	Engineer, Mixing
Frampton Comes Alive! [DVD Audio] (2003)	Mixing

Vince Gill

When Love Finds You (1994)	Engineer
High Lonesome Sound (1996)	Engineer
Key (1998)	Engineer, Mixing

Nanci Griffith

Little Love Affairs (1988)	Engineer, Mastering, Mixing

Wynonna Judd

Wynonna (1992)	Engineer, Overdubs, Mastering
Tell Me Why (1993)	Engineer, Mastering, Mixing
Revelations (1996)	Engineer, Mixing
Collection (1997)	Mastering
Other Side (1997)	Mixing
New Day Dawning (2000)	Mixing

Robert Earl Keen Jr.

Gravitational Forces (2001)	Mixing

Toby Keith

How Do You Like Me Now? (1999)	Mixing

Mark Knopfler

Golden Heart (1996)	Producer, Engineer, Mixing
Wag the Dog (1998)	Producer
Sailing to Philadelphia (2000)	Producer, Engineer, Mixing
The Ragpicker's Dream (2002)	Producer, Engineer, Mixing
Shangri-La (2004)	Producer, Engineer, Mixing

Lyle Lovett

Lyle Lovett & His Large Band (1989)	Engineer, Mixing

Martina McBride

Evolution (1997)	Mixing

Reba McEntire

Have I Got a Deal for You (1985)	Engineer
Whoever's in New England (1986)	Mixing
What Am I Gonna Do About You (1986)	Engineer
Last One to Know (1987)	Mixing
Merry Christmas to You (1988)	Mixing
Greatest Hits, Vol. 2 (1993)	Engineer, Mixing

Dolly Parton

For God and Country (2003)	Engineer, Digital Editing, Mixing

George Strait

Easy Come Easy Go (1993)	Engineer, Mastering, Mixing
Blue Clear Sky (1996)	Mixing
Carrying Your Love with Me (1997)	Mixing
One Step at a Time (1998)	Engineer, Mixing
Merry Christmas Wherever You Are (1999)	Engineer, Mixing

Latest Greatest Straitest Hits (2000)	Engineer
George Strait (2000)	Engineer
Pam Tillis	
Sweetheart's Dance (1994)	Mixing
Greatest Hits (1997)	Mixing
Thunder and Roses (2001)	Mixing
Travis Tritt	
Down the Road I Go (2000)	Mixing
My Honky Tonk History (2004)	Mixing
Strong Enough (2002)	Mastering, Mixing
Trisha Yearwood	
Songbook: A Collection of Hits (1997)	Mixing
Where Your Road Leads (1998)	Mixing
Real Live Woman (2000)	Mixing
Original Soundtrack	
Twister (1996)	Producer
Horse Whisperer (1998)	Engineer, Mixing
Prince of Egypt (Nashville) (1998)	Engineer, Mixing

Kenny Aronoff . . . .

Garth Brooks	
In the Life of Chris Gaines (1999)	Drums
Belinda Carlisle	
Her Greatest Hits (1992)	Percussion, Drums
Mary-Chapin Carpenter	
Stones in the Road (1994)	Percussion, Drums
Joe Cocker	
Greatest Hits [EMI] (1998)	Drums
Shawn Colvin	
Cover Girl (1994)	Percussion, Drums
Marshall Crenshaw	
Good Evening (1989)	Percussion, Drums
Life's Too Short (1991)	Drums
Live: My Truck Is My Home (1994)	Drums
Rodney Crowell	
Jewel of the South (1995)	Drums
Neil Diamond	
In My Lifetime (1996)	
Celine Dion	
Falling into You (1996)	Drums
Let's Talk About Love [US] (1997)	Drums
All the Way: A Decade of Song (1999)	Drums
Bob Dylan	
Under the Red Sky (1990)	Drums
Bob Dylan 30th Anniversary Concert (1993)	Drums
Greatest Hits, Vol. 3 [US] (1994)	Drums
Heart Land (2003)	Drums
Melissa Etheridge	
Your Little Secret (1995)	Drums

Breakdown (1999)	Drums, Marimba, Shaker
Angels Would Fall (1999)	Drums, Marimba
Skin (2001)	Drums
Lucky (2004)	Percussion, Drums, Tambourine
John Fogerty	
Blue Moon Swamp (1997)	Drums
Premonition (1998)	Drums
Glenn Frey	
Solo Collection (1995)	Drums
Indigo Girls	
Nomads Indians Saints (1990)	Percussion, Drums, Drums (African), Percussion (African)
Rites of Passage (1992)	Percussion, Drums
4.5: The Best of the Indigo Girls (1995)	Percussion, Drums
Retrospective (2000)	Percussion, Drums
Joe Jackson	
Heaven & Hell (1997)	Drums
B.B. King	
King of the Blues [Box] (1992)	Drums
Lyle Lovett	
I Love Everybody (1994)	Drums
Ricky Martin	
Ricky Martin (1999)	Drums
Sound Loaded (2000)	Drums
John Cougar Mellencamp	
Nothin' Matters & What If It Did (1980)	Percussion, Drums, Vibraphone
American Fool (1982)	Percussion, Drums
Uh-Huh (1983)	Percussion, Drums
Scarecrow (1985)	Drums, Tambourine, Vocals (bckgr), Vibraphone
Lonesome Jubilee (1987)	Dulcimer, Conga, Drums, Tambourine, Vocals (bckgr), Vibraphone
Big Daddy (1989)	Percussion, Drums, Vocals (bckgr)
Whenever We Wanted (1991)	Percussion, Drums, Vibraphone
Human Wheels (1993)	Bongos, Conga, Drums, Maraccas, Tambourine, Drums (African), Claves, Djembe, Rainstick, Shaker, Guiro, Metal
Dance Naked (1994)	Percussion, Drums
Mr. Happy Go Lucky (1996)	Percussion, Drums, Vibraphone, Loops
Best That I Could Do (1978-1988) (1997)	Drums, Vocals (bckgr), Vibraphone, Dulcimer (Hammer)
Dance Naked [Bonus CD] (1999)	Percussion, Drums
Randy Newman	
Faust (1995)	Drums
Stevie Nicks	
Street Angel (1993)	Drums, Tambourine
Iggy Pop	
Brick by Brick (1990)	Drums
The Rolling Stones	
Bridges to Babylon (1997)	
Bob Seger	
Fire Inside (1991)	Drums
It's a Mystery (1995)	Drums
Rod Stewart	
Spanner in the Works (1995)	Drums

Dave Aron . . . .

Bobby Brown
Bobby (1992)   Mixing
Doggy's Angels
Pleezbalevit (2000)   Engineer
Carmen Electra
Carmen Electra (1993)   Mixing Assistant, Assistant Producer, Assistant
Kurupt
Space Boogie: Smoke Oddessey (2001)   Engineer, Mixing, Mixing Engineer
Barrington Levy
Living Dangerously (1998)   Producer, Engineer, Mixing
Lil' J
All About J (2002)   Programming, Mixing
MC Eiht Featuring CMW
Last Man Standing (1997)   Mixing
Prince & The New Power Generation
My Name Is Prince (1992)   Mixing
7 (1992)   Engineer
Snoop Dogg
Tha Last Meal (2000)   Mixing
Doggfather (2001)   Engineer, Mixing
Paid tha Cost to Be da Bo$$ (2002)   Engineer, Mixing
R&G (Rhythm & Gangsta): The Masterpiece (2004)   Mixing
Tha Eastsidaz
Tha Eastsidaz (2000)   Engineer
Duces n' Trays: The Old Fashioned… (2001)   Mixing
2 Pac
All Eyez on Me (1996)   Engineer, Mixing
2 Pac & Outlawz
Still I Rise (1999)   Engineer
Rob Wasserman
Space Island (2000)   Clarinet, Engineer
Original Soundtrack
Thin Line Between Love and Hate (1996)   Engineer
Rush Hour (1998)   Mixing

Michael Brauer . . . .

Aerosmith
Pandora's Box (1991)   Remixing
Box of Fire (1994)   Mixing
Regina Belle
Passion (1993)   Mixing
Baby Come to Me: The Best of… (1997)   Mixing
Tony Bennett
MTV Unplugged (1994)   Mixing
Essential: Retrospective (1999)   Mixing
Breaking Benjamim
We Are Not Alone (2004)   Mixing

James Brown
Love Over-Due (1991)   Engineer, Mixing
Jeff Buckley
Live at Sin-E [US EP] (1993)   Mixing
David Byrne
David Byrne (1994)   Mixing
Coldplay
Acoustic CD (2000)   Mixing
Parachutes (2000)   Mixing
Trouble (2001)   Mixing
Don't Panic (2001)   Mixing
X&Y (2005)   Mixing
Shawn Colvin
Fat City (1992)   Mixing
Cover Girl (1994)   Mixing
Bob Dylan
Bootleg Series, Vol. 4: Live 1966… (1998)   Mixing
Dionne Farris
Wild Seed—Wild Flower (1995)   Mixing
Fishbone
Reality of My Surroundings (1991)   Mixing
Aretha Franklin
Jump to It (1982)   Engineer, Mixing
Get It Right (1983)   Engineer, Mixing
Who's Zoomin' Who? (1985)   Mixing
Greatest Hits (1980-1994) (1994)   Engineer, Mixing
Billy Joel
Complete Hits Collection 1974-1997 (1997)   Mixing
Aimee Mann
Lost In Space (2002)   Mixing
Paul McCartney
Back In The USA (2002)   Mixing
In Red Square (2005)   Mixing
My Morning Jacket
Acoustic Citsuoca: Live At The Startime Pavilion (2004)   Mixing
The New Radicals
Maybe You've Been Brainwashed Too (1998)   Mixing
Prefab Sprout
From Langley Park to Memphis (1988)   Engineer
Rachid
Prototype (1998)   Mixing
Pride (1998)   Mixing
Simon & Garfunkel
Old Friends: Live On Stage [DVD] (2004)   Mixing
Rod Stewart
Human (2000)   Mixing
Toad the Wet Sprocket
P.S.: A Toad Retrospective [US] (1999)   Remixing
Luther Vandross
Never Too Much (1981)   Engineer, Mixing

Forever, For Always, For Love (1982)	Engineer, Mixing
Always & Forever: The Classics (1998)	Engineer, Mixing
Ultimate Luther Vandross (2001)	Engineer, Mixing
Was (Not Was)	
Born to Laugh at Tornados (1983)	Engineer
What Up, Dog? (1988)	Engineer
Grover Washington, Jr.	
Soulful Strut (1996)	Mixing
Prime Cuts: The Greatest Hits (1999)	Mixing
Original Soundtrack	
White Men Can't Jump (1992)	Mixing
Blue in the Face [Luaka Bop] (1995)	Mixing
Soundtrack	
Touched By an Angel: The Album (1998)	Mixing
Various Artists	
Bonnaroo Music Festival 2004 (2005)	Mixing
Space: Ibiza 2004 (2004)	Mixing

David Briggs . . . .

Australian Crawl	
Crawl File (1994)	Producer
Nick Cave & the Bad Seeds	
Henry's Dream (1992)	Producer, Mixing
Best of Nick Cave & the Bad Seeds (1998)	Producer
Crazy Horse	
Crazy Horse (1971)	Engineer
Crazy Moon [Raven] (1978)	Engineer, Associate Producer
Grin	
Grin (1971)	Producer
Grin-1+1 (1972)	Producer
Hi	Producer
Marty Haggard	
Borders & Boundaries (1996)	Producer
Nils Lofgren & Grin	
Nils Lofgren (1975)	Producer, Engineer
Willie Nelson	
Shotgun Willie/Phases & Stages (1974)	Producer
Half Nelson (1985)	Producer
Revolutions of Time (1995)	Synthesizer, Keyboards, Producer
Royal Trux	
Thank You (1995)	Producer
Tom Rush	
Wrong End of the Rainbow (1970)	Producer
Spirit	
Twelve Dreams of Dr. Sardonicus (1970)	Producer
Feedback (1972)	Producer
Best of Spirit (1973)	Producer
Time Circle (1991)	Producer

Neil Young

Neil Young (1969)	Producer
After the Gold Rush (1970)	Producer
After the Gold Rush/Harvest (1973)	Producer
Tonights The Night (1974)	
Zuma (1975)	Producer
Comes a Time (1978)	Producer
Trans (1983)	Producer
Old Ways (1985)	Producer
Lucky Thirteen (1993)	Producer, Remixing
Unplugged (1993)	Producer

Neil Young & Crazy Horse

Everybody Knows This Is Nowhere (1969)	Producer, Engineer
Live Rust (1979)	Producer
Rust Never Sleeps (1979)	Producer
Life (1987)	Producer
Mansion on the Hill (1990)	Producer
Ragged Glory (1990)	Producer, Mixing
Arc (1991)	Engineer
Weld (1991)	Producer, Engineer, Mixing
Sleeps With Angels (1994)	Producer

Original Soundtrack

Jerry Maguire (1996)	Producer

Terry Brown . . . .

Blue Rodeo

Outskirts (1987)	Producer

The Bonzo Dog Band

Urban Spaceman (1969)	Engineer

Cirque du Soleil

Zumanity (2005)	Engineer, Mixing

Crowbar

Best of Crowbar (1996)	Engineer

Cutting Crew

Broadcast (1986)	Producer, Engineer, Mixing

Funkadelic

America Eats Its Young (1972)	Engineer

Jimi Hendrix Experience

Axis: Bold as Love (1967)	Engineer

Moist

Silver (1994)	Mixing

Rush

Rush (1974)	Remixing
Caress of Steel (1975)	Arranger, Producer
Fly by Night (1975)	Arranger, Producer, Engineer
All the World's a Stage (1976)	Producer, Engineer
2112 (1976)	Arranger, Producer, Engineer
Farewell to Kings (1977)	Producer, Engineer, Mixing
Archives (1978)	Producer

Hemispheres (1978)	Arranger, Producer, Engineer, Mixing
Permanent Waves (1980)	Arranger, Producer, Mixing
Moving Pictures (1981)	Arranger, Producer
Exit…Stage Left (1981)	Producer
Signals (1982)	Arranger, Producer
Big Money (1988)	Producer
Chronicles (1991)	Producer
Roll the Bones [Single #2] (1991)	Producer
Retrospective, Vol. 1 (1974-1980) (1997)	Producer
Retrospective, Vol. 2 (1981-1987) (1997)	Producer
Different Stages (1998)	Engineer

Tiles

Window Dressing (2004)	Arranger, Producer, Engineer, Mixing

Traffic

Traffic (1968)	Engineer

Various Artists

More American Graffiti [1976] (1976)	Producer

Tony Brown ·

Jimmy Buffett

Boats, Beaches, Bars & Ballads (1992)	Producer
Beach House on the Moon (1999)	Producer

Rodney Crowell

Keys to the Highway (1989)	Producer
Diamonds & Dirt (1989)	Producer
Let the Picture Paint Itself (1994)	Producer

Steve Earle

Guitar Town (1986)	Producer
Exit O (1987)	Producer
Copperhead Road (1988)	Producer

Joe Ely

Love & Danger (1992)	Producer

Vince Gill

When I Call Your Name (1989)	Producer
Pocket Full of Gold (1991)	Producer
I Still Believe in You (1992)	Producer
Souvenirs (1995)	Producer
High Lonesome Sound (1996)	Producer
Key (1998)	Producer

Nanci Griffith

MCA Years: a Retrospective (1993)	Producer

Emmylou Harris

Blue Kentucky Girl (1979)	Piano, Keyboards
Christmas Album (Light in the Stable) (1979)	Clavinet
Cimarron (1981)	Piano, Keyboards
Evangeline (1981)	Keyboards
Anthology: The Warner/Reprise Years. (2001)	Piano, Keyboards

Billy Joel

Greatest Hits, Vol. 3 (1997)	Producer

Wynonna Judd

Wynonna (1992)	Producer
Tell Me Why (1993)	Producer
Revelations (1996)	Producer
Collection (1997)	Producer

Lyle Lovett

Pontiac (1987)	Producer
Lyle Lovett & His Large Band (1989)	Producer

Mac McAnally

Live & Learn (1992)	Producer

Reba McEntire

For My Broken Heart (1991)	Producer
Greatest Hits, Vol. 2 (1993)	Producer

Todd Snider

Songs for the Daily Planet (1994)	Producer

George Strait

Strait Out of the Box (1995)	Producer
Blue Clear Sky (1996)	Producer
One Step at a Time (1998)	Producer
Latest Greatest Straitest Hits (2000)	Producer

Chely Wright

Let Me In (1997)	Piano, Producer
Shut Up and Drive (1997)	Producer
Single White Female (1999)	Producer

Trisha Yearwood

Songbook: A Collection of Hits (1997)	Producer
Where Your Road Leads (1998)	Producer

Original Soundtrack

Firm (1993)	Producer
Horse Whisperer (1998)	Producer
Prince of Egypt (Nashville) (1998)	Producer

Greg Calbi . . . .

Susana Baca

Eco de Sombras: Echo of Shadows (2000)	Mastering

Tony Bennett

Playground (1998)	Mastering

David Byrne

Look into the Eyeball (2001)	Mastering

Deep Purple

Machine Head (1972)	Mastering

Dire Straits

Making Movies (1980)	Mastering

Bob Dylan

Oh Mercy (1989)	Mastering
MTV Unplugged (1995)	Mastering
Bootleg Series, Vol. 4: Live 1966 … (1998)	Mastering

Brian Eno-David Byrne

My Life in the Bush of Ghosts (1981)	Mastering

Brian Eno

Ambient 4: On Land (1982)   Mastering

Apollo: Atmospheres & Soundtracks (1983)   Mastering

Fountains of Wayne

Fountains of Wayne (1996)   Mastering

Bill Frisell

Nashville (1995)   Mastering

Good Dog, Happy Man (1999)   Mastering

Ghost Town (2000)   Mastering

Elton John

Muse (1999)   Mastering

Lenny Kravitz

Let Love Rule (1989)   Mastering

Mama Said (1991)   Mastering

Are You Gonna Go My Way? (1993)   Mastering

Circus (1995)   Mastering

k.d. lang

Drag (1997)   Mastering

Daniel Lanois

Acadie (1989)   Mastering

For The Beauty of Wynona (1993)   Mastering

John Lennon

Walls and Bridges (1974)   Mastering

Manhattan Transfer

Spirit of St. Louis (2000)   Mastering

Medeski, Martin & Wood

Combustication (1998)   Mastering

Tom Petty & the Heartbreakers

Damn the Torpedoes (1979)   Mastering

Hard Promises (1981)   Mastering

The Ramones

Ramones (1976)   Mastering

Rocket to Russia (1977)   Mastering

Road to Ruin (1978)   Mastering

Lou Reed

New Sensations (1984)   Mastering

Simon & Garfunkel

Concert in Central Park Mastering

Greatest Hits (2001)   Mastering

Paul Simon

Rhythm of the Saints (1990)   Mastering

Paul Simon Anthology (1999)   Mastering

Patti Smith

Masters [Box] (1996)   Mastering

Smithereens

Especially for You (1986)   Mastering

Sonic Youth

Washing Machine (1995)   Mastering

Thousand Leaves (1998)   Mastering

Bruce Springsteen
Born to Run (1975)   Mastering
Greatest Hits [Columbia] (1995)   Mastering
Talking Heads
Remain in Light (1980)   Mastering
Popular Favorites 1984-1992 (1992)   Mastering
James Taylor
Never Die Young (1988)   Digital Remastering
New Moon Shine (1991)   Digital Remastering
Greatest Hits, Vol. 2 (2000)   Digital Remastering
Luther Vandross
Always & Forever: The Classics (1998)   Mastering
Violent Femmes
Add It Up (1981-1993) (1993)   Mastering
Rufus Wainwright
Poses (2001)   Mastering
Warren Zevon
Life'll Kill Ya (2000)   Mastering
New Broadway Cast
Rocky Horror Show [New Broadway Production] (2001)   Mastering
Original Soundtrack
Sling Blade (1996)   Mastering
Velvet Goldmine (1998)   Mastering
Wonder Boys [Soundtrack] (2000)   Mastering

Ian Caple . . . .

a-ha
Lifelines (2002)   Producer
Jean-Luis Aubert
Stockholm (1998)   Mixing
Buffseeds
Picture Show (2004)   Producer, Mixing
Sparkle Me [EP] (2003)   Producer, Mixing
Julian Cope
Leper Skin (1999)   Engineer
Cousteau
Cousteau (2000)   Producer, Mixing
Faithless
Back to Mine (2001)   Engineer
Low Pop Suicide
Death of Excellence (1995)   Engineer, Mixing
Malacoda
Cascade (1997)   Producer, Engineer
The Mekons
Honky Tonkin' (1987)   Mixing
Curse of the Mekons (1991)   Producer, Engineer
I Have Been to Heaven and Back (1999)   Engineer
Where Were You? (1999)   Engineer, Mixing

Stina Nordenstam
People Are Strange (1998)   Keyboards, Programming, Producer, Engineer
Yoko Ono
Rising Mixes (1996)   Engineer
The Psyclone Rangers
Beatin' on the Bat Pole (1996)   Engineer
Shriekback
Oil & Gold (1985)   Engineer
Sky Cries Mary
Exit at the Axis (1991)   Engineer, Mixing
This Timeless Turning (1994)   Producer, Engineer, Mixing
Fresh Fruits for the Revolution (1998)   Engineer
Suede
Sci-Fi Lullabies (1997)   Producer
Film Star #1 [single] (1997)   Producer
3 Mustaphas 3
Shopping (1987)   Engineer, Mixing
Yann Tiersen
L'Absente (2001)   Engineer, Mixing
Tindersticks
Tindersticks (1993)   Producer, Engineer
Tindersticks [II] (1995)   Engineer, Mixing
Curtains (1997)   Engineer
Simple Pleasure (1999)   Engineer, Mixing
Can Our Love… (2001)
Waiting for the Moon (2003)   Producer
Tricky Vs. the Gravediggaz
Hell [EP] (1995)   Mixing
Tricky
Pre-Millennium Tension (1996)   Engineer, Mixing
Ruff Guide (2002)   Engineer, Mixing
Nénette et Boni [Canada Bonus CD] (2004)   Engineer, Mixing
Vitro
Distort (1999)   Producer, Original Album Producer
Various Artists
Born to Choose (1993)   Producer

Ed Cherney...

Jann Arden
Time for Mercy (1993)   Producer, Engineer, Mixing, Vocals (bckgr)
Living Under June (1995)   Producer, Engineer, Mixing, Arranger, Vocals (bckgr)
Happy? (1998)   Producer, Engineer, Mixing
The B-52's
Good Stuff (1992)   Engineer
Jackson Browne
Next Voice You Hear: The Best of Jackson Browne (2001)   Mixing
Eric Clapton
Rush (1992)   Engineer

Clapton Chronicles (2000)	Engineer, Mixing
Ry Cooder	
Get Rhythm (1987)	Engineer, Mixing
Bob Dylan	
Under the Red Sky (1990)	Engineer, Mixing
MTV Unplugged (1995)	Mixing
The Fabulous Thunderbirds	
This Night in L.A. (2001)	Producer, Engineer, Mixing
Live (2001)	Producer, Engineer, Mixing
Goo Goo Dolls	
Gutterflower (2002)	Mixing
Buddy Guy	
Blues Singer (2003)	Mixing
Hootie & the Blowfish	
Hootie & the Blowfish (2003)	Engineer, Mixing
Billy Joel	
Greatest Hits, Vol. 1, 2 & 3 (2000)	Engineer
Elton John	
To Be Continued… (1990)	Mixing
Duets (1993)	Engineer, Mixing
Keb' Mo'	
Big Wide Grin (2001)	Mixing
Robert Earl Keen, Jr.	
Farm Fresh Onions (2003)	Mixing
Little Feat	
Ain't Had Enough Fun (1995)	Producer, Engineer
Hotcakes and Outtakes: 30 Years of Little Feat (2000)	Producer, Engineer, Assistant Engineer, Production Consultant
Bette Midler	
Bette (2000)	Engineer, Mixing
Randy Newman	
Faust (1995)	Engineer
Lee Roy Parnell	
Hits And Highways Ahead (1999)	Producer, Mixing
Iggy Pop	
Brick by Brick (1990)	Engineer, Mixing, Vocals
Bonnie Raitt	
Nick of Time (1989)	Engineer, Mixing
Luck of the Draw (1991)	Engineer, Mixing
Longing in Their Hearts (1994)	Engineer
Road Tested (1995)	Producer, Engineer, Mixing
The Rolling Stones	
Stripped (1995)	Engineer
Bridges to Babylon (1997)	Engineer
No Security (1998)	Engineer
Live Licks (2004)	Engineer
Bob Seger	
Fire Inside (1991)	Engineer, Mixing
Pops Staples	
Peace to the Neighbourhood (1992)	Producer, Engineer

Ringo Starr

Time Takes Time (1992)	Engineer, Remixing, Mixing
Weight of the World (1992)	Engineer

Barbra Streisand

Emotion (1984)	Engineer

The Wallflowers

Red Letter Days (2002)	Mixing

Various Artists

Woodstock 94 (1994)	Engineer

Bob Clearmountain . . . .

Bryan Adams

Cuts Like a Knife (1983)	Vocals (bckgr), Producer, Engineer
Reckless (1984)	Vocals (bckgr), Producer, Engineer
So Far So Good (1993)	Producer, Mixing
MTV Unplugged (2002)	Engineer, Mixing
Room Service (2004)	Engineer, Mixing

Aerosmith

O, Yeah Ultimate Hits (2002)	Mixing

Tori Amos

Boys for Pele (1996)	Mixing

Laurie Anderson

Strange Angels (1989)	Mixing

David Bowie

Let's Dance (1983)	Engineer, Mixing

Tracy Chapman

Matters of the Heart (1992)	Mixing

Chic

C'est Chic (1978)	Engineer, Mixing

The Church

Under the Milky Way: The Best of The Church (1999)	Producer, Mixing

Shawn Colvin

Few Small Repairs (1996)	Mixing
Whole New You (2001)	Mixing

The Counting Crows

Across a Wire: Live in New York (1998)	Mixing

Crowded House

Recurring Dream: The Very Best of Crowded House (1998)	Mixing

The Cure

Galore (1997)	Mixing
Join The Dots: B-Sides & Rarities, 1978-2001 (2004)	Mixing

Dire Straits

On Every Street (1991)	Mixing

Fastball

Keep Your Wig On (2004)	Mixing

Bryan Ferry

Frantic (2002)	Producer, Mixing

Finn Brothers

Evveryone Is Here (2004)	Mixing

Five For Fighting
America Town (2000)   Mixing
Battle For Everything (2004)   Mixing
John Fogerty
Blue Moon Swamp (2002)   Mixing
Déjà vu All Over Again (2004)   Mixing
Hall & Oates
Very Best of Hall & Oates (2001)   Producer, Mixing
Ballads Collection (2001)   Producer, Mixing
Indigo Girls
All That We Let In (2005)   Mixing
Rarities (2005)   Mixing
INXS
Kick (1987)   Engineer, Mixing
Welcome to Wherever You Are (1992)   Mixing
Shine Like It Does: The Anthology (2001)   Mixing
King Crimson
3 of a Perfect Pair (1984)   Mixing
Paul McCartney
Tripping the Live Fantastic (1990)   Producer, Engineer, Mixing
Willie Nelson
Across the Borderline (1993)   Mixing
The Pretenders
Get Close (1986)   Producer, Mixing
Singles (1987)   Producer, Mixing
Public Image Ltd.
Greatest Hits, So Far (1990)   Mixing
The Rezillos
Can't Stand the Rezillos (1978)   Producer, Engineer, Mixing
Robbie Robertson
Robbie Robertson (1987)   Mixing
Music for the Native Americans (1994)   Mixing
The Rolling Stones
Voodoo Lounge (1994)   Mixing
Stripped (1995)   Mixing
Bridges to Babylon (1997)   Mixing
Forty Licks (2002)   Mixing
Live Licks (2004)   Mixing
Roxy Music
Avalon (1982)   Engineer, Mixing
Avalon (SACD surround version 2004)   Mixing
Semisonic
Feeling Strangely Fine (1998)   Mixing
All About Chemistry (2001)   Mixing
Sixpence None the Richer
Sixpence None the Richer (1997)   Mixing
Bruce Springsteen
Born in the U.S.A. (1984)   Mixing
Live 1975-1985 (1986)   Mixing
Tunnel of Love (1987)   Mixing

Greatest Hits [Columbia] (1995)	Mixing
Live in New York City (2001)	Mixing
In Concert (2004)	Mixing
Tears for Fears	
Seeds of Love (1989)	Mixing
Universal Masters Collection (2001)	Remixing
They Might Be Giants	
User's Guide To They Might Be Giants (2005)	Mixing
Tina Turner	
Break Every Rule (1986)	Producer, Engineer, Mixing
Rufus Wainwright	
Poses (2002)	Mixing
David Werner	
David Werner (1979)	Producer, Engineer, Mixing
Original Soundtrack	
That Thing You Do (1996)	Mixing
Hope Floats [Original Soundtrack] (1998)	Mixing
Scream 3 [Original Soundtrack] (2000)	Mixing
Various Artists	
Sun City: Artists United Against Apartheid (1985)	Mixing
Secret Policeman's Third Ball: The (1987)	Producer, Mixing
Folkways: A Vision Shared (1988)	Mixing
Woodstock 94 (1994)	Producer, Engineer
Saturday Night Live: 25 Years (1999)	Mixing

Peter Collins . . . .

Beth Nielsen Chapman	
Look (2005)	Producer
Alice Cooper	
Hey Stoopid (1991)	Producer
The Divinyls	
Underworld (1996)	Producer
Nanci Griffith	
Flyer (1994)	Producer
Clock Without Hands (2001)	Producer
Indigo Girls	
Indigo Girls (1989)	Original Recording Producer
Rites of Passage (1992)	Producer, Original Recording Producer
Swamp Ophelia (1994)	Producer
Retrospective (2000)	Producer, Original Recording Producer
Jewel	
Foolish Games (1998)	Producer
Spirit (1998)	Producer
Down So Long (1999)	Producer
Elton John & Tim Rice	
Aida (1999)	Producer
Lisa Loeb	
Hello Lisa (2002)	Producer
Cake and Pie (2002)	Producer

Shawn Mullins
Soul's Core (1998)   Producer
Queensryche
Operation: Mindcrime (1988)   Producer
Empire (1990)   Producer
LeAnn Rimes
I Need You (2001)   Producer
Rush
Power Windows (1985)   Arranger, Producer
Hold Your Fire (1987)   Arranger, Producer
Big Money (1988)   Producer
Chronicles (1991)   Producer
Counterparts (1993)   Producer
Test for Echo (1996)   Arranger, Producer
Retrospective, Vol. 2 (1981-1987) (1997)   Producer
The Brian Setzer Orchestra
Dirty Boogie (1998)   Producer
Vavoom! (2000)   Producer
Tracey Ullman
Best of Tracey Ullman (1991)   Producer
Original Soundtrack
Wayne's World (1992)   Producer
Philadelphia [Original Soundtrack] (1993)   Producer

Mike Couzzi . . . .

Christina Aguilera
Mi Reflejo (2000)   Mixing
Azucar Moreno
Amor (1994)   Mixing
Olé (1998)   Engineer, Mixing
Amen (2000)   Engineer
Luis Enrique
Genesis (1996)   Engineer, Mixing
Gloria Estefan
Into the Light (1991)   Mixing
Greatest Hits (1992)   Mixing
Mi Tierra (1993)   Mixing
Destiny (1996)   Engineer
Wrapped (2003)   Engineer
Unwrapped (2003)   Engineer
Exposé
Exposure (1986)   Engineer, Mixing
What You Don't Know (1989)   Engineer, Mixing
Expose (1992)   Engineer
Greatest Hits (1995)   Engineer, Mixing
Luis Guerra Y 440
Ni Es Lo Mismo Ni Es Igual (1998)   Engineer

José José

Mujeriego (1996)	Engineer
35 Aniversario, Vol. 7 (1998)	Engineer, Mixing
35 Aniversario, Vol. 6 (1998)	Mixing

Melina Leon

Corazon de Mujer (2001)	Engineer, Mezcla

MDO

Subir Al Cielo (2001)	Producer, Mixing Engineer

Ednita Nazario

Sin Limite (2001)	Engineer, Mixing

Roberto Perera

Passions, Illusions and Fantasies (1991)	Engineer
Dreams & Desires (1992)	Engineer
Seduction (1994)	Engineer
Harp and Soul (1996)	Engineer

Pet Shop Boys

Discography: The Complete Singles Collection (1991)	Engineer, Mixing
PopArt (2003)	Engineer, Mixing

Jose Luis Rodriguez

En Ritmo 2: Fiesta (1999)	Engineer

Jon Secada

Jon Secada (1992)	Vocals (bckgr), Engineer, Mixing
Si Te Vas (1994)	Mezcla

Frank Sinatra

Duets II (1994)	Engineer

Olga Tanon

Te Acordaras de Mi (1998)	Mixing

Tommy Torres

Estar de Moda, No Esta de Moda (2004)	Engineer
Tommy Torres (2001)	Engineer

Jaci Velasquez

Llegar a Ti (1999)	Mixing
Mi Corazon (2001)	Mixing, Mixing Engineer

Yolandita

Siento (1999)	Engineer, Mixing, Recording Technician

Charlie Zaa

Ciego de Amor (2000)	Mixing Engineer

Original Soundtrack

When We Were Kings (1997)	Engineer

Various Artists

2000 Latin Grammy Nominees (2000)	Engineer

Gail Davies . . . .

Gail Davies selected artistic discography:

1978	Gail Davies
1980	The Game
1980	I'll Be There
1982	Giving Herself Away
1983	What Can I Say

1984	Where is a Woman to Go
1986	Wild Choir
1989	Pretty Words
1990	The Other Side of Love
2001	Live & Unplugged at the Station Inn
1991	The Best of Gail Davies
1998	Greatest Hits [Little Chickadee]
1998	Greatest Hits [Koch]

Hoyt Axton

Southbound (1975)	Vocals

Glen Campbell

Legacy 1961-2002 (2003)	Vocals

Paul Craft

Brother Jukebox (1998)	Vocals

Lacy J. Dalton

Dream Baby (1983)	Vocals

Rosie Flores

Speed of Sound (2001)	Vocals (bckgr)
Where Does the Time Go (2003)	Harmony Vocals

Emmylou Harris

Ballad of Sally Rose (1985)	Vocals, Vocals (bckgr)
Portraits (1996)	Vocals (bckgr)
Anthology: The Warner/Reprise Years (2001)	Vocals (bckgr)

Hugh Moffatt

Life of a Minor Poet (1996)	Harmony Vocals, Executive Producer

The Whites

Greatest Hits (1987)	Composer

Dwight Yoakam

Dwight's Used Records (2004)	Producer

Neil Young

Old Ways (1985)	Vocals, Vocals (bckgr)
Lucky Thirteen (1993)	Vocals (bckgr)

Various Artists

Kerrville Folk Festival: 25th Anniversary Album (1998)	Guitar, Vocals, Mixing Producer
Kerrville Folk Festival (2000)	Guitar, Vocals, Mixing Producer

Jim Dickinson . . . .

Duane Allman

Anthology, Vol. 2 (1974)	Guitar, Piano

Big Star

Third/Sister Lovers (1978)	Producer, Engineer, Mellotron, Bass, Guitar, Drums, Keyboards

Delaney & Bonnie Bramlett

To Bonnie from Delaney (1970)	Piano

Alex Chilton

Like Flies on Sherbert (1979)	Producer

Clawhammer

Hold Your Tongue (And Say Apple) (1997)	Producer, Mixing

Ry Cooder

Into the Purple Valley (1971)	Piano, Producer

Boomer's Story (1972)	Bass, Piano, Vocals, Producer
Long Riders (1980)	Organ, Piano, Harmonium, Producer
Slide Area (1982)	Organ, Piano, Keyboards, Piano (Electric), Producer
Alamo Bay (1985)	Piano, Producer
Blue City (1986)	Piano, Drums, Keyboards, Producer
Crossroads (1986)	Organ, Guitar, Piano, Vocals, Dolceola
Paris, Texas (1989)	
Music by Ry Cooder (1995)	Organ, Piano

James Luther Dickinson

Free Beer Tomorrow (2002)	Producer, Mixing, Vocals, Keyboards

Bob Dylan

Time Out of Mind (1997)	Keyboards

John Eddie

Who the Hell Is John Eddie? (2003)	Keyboards, Producer, Mixing
Let Me Down Hard (2003)	Producer

The Flamin' Groovies

Teenage Head (1971)	Piano
Still Shakin' (1976)	Piano

Steve Forbert

Evergreen Boy (2000)	Producer, Keyboards

Aretha Franklin

Spirit in the Dark (1970)	Keyboards

G. Love & Special Sauce

Coast to Coast Motel (1995)	Producer, Piano (Electric)

Arlo Guthrie

Hobo's Lullaby (1972)	Keyboards

Alvin Youngblood Hart

Start with the Soul (2000)	Producer
Down in the Alley (2002)	Producer, Mixing

John Hiatt

Master Of Disaster (2005)	Producer, Keyboards

Toots Hibbert

Toots in Memphis (1988)	Producer, Keyboards

Jason & the Scorchers

Fervor EP (1983)	Producer

Los Lobos

Cancionero: Mas y Mas (2000)	Piano

Mudhoney

Tomorrow Hit Today (1998)	Keyboards, Producer
March to Fuzz (2000)	Producer

Phineas Newborn

Solo Piano (1974)	Engineer

North Mississippi Allstars

51 Phantom (2001)	Piano, Producer, Omnichord, Dolceola
Polaris (2003)	Piano, Mellotron, Omnichord, Fuzz-wah
Hill Country Revue: Live at Bonnaroo (2004)	Organ, Keyboards, Vocals, Liner Notes, Mixing, Post Production
Electric Blue Watermelon (2005)	Producer, Keyboards

Poi Dog Pondering

Wishing Like a Mountain & Thinking (1989)	Conductor, Horn (Alto), Horn Arrangements

Primal Scream

Give Out But Don't Give Up (1994) — Keyboards

The Radiators

Total Evaporation (1990) — Producer

New Dark Ages (1995) — Mixing

The Replacements

Pleased to Meet Me (1987) — Producer

All For Nothing/Nothing for All (1997) — Producer

The Rolling Stones

Sticky Fingers (1971) — Piano

Royal Fingerbowl

Greyhound Afternoons (2000) — Producer

Calvin Russell

Soldier (1997) — Organ, Piano, Vocals (bckgr), Producer, Mixing

Calvin Russell (1997) — Keyboards, Producer

Jon Spencer Blues Explosion

Acme (1998) — Mixing

Xtra Acme USA (1999) — Mixing

T-Model Ford

Bad Man (2002) — Producer, Liner Notes

The Texas Tornados

4 Aces (1996) — Piano, Producer

Little Bit Is Better Than Nada (1997) — Producer

True Believers

True Believers (1986) — Piano, Producer

Hard Road — Piano, Producer

Jerry Jeff Walker

Bein' Free (1970) — Dobro, Guitar, Piano, Keyboards, Tack Piano, Mouth Bow

Weddings Parties Anything

Trophy Night: The Best of Weddings (1998) — Producer

Original Soundtrack

Dead Man Walking (1996) — Piano

Tin Cup (1996) — Producer

Can't Hardly Wait (1998) — Producer

Richard Dodd . . . .

Big & Rich

Horse of a Different Color (2004) — Mastering

Billy Pilgrim

Bloom (1995) — Producer, Engineer, Mixing, Mastering, Keyboards

Brooks & Dunn

Very Best Of Brooks & Dunn (2004) — Mastering

Marty Brown

Cryin', Lovin', Leavin' (1994) — Engineer, Mixing

Johnny Cash

American III: Solitary Man (2000) — Engineer

Clannad

Pastpresent (1989) — Producer, Engineer

Anam (1990) — Producer

Themes (1996)	Producer
Rogha: The Best of Clannad (1997)	Producer, Engineer
Sheryl Crow	
Globe Sessions (1998)	Mixing
Sweet Child O' Mine [US] (1999)	Mixing
Roger Daltrey	
Martyrs & Madmen: The Best of Roger Daltrey (1997)	Engineer
Francis Dunnery	
Tall Blonde Helicopter (1995)	Producer, Engineer, Mixing
Steve Earle	
I Feel Alright (1996)	Producer, Engineer, Mixing
Electric Light Orchestra	
Zoom (2001)	Engineer
John Entwistle	
Thunderfingers: The Best of John Entwistle (1996)	Engineer
Steve Forbert	
Evergreen Boy (2000)	Mixing
Mary Gauthier	
Mercy Now (2005)	Mastering
Green Day	
Redundant (1998)	Mixing
Nimrod (1999)	Mixing
Take 2 (2000)	Mixing
George Harrison	
Cloud Nine (1987)	Engineer
John Hiatt	
Tiki Bar Is Open (2001)	Mixing
Jars Of Clay	
Furthermore: From The Studio/From The Stage (2003)	Mastering
Little River Band	
No Reins (1986)	Producer
Reminiscing (1992)	Producer
Delbert McClinton	
Nothing Personal (2001)	Tambourine, Mixing
Room To Breathe (2002)	Mixing, Mastering
Tift Merritt	
Tambourine (2004)	Mastering
Bill Miller	
Ghostdance (1999)	Producer, Engineer, Mixing, Vocals (bckgr)
Shawn Mullins	
Music from the Motion Picture Big Daddy (1999)	Mixing
First Ten Years (1999)	Mixing
Roy Orbison	
Mystery Girl (1989)	Engineer
King of Hearts (1992)	Engineer, Mixing
Tom Petty	
Wildflowers (1994)	Engineer, Mixing
Tom Petty & the Heartbreakers	
Into the Great Wide Open (1991)	Engineer, Mixing
Playback (1995)	Engineer, Mixing

Songs and Music from "She's The One" (1996)	Mixing
The Last DJ (2002)	Engineer, Mixing, Mastering
Red Hot Chili Peppers	
Greatest Hits (2003)	Mixing
Boz Scaggs	
Some Change (1994)	Engineer, Mixing
Fade Into Light (1999)	Mixing
South Park	
Chef Aid: The South Park Album (1998)	Mixing
Ringo Starr	
Time Takes Time (1992)	Engineer
Weight of the World (1992)	Engineer, Mixing
The Traveling Wilburys	
Traveling Wilburys, Vol. 1 (1988)	Engineer
Keith Urban	
Ranch (1997)	Mixing
In The Ranch (2004)	Mixing
Wilco	
A.M. (1995)	Mixing
Original Soundtrack	
Patriot Games (1992)	Producer
I Shot Andy Warhol (1996)	Mixing
Horse Whisperer (1998)	Mixing

Jerry Douglas . . . .

Jerry Douglas selected artist discography:

1979	Fluxology
1982	Fluxedo
1986	Under the Wire
1987	Changing Channels
1987	Everything Is Gonna Work out Fine
1989	Plant Early
1992	Slide Rule
1994	Skip, Hop & Wobble
1996	Yonder
1998	Restless on the Farm
2002	Lookout For Hope
Acoustic Alchemy	
Beautiful Game (2000)	Dobro
Garth Brooks	
Ropin' the Wind (1991)	Dobro
In Pieces (1993)	Dobro
Limited Series (1998)	Dobro
T-Bone Burnett	
T-Bone Burnette (1986)	Dobro, Guitar (Steel), Lap Steel Guitar
Sam Bush	
Glamour & Grits (1996)	Dobro
Howlin' at the Moon (1998)	Dobro, Lap Steel Guitar
Ice Caps: Peaks of Telluride (2000)	Dobro, Lap Steel Guitar

Rosanne Cash	
Interiors (1990)	Dobro
Steve Earle	
Copperhead Road (1988)	Dobro
Béla Fleck	
Natural Bridge (1982)	Dobro
Tales from the Acoustic Planet (1994)	Guitar
Bluegrass Sessions: Tales From the (1999)	Dobro
Little Worlds (2003)	Dobro, Lap Steel Guitar
Dan Fogelberg	
High Country Snows (1985)	Dobro, Guitar, Vocals
Bill Frisell	
Nashville (1995)	Dobro
A-Collection (2000)	Dobro
Vince Gill	
High Lonesome Sound (1996)	Dobro
Emmylou Harris	
Anthology: The Warner/Reprise Years (2001)	Dobro
Roses in the Snow [Expanded] (2002)	Dobro
Faith Hill	
Take Me As I Am (1994)	Dobro
George Jones	
Bradley Barn Sessions (1994)	Dobro
Jorma Kaukonen	
Blue Country Heart (2002)	Dobro, Weissenborn
Alison Krauss	
I've Got That Old Feeling (1990)	Dobro, Producer
Now That I've Found You: A Collection (1995)	Dobro, Guitar, Producer
Forget About It (1999)	Dobro, Lap Steel Guitar
New Favorite (2001)	Dobro, Lap Steel Guitar
Leftover Salmon	
Nashville Sessions (1999)	Dobro
Patty Loveless	
When Fallen Angels Fly (1994)	Slide Guitar
Trouble with the Truth (1996)	Dobro, Lap Steel Guitar
Long Stretch of Lonesome (1997)	Lap Steel Guitar
Strong Heart (2000)	Dobro, Lap Steel Guitar
Lyle Lovett	
Step Inside This House (1998)	Dobro, Weissenborn
Del McCoury	
Deeper Shade of Blue (1993)	Dobro, Guitar, Producer
Cold Hard Facts (1996)	Dobro, Producer, Engineer, Mixing
Natalie MacMaster	
Blueprint (2003)	Dobro
The Nashville Bluegrass Band	
Boys Are Back in Town (1990)	Producer
Home of the Blues (1991)	Dobro, Producer
Waitin' for the Hard Times to Go (1993)	Dobro, Producer
Unleashed (1995)	Producer

The Nitty Gritty Dirt Band
Will the Circle Be Unbroken, Vol. 2 (1989)   Dobro
Maura O'Connell
Blue Is the Colour of Hope (1992)   Dobro, Guitar (Steel), Producer
Stories (1995)   Dobro, Guitar (Steel), Vocals, Producer
Wandering Home (1997)   Dobro, Arranger, Producer, Lap Steel Guitar
Don't I Know (2004)   Dobro, Producer, Lap Steel Guitar
Mark O'Connor
New Nashville Cats (1991)   Dobro
Heroes (1993)   Dobro, Guitar (Steel), Lap Steel Guitar
Mark O'Connor/Yo-Yo Ma/Wynton Marsalis
Liberty (1997)   Dobro
Dolly Parton
Grass Is Blue (1999)   Dobro, Harmony Vocals
Phish
Farmhouse (2000)   Dobro
Tony Rice
California Autumn (1975)   Dobro
Tony Rice (1977)   Dobro
Manzanita (1979)   Dobro
Bluegrass Album, Vol. 4 (1984)   Dobro, Baritone (Vocal)
Cold on the Shoulder (1984)   Dobro
Peter Rowan
Dust Bowl Children (1990)   Producer
All on a Rising Day (1991)   Dobro, Guitar, Vocals, Producer
Paul Simon
Paul Simon Anthology (1999)   Dobro
Ricky Skaggs
Sweet Temptation (1979)   Dobro
Highways & Heartaches (1982)   Dobro
Bluegrass Rules! (1997)   Dobro
Soldier of the Cross (1999)   Slide Guitar
History of the Future (2001)   Fiddle
Sing the Songs of Bill Monroe (2002)   Dobro
James Taylor
New Moon Shine (1991)   Dobro
Randy Travis
Greatest Hits, Vol. 1 (1992)   Dobro
Greatest Hits, Vol. 2 (1992)   Dobro
Worship & Faith (2003)   Dobro
The Whites
Lifetime in the Making (2000)   Dobro, Producer
Original Soundtrack
Horse Whisperer (1998)   Weissenborn
O Brother, Where Art Thou? (2000)   Dobro

Gus Dudgeon ·

Joan Armatrading
Whatever's For Us (1972)   Producer

Audience
House On The Hill (1971)   Producer
Lunch (1972)
Bonzo Dog Band
Tadpoles (1969)   Producer
Urban Spacemen (1969)   Producer
Beast of the Bonzos(1970)   Producer
David Bowie
Man Of Words, Man Of Music (Space Oddity) (1969)   Producer
Fairport Convention
Jewel In The Crown (1995)   Mixing
Elton John
Empty Sky (1969)   Producer
Elton John (1970)   Producer
11-17-70 (1971)   Producer
Friends (1971)   Producer
Tumbleweed Connection (1971)   Producer
Madman Across The Water (1971)   Producer
Honky Chateau (1972)   Producer
Don't Shoot Me, I'm Only The Piano Player (1973)   Producer
Goodbye Yellow Brick Road (1973)   Producer
Caribou (1974)   Producer
Caotain Fantastic and the Brown Dirt Cowboy (1975)   Producer
Rock Of The Westies (1975)   Producer
Blue Moves (1976)   Producer
Here And There (1976)   Producer
John Kongos
John Kongos (1971)   Producer, Percussion
John Mayal (& The Bluesbreakers)
Bluesbreakers with Eric Clapton (1966)   Engineer
Chris Rea
Whatever Happened to Benny Santini? (1978)   Producer, Percussion
Jennifer Rush
Heart Over Mind (1987)   Producer
The Sinceros
Pet Rock (1981)   Producer
Legs Larry Smith
Springtime For Hitler (2001)   Producer
Ten Years After
Ten Year After (1967)   Engineer
XTC
Nonesuch (1992)   Producer

Steve Ebe . . . .

Libbi Bosworth
Outskirts of You (1997)   Drums
George Ducas
Where I Stand (1997)   Drums

Floating Men
Haunting (2004) — Drums
Tommy Hoehn
I Do Love the Light (1981) — Drums
Of Moons & Fools (1997) — Drums
Donna Mogavero
Out of the Nest (1999) — Drums
John Mohead
Mary's Porch (1998) — Drums
Ross Rice
Umpteen (1997) — Drums
Jason Ringenberg
Empire Builders (2004) — Drums
Day at the Farm With Farmer Jason (2003) — Drums
Adrienne Young & Little Sadie
Plow to the End of the Row (2004) — Drums

Danny Elfman . . . .

Oingo Boingo
Only a Lad (1981) — Guitar, Guitar (Rhythm), Vocals
Nothing to Fear (1982) — Guitar, Guitar (Rhythm), Vocals
Good for Your Soul (1983) — Guitar, Guitar (Rhythm), Vocals
Dead Man's Party (1985) — Guitar, Guitar (Rhythm), Vocals, Producer
Boi-ngo (1987) — Guitar, Guitar (Rhythm), Vocals, Producer
Boingo Alive (1988) — Guitar, Guitar (Rhythm), Vocals, Producer
Skeletons in the Closet (Best Of) (1989) — Guitar, Guitar (Rhythm), Vocals
Dark at the End of the Tunnel (1990) — Guitar, Vocals, Producer
Best O' Boingo (1992) — Guitar, Guitar (Rhythm), Vocals, Producer, Engineer, Mixing
Boingo (1994) — Guitar, Arranger, Vocals, Producer
Farewell (1996) — Guitar, Vocals, Producer, Liner Notes
Anthology (1999) — Percussion, Guitar (Rhythm), Programming, Vocals, Producer
Skeletons in the Closet — Guitar, Vocals
Original Soundtrack
Beetlejuice (1988) — Composer, Producer
Forbidden Zone (1980) — Composer, Vocals, Liner Notes
Beverly Hills Cop (1984) — Composer, Producer
Weird Science (1985) — Composer, Producer
Sommersby (1993) — Composer, Producer
Nightmare Before Christmas (1993) — Composer, Lyre, Vocals, Producer
Mission: Impossible (1996) — Composer, Producer
Mars Attacks (1997) — Composer, Producer
Good Will Hunting (1997) — Producer, Orchestral Arrangements
Men in Black (1997) — Composer, Producer
Civil Action (1998) — Composer, Producer
Sleepy Hollow (1999) — Composer, Producer
Planet of the Apes (2001) — Composer, Producer
Spider Man (2002) — Composer, Producer
Men In Black 2 (2002) — Composer, Producer
Hulk (2003) — Composer, Producer

Chicago (2003)	Composer, Producer
Big Fish (2003)	Composer, Producer
Spider Man 2 (2004)	Composer, Producer
Charlie & The Chocolate Factory (2005)	Composer, Producer
Corpse Bride (2005)	Composer, Producer
Charlotte's Web (2006)	Composer, Producer
A Day With Wilbur Robinson (2006)	Composer, Producer

Ellen Fitton

The Bee Gees

E.S.P. (1987)	Engineer

Michael Bolton

This Is the Time: The Christmas Album (1996)	Engineer

David Byrne

Rei Momo (1989)	Assistant Engineer

Charlotte Church

Charlotte Church (1999)	Editing
Dream a Dream (2000)	Editing Engineer

Michael Crawford

On Eagle's Wings (1998)	Engineer

Foreigner

Unusual Heat (1991)	Assistant Engineer

Chaka Khan

Destiny (1986)	Assistant Engineer

Ladysmith Black Mambazo

Two Worlds One Heart (1991)	Assistant Engineer

Branford Marsalis

Creation (2001)	Editing

Johnny Mathis

Global Masters (1997)	Remixing, Mastering

Bobby McFerrin/Chick Corea

Mozart Sessions (1996)	Assistant Engineer

Bette Midler

3 for One (2000)	Assistant Engineer

Mormon Tabernacle Choir

More Greatest Hits (1995)	Engineer
Great Thanksgiving (1995)	Reissue Engineer

Frank Sinatra

Swing and Dance with Frank Sinatra (1996)	Digital Mastering, Archival Restoration

Dionne Warwick

Sings Cole Porter (1989)	Assistant Engineer

Original Soundtrack

Fantasia 2000 (1999)	Assistant Engineer

Pat Foley

Redskins

Neither Washington nor Moscow (1986)	Producer

The Untouchables
Wild Child (1985)   Producer
Original Soundtrack
Letter to Brezhnev (1985)   Producer
Various Artists
Stiff, Stiffer, Stiffest: A Stiff Records Collection (2001)   Producer

Mark Freegard . . . .

The Breeders
Safari (1992)   Remixing
Last Splash (1993)   Producer, Engineer
Cranes
Population 4 (1997)   Producer , Piano, Vocals (bckgr)
EP Collection, Vols. 1-2 (1997)   Producer
Del Amitri
Waking Hours (1989)   Producer
Hatful of Rain: The Best of Del Amitri (1998)   Producer, Engineer
Dillon Fence
Living Room Scene (1994)   Producer
Erasure
EBX, Pt. 2 (1999)   Remixing
Machines of Loving Grace
Burn Like Brilliant Trash (1992)   Engineer
Madder Rose
Panic On (1994)   Producer, Engineer, Mixing, Mini Moog
Marilyn Manson
Lest We Forget: The Best Of (2004)   Mixing
Marillion
Script for a Jester's Tear (1983)   Engineer
Misplaced Childhood (1985)   Mixing Engineer
Brief Encounter (1986)   Engineer
Singles Boxset (2000)   Engineer, Mixing
Maria McKee
Life Is Sweet (1996)   Producer, Engineer, Mixing
New Model Army
No Rest for the Wicked (1985)   Producer, Engineer
Pale Saints
Slow Buildings (1994)   Producer, Engineer
Ride
OX4: The Best of Ride (2002)   Mixing
Tarantula [2001 Bonus Tracks] (2001)   Mixing
Ride [Box Set] (2001)   Mixing
Sisters of Mercy
Vision Thing (1990)   Engineer
Pete Townshend
All the Best Cowboys Have Chinese Eyes (1982)   Assistant Engineer

Don Gehman . . . .

Better Than Ezra
Friction, Baby (1996)   Producer, Engineer, Mixing
Blues Traveler
Truth Be Told (2003)   Arranger, Producer, Mixing
Tracy Chapman
New Beginning (1995)   Producer, Engineer, Mixing
Give Me One Reason (1996)   Producer, Engineer, Mixing
Cock Robin
Best of Cock Robin (1998)   Producer
Firefall
Elan (1978)   Engineer, Mixing
Nanci Griffith
Blue Roses from the Moons (1997)   Producer, Engineer, Mixing
Other Voices, Too (A Trip Back to…) (1998)   Producer, Engineer
Hootie & the Blowfish
Cracked Rear View (1994)   Producer, Engineer, Mixing
Fairweather Johnson (1996)   Producer, Engineer, Mixing
Musical Chairs (1998)   Producer, Engineer, Mixing
Scattered, Smothered and Covered (2000)   Producer, Engineer, Remixing, Mastering, Mixing
Bruce Hornsby & the Range
Night on the Town (1990)   Producer
Across the River (1990)   Producer
Joy Division
Love Will Tear Us Apart (1995)   Mixing
Phil Lesh
There and Back Again (2002)   Producer, Mixing
Mason's Children (2002)   Producer, Mixing
John Cougar Mellencamp
John Cougar (1979)   Engineer
American Fool (1982)   Producer, Engineer
Scarecrow (1985)   Producer, Engineer, Mixing
Lonesome Jubilee (1987)   Producer, Engineer
Best That I Could Do (1978-1988) (1997)   Producer, Engineer
Rough Harvest (1999)   Producer
Cuttin' Heads (2001)   Engineer, Mixing
R.E.M.
Lifes Rich Pageant (1986)   Producer, Engineer
Dead Letter Office (1987)   Producer
Eponymous (1988)   Producer
Brian Setzer
Knife Feels Like Justice (1986)   Producer, Engineer, Mixing
Stephen Stills
Stills (1975)   Engineer
Illegal Stills (1976)   Producer, Mixing
Turnin' Back the Pages (2003)   Producer, Engineer, Mixing
Stills-Young
Long May You Run (1976)   Producer, Engineer, Mixing

Barbra Streisand
Guilty (1980)   Engineer
Emotion (1984)   Mixing
The Subdudes
Subdudes (1989)   Producer
Treat Her Right
Tied to the Tracks (1989)   Producer
Original Soundtrack
La Bamba (1987)   Producer
Footloose [Expanded Edition] (1998)   Producer
Various Artists
Folkways: A Vision Shared (1988)   Producer

Bud Graham ·

David Bromberg
Demon in Disguise (1972)   Engineer
Chicago
At Carnegie Hall, Vols. 1-4… (1971)   Engineer
John Coltrane With Archie Shepp
New Thing at Newport (1965)   Engineer
Miles Davis/John Coltrane
Complete Columbia Recordings (1999)   Engineer
Placido Domingo
Man of La Mancha (1996)   Engineer, Mixing
Gil Evans
Priestess (1977)   Engineer
Branford Marsalis
Romances for Saxophone (1986)   Engineer
Wynton Marsalis
Carnival (1987)   Engine
London Concert: Haydn/Hummel/Mozart/Fasch (2004)   Engineer
Mormon Tabernacle Choir
American Tribute (1990)   Engineer
Voices in Harmony (1990)   Engineer
Rock of Ages: 30 Favorite Hymns (1992)   Engineer
Great Thanksgiving (1995)   Engineer
Stars & Stripes Forever   Engineer
Michael Tilson Thomas
Of Thee I Sing/Let 'em Eat Cake (1987)   Remixing
John Williams
Joy to the World (1991)   Engineer
Green Album   Engineer
Music for Stage and Screen   Engineer, Mixing
Original Broadway Cast
Sound of Music [Original Broadway Cast] (1959)   Engineer
Annie [Original Broadway Cast] (1977)   Engineer
Camelot [Original Broadway Cast] (1998)   Engineer
Original Soundtrack
Irma La Douce [Sony] (1960)   Engineer

Manhattan (1978)	Engineer
Annie [Original Soundtrack] (1982)	Engineer

Jay Graydon . . . .

Air Supply
Ultimate Collection (2000) — Producer
George Benson
George Benson Anthology (2000) — Producer, Synthesizer, Guitar, Arranger
Christopher Cross
Christopher Cross (1980) — Guitar
DeBarge
Rhythm of the Night (1985) — Producer, Engineer, Guitar, Songwriter, Arranger
El DeBarge with DeBarge
Heart Is Not So Smart (1985) — Guitar, Arranger, Producer, Engineer
El DeBarge (1986) — Producer, Engineer, Synthesizer, Guitar, Songwriter, Arranger
Gemini (1989) — Producer, Engineer, Synthesizer, Guitar, Songwriter Arranger
Earth, Wind & Fire
Eternal Dance [Box Set] (1992) — Songwriter
Béla Fleck & The Flecktones
Bela Fleck & The Flecktones (1990) — Guitar
David Foster
Touch of David Foster (1998) — Synthesizer, Guitar, Songwriter, Arranger, Producer, Rhythm Arrangements

Aretha Franklin
Queen of Soul: The Atlantic Years (1993) — Guitar
Art Garfunkel
Lefty (1988) — Synthesizer, Guitar, Producer, Engineer
Marvin Gaye
I Want You (1976) — Guitar
Jay Graydon
Bebop (2001) — Guitar
Al Jarreau
Best of Al Jarreau (1996) — Synthesizer, Bass, Guitar, Songwriter, Arranger, Guitar (Electric), Programming, Producer, Rhythm Arrangements

Manhattan Transfer
Mecca for Moderns (1981) — Synthesizer, Guitar, Songwriter, Arranger, Producer, Engineer
Anthology: Down in Birdland (1992) — Guitar, Songwriter, Arranger, Guitar (Electric), Vocals, Producer, Horn Arrangements

Johnny Mathis
Friends in Love (1982) — Songwriter, Conductor, Producer, Engineer
Love Songs (1988) — Songwriter, Producer
Kenny Rogers
Greatest Hits [EMI America] (1980) — Arranger, Producer
They Don't Make 'em Like They Used (1986) — Synthesizer, Guitar, Songwriter, Arranger, Drums, Producer
Steely Dan
Aja (1977) — Guitar
Decade of Steely Dan (1985) — Guitar
Citizen Steely Dan (1993) — Guitar

Barbra Streisand

Lazy Afternoon (1975)	Guitar (Electric)
Streisand Superman (1977)	Guitar
Songbird (1978)	Guitar
Wet (1979)	Guitar

Donna Summer

On the Radio (Greatest Hits) (1979)	Guitar, Songwriter
She Works Hard for the Money (1983)	Guitar, Songwriter

Dionne Warwick

Friends in Love (1982)	Synthesizer, Guitar, Percussion, Songwriter, Arranger, Producer, Engineer
Dionne Warwick Greatest Hits (1989)	Producer

Original Soundtrack

Grease [Original Soundtrack] (1978)	Guitar
Ghostbusters (1984)	Songwriter, Producer, Engineer
St. Elmo's Fire (1987)	Guitar, Songwriter, Arranger, Composer, Producer,
Caddyshack 2 (1988)	Producer

Original TV Soundtrack

Miami Vice II (1986)	Producer, Engineer

Paul Grupp . . . .

Boston

Boston (1976)	Engineer

Charlie Daniels Band

Million Mile Reflections (1979)	Engineer
Roots Remain (1996)	Engineer
Volunteer Jam, Vol. 7 (1997)	Producer, Engineer

Johnny Lee

Lookin' for Love (1980)	Engineer

Little River Band

Diamantina Cocktail (1976)	Engineer, Remixing
Sleeper Catcher (1978)	Engineer
World Wide Love (1991)	Engineer
Reminiscing (1992)	Engineer

Taj Mahal

Music Fuh Ya' (Music Para Tu) (1977)	Producer, Engineer
Martin Scorsese Presents the Blues: Taj Mahal (2003)	Producer
Sing a Happy Song: The Warner Bros. Recordings (2001)	Mixing

Roger McGuinn

Roger McGuinn & His Band (1975)	Engineer
Born to Rock & Roll (1992)	Engineer

Michael Murphey

Lone Wolf (1978)	Engineer

Ozark Mountain Daredevils

Ozark Mountain Daredevils (1980)	Percussion, Engineer

Bernadette Peters

I'll Be Your Baby Tonight (1996)	Engineer

Pure Prairie League

Two Lane Highway (1975)	Engineer
If the Shoe Fits (1976)	Engineer

Quarterflash

Harden My Heart: The Best of Quarterflash (1997)	Engineer

REO Speedwagon

You Can Tune a Piano, But You Can't Tuna Fish (1978)	Producer, Engineer, Audio Engineer
Hits (1988)	Producer

Linda Ronstadt

Different Drum (1974)	Engineer
Greatest Hits, Vol. 1 (1998)	Engineer
Merry Little Christmas (2000)	Engineer

Carly Simon

Coming Around Again (1987)	Engineer

The Simpsons

Simpsons Sing the Blues (1990)	Engineer
Yellow Album (1998)	Engineer, Mixing

Paul Stanley

Paul Stanley (1978)	Engineer

Livingston Taylor

Carolina Day: The Collection (1970, 1998)	Engineer

Various Artists

Volunteer Jam 6 (1980)	Producer, Engineer
Volunteer Jam 7 (1981)	Producer, Engineer

Original Soundtrack

Urban Cowboy (1980)	Engineer
Fast Times at Ridgemont High (1982)	Engineer
Streets of Fire (1984)	Engineer
Cry Baby (1990)	Engineer, Engineering Supervisor, Supervising Engineer
Hope Floats [Original Soundtrack] (1998)	Engineer

John Guess . . . .

Blackhawk

Sky's the Limit (1998)	Mixing

Suzy Bogguss

Aces (1991)	Engineer

Captain Beefheart and the Magic Band

Unconditionally Guaranteed (1974)	Engineer
Dust Blows Forward: An Anthology (1999)	Engineer

Larry Carlton

Playing/Singing (1973)	Producer

Jeff Carson

Butterfly Kisses (1997)	Mixing

Linda Davis

Shoot for the Moon (1994)	Producer, Mixing
Some Things Are Meant to Be (1996)	Producer, Engineer, Mixing
I'm Yours (1998)	Producer, Engineer

Dixie Chicks

Wide Open Spaces (1998)	Mixing
Fly (1999)	Mixing

Vince Gill

Pocket Full of Gold (1991)	Engineer, Mixing

I Still Believe in You (1992)   Engineer, Mixing
Toby Keith
Greatest Hits, Vol. 1 (1998)   Mixing
Pull My Chain [Enhanced] (2001)   Engineer
Patty Loveless
Only What I Feel (1993)   Mixing
When Fallen Angels Fly (1994)   Mixing
Long Stretch of Lonesome (1997)   Mixing
Strong Heart (2000)   Mixing, Tracking
Reba McEntire
For My Broken Heart (1991)   Engineer, Mastering, Mixing
Greatest Hits, Vol. 2 (1993)   Engineer
What If It's You (1996)   Producer, Engineer, Mixing
John Michael Montgomery
Kickin' It Up (1994)   Engineer
Lorrie Morgan
Greatest Hits (1995)   Engineer, Mastering, Mixing
Dolly Parton
For God and Country (2003)   Mixing
Kenny Rogers
42 Ultimate Hits (2004)   Producer
Back to the Well [Sanctuary] (2003)   Producer, Engineer, Mixing
Frank Sinatra
Some Nice Things I've Missed (1973)   Remixing, Mixing
Rod Stewart
Camouflage (1984)   Engineer, Remixing
George Strait
Pure Country (1992)   Mixing
Latest Greatest Straitest Hits (2000)   Mixing
Keith Urban
In the Ranch (2004)   Mixing
Keith Urban/The Ranch (2003)   Mixing
Lari White
Best of Lari White (1997)   Producer
Kelly Willis
One More Time: The MCA Recordings (2000)   Producer
Chely Wright
Let Me In (1997)   Engineer
Michelle Wright
For Me It's You (1996)   Producer, Mixing
Reasons Why (1997)   Producer, Mixing
Greatest Hits (2000)   Producer, Mixing
Original Soundtrack
Prince of Egypt (Nashville) (1998)   Engineer, Mixing
Various Artists
USA for Africa: We Are the World (1985)   Engineer

Robert Hall. . . . .

Nancy Apple
Outside the Lines (2001)   Drums
Freeworld
You Are Here (1996)   Drum Technician
Diversity (1999)   Drum Technician
Celia McRee
Passion (1994)   Drums
REM
Green (1988)   Drum Technician
Automatic For The People (1992)   Drum Technician
Keith Sykes
Advanced Medication for the Blues (1998)   Drums
Zuider Zee
Zuider Zee (1975)   Drums

John Hampton . . . .

The Afghan Whigs
Gentlemen (1993)   Engineer
Luther Allison
Soul Fixin' Man (1994)   Mixing
Blue Streak (1995)   Mixing
Audio Adrenaline
Bloom (1996)   Percussion, Producer, Engineer, Mixing
Some Kind of Zombie (1997)   Producer
8 Great Hits (2004)   Producer
Hit Parade (2001)   Producer
BR5-49
Big Backyard Beat Show (1998)   Mixing
Big Tent Revival
Open All Nite (1996)   Producer, Engineer
Amplifier (1998)   Producer
Choose Life (1999)   Mixing
Marty Brown
High & Dry (1991)   Engineer, Mixing
Wild Kentucky Skies (1993)   Mixing
Cryin', Lovin', Leavin' (1994)   Mixing
Alex Chilton
Like Flies on Sherbert (1979)   Engineer, Mixing
High Priest/Feudalist Tarts/No Sex (1987)   Engineer
The Cramps
Songs the Lord Taught Us (1980)   Engineer
Psychedelic Jungle/Gravest Hits (1981)   Engineer
Robert Cray
Heavy Picks: The Robert Cray Collection (1999)   Mixing

dc Talk
Welcome to the Freak Show (1997)   Mixing
James Luther Dickinson
Free Beer Tomorrow (2002)   Mixing
Gin Blossoms
New Miserable Experience (1992)   Producer, Engineer, Mixing
Outside Looking In: The Best of Gin Blossoms (1999)   Producer, Engineer, Mixing
Toots Hibbert
Toots in Memphis (1988)   Engineer
Idle Wilds
Dumb, Gifted and Beautiful (1995)   Producer, Engineer
B.B. King
Blues Summit (1993)   Mixing
Little Texas
Big Time (1993)   Engineer, Mixing
Kick a Little (1994)   Engineer, Mixing
Little Texas [1997] (1997)   Engineer, Mixing
Lynyrd Skynyrd
Lynyrd Skynyrd 1991 (1991)   Engineer
Mr. Henry
Jackhammer (1998)   Producer, Engineer, Mixing
Mudhoney
Tomorrow Hit Today (1998)   Engineer
North Mississippi Allstars
51 Phantom (2001)   Mixing
The Replacements
Pleased to Meet Me (1987)   Engineer, Mixing
All For Nothing/Nothing for All (1997)   Engineer, Mixing
Kim Richey
Kim Richey (1995)   Mixing
Sid Selvidge
Twice Told Tales (1993)   Producer, Engineer, Mixing
Smalltown Poets
Smalltown Poets (1997)   Producer, Engineer
Listen Closely (1998)   Producer, Engineer, Mixing
Snider
Viva Satellite (1998)   Producer, Engineer
Aaron Tippin
Greatest Hits and the Some (1997)   Mixing
Travis Tritt
It's All About to Change (1991)   Engineer, Mixing
T-r-o-u-b-l-e (1992)   Mixing
Vaughan Brothers
Family Style (1990)   Engineer
Jimmie Vaughan
Strange Pleasure (1995)   Engineer, Mixing
Out There (1998)   Producer
Do You Get the Blues (2001)   Engineer, Mixing

Joe Hardy. . . . .

Jimmy Barnes
Hits (1996)   Producer, Engineer
Bloodline
Bloodline (1994)   Producer, Engineer, Mixing
C.J. Chenier
I Ain't No Playboy (1992)   Organ, Guitar, Producer, Engineer, Mixing
Tom Cochrane
Mad Mad World (1992)   Percussion, Producer, Engineer, Mixing
Steve Earle
Copperhead Road (1988)   Engineer
The Hard Way (1990)   Producer, Engineer
The Georgia Satellites
Let It Rock: The Best of the Georgia Satellites (1993)   Producer
The Jeff Healey Band
Feel This (1992)   Percussion, Keyboards, Producer, Engineer, Mixing
Master Hits: Jeff Healey Band (1999)   Producer
The Hooters
Out of Body (1993)   Producer, Engineer, Mixing, Digital Engineer
Colin James
Sudden Stop (1990)   Producer, Engineer, Mixing
Colin James & the Little Big Band (1998)   Arranger, Producer, Engineer, Mixing
Tommy Keene
Based on Happy Times (1989)   Producer, Engineer, Organ, Strings, Guitar (Bass)
Michael McDermott
Michael McDermott (1996)   Producer, Engineer, Mixing
Last Chance Lounge (2000)   Producer, Engineer, Mixing, Bass, Guitar, Vocals
Ashes (2004)   Programming, Multi Instruments, Producer, Engineer, Mixing, Instrumentation
Kim Mitchell
Itch (1994)   Producer, Engineer, Mixing
The Radiators
Zig-Zaggin' Through Ghostland (1989)   Producer, Engineer, Mixing
The Replacements
Pleased to Meet Me (1987)   Engineer, Mixing
All For Nothing/Nothing for All (1997)   Engineer, Mixing
.38 Special
Resolution (1997)   Producer, Mixing
Anthology (2001)   Producer
38 Special
Anthology (2001)   Producer
Drivetrain (2004)   Mixing
Tora Tora
Surprise Attack (1989)   Producer, Engineer
ZZ Top
Afterburner (1985)   Engineer
Greatest Hits (1992)   Engineer
Antenna (1994)   Engineer, Mixing
One Foot in the Blues (1994)   Engineer
Rhythmeen (1996)   Engineer, Mixing

XXX (1999)	Engineer, Mixing, Recording
Mescalero (2003)	Engineer, Mixing
Original Soundtrack	
Bill & Ted's Excellent Adventure	Producer

Roger Hawkins . . . .

Duane Allman	
Anthology (1972)	Drums
Anthology, Vol. 2 (1974)	Drums
Gregg Allman	
Searching for Simplicity (1997)	Conga, Timbales
James Brown	
Star Time (1991)	Drums
Jimmy Buffett	
Beach House on the Moon (1999)	Drums
Eric Clapton	
Money and Cigarettes (1983)	Drums
Aretha Franklin	
Aretha Arrives (1967)	Drums
Aretha Now (1968)	Drums
Lady Soul (1968)	Drums
Soul '69 (1969)	Drums
Spirit in the Dark (1970)	Drums
Queen of Soul: The Atlantic Years (1993)	Drums
Art Garfunkel	
Breakaway (1975)	Drums
Watermark (1977)	Drums
Etta James	
Tell Mama (1968)	Drums
Seven Year Itch (1989)	Drums
Delbert McClinton	
Second Wind (1978)	Drums
Willie Nelson	
Phases and Stages (1974)	Drums
Laura Nyro	
Christmas and the Beads of Sweat (1970)	Drums
Gonna Take a Miracle (1971)	Percussion
Penn	
Do Right Man (1994)	Drums, Percussion
Wilson Pickett	
Man and a Half: The Best of Wilson Pickett (1992)	Drums
Primal Scream	
Give Out But Don't Give Up (1994)	Drums
Linda Ronstadt	
Linda Ronstadt (1971)	Drums
Leon Russell	
And the Shelter People (1971)	Drums
Leon Russell & the Shelter People (1971)	Drums

Boz Scaggs

Boz Scaggs (1969)	Drums
My Time (1972)	Drums
Hits! (1980)	Drums

Bob Seger

Back in '72 (1973)	Drums
Beautiful Loser (1975)	Percussion, Drums, Producer
Night Moves (1976)	Drums, Percussion
Stranger in Town (1978)	Percussion, Drums
Against the Wind (1980)	Percussion, Drums
The Distance (1982)	Drums

Paul Simon

There Goes Rhymin' Simon (1973)	Percussion, Drums
Still Crazy After All These Years (1975)	Drums

Rod Stewart

Atlantic Crossing (1975)	Percussion, Drums
Night on the Town (1976)	Drums

Traffic

Shoot Out at the Fantasy Factory (1973)	Drums
Traffic: On the Road (1973)	Drums

Tony Joe White

Best of Tony Joe White (1973)	Drums, Percussion

Bobby Womack

Communication (1971)	Percussion, Drums
Understanding (1972)	Percussion, Drums
Facts of Life (1973)	Drums

Bob Hodas . . . .

William Ackerman

Imaginary Roads (1990)	Engineer

Emily Bezar

Grandmothers Tea Leaves (1994)	Engineer, Mixing
Moon in Grenadine (1996)	Engineer, Mixing

Jim Chappell

Nightsongs and Lullabies (1991)	Engineer, Mixing

Tim Clark

Tales of the Sun People (1990)	Mixing

Ferron

Not a Still Life (1992)	Engineer

Billy Harper

Live on Tour in the Far East, Vol.1 (1994)	Engineer
Live on Tour in the Far East, Vol. 2 (1995)	Engineer
Live on Tour in the Far East, Vol. 3 (1995)	Engineer

Mickey Hart/Airto/Flora Purim

Däfos (1983)	Technical Assistance

Mickey Hart/Henry Wolff/Nancy Hennings

Yamantaka (1983)	Engineer, Mixing

Barbara Higbie

Signs of Life (1990)	Engineer, Mixing

232

Osamu Kitajima
Behind the Light (1991)   Engineer, Mixing
Michael Manring
Toward the Center of the Night (1989)   Engineer
The Modern Mandolin Quartet
Intermezzo (1990)   Engineer, Editing
Amy X Neuburg
Songs 91 to 85 (1996)   Mixing
San Francisco Gay Men's Chorus
How Fair This Place (1991)   Engineer

Chris Huston. . . . .

The Bar-Kays
Soul Finger (1967)   Engineer
Blood, Sweat & Tears
Nuclear Blues (1980)   Engineer
Tim Buckley
Greetings from L.A. (1972)   Engineer, Remixing
Morning Glory: The Tim Buckley… (2001)   Engineer
Eric Burdon & War
Best of Eric Burdon & War (1996)   Engineer
War [1971] (1971)   Engineer
World Is a Ghetto (1972)   Engineer
Deliver the Word (1973)   Engineer
Why Can't We Be Friends (1975)   Engineer
Greatest Hits [United Artists] (1976)   Engineer
Grooves & Messages: Greatest Hits (1999)   Producer, Engineer
Robben Ford
Discovering the Blues (1972)   Engineer
Schizophonic (1976)   Producer, Engineer
Anthology: The Early Years (2001)   Producer, Engineer
The Fugs
Fugs Second Album (1993)   Engineer
H.P. Lovecraft
H.P. Lovecraft II (1968)   Engineer
Led Zeppelin
Complete Studio Recordings (1993)   Engineer
The Nazz
Nazz (1968)   Associate Producer
Lee Oskar
The Best Of Lee Oskar (1992)   Engineer

Dennis Hysom . . . .

Dennis Hysom discography:
1992   The Wooleycat's Favorite Nursery Rhymes
1996   Ancient Voices
2001   Glacier Bay
2001   Ocean Planet

2001	Caribbean
2001	Bayou
2001	Prairie
2001	Song Play Hooray
2001	The Wooleycat's Favorite Fairy Tales

Joanie Bartels
Jump for Joy — Vocals

Karan Casey
Seal Maiden: A Celtic Musical (2000) — Sound Design

Russil Paul
Bhava Yoga (2000) — Natural Sounds

Various Artists
Healing Music Project (2000) — Sound Effects
Healing Music Project: Radiance (2004) — Natural Sounds

Wayne Jackson . . . .

Duane Allman
Anthology, Vol. 2 (1974) — Trumpet

Booker T. & the MG's
Very Best of Booker T. & the MG's (1994) — Trumpet

The Box Tops
Best of the Box Tops: Soul Deep (1996) — Horn Arrangements

Jimmy Buffett
Boats, Beaches, Bars & Ballads (1992) — Trombone, Trumpet

Ray Charles
Genius & Soul: The 50th Anniversary Box Set (1949) — Trumpet

Joe Cocker
Live! (1990) — Trumpet, Horn

Robert Cray
Heavy Picks: The Robert Cray Collection (1999) — Trombone, Trumpet

Dr. John
Sun, Moon & Herbs (1971) — Horn

The Doobie Brothers
Greatest Hits (2001) — Trumpet

En Vogue
Funky Divas (1992) — Rap

Eddie Floyd
Knock on Wood (1967) — Trumpet

Aretha Franklin
Queen of Soul: The Atlantic Years (1993) — Trumpet, Sax (Tenor)

Peter Gabriel
So (1986) — Trumpet, Cornet, Horn Arrangements

Al Green
Anthology (1997) — Trumpet

Billy Joel
Storm Front (1989) — Horn

Albert King
Born Under a Bad Sign (1967) — Horn

B.B. King
King of the Blues [Box] (1992)   Horn
Mark Knopfler
Sailing to Philadelphia (2000)   Trumpet
Jerry Lee Lewis
All Killer, No Filler: The Jerry Lewis Anthology (1993)   Trumpet
Little Feat
Hotcakes and Outtakes: 30 Years of (2000)   Trumpet
Nick Lowe
Convincer (2001)   Trumpet
Manhattan Transfer
Jukin' (1969)   Trumpet, Flugelhorn
The Mar-Keys
Great Memphis Sound (1966)   Trumpet
The Memphis Horns
Memphis Horns [Telarc] (1971)   Trombone, Trumpet, Horn
High on Music (1976)   Horn
Get up and Dance (1977)   Horn
Memphis Horns Band 2 (1978)   Horn
Welcome To (1979)   Horn
Flame Out (1992)   Trombone, Trumpet, Producer
Memphis Horns with Special Guests (1995)   Trombone, Trumpet
Willie Nelson
Shotgun Willie (1973)   Trumpet
Ann Peebles
Best of Ann Peebles: The Hi Years (1996)   Trumpet
Dan Penn
Do Right Man (1994)   Trumpet
Wilson Pickett
Man and a Half: The Best of Wilson Pickett (1992)   Trumpet
Elvis Presley
Memphis Record (1987)   Trumpet
Primal Scream
Vanishing Point (1997)   Trumpet
John Prine
Common Sense (1975)   Horn
Bonnie Raitt
Longing in Their Hearts (1994)   Trombone, Trumpet
Otis Redding
Otis! The Definitive Otis Redding (1993)   Trumpet
Sting
Mercury Falling (1996)   Trumpet
James Taylor
Mud Slide Slim and the Blue Horizon (1971)   Horn
Carla Thomas
Gee Whiz: The Best of Carla Thomas (1994)   Trumpet
Rufus Thomas
Funky Chicken [Stax] (1969)   Trumpet, Arranger
Tony Joe White
Best of Tony Joe White (1973)   Trumpet

Steve Winwood
The Finer Things (1995)   Trombone, Trumpet

David Kahne . . . .

The Bangles
Bangles (1982)   Producer, Engineer
All Over the Place (1984)   Producer, Engineer
Different Light (1986)   Producer
Tony Bennett
Steppin' Out (1993)   Producer
MTV Unplugged (1994)   Producer
Here's to the Ladies (1995)   Producer
Shawn Colvin
Fat City (1992)   Producer
Cover Girl (1994)   Bass, Keyboards, Programming, Producer, Mixing
Dick Dale & the Del-Tones
King of the Surf Guitar: The Best of Dick Dale (1989)   Producer
Fishbone
Truth & Soul (1988)   Producer, Engineer
Reality of My Surroundings (1991)   Producer, Associate Producer
Fishbone 101: Nuttasaurusmeg Fossil Fuelin (1996)   Producer
Greg Garing
Alone (1997)   Keyboards, Programming, Producer, Engineer, Mixing
Imogen Heap
I Megaphone (1998)   Producer, Engineer, Mixing
k.d. lang
Invincible Summer (2000)   Producer, Mixing
Paul McCartney
Back in the World (2002)   Producer, Mixing
From a Lover to a Friend [CD #1] (2001)   Synthesizer, Guitar, Programming, Producer, Sampling
Freedom (2001)   Producer
Driving Rain (2001)   Synthesizer, Guitar, Guitar (Electric), Organ (Hammond), Programming,
                                Producer, Sampling, Mixing, Wurlitzer, Roland Synthesizer, String Samples
Stevie Nicks
Trouble in Shangri-La (2001)   Keyboards, Programming, Producer
Menace to Sobriety (2000)   Producer, Mixing
Orgy
Vapor Transmission (2000)   Producer, Mixing
Presidents of the United States of America
Presidents of the United States of America (1995)   Mixing
Red Rockers
Good As Gold (1983)   Producer, Engineer
Romeo Void
Instincts (1984)   Producer, Engineer
Warm, In Your Coat (1992)   Producer
Soul Coughing
Irresistible Bliss (1996)   Producer, Mixing
Sublime
Sublime (1996)   Organ, Producer, Mixing

What I Got [7 Song EP] (1997)   Producer
Doin' Time (1997)   Producer
Greatest Hits (1999)   Organ, Producer, Mixing
Sugar Ray
Floored (1997)   Keyboards, Programming, Producer, Engineer, Mixing
14:59 (1999)   Programming, Producer, Engineer, Mastering, Mixing
Sugar Ray (2001)   Programming, Producer, Mixing
In the Pursuit of Leisure (2003)   Programming, Producer, Engineer, Mixing
Matthew Sweet
Inside (1986)   Producer, Guitar (Acoustic), Keyboards
Translator
Everywhere That We Were: The Best of Translator (1996)   Producer
Original Soundtrack
American Pie (1999)   Programming, Producer, Engineer, Mixing
Original Television Soundtrack
King of the Hill (1999)   Programming, Producer, Mixing
Touched By an Angel: The Album (1998)   Producer
Various Artists
Folkways: A Vision Shared (1988)   Producer, Engineer

Michael Kamen

Bryan Adams
18 'til I Die (1996)   Piano, String Arrangements
MTV Unplugged (1997)   Conductor, String Arrangements
David Bowie
David Live (1974)   Keyboards, Oboe, Piano (Electric), Moog Synthesizer
Sound + Vision [Box Set] (1989)   Piano, Oboe
Liona Boyd
Persona (1988)   Producer, Arranger, Strings, Bass, Percussion, Piano, Shakuhachi, Drums, Keyboards, Oboe, Wind, Choir, Chorus, Bells
Kate Bush
Sensual World (1989)   Arranger, Orchestration
Red Shoes [US] (1993)   Orchestration
This Woman's Work [Box Set] (1998)   Arranger
Eric Clapton
24 Nights (1991)   Conductor
Def Leppard
Retro Active (1993)   Strings, Arranger
Eurythmics
Touch (1983)   Conductor, String Arrangements
Be Yourself Tonight (1985)   Strings, Celeste
Revenge (1986)   Strings, Conductor, Orchestration
Indigo Girls
Rites of Passage (1992)   Conductor, String Arrangements
Metallica
Metallica (1991)   Arranger
S&M (1999)   Arranger, Conductor, Producer, Liner Notes, Orchestration
New York Rock & Roll Ensemble
Faithful Friends (1969)   Guitar, Keyboards, Vocals, Wind

Reflections (1970)	Keyboards, Oboe
Roll Over (1971)	Organ, Guitar, Piano, Keyboards, Oboe, Vocals, Wind
Freedomburger (1972)	Guitar, Keyboards, Vocals
Tom Petty	
Wildflowers (1994)	Conductor, Orchestration
Pink Floyd	
Wall (1979)	Orchestral Arrangements
Final Cut (1983)	Piano, Arranger, Conductor, Harmonium, Keyboards
Shine On (1992)	Arranger, Orchestral Arrangements
Division Bell (1994)	Arranger, Orchestration
Queen	
Kind of Magic (1986)	Orchestration
Greatest Hits, Vol. 2 (1991)	Orchestral Arrangements
Queensryche	
Warning (1984)	Arranger, Conductor
Operation: Mindcrime (1988)	Cello, Choir, Chorus
Sting	
Fields of Gold: The Best of Sting… (1994)	Producer
Roger Waters	
Pros and Cons of Hitch Hiking (1984)	Piano, Arranger, Conductor, Drums, Producer
Wall: Live in Berlin, 1990 (1990)	Conductor, Orchestration
Amused to Death (1992)	Arranger, Conductor
Original Score	
Mr. Holland's Opus [Score] (1996)	Piano, Strings, Conductor, Producer, Orchestration
Bordello of Blood [Score] (1996)	Executive Score Producer
Brazil (1985)	Arranger, Conductor, Producer, Liner Notes, Orchestration
Lethal Weapon (1987)	Keyboards
Lethal Weapon 2 (1989)	Producer, Kurzweil Synthesizer
Die Hard 2: Die Harder (1990)	Composer, Conductor, Producer,
Lethal Weapon 3 (1992)	Conductor, Keyboards, Producer
Die Hard with a Vengeance (1995)	Composer
Digital Highlander: the Final Dimension (1995)	Conductor, Producer, Orchestration
What Dreams May Come (1998)	Conductor, Oboe, Orchestra,
X-Men (2000)	Producer, Score Conductor

Ken Kessie . . . .

Greg Adams	
Hidden Agenda (1995)	Producer, Engineer, Mixing, Bass, Arranger, Drums, Keyboards,
All-4-One	
And the Music Speaks (1995)	Mixing
Assia	
Chercheuse d'Or (2001)	Engineer, Drum Programming, Realization
The Barrio Boyzz	
Crazy Coolin' (1992)	Mixing
Bell Biv Devoe	
WBBD-Bootcity! [Re-mix Album] (1991)	Engineer
Regina Belle	
Baby Come to Me: The Best of Regina Belle (1997)	Mixing

The Braxton Brothers
Now & Forever (1999)   Mixing
Brownstone
From the Bottom Up (1995)   Producer, Engineer, Mixing
En Vogue
Born to Sing (1990)   Engineer
Funky Divas (1992)   Mixing
EV3 (1997)   Engineer, Mixing
Masterpiece Theatre (2000)   Mixing
Journey
Departure (1980)   Engineer, Assistant Engineer, Mixing Assistant
Bobby McFerrin
Bobby McFerrin (1982)   Engineer
New Kids on the Block
Face the Music (1994)   Guitar, Mixing
Ce Ce Peniston
Thought 'Ya Knew (1994)   Mixing
Billy Preston
On the Air (1996)   Engineer, Mixing
Carlos Santana
Havana Moon (1983)   Engineer
Sister Sledge
All American Girls (1981)   Engineer
Sylvester
Do Ya Wanna Funk (1982)   Mixing
Greatest Hits (1983)   Producer
Tony! Toni! Toné!
Revival (1990)   Engineer, Mixing
Sons of Soul (1993)   Mixing
House of Music (1996)   Engineer, Mixing
Tower of Power
What Is Hip?: The Tower of Power Anthology (1999)   Engineer, Mixing
The Tubes
Outside/Inside (1983)   Engineer
Narada Michael Walden
Ecstasy's Dance: The Best of Michael Narada Walden (1996)   Engineer
Jody Watley
Affairs of the Heart (1991)   Mixing
Original Soundtrack
Apocalypse Now (1979)   Engineer
Apocalypse Now Redux (2001)   Engineer

Richard King. . . . .

American Boy Choir
Carol (1996)   Mixing, Balance Engineer
Bang on a Can
Industry (1995)   Engineer
Cheating, Lying, Stealing (1996)   Engineer

Joshua Bell/Philharmonica Orchestra/David Zinman

West Side Story Suite (2001)	Engineer

James Carter

Gardenias for Lady Day (2003)	Mixing

Miles Davis

Live at the Fillmore East (2001)	Mixing

Placido Domingo

Man of La Mancha (1996)	Editing
Christmastime in Vienna (1999)	Mixing

Billy Joel

Fantasies & Delusions (2001)	Engineer, Mastering

Yo-Yo Ma

Protecting Veil/Wake up & Die (1998)	Engineer
Solo (1999)	Engineer
Obrigado Brazil (2003)	Engineer
Obrigado Brazil Live in Concert (2004)	Engineer, Mastering
Sounds of Yo-Yo Ma (2004)	Reissue Engineer

Yo-Yo Ma/Frank/Winter/Waterston

Lulie the Iceberg (1999)	Engineer

Yo-Yo Ma & the Silk Road Ensemble

Silk Road Journeys: When Strangers Meet (2002)	Engineer
Silk Road Journeys: Beyond the Horizon (2004)	Engineer, Mixing

Wynton Marsalis

Fiddler's Tale (1999)	Engineer

Charles Mingus

Soul Fusion (1978)	Engineer

Mormon Tabernacle Choir

More Greatest Hits: 19 Best Loved Favorites (1995)	Engineer
Around the World: A Musical Journey (1996)	Engineer, Reissue Producer
Stars & Stripes Forever	Producer, Engineer

Jessye Norman/Ann Schein

Seven Early Songs/Altenberg Songs/Youthful Songs (1995)	Engineer

Mark O'Connor/Ma/Marsalis/Taylor

Liberty (1997)	Mixing

Arcadi Volodos

Live at Carnegie Hall (1999)	Engineer

Grover Washington, Jr.

Aria (2000)	Engineer

John Williams

Joy to the World (1991)	Editing

Original Broadway Cast

Camelot (1998)	Engineer

Original Soundtrack

Crouching Tiger Hidden Dragon (2000)	Engineer, Mixing

Craig Krampf . . . .

Alabama

Pass It on Down (1990)	Percussion, Drums
American Pride (1992)	Percussion, Drums

240

Cheap Seats (1993)	Percussion, Drums
In Pictures (1995)	Drums
Joan Armatrading	
Key (1983)	Drums
Kim Carnes	
Gypsy Honeymoon: Best of Kim Carnes (1993)	Drums, Vocals (bckgr), Drum Programming
Cher	
Cher (1987)	Drums, Drum Programming
Ashley Cleveland	
Big Town (1991)	Producer, Mixing, Percussion, Drums, Vocals (bckgr)
Bus Named Desire (1993)	Producer, Drums
Alice Cooper	
Zipper Catches Skin (1982)	Drums
Disappear Fear	
Disappear Fear (1994)	Producer, Percussion, Drums
Melissa Etheridge	
Melissa Etheridge (1988)	Producer, Percussion, Drums
The Features	
Exhibit A (2004)	Producer
Nick Gilder	
Best of Nick Gilder: Hot Child in the City (2001)	Percussion, Drums
Buddy Guy	
Sweet Tea (2001)	Percussion
Col. Bruce Hampton	
Fiji Mariners (1996)	Drums
Will Kimbrough	
Home Away (2002)	Percussion, Drums
Patty Loveless	
Trouble with the Truth (1996)	Drums
Strong Heart (2000)	Percussion, Drums
The Motels	
All 4 One (1982)	Percussion, Drums
Little Robbers (1983)	Drums
Dolly Parton	
Rainbow (1988)	Drums, Producer, Drum Overdubs
Steve Perry	
Greatest Hits + Five Unreleased (1998)	Producer, Drums
Santana	
Beyond Appearances (1985)	Drums
Son Volt	
Trace (1995)	Drums
Townes Van Zandt	
Far Cry from Dead (1999)	Cymbals, Drums, Tambourine, Triangle, Bells, Drums (Snare)
Warren Zevon	
Sentimental Hygiene (1987)	Drums
I'll Sleep When I'm Dead (Anthology) (1996)	Drums

Bob Kruzen . . . .

Gil Clark
Ridin' On (2000)   Producer, Engineer, Mixing
Willy DeVille
Horse of a Different Color (2001)   Engineer, Mixing
Steve Forbert
Evergreen Boy (2000)   Engineer

Daniel Lanois . . . .

Brian Blade
Brian Blade Fellowship (1998)   Producer, Photography, Mando-Guitar
Perceptual (2000)   Guitar (Acoustic), Guitar, Pedal Steel Guitar
Harold Budd & Brian Eno
Ambient 2: The Plateaux of Mirrors (1980)   Engineer
Pearl (1984)   Producer
Bella Vista (2003)   Producer, Liner Notes, Cover Photo
Bob Dylan
Oh Mercy (1989)   Dobro, Guitar, Producer, Omnichord, Mixing, Lap Steel Guitar
Bootleg Series, Vols. 1-3: Rare &... (1991)   Bass, Guitar, Percussion, Guitar (12 String), Producer
Time Out of Mind (1997)   Guitar, Guitar (Rhythm), Producer, Photography, Mando-Guitar
Love Sick [US] (1997)   Producer
Brian Eno
Ambient 4: On Land (1982)   Engineer, Equalization
Apollo: Atmospheres & Soundtracks (1983)   Producer
Eno Box I: Instrumentals (1994)   Producer
More Music For Films (2005)   Producer
Roger Eno
Voices (1985)   Producer
Marianne Faithfull
Vagabond Ways (1999)   Organ, Bass, Guitar, Percussion, Drums, Producer, Drums (Snare), Loops, Loop
Peter Gabriel
Birdy (1985)   Producer
So (1986)   Guitar, Percussion, Tambourine, Guitar (12 String), Producer, Engineer
Shaking the Tree: Sixteen Golden... (1990)   Drums, Producer
Us (1992)   Guitar, Vocals, Producer, Shaker
OVO: Millennium Show (2000)   Engineer
Up, (Japan Bonus CD) (2002)   Guitar, Percussion, Sampling
Emmylou Harris
Wrecking Ball (1995)   Dulcimer, Guitar (Acoustic), Bass, Mandolin, Percussion, Guitar (Electric),
                                      Producer, Chant, Harmony Vocals, Bass Pedals
Stumble Into Grace (2003)   Pedal Steel, Vocals, Orchestra
Hothouse Flowers
Home (1990)   Dobro, Producer
Martha and the Muffins
Then Again: A Retrospective (1998)   Producer
Willie Nelson
Teatro (1998)   Mandolin, Producer, Omnichord, Photography

The Neville Brothers
Yellow Moon (1989)   Guitar, Keyboards, Vocals (bckgr), Producer, Mixing
Brother's Keeper (1990)   Guitar
AaronNeville
Ultimate Collection (2001)   Producer
Paul Oakenfold
Ibiza (2001)   Producer
Robbie Robertson
Robbie Robertson (1987)   Bass, Guitar, Percussion, Vocals, Vocals (bckgr), Producer, Omnichord
Ron Sexsmith
Ron Sexsmith (1995)   Guitar (Electric), Producer, Photography
Billy Bob Thorton
Edge of the World (2003)   Bass, Guitar, Percussion, Pedal Steel, Guitar (Electric), Sitar, Producer,
Omnichord
U2
Unforgettable Fire (1984)   Vocals, Producer, Engineer, Treatments
Joshua Tree (1987)   Guitar (Rhythm), Tambourine, Vocals (bckgr), Producer, Omnichord
Rattle and Hum (1988)   Engineer
Achtung Baby (1991)   Guitar, Percussion, Producer, Mixing
Zooropa (1993)   Engineer
Best of 1980-1990 (1998)   Producer, Engineer, Mixing
All That You Can't Leave Behind (2000)   Guitar, Vocals (bckgr), Producer, Mixing
How To Dismantle An Atomic Bomb, (Bonus Track), (CD + DVD Deluxe Edition)(2004)   Guitar,
Mandolin, Pedal Steel, Producer, Shaker

Original Soundtrack
9 1/2 Weeks (1988)   Producer, Engineer
Philadelphia [Original Soundtrack] (1993)   Producer
Trainspotting (1996)   Producer
Sling Blade (1996)   Bass, Guitar, Arranger, Producer, Engineer, Loops, Omnichord
Good Will Hunting (1997)   Producer
Wonder Boys [Soundtrack] (2000)   Producer
High Fidelity (2000)   Producer
Tomb Raider (2001)   Producer
Television Soundtrack
Touched By an Angel: The Album (1998)   Producer

Brian Lee. . . . .

Cindy Bullens
Somewhere Between Heaven & Earth (1999)   Engineer
Rick Danko Band
Live on Breeze Hill (1999)   Mastering
The Gipsy Kings
Best of the Gipsy Kings   Mastering
Juliana Hatfield
Juliana's Pony: Total System… (2000)   Mastering
Beautiful Creature (2000)   Mastering
Journey
Infinity (1978)   Remastering
Evolution (1979)   Remastering

Departure (1980)	Remastering
Captured (1981)	Remastering
Escape (1981)	Remastering
Raised on Radio (1986)	Remastering
Ali Akbar Khan/Asha Bhosle/Swapan Chaudhuri	
Legacy: 16th-18th Century Music From India (1998)	Mastering
Moore	
Strangest Places (1997)	Mastering
Ozzy Osbourne	
Diary of a Madman (1981)	Remastering
Bark at the Moon (1983)	Remastering
Tribute (1987)	Remastering
No Rest for the Wicked (1989)	Remastering
No More Tears (1991)	Remastering
Rush	
2112 (1976)	Remastering
Moving Pictures (1981)	Remastering
Exit…Stage Left (1981)	Remastering
Signals (1982)	Remastering
Power Windows (1985)	Remastering
Retrospective, Vol. 1 (1974-1980) (1997)	Remastering
Retrospective, Vol. 2 (1981-1987) (1997)	Remastering
Bruce Springsteen	
Chimes of Freedom (1988)	Remastering
Greatest Hits [Columbia] (1995)	Editing
Billy Squier	
Reach for the Sky: The Anthology (1996)	Mastering
Stevie Ray Vaughan & Double Trouble	
Live at Carnegie Hall (1997)	Mastering
Yamantaka Trochu	
Diamond Path: Rituals of Tibetan Buddhism (1998)	Mastering

Bob Ludwig . . . .

Bryan Adams	
Reckless (1984)	Mastering
So Far So Good (1993)	Mastering
Anthrax	
Persistence of Time (1990)	Mastering
The B-52's	
Time Capsule (1998)	Mastering
Barenaked Ladies	
Everything To Everyone (2003)	Mastering
Beck	
Odelay (1996)	Mastering, Photography
Mutations (1998)	Mastering
Sea Change (2002)	Mastering
Guero (2005)	Mastering
Tony Bennett	
Astoria: Portrait of the Artist (1990)	Mastering

Mariah Carey

#1's (1998)   Mastering

Glitter (2001)   Mastering

Tracy Chapman

Matters of the Heart (1992)   Mastering

Telling Stories (2000)   Mastering

Eric Clapton

Clapton Chronicles: Best of 1981-1999 (1999)   Mastering

Reptile (2001)   Mastering

Elvis Costello

Spike (1989/2001)   Mastering/Remastering

All This Useless Beauty (1996/2001)   Mastering/Remastering

Sheryl Crow

Sheryl Crow (1996)   Mastering

Globe Sessions (1998)   Mastering

Def Leppard

Hysteria (1987)   Mastering

Rock Of Ages: The Definitive Collection (2005)   Mastering

Dire Straits

Making Movies (1980)   Remastering

Love over Gold (1982)   Remastering

The Ditty Bops

Ditty Bops (2004)   Mastering

Gloria Estefan

Greatest Hits (1992)   Mastering

Greatest Hits, Vol. 2 (2001)   Mastering

Melissa Etheridge

Yes I Am (1993)   Mastering

Breakdown (1999)   Mastering

Everclear

Sparkle & Fade (1995)   Mastering, Sequencing

So Much for the Afterglow (1997)   Mastering

Donald Fagen

Nightfly (1982)   Mastering

Flaming Lips

Yoshimi Battles The Pink Robots (CD/DVDAudio) (2003)   Mastering

Foo Fighters

Colour and the Shape (1997)   Mastering

There Is Nothing Left to Lose (1999)   Mastering

One By One (2003)   Mastering

In Your Honor (2005)   Mastering

Peter Frampton

Greatest Hits (1996)   Remastering

Frampton Comes Alive: 25th Anniversary (2001)   Mastering

Goo Goo Dolls

Ego Opinion Art & Commerce (2001)   Mastering

Hole

Live Through This (1994)   Mastering

Janet Jackson

Design of a Decade: 1986-1996 (1995)   Mastering

k.d. lang
Invincible Summer (2000)   Mastering
Jennifer Lopez
On the 6 (1999)   Mastering
John Mayer
Heavier Things (DualDisc) (2005)   Mastering
Paul McCartney
Tripping the Live Fantastic (1990)   Mastering
Megadeth
Capitol Punishment: The Megadeth Years (2000)   Digital Remastering
John Cougar Mellencamp
Scarecrow (1985)   Mastering
Human Wheels (1993)   Mastering
Natalie Merchant
Tigerlily [DVD Audio] (2000)   Mastering
In Utero (1993)   Mastering
Nine Inch Nails
Downward Spiral (DualDisc) (2004)   Mastering
No Doubt
Return of Saturn (2000)   Mastering
Pearl Jam
Ten (1991)   Mastering
No Code (1996)   Mastering
Tom Petty & the Heartrbreakers
Let Me Up (I've Had Enough) (1987)   Mastering
Phish
Slip, Stitch & Pass (1997)   Mastering
Farmhouse (2000)   Mastering
Siket Disc (2000)   Mastering
Queensryche
Operation: Mindcrime (1988)   Mastering
Radiohead
Amnesiac (2001)   Mastering
Rage Against the Machine
Rage Against the Machine (1992)   Mastering
Evil Empire (1996)   Mastering
Bonnie Raitt
Fundamental (1998)   Mastering
Lou Reed
Definitive Collection (1999)   Mastering
R.E.M.
Document (1987)   Mastering, Remastering
Green (CD/DVD Audio) (2005)   Mastering
New Adventures In Hi-Fi (CD/DVD Audio) 2005   Mastering
Reveal (2001)   Mastering
Reveal (CD/DVD Audio) (2005)   Mastering
The Replacements
Don't Tell a Soul (1989)   Mastering
All For Nothing/Nothing for All (1997)   Digital Mastering

The Rolling Stones

Love You Live (1977)	Mastering
Some Girls (1978)	Remixing

Boz Scaggs

Dig (2001)	Mastering

Paul Simon

Songs from the Capeman (1997)	Mastering
You're the One (2000)	Mastering

Bruce Springsteen

Born to Run (1975)	Remastering
Born in the U.S.A. (1984)	Mastering
Live 1975-1985 (1986)	Mastering
Tunnel of Love (1987)	Mastering
Greatest Hits [Columbia] (1995)	Remastering

Steely Dan

Greatest Hits (1979)	Mastering

Sting

Ten Summoner's Tales (1993)	Mastering
Fields of Gold: The Best of Sting (1994)	Remastering

Talking Heads

Stop Making Sense (1984)	Mastering
Best of Talking Heads (1992)	Digital Remastering

Rob Thomas

Something To Be (2005)	Mastering

Stevie Ray Vaughan

Sky Is Crying (1991)	Mastering
Live at Carnegie Hall (1997)	Mastering

Caetano Veloso

Livros (1998)	Mastering

The Who

Quadrophenia (1973)	Remastering, Reissue Remastering
Who By Numbers (1975)	Remastering

XTC

Nonsuch (1992)	Mastering
Wasp Star (Apple Venus, Pt. 2) (2000)	Mastering

ZZ Top

Eliminator (1983)	Engineer
Afterburner (1985)	Engineer
Greatest Hits (1992)	Engineer

Original Score

A.I. Artificial Intelligence (2001)	Mastering
Brazil (1985)	Mastering
Short Cuts (1993)	Mastering
Dead Man Walking (1996)	Mastering
X-Files (1998)	Mastering

Cookie Marenco . . . .

Scott Amendola Band

Scott Amendola Band (2005)	Producer, Mastering, Mixing, Engineering

Peter Apfelbaum
Jodoji Brightness (1992) Engineer, Mixing
Luminous Charms (1996) Engineer, Mixing
Andre Bush
Invisible City (1999) Engineer, Mastering, Mixing
Garrick Davis
Glass Half Full (2001) Tamboura, Producer, Mixing
Alex DeGrassi
Deep at Night (1983) Producer, Engineer, Editing
Windham Hill Retrospective (1992) Producer, Engineer
Brigitte DeMeyer
Nothing Comes Free (2003) Producer, Engineer, Mixing
Fieldwork
Your Life Flashes (2002) Producer, Engineer, Mastering, Mixing
Tony Furtado
Full Circle (1994) Producer
Roll My Blues Away (1997) Producer, Engineer, Mixing
Tony Furtado & Dirk Powell (1999) Producer, Engineer
Tony Furtado Band (2000) Producer, Engineer, Mixing
American Gypsy (2002) Producer, Engineer
Danny Glover w/ Ladysmith Black Mambazo
How the Leopard Got His Spots (1989) Producer, Mixing
Glover & Taj Mahal
Brer Rabbit and the Wonderful Tar Baby (1989) Engineer
James Gregory
Search (1998) Engineer, Mastering, Mixing
Charlie Haden Quartet West
Haunted Heart (1991) Engineer
Charlie Haden
Always Say Goodbye (1993) Engineer
Art Hirahara
Edge of This Earth (2004) Engineer, Mixing
Vijay Iyer
Memorophilia (1995) Engineer
Architextures (1998) Engineer, Mixing
Jon Jang/Max Roach/Jiebing
Beijing Trio (1998) Engineer, Mastering
The Modern Mandolin Quartet
Intermezzo (1990) Producer
Glen Moore
Dragonetti's Dream (1996) Producer, Mixing
Nude Bass Ascending (1999) Producer, Engineer, Mixing, Assembly
Oregon
Troika (1993) Engineer, Editing, Mixing
Jack Perla
Swimming Lessons for the Dead (1999) Producer, Engineer, Mastering
Meg Ryan w/Art Land
Red Riding Hood & Goldilocks Vocals, Producer, Mixing
Tony Trischka
New Deal (2003) Producer, Engineer

Turtle Island String Quartet
Skylife (1990)   Producer
Shock to the System (1990)   Producer
Natalia Zukerman
Mortal Child (2001)   Accordion, Producer, Engineer, Mastering, Mixing
Original Soundtrack
Winter Solstice on Ice (1999)   Engineer

Andrew Mendelson . . . .

Adrian Belew
Side One (2005)   Mastering
Side Two (2005)   Mastering
Big & Rich
(Upcoming album—untitled) 2005   Mastering
Johnny Cash
Silver (SACD Surround) (2003)   Mastering
Kenny Chesney
Be As You Are (Song From An Old Blue Chair) (2005)   Mastering
Cowboy Troy
Loco Mottive (2005)   Mastering
Shelly Fairchild
Ride (2005)   Mastering
Emmylou Harris
Pieces Of The Sky (2004)   Digital Editing
Quarter Moon In A Ten Cent Town (2004)   Digital Editing
Elite Hotel (2004)   Digital Editing
Luxury Liner (2004)   Digital Editing
Roses In The Snow (DVD Audio Surround) (2006)   Mastering
Jump 5
Dreaming In Color (2004)   Mastering
Very Best Of (2005)   Mastering
Los Tigres Del Norte
Reina del Sur (2002)   Mastering
Cerys Matthews
Cockahoop (2003)   Mastering
MercyMe
MercyMe Love (surround) (2004)   Mastering
Ricky Skaggs (& Kentucky Thunder)
Live At The Charleston Music Hall (2003)   Mastering
Brand New Strings (2004)   Mastering
Holly Williams
Ones We Never Knew (2004)   Mastering
Gretchen Wilson
All Jacked Up (2005)   Mastering

Skidd Mills . . . .

Bernard Allison
Times Are Changing (1998)   Engineer, Mixing

Audio Adrenaline
Some Kind of Zombie (1997)   Mixing
Big Tent Revival
Choose Life (1999)   Engineer
Big Tent Revival Live (2001)   Mixing
Bobgoblin
Twelve-Point Master Plan [ecd] (1997)   Mixing
Clear
Clear (1998)   Guitar, Organ (Hammond), Producer, Engineer, Mastering, Mixing
Deborah Coleman
Soft Place to Fall (2000)   Engineer, Mixing
Robert Cray
Sweet Potato Pie (1997)   Engineer, Mixing
Dirty Americans
Strange Generation (2004)   Engineer, Mixing
George Ducas
George Ducas (1995)   Mixing
Joe, Marc's Brother
Debut of Joe, Marc's Brother (1996)   Engineer, Mixing
The Killjoys
Gimme Five (1996)   Engineer
B.B. King
Blues Summit (1993)   Assistant Engineer, Mixing
Pseudopod
Pseudopod (2002)   Engineer
Riddlin' Kids
Stop the World (2004)   Engineer, Mixing
Saliva
Survival of the Sickest (2004)   Engineer, Mixing
Seven Day Jesus
Seven Day Jesus (1998)   Mixing
Sister Hazel
Lift (2004)   Synthesizer, Organ (Hammond), Producer, Engineer, Fender, Rhodes,
                                                                       String Arrangements, Mixing
Live Live (2004)   Mixing
Skillet
Skillet (1996)   Producer, Engineer, Mixing
Hey You, I Love Your Soul (1998)   Producer, Engineer
Invincible (2000)   Guitar, Producer, Loops
Alien Youth (2001)   Producer, Mixing
Collide (2003)   Engineer
Smalltown Poets
Smalltown Poets (1997)   Engineer, Mixing
Listen Closely (1998)   Percussion, Engineer, Mixing
Todd Snider
Viva Satellite (1998)   Assistant Engineer
Spacehog
Hogyssey (2001)   Engineer
Third Day
Wire (2004)   Engineer

The Vanished
Favorite Scar (2005)   Producer, Engineer, Mixing

Doug Mitchell . . . .

Michel Genest
Ascension (1985)   Engineer
Leah Wolfsong
Songs of the Circle (2000)   Engineer, Mixing, Mastering, Vocals,
Original Soundtrack
Babe [Original Soundtrack] (1995)   Executive Producer
Babe: Pig in the City (1998)   Executive Producer
Various Artists
Narada Sampler, Vol. 2 (1986)   Producer, Engineer
Narada: Lotus Sampler #2 (1986)   Engineer
Narada Sampler, Vol. 3 (1988)   Engineer

Clif Norrell . . . .

Jeff Buckley
Grace (1994)   Engineer
Echo & the Bunnymen
Crystal Days: 1979-1999 (2001)   Mixing
Macy Gray
Trouble With Being Myself [Japan Bonus Tracks] (2003)   Engineer
Hayden
Closer I Get (1998)   Engineer, Mixing
John Hiatt
Perfectly Good Guitar (1993)   Engineer
Greatest Hits & More (2001)   Mixing
Home Grown
Act Your Age (1998)   Producer
Indigo Girls
Indigo Girls (1989)   Engineer
Nomads Indians Saints (1990)   Engineer
Inspiral Carpets
Cool As (2003)   Engineer
Jayhawks
Tomorrow the Green Grass (1995)   Engineer
Jewel
0304 (2003)   Engineer
No Doubt
Rock Steady (2002)   Engineer
The Pixies
Debaser Live [EP] (2003)   Mixing
Refreshments
Fizzy Fuzzy Big & Buzzy (1996)   Producer, Engineer, Mixing, Trumpet
The Replacements
All Shook Down (1990)   Engineer

Rollins Band

Come In & Burn (1997)	Engineer, Mixing
Get Some Go Again (2000)	Engineer, Mixing
Nice (2001)	Trumpet, Engineer, Mixing

Rush

Test for Echo (1996)	Engineer

Saliva

Back Into Your System (2002)	Mixing

Weezer

Pinkerton (1996)	Engineer

Widespread Panic

Bombs & Butterflies (1997)	Mixing

You Am I

Dress Me Slowly (2001)	Producer, Engineer, Mixing

Original Soundtrack

Singles (1992)	Mixing
So I Married an Axe Murderer (1993)	Engineer
Speed (1994)	Engineer
American Werewolf in Paris (1997)	Producer
Man on the Moon (1999)	Mixing

Mark O'Connor . . . .

Mark O'Connor Catalog:

1976	Pickin' in the Wind
1978	Markology
1980	On the Rampage
1981	Soppin' the Gravy
1982	False Dawn
1985	Contest Fiddling, Championship Style
1986	Meanings Of…
1988	Stone from Which the Arch Was Made
1988	Elysian Forest
1989	On the Mark
1990	Championship Years
1991	The New Nashville Cats
1993	The Night Before Christmas
1993	Heroes
1994	Johnny Appleseed
1994	Johnny Appleseed
1995	The Fiddle Concerto
1997	Liberty
1998	Midnight on the Water
2001	Hot Swing!
2001	American Seasons
2001	Fanfare for the Volunteer: Three Pieces for…
2001	National Junior Fiddle Champion
2001	Retrospective
2001	Caprices No.'s 1-6
2003	In Full Swing

2004

Mark O'Connor's Hot Swing Trio

	Crossing Bridges (live)

Hot Swing! (2001) — Violin, Producer, Photography

In Full Swing (2003) — Violin, Arranger, Producer

Chet Atkins

Stay Tuned (1985) — Fiddle, Violin

Chet Atkins with Mark Knopfler

Neck & Neck (1990) — Fiddle, Mandolin

T-Bone Burnett

Criminal Under My Own Hat (1992) — Mandolin, Violin

Rosanne Cash

Hits 1979-1989 (1989) — Fiddle

Interiors (1990) — Mandolin, Violin

Rodney Crowell

Diamonds & Dirt (1989) — Fiddle, Mandolin

The Dixie Dregs

Industry Standard (1982) — Violin

Béla Fleck

Natural Bridge (1982) — Fiddle, Guitar, Viola, Guitar (12 String)

Daybreak (1988) — Fiddle, Guitar, Viola

Stephane Grappelli

Live 1992 (1992) — Guitar, Violin

Stephane Grappelli/David Grisman

Stephane Grappelli and David Grisman (1994) — Guitar, Violin

Nanci Griffith

MCA Years: a Retrospective (1993) — Guitar (Acoustic), Fiddle, Mandolin, Violin, Viola

David Grisman

Mondo Mando (1981) — Guitar, Violin

Dawg '90 (1990) — Fiddle

DGQ-20 (1996) — Guitar, Mandolin, Violin

Emmylou Harris

Angel Band (1987) — Fiddle, Viola, Mandola

Bluebird (1988) — Mandolin

John Hartford

Gum Tree Canoe (1987) — Fiddle, Guitar, Mandolin

Mark Johnson & Clawgrass

Bridging the Gap (1997) — Arranger

Lyle Lovett

Lyle Lovett & His Large Band (1989) — Fiddle, Mandola

I Love Everybody (1994) — Violin

Yo-Yo Ma/Edgar Meyer/Mark O'Connor

Appalachia Waltz (1996) — Mandolin, Violin, Producer

Manhattan Transfer

Swing (1997) — Violin

Willie Nelson

Across the Borderline (1993) — Violin

The Nitty Gritty Dirt Band

Will the Circle Be Unbroken, Vol. 2 (1989) — Fiddle, Mandolin

James Taylor

Greatest Hits, Vol. 2 (2000) — Fiddle, Violin

Randy Travis

Greatest Hits, Vol. 1 (1992)	Fiddle, Mandolin
Greatest Hits, Vol. 2 (1992)	Fiddle, Mandolin

Townes Van Zandt

At My Window (1987)	Fiddle, Mandolin, Violin

Doc Watson

Elementary Doc Watson (1972)	Fiddle, Mandolin
Riding the Midnight Train (1984)	Fiddle
Portrait (1988)	Fiddle

Doc & Merle Watson

Watson Country (1996)	Fiddle, Mandolin

Eddie Offord . . . .

Brian Auger's Oblivion Express

Best of Brian Auger's Oblivion Express (1996)	Engineer

Baker Gurvitz Army

Hearts on Fire (1976)	Producer, Engineer

Elizabeth Barraclough

Elizabeth Barraclough (1978)	Engineer

Valerie Carter

Way It Is (1996)	Producer, Engineer, Mixing

The Dixie Dregs

Industry Standard (1982)	Producer

Julie Driscoll/Brian Auger

Street Noise (1968)	Engineer
Tinsley Ellis	
Cool on It (1986)	Producer, Engineer
Storm Warning (1994)	Producer, Engineer

Tinsley Ellis

Hell or High Water (2002)	Producer, Engineer, Mixing

Emerson, Lake & Palmer

Emerson, Lake & Palmer (1970)	Engineer
Tarkus (1971)	Engineer
Pictures at an Exhibition (1972)	Engineer
Trilogy (1972)	Engineer

Levon Helm

Levon Helm & the RCO All-Stars (1977)	Engineer

Bill Laswell

Deconstruction: Celluloid Recordings (1993)	Engineer

John Lennon

Imagine (1971)	Engineer

McLaughlin

Extrapolation (1969)	Engineer

Yoko Ono

Yoko Ono/Plastic Ono Band (1970)	Engineer
Fly (1971)	Engineer

Platinum Blonde

Alien Shores (1985)	Producer, Engineer

Andy Pratt
Motives (1979)   Producer, Engineer
Terry Reid
River (1973)   Producer
David Sancious
True Stories (1978)   Producer, Engineer
Just As I Thought (1980)   Producer, Engineer
Billy Squier
Tale of the Tape (1980)   Producer
311
Music (1993)   Producer, Engineer
Grassroots (1994)   Producer, Engineer
Wet Willie
Greatest Hits (1977)   Producer, Engineer, Mixing
Yes
Yes Album (1971)   Producer, Engineer
Fragile (1972)   Producer, Engineer
Close to the Edge (1972)   Producer
Relayer (1974)   Producer, Engineer
Drama (1980)   Producer
Classic Yes (1981)   Producer
Yesyears (1991)   Producer, Engineer

John Ottman . . . .

Original Soundtrack
Urban Legends: Final Cut (2000)   Producer, Orchestration
Cable Guy (1996)   Producer
Incognito (1998)   Producer, Fender Rhodes
Apt Pupil (1998)   Vocals, Producer
Lake Placid (1999)   Producer, Orchestration
Bubble Boy (2001)   Original Score, Producer, Orchestration
Eight Legged Freaks (2002)   Original Score Producer, Executive Producer, Orchestration
Gothika (2003)   Original Score Producer, Orchestration, Synthesizer Programming
Point of Origin (2003)   Arranger, Producer, Performer, Liner Notes
X-Men, Vol. 2 (2003)   Score Orchestration
Trapped (2002)   Synthesizer, Piano, Orchestration, Score Producer
Cellular (2004)   Producer, Orchestration, Synthesizer Programming
Ultra Noir (2004)   Producer
Hide and Seek (2005)   Producer, Orchestration

Tim Palmer . . . .

Better Than Ezra
Closer (2001)   Mixing
Big Country
Best of Big Country (1994)   Producer
The Cure
Wild Mood Swings (1996)   Mixing
Strange Attraction (1996)   Mixing

Dance Hall Crashers
Blue Plate Special (1998)   Producer, Mixing
Goldfinger
Stomping Ground (2000)   Producer
Open Your Eyes (2002)   Mixing
Heatwave
Best of Heatwave: Always & Forever (1996)   Engineer
Faith Hill
Cry (2002)   Mixing
House of Love
Best Of (1998)   Mixing
James
Gold Mother (1990)   Remixing
James (1990)   Remixing
Seven (1992)   Mixing
Kajagoogoo
Too Shy: The Singles…& More (1993)   Producer
Live
V (2001)   Mixing
The Mission UK
God's Own Medicine (1986)   Producer
Carved in Sand (1990)   Producer
Mother Love Bone
Stardog Champion (1990)   Mixing
Ozzy Osbourne
Essential Ozzy Osbourne (2003)   Producer
Prince of Darkness (2005)   Producer
Pearl Jam
Ten (1991)   Percussion, Engineer, Mixing
Robert Plant
Little by Little (1985)   Producer, Engineer
Shaken 'N' Stirred (1985)   Producer, Engineer
Now & Zen (1988)   Producer
Sixty Six to Timbuktu (2003)   Producer
Sepultura
Against (1998)   Mixing
Tears for Fears
Tears Roll Down: Greatest Hits (1992)   Producer
Texas
Song Book: Best of Texas (2001)   Producer
Tin Machine
Tin Machine (1989)   Producer, Mixing
Tin Machine II (1991)   Producer
You Belong in Rock N' Roll (1991)   Producer, Mixing
U2
All That You Can't Leave Behind (2000)   Engineer, Mixing
Original Soundtrack
Bill & Ted's Bogus Journey (1991)   Producer
American Pie (1999)   Producer, Mixing
Tomb Raider (2001)   Mixing

Eric Paul . . . .

Johnny Bush
Sings Bob Wills (2000)   Engineer
Clem Snide
Your Favorite Music (2000)   Drums
Ghost of Fashion (2001)   Percussion, Drums, Whistle
Valerie Duchateau
America (1995)   Engineer
Kinky Friedman
Pearls In the Snow   Engineer
Gaither Vocal Band
Homecoming (1991)   Engineer
David Gates
Love is Always Seventeen (1994)   Engineer
John Gorka
Out of the Valley (1994)   Engineer
Between Five and Seven (1996)   Engineer
Emmylou Harris
Bluebird (1988)   Assistant Engineer
Vince Hatfield
Take It Easy on Yourself (2003)   Producer, Mixing
The Highwaymen
Highwaymen 2 (1990)   Assistant Engineer
Shelley Laine
Skipping Stones (2001)   Producer, Engineer
Back to Austin (2002)   Producer, Engineer, Mixing
Charlie McCoy
Precious Memories (1998)   Engineer
Willie Nelson
Red Headed Stranger (1975)   Engineer
Horse Called Music (1989)   Engineer
Six Hours at Pedernales (1995)   Engineer
Just One Love (1996)   Engineer, Mixing
Billy Joe Shaver
Billy and the Kid (2004)   Engineer
Townes Van Zandt
Far Cry from Dead (1999)   Producer, Engineer, Assistant Engineer
Texas Rain (2001)   Engineer
Don Walser
Here's to Country Music (1999)   Engineer
Chris Webster
Drive (1999)   Engineer
Original Soundtrack
Ballad of the Sad Cafe (1991)   Engineer
Various Artists
Poet: Tribute to Townes Van Zandt (2001)   Producer

Rik Pekkonen . . . .

Booker T. & the MG's	
McLemore Avenue (1970)	Engineer
Garth Brooks	
In the Life of Chris Gaines (1999)	Engineer
Jackson Browne	
I'm Alive (1993)	Engineer
Solomon Burke	
Make Do With What You Got (2005)	Engineer
Carlton	
Collection (1988)	Engineer, Remixing, Mixing
Chick Corea Elektric Band	
To the Stars (2004)	Mixing
The Jazz Crusaders	
Best of the Crusaders [Blue Thumb] (1969)	Engineer
The Crusaders	
2nd Crusade (1972)	Engineer
Scratch (1975)	Engineer
Street Life (1979)	Engineer, Mixing
Healing the Wounds (1991)	Engineer
The Dixie Dregs	
Free Fall (1977)	Engineer, Associate Producer, Mixing
Dr. John	
N'Awlinz: Dis Dat or d'Udda (2004)	Engineer, Mixing
Joe Jackson	
Body & Soul (1984)	Engineer
B.B. King	
Let the Good Times Roll: The Music of Louie Jordan (1999)	Engineer, Mixing
Leo Kottke	
My Father's Face (1989)	Engineer, Mixing
Ladysmith Black Mambazo	
Two Worlds One Heart (1991)	Engineer
Jeff Lorber	
Definitive Collection (2000)	Producer
Lyle Lovett	
Smile (2003)	Engineer, Mixing
Ricky Martin	
Vuelve (1998)	Engineer
Ricky Martin [US 1999] (1999)	Engineer
Jim Morrison	
American Prayer (1978)	Engineer
Aaron Neville	
To Make Me Who I Am (1997)	Engineer
Iggy Pop	
Avenue B [US] (1999)	Mixing
Ringo Starr	
Time Takes Time (1992)	Engineer, Mixing
Liz Story	
Gift (1994)	Engineer

Barbra Streisand
Emotion (1984)   Engineer

T. Rex
Electric Warrior (1971)   Engineer

Travis Tritt
Restless Kind (1996)   Engineer, Mixing

Neil Young
Neil Young (1969)   Engineer

Original Soundtrack
Toy Story (1995)   Engineer, Mixing
That Thing You Do (1996)   Engineer
Hope Floats [Original Soundtrack] (1998)   Engineer

Csaba Petocz . . . .

Philip Aaberg
Upright (1980)   Engineer, Mixing

Blackhawk
Greatest Hits (2000)   Recorder

Larry Carlton
Sapphire Blue Engineer (2004)   Mixing

Camper Van Beethoven
Key Lime Pie (1989)   Engineer, Mixing

Peter Cetera
Peter Cetera Collection (2001)   Engineer, Mixing

Kenny Chesney
In My Wildest Dreams (1994)   Engineer
All I Need to Know (1995)   Engineer

Stanley Clarke
Find Out! (1985)   Engineer
Hideaway (1986)   Engineer
If This Bass Could Only Talk (1988)   Engineer

Kelly Clarkson
Thankful (2003)   Engineer

Elvis Costello/The Imposters
Delivery Man (2004)   Engineer

Cracker
Golden Age (1996)   Engineer
Gentleman's Blues (1998)   Engineer

Alecia Elliott
I'm Diggin' It (2000)   Engineer

Vince Gill
Way Back Home (1987)   Engineer

Howard Hewett
Very Best of Howard Hewett (2001)   Engineer, Mixing

Etta James
Love's Been Rough on Me (1997)   Engineer

Al Jarreau
Breakin' Away (1981)   Engineer

Elton John
Duets (1993)   Engineer
Lynyrd Skynyrd
Endangered Species (1994)   Engineer
Mindy McCready
I'm Not So Tough (1999)   Producer, Engineer
Metallica
Garage Inc. (1998)   Engineer
John Michael Montgomery
What I Do the Best (1996)   Producer, Engineer, Mixing
Greatest Hits (1997)   Producer, Overdubs, Mixing
Leave a Mark (1998)   Producer
Friends   Producer
Lorrie Morgan
Merry Christmas from London (1993)   Engineer, Mixing
Ted Nugent
Nugent (1982)   Engineer
Oingo Boingo
Dark at the End of the Tunnel (1990)   Engineer
Rimes
Blue (1996)   Mixing
Sittin' on Top of the World… (2000)   Engineer
Self
Breakfast with Girls (1999)   Mixing
Frank Sinatra
Duets II (1994)   Engineer
The Temptations
To Be Continued… (1986)   Engineer
Jennifer Warnes
Famous Blue Raincoat (1987)   Engineer
Jody Watley
Jody Watley (1987)   Engineer
Chely Wright
Woman in the Moon (1994)   Engineer

Jeff Powell . . . .

The Afghan Whigs
Gentlemen (1993)   Engineer, Mixing
Love (1996)   Engineer, Mixing, Vocals
1965 (1998)   Engineer
Luther Allison
Soul Fixin' Man (1994)   Engineer
Reckless (1997)   Engineer
The Allman Brothers Band
Shades of Two Worlds (1991)   Engineer
Big Star
Columbia: Live at Missouri (1993)   Mixing Assistant
Cory Branan
Hell You Say (2002)   Producer, Engineer, Mixing

Marty Brown
High & Dry (1991)   Engineer, Mixing Assistant
Five Way Friday
Run Like This (2000)   Producer, Engineer, Mixing
Jolene
Hell's Half Acre (1996)   Producer, Engineer, Mixing
In the Gloaming (1998)   Producer, Engineer, Mixing
Antic Ocean (2000)   Producer
Rob Jungklas
Arkadelphia (2003)   Piano, Producer, Engineer, Mixing
B.B. King
Blues Summit (1993)   Engineer
Little Texas
First Time for Everything (1992)   Engineer
Big Time (1993)   Engineer
Lodestar
Jehovahcaine (1998)   Producer, Mixing
Lynyrd Skynyrd
Lynyrd Skynyrd 1991 (1991)   Engineer
Pawtuckets
Dogsbody Factotum (2001)   Producer, Mixing
Cheer Up (1996)   Producer, Engineer, Mixing
Primal Scream
Give Out But Don't Give Up (1994)   Engineer
RiverBluff Clan
Two Quarts Low (1998)   Producer, Engineer, Mixing
Scrawl
Travel on, Rider (1996)   Producer, Engineer
16 Horsepower
Heel on the Shovel (1995)   Engineer, Mixing
Sackcloth 'n' Ashes (1996)   Engineer, Mixdown Engineer
Low Estate (1998)   Engineer
Tonic
Sugar (1999)   Engineer
Travis Tritt
It's All About to Change (1991)   Engineer
The Twilight Singers
Blackberry Belle (2003)   Engineer
Vaughan Brothers
Family Style (1990)   Engineer
Stevie Ray Vaughan
Sky Is Crying (1991)   Engineer
Live at Carnegie Hall (1997)   Mixing
Original Television Show
King of the Hill (1999)   Engineer, Mixing

Denny Purcell . . . .

Chet Atkins & Tommy Emmanuel
Day Finger Pickers Took Over the World (1997)   Mastering

Garth Brooks	
Garth Brooks (1989)	Mastering
No Fences (1990)	Mastering
Ropin' the Wind (1991)	Mastering
Chase (1992)	Mastering
In Pieces (1993)	Mastering
Fresh Horses (1995)	Mastering
Sevens (1997)	Mastering
Limited Series (1998)	Mastering
Double Live (1998)	Mastering
In the Life of Chris Gaines (1999)	Mastering
Garth Brooks & the Magic of… (1999)	Mastering
Dire Straits	
Sultans of Swing: The Very Best of (1998)	Mastering
Dixie Chicks	
Wide Open Spaces (1998)	Mastering
Fly (1999)	Mastering
Béla Fleck & The Flecktones	
Flight of the Cosmic Hippo (1991)	Mastering
Bluegrass Sessions: Tales From the (1999)	Mastering
Greatest Hits of the 20th Century (1999)	Mastering
Outbound (2000)	Mastering
Vince Gill	
High Lonesome Sound (1996)	Mastering
Key (1998)	Mastering
Let's Make Sure We Kiss Goodbye (2000)	Mastering
Emmylou Harris	
Brand New Dance (1990)	Mastering
Songs of the West (1994)	Mastering, Sequencing
Mark Knopfler	
Cal (1984)	Remastering
Golden Heart (1996)	Mastering
Sailing to Philadelphia (2000)	Mastering
Alison Krauss	
Now That I've Found You: A Collection (1995)	Mastering
Willie Nelson	
Always on My Mind (1982/1997)	Mastering/Remastering
16 Biggest Hits (1998)	Mastering
Oh Boy Records Classics Presents: Willie Nelson (2000)	Mastering
Mark O'Connor	
Heroes (1993)	Mastering
Midnight on the Water (1998)	Mastering
Dolly Parton	
Hungry Again (1998)	Mastering
Super Hits [1999] (1999)	Mastering
John Prine	
Live on Tour (1997)	Mastering
In Spite of Ourselves (1999)	Mastering
Ricky Skaggs	
Bluegrass Rules! (1997)	Mastering

Ricky Skaggs and Kentucky Thunder
Soldier of the Cross (1999) — Mastering
History of the Future (2001) — Mastering
George Strait
Blue Clear Sky (1996) — Mastering
One Step at a Time (1998) — Mastering
Latest Greatest Straitest Hits (2000) — Mastering, Project Assembly
George Strait (2000) — Mastering
Take 6
Greatest Hits (1999) — Mastering
Townes Van Zandt
Far Cry from Dead (1999) — Mastering
Trisha Yearwood
Hearts in Armor (1992) — Mastering
Song Remembers When (1993) — Mastering
Sweetest Gift (1994) — Mastering
Where Your Road Leads (1998) — Mastering
Neil Young & Crazy Horse
Comes a Time (1978) — Engineer
Neil Young
Old Ways (1985) — Mastering
Silver & Gold (2000) — Mastering, Transfers
Original Soundtrack
Happy Texas (1999) — Mastering
Television Soundtrack
Touched By an Angel: The Album (1998) — Mastering
Various Artists
Class of '55: Memphis Rock & Roll Trio (1986) — Mastering

Norbert Putnam . . . .

Addrisi Brothers
We've Got to Get It on Again (1972) — Guitar (Bass), Producer
Eric Andersen
Blue River (1972) — Bass, Producer
Stages: The Lost Album (1973) — Bass, Cello, Guitar (Bass), Producer, Bass (Upright), Mixing
Area Code 615
Area Code 615 (1969) — Bass
Trip in the Country (1970) — Bass
Joan Baez
Blessed Are (1971) — Bass, Arranger, Producer
Where Are You Now, My Son? (1973) — Producer
Jimmy Buffett
Changes in Latitudes, Changes in Attitudes (1977) — Producer, String Arrangements
Son of a Son of a Sailor (1978) — Bass, Producer
You Had to Be There (1978) — Producer
Volcano (1979) — Bass, Producer
Coconut Telegraph (1981) — Producer
Somewhere over China (1982) — Bass, Producer, Bass (Upright), Casio
Boats, Beaches, Bars & Ballads (1992) — Producer

Donovan
Troubadour: The Definitive Anthology (1992)   Bass, Producer
The Flying Burrito Brothers
Flying Again (1975)   Producer
Dan Fogelberg
Home Free (1973)   Bass, Cello, Producer
Netherlands (1977)   Producer, Bass
Twin Sons of Different Mothers (1978)   Producer, Bass
Phoenix (1980)   Bass, Producer
Portrait: The Music of Dan Fogelberg (1997)   Bass, Producer
Steve Goodman
No Big Surprise: Anthology (1994)   Producer, Bass
Dobie Gray
Soul Days (2000)   Organ, Arranger, Director, Horn Arrangements, String Arrangements, Mixing
Jim Hall
Touch You (1980)   Strings, Producer
Cadillac Tracks (1982)   Producer
John Hiatt
Warming Up to the Ice Age (1985)   Producer, Engineer
Waylon Jennings
Ladies Love Outlaws [RCA] (1972)   Bass
Kris Kristofferson
Silver Tongued Devil and I (1971)   Bass
Henry Mancini
Mancini Country (1970)   Bass Fiddle
Manhattan Transfer
Jukin' (1969)   Bass
The Mighty Clouds of Joy
Catching On (1972)   Producer, Engineer
The Monkees
Greatest Hits (1999)   Bass
The New Riders of the Purple Sage
Adventures of Panama Red (1973)   Bass, Arranger, Producer, Remixing
Wasted Tasters (1998)   Producer
Mickey Newbury
Mickey Newbury Collection (1998)   Bass, Producer
The Nitty Gritty Dirt Band
Let's Go (1982)   Producer
Elvis Presley
That's the Way It Is (1970)   Bass, Arranger, Horn Arrangements, String Arrangements
He Touched Me (1972)   Bass
Artist of the Century (1999)   Bass
Linda Ronstadt
Silk Purse (1970)   Bass
Greatest Hits, Vol. 1 (1998)   Bass, Arranger, Harpsichord
Buffy Sainte-Marie
Quiet Places (1973)   Bass, Producer
Native North American Child: An Odyssey (1974)   Producer
Tony Joe White
Best of Tony Joe White (1973)   Bass

Benny Quinn . . . .

Alabama
Essential (1998)   Digital Remastering
Chet Atkins
Chet Atkins Picks on the Beatles (1965)   Digital Remastering
Master & His Music (2001)   Mastering
Big Ass Truck
Kent (1996)   Mastering
Who Let You in Here? (1998)   Mastering
Tracy Byrd
It's About Time (1999)   Mastering
Ten Rounds (2001)   Mastering
Guy Clark
Essential (1997)   Digital Remastering
Patsy Cline
Essential Patsy Cline (1997)   Remastering, Digital Remastering
The Dixie Dregs
Bring 'em Back Alive (1992)   Mastering
Vince Gill
Super Hits (1996)   Digital Remastering
Waylon Jennings
Essential Waylon Jennings (1996)   Digital Remastering
Neal McCoy
Super Hits (2000)   Remastering
Mindy McCready
I'm Not So Tough (1999)   Mastering
Dolly Parton
Super Hits [1996] (1996)   Remastering
For God and Country (2003)   Mastering
Elvis Presley
Blue Christmas (1992)   Mastering, Mixing, Restoration
Shaver
Tramp on Your Street (1993)   Mastering
SHeDAISY
Whole SHeBANG — All Mixed Up (2001)   Mastering
Pam Tillis
Thunder and Roses (2001)   Mastering
Travis Tritt
No More Looking over My Shoulder (1998)   Mastering
Down the Road I Go (2000)   Mastering
My Honky Tonk History (2004)   Mastering
Keith Whitley
Wherever You Are Tonight (1995)   Producer, Mastering, Mixing, Digital Transfers
Widespread Panic
Space Wrangler (1988)   Mastering
Everyday (1993)   Mastering
Ain't Life Grand (1994)   Mastering
Webb Wilder
It Came from Nashville (1993)   Mastering

Trevor Rabin . . . .

(Solo albums)
Beginnings (2003)	Multi Instruments, Producer
Live in L.A. (2003)	Guitar, Vocals

Michael Jackson
History: Past, Present and Future (1995)	Guitar

Manfred Mann's Earth Band
Best of Manfred Mann's Earth Band (1996)	Guitar, Associate Producer

John Miles
Transition (1985)	Producer

Rabbitt
Boys Will Be Boys [Bonus Tracks] (2004)	Synthesizer, Guitar, Arranger, Keyboards, Vocals, Producer, Group Member

Paul Rodgers
Tribute to Muddy Waters (1993)	Guitar

Seal
Seal [1991] (1991)	Guitar

Tina Turner
Wildest Dreams (1996)	Guitar, Vocals (bckgr)

Rick Wakeman
Return to the Centre of the Earth (1999)	Guitar, Vocals, Engineer
90125 (1983)	Guitar, Keyboards, Vocals
90125 Live: The Solos (1985)	Guitar, Vocals
Big Generator (1987)	Guitar, Keyboards, Vocals (bckgr), Producer, Engineer, String Arrangements, Mixing
Union (1991)	Vocals, Multi Instruments, Producer, Engineer
Talk (1994)	Guitar, Keyboards, Programming, Vocals, Producer, Engineer

Original Score
Twister [Score] (1996)	Guitar
Armageddon [Score] (1998)	Producer, Engineer, Mixing
Con Air (1997)	Producer, Orchestration
Enemy of the State (1998)	Producer
Remember the Titans (2000)	Arranger, Producer
Rock Star (2001)	Producer
Bad Company (2002)	Producer
Banger Sisters (2002)	Producer
National Treasure (2004)	Orchestration

Phil Ramone . . . .

Burt Bacharach
Look of Love: The Burt Bacharach Collection (1998)	Producer, Associate Producer

The Band
Rock of Ages (1972)	Engineer

Michael Bolton
Timeless: The Classics, Vol. 2 (1999)	Producer

Chicago
Chicago's Greatest Hits, Vol. 2 (1981)	Producer

If You Leave Me Now (1982)	Producer
Natalie Cole	
Snowfall on the Sahara (1999)	Producer
Greatest Hits, Vol. 1 (2000)	Producer
John Coltrane	
Coltrane Legacy (1959)	Engineer
Olé Coltrane (1961)	Engineer
Bob Dylan & the Band	
Before the Flood (1974)	Engineer
Bob Dylan	
Blood on the Tracks (1975)	Engineer
Gloria Estefan	
Greatest Hits (1992)	Mixing
Everything But the Girl	
Best of Everything But the Girl (1996)	Producer, Engineer
Kenny G	
Greatest Hits [US] (1982)	Producer, Post Production
Art Garfunkel	
Breakaway (1975)	Producer
Watermark (1977)	Producer
Stan Getz/Joao Gilberto	
Getz/Gilberto (1963)	Engineer
Dave Grusin	
Presents: West Side Story (1997)	Producer
Julio Iglesias	
My Life: Greatest Hits (1998)	Producer
Billy Joel	
Stranger (1977)	Producer, Engineer
52nd Street (1978)	Producer, Remixing
Glass Houses (1980)	Producer
Songs in the Attic (1981)	Producer, Remixing
Nylon Curtain (1982)	Producer
Innocent Man (1983)	Producer
The Bridge (1986)	Producer, Photography
Lenningrad (1991)	Executive Music Supervisor
Elton John	
11-17-70 (1971)	Engineer
One Night Only (2000)	Producer
Elton John & Tim Rice	
Aida (1999)	Producer, Executive Producer
Quincy Jones	
Greatest Hits (1996)	Producer
Reel Quincy Jones (1999)	Producer
Barry Manilow	
Singin' with the Big Bands (1994)	Producer
Manilow Sings Sinatra (1998)	Producer
Paul McCartney	
Press to Play (1986)	Producer, Engineer, Mixing
Sinéad O'Connor	
So Far…The Best of Sinéad O'Connor (1997)	Producer

Luciano Pavarotti

For War Child (1996)	Producer
Pavarotti & Friends for Cambodia & Tibet (2000)	Producer

Diane Schuur

Friends for Schuur (2000)	Producer

The Brian Setzer Orchestra

Dirty Boogie (1998)	Producer

Simon & Garfunkel

Concert in Central Park (1982)	Producer
Old Friends (1997)	Producer

Paul Simon

Paul Simon (1972)	Engineer
There Goes Rhymin' Simon (1973)	Producer, Engineer
Still Crazy After All These Years (1975)	Producer, Engineer
One Trick Pony (1980)	Producer, Engineer

Frank Sinatra

Sinatra 80th — Live in Concert (1981)	Producer, Remixing
L.A. Is My Lady (1984)	Engineer, Mixing
Duets, Vol. 1-2 (1993/1994)	Producer

Phoebe Snow

Very Best of Phoebe Snow (2001)	Producer, Engineer, Mixing

Ringo Starr

Time Takes Time (1992)	Producer

Barbara Streisand & Kris Kristofferson

Star Is Born (1976)	Producer, Engineer
Barbra Streisand Greatest Hits…and More (1989)	Producer

U2

Stay (Faraway, So Close) [US] (1993)	Producer

Original Soundtrack

Star Is Born [United Artists] (1976)	Engineer
Flashdance [Original Soundtrack] (1983)	Producer
Ghostbusters (1984)	Producer

Nile Rodgers . . . .

All-4-One

On and On (1998)	Producer

Laurie Anderson

Home of the Brave (1986)	Producer, Guitar, Keyboards

The B-52's

Time Capsule (1998)	Producer

Philip Bailey

Inside Out (1990)	Producer, Guitar, Keyboards, Vocals

Jeff Beck

Flash (1985)	Producer

David Bowie

Let's Dance (1983)	Producer, Guitar, Arranger, Mixing Assistant
Black Tie White Noise [Expanded] (2004)	Guitar, Choir, Chorus, Producer, Mixing

Chic

Chic (1977)	Guitar, Arranger, Vocals

C'est Chic (1978)	Guitar, Arranger, Conductor, Producer
Risque (1979)	Guitar, Arranger, Conductor, Producer
Real People (1980)	Guitar, Producer
Chic Chic (1981)	Guitar
Take It Off (1981)	Guitar, Arranger, Conductor, Vocals, Producer
Believer (1984)	Guitar
Very Best of Chic (2000)	Producer

Phil Collins

White Nights (1985)	Producer, Composer

The Dandy Warhols

Welcome to the Monkey House (2003)	Guitar (Rhythm)

Duran Duran

Arena (1984)	Producer
Notorious (1986)	Producer
Decade: Greatest Hits (1989)	Producer, Mixing
Strange Behaviour (1999)	Producer, Mixing

Sheena Easton

World of Sheena Easton: The Singles Collection (1993)	Producer

Deborah Harry

Most of All: Best Of Deborah Harry (1999)	Producer

INXS

Swing (1984)	Producer

Michael Jackson

History: Past, Present and Future, (1995)	Guitar

Mick Jagger

She's the Boss (1985)	Producer, Guitar

Al Jarreau

L Is for Lover (1986)	Producer, Guitar, Keyboards, Vocals (bckgr), Vocoder, Keyboard Bass

Madonna

Like a Virgin (1984)	Guitar, Producer, Synclavier
Immaculate Collection (1990)	Producer

Eddie Murphy

So Happy (1989)	Producer, Guitar, Vocals (bckgr)

Robert Plant

Sixty Six to Timbuktu (2003)	Guitar

Diana Ross

Diana (1980)	Producer, Arranger, Writer
One Woman: The Ultimate Collection (1994)	Producer, Arranger, Conductor

David Lee Roth

Your Filthy Little Mouth (1994)	Producer

Sister Sledge

Best of Sister Sledge (1973-1985) (1992)	Producer

Britney Spears

Britney (2001)	Guitar

Joss Stone

Mind, Body & Soul (2004)	Guitar

Thompson Twins

Greatest Hits (1996)	Producer

Vaughan Brothers

Family Style (1990)	Guitar, Producer, Horn Arrangements, Mixing

Jimmie Vaughan

Strange Pleasure (1995)	Guitar (Rhythm), Producer
Out There (1998)	Producer

Original Soundtrack

Gremlins (1984)	Producer
Thelma & Louise (1991)	Producer
Public Enemy (1999)	Executive Producer
Maid in Manhattan (2002)	Producer
In-Laws (2003)	Producer
Outlaw Vollyball: Xbox Original Soundtrack (2003)	Executive Producer
Halo 2, Vol. 1 (2004)	Vocals, Producer, Supervisor

Elliot Scheiner . . . .

Aerosmith

Nine Lives (1997)	Engineer

Ashford & Simpson

Solid (1984)	Producer

Beck

Sea Change (2002)	Surround Mix
Guero [Deluxe Version] (2005)	Surround Mix

George Benson

George Benson Anthology (2000)	Engineer, Mixing

Jimmy Buffett

Boats, Beaches, Bars & Ballads (1992)	Producer

Natalie Cole

Stardust (1996)	Engineer

Bob Dylan

Blood on the Tracks [Remastered] (2003)	Mixing
Bob Dylan - Limited Edition Hybrid SACD Set (2003)	Mixing

The Eagles

Hell Freezes Over (1994)	Producer, Engineer, Mixing
Selected Works: 1972-1999 (2000)	Producer, Engineer, Mixing

Donald Fagen

Nightfly (1982)	Tracking, Mix Down

Fleetwood Mac

Dance (1997)	Producer, Engineer, Mixing

Dan Fogelberg

River of Souls (1993)	Engineer, Mixing

John Fogerty

Premonition (1998)	Producer, Engineer, Mixing

Glenn Frey

Solo Collection (1995)	Producer, Engineer, Mixing

Faith Hill

Cry (2002)	Remixing

Bruce Hornsby & The Range

Way It Is (1986)	Producer, Engineer, Mixing

Billy Joel

Songs in the Attic (1981)	Engineer, Remixing
Complete Hits Collection 1974-1997 (1997)	Engineer, Remixing

Rickie Lee Jones
Pirates (1981) — Engineer
Manhattan Transfer
Bop Doo-Wopp (1983) — Engineer
Vocalese (1985) — Engineer, Remixing, Mixing
Queen
Night at the Opera [DTS] (2002) — Mixing
R.E.M.
Around the Sun [CD/DVD Audio] (2005) — Surround Mix
Automatic for the People [CD/DVD] (2005) — Re-mix Producer
Green [CD+DVD] (2005) — Re-mix Producer
Monster [CD/DVD Audio] (2005) — Producer
Out of Time [CD/DVD Audio] (2005) — Surround Mix
Up [CD+DVD] (2005) — Re-mix Producer
Ricky Martin
Ricky Martin (1999) — Engineer
matchbox twenty
Show: A Night In The Life Of Matchbox Twenty (2004) — Engineer
Michael McDonald
Voice of Michael McDonald (2001) — Producer, Engineer, Mixing
Bobby McFerrin
Best of Bobby McFerrin (1985) — Engineer
Van Morrison
Moondance (1970) — Engineer
New York Voices
Sing, Sing, Sing (2000) — Producer, Engineer, Mixing Engineer
Roy Orbison
Black & White Night (1998) — Remixing
David Sanborn
Straight to the Heart (1984) — Engineer, Mixing
Boz Scaggs
Come on Home (1997) — Engineer
My Time: The Anthology (1969-1997) (1997) — Producer
Dig (2001) — Mixing
Frank Sinatra
L.A. Is My Lady (1984) — Remixing, Assistant Engineer, Mixing Assistant
Phoebe Snow
Very Best of Phoebe Snow (2001) — Producer
Steely Dan
Aja (1977) — Engineer
Greatest Hits (1979) — Engineer, Package Development
Citizen Steely Dan (1993) — Engineer
Two Against Nature (2000) — Engineer
Barbra Streisand
Mirror Has Two Faces (1996) — Engineer, Mixing
Toto
Tambu (1995) — Producer, Engineer, Chant, Mixing
Mindfields (1999) — Producer, Engineer, Mixing
Livefields (1999) — Producer, Engineer, Mixing

Loudon Wainwright III
Atlantic Recordings (2000)   Engineer
Original Soundtrack
Thelma & Louise (1991)   Producer

Eric Schilling ·

Babyface
Closer Look (1991)   Producer, Remixing
Michael Bolton
Timeless: The Classics, Vol. 2 (1999)   Engineer
Cachao
Master Sessions, Vol. 1 (1994)   Engineer
Master Sessions, Vol. 2 (1995)   Engineer, Mixing
Cuba Linda (2000)   Engineer, Mixing
Natalie Cole
Greatest Hits, Vol. 1 (2000)   Engineer, Mixing
Crosby Stills & Nash
Live It Up (1990)   Engineer
Gloria Estefan & Miami Sound Machine
Primitive Love (1986)   Engineer, Mixing
Gloria Estefan
Greatest Hits (1992)   Engineer, Mixing
Mi Tierra (1993)   Engineer, Mixing
Turn the Beat Around (1994)   Arranger, Programming, Engineer, Mixing
Destiny (1996)   Engineer
Gloria! (1998)   Engineer
Greatest Hits, Vol. 2 (2001)   Arranger, Engineer
Unwrapped (2003)   Engineer
Wrapped (2003)   Engineer
Dave Grusin
Presents: West Side Story (1997)   Engineer
Guaco
Como Era Y Como Es (1999)   Mixing Engineer
Juan Luis Guerra Y 440
Ni Es Lo Mismo Ni Es Igual (1998)   Engineer, Mixing
Happy the Man
Muse Awakens (2004)   Mixing
Idale
Perdidos en el Eden (2000)   Programming, Vocal Director, Mixing Engineer
Julio Iglesias
Noche de Cuatro Lunas (2000)   Engineer, Overdub Engineer, Tracking, Mezcla
Elton John
One Night Only (2000)   Engineer
Patricia Kaas
Dans Ma Chair (1997)   Engineer, Mixing
Longbox (2001)   Mixing
Barry Manilow
Swing Street (1987)   Engineer, Mixing
Another Life (1995)   Engineer

Ricky Martin
Sound Loaded (2000)   Engineer
Nana Mouskouri
Nana Latina (1996)   Engineer, Mixing
Rosie O'Donnell
Rosie Christmas (1999)   Engineer
Arturo Sandoval
Hot House (1998)   Engineer, Mastering, Mixing
Jon Secada
Heart, Soul & a Voice (1994)   Engineer
Si Te Vas (1994)   Engineer, Mezcla
Secada (1997)   Engineer, Production Coordination, Mixing
Shakira
MTV Unplugged (2000)   Mixing
Frank Sinatra
Duets, Vol. 1-2 (1993/1994)   Engineer, Mixing

Ken Scott . . . .

America
America (1972)   Engineer
The Beatles
Anthology 2 (1996)   Engineer
Anthology 3 (1996)   Engineer
Jeff Beck
There And Back (1980)   Producer
David Bowie
Hunky Dory (1971)   Producer
Ziggy Stardust (1972)   Producer
Pin Ups (1973)   Producer
Stanley Clarke
Stanley Clarke (1974)   Engineer
Journey To Love (1975)   Producer, Engineer
School Days (1976)   Producer, Engineer, Re-mix engineer
Billy Cobham
Spectrum (1973)   Engineer, Remixing
Dada
Puzzle (1992)   Producer, Engineer, Mixing
Devo
Duty Now For The Future (1979)   Producer, Engineer
Dixie Dregs
What If (1978)   Producer, Engineer
Night Of The Living Dregs (1979)   Producer, Engineer
Gamma
Gamma 1 (1979)   Producer, Engineer
George Harrison
All Things Must Pass (1970)   Engineer
Elton John
Honky Chateau (1972)   Engineer
Don't Shoot Me, I'm Only The Piano Player (1973)   Engineer

Kansas
Vinyl Confessions (1982)   Producer, Engineer
Level 42
World Machine (1985)   Producer
Mahavishnu Orchestra
Birds Of Fire (1972)   Engineer
Visions Of The Emerald Beyond (1974)   Producer, Engineer
Missing Persons
Spring Session M (1982)   Producer, Engineer
Harry Nilsson
Son Of Schmilsson (1972)   Balance Engineer
Jeffrey Osborne
Only Human (1991)   Producer, Keyboards
Procol Harum
Salty Dog (1969)   Engineer
Lou Reed
Transformer (1972)   Engineer, Mixing
Supertramp
Crime Of The Century (1974)   Producer
Crisis, What Crisis? (1975)   Producer
Tangerine Dream
Risky Business (1984)   Producer
The Tubes
Young And Rich (1976)   Producer

Allen Sides . . . .

Aerosmith
Just Push Play (2001)   Engineer
Eric Clapton
Clapton Chronicles: Best of 1981-1999 (2000)   Engineer
Phil Collins
Testify (2002)   Engineer, Mixing
Ry Cooder
Slide Area (1982)   Engineer
Paris, Texas (1989)   Engineer
Neil Diamond
In My Lifetime (1996)   Engineer
Ella Fitzgerald
Best Is Yet to Come (1982)   Engineer
Foo Fighters
There Is Nothing Left to Lose (1999)   Engineer
Aretha Franklin
So Damn Happy (2003)   Engineer, Mixing
Goo Goo Dolls
Dizzy up the Girl (1998)   Engineer
Ego Opinion Art & Commerce (2001)   Engineer
Gutterflower (2002)   Engineer
Green Day
Warning (2000)   Studio Consultant

Don Henley

Building the Perfect Beast (1984)	Engineer

John Lee Hooker

Mr. Lucky (1991)	Engineer
Best of Friends (1998)	Engineer, Mixing

Ron Isley/Burt Bacharach

Here I Am: Ron Isley Sings Burt Bacharach (2003)	Engineer, Mixing

Little Village

Little Village (1992)	Engineer

Lyle Lovett

Smile (2003)	Engineer, Mixing

Barry Manilow

Swing Street (1987)	Engineer, Mixing
Because It's Christmas (1990)	Engineer, Mixing

Joni Mitchell

Travelogue (2002)	Mixing

Michael McDonald

Motown Two (2004)	Engineer

Bonnie McKee

Trouble (2004)	Producer, Engineer

The Polyphonic Spree

Hold Me Now (2004)	Engineer
Together We're Heavy (2004)	Engineer

Lisa Marie Presley

Now What (2005)	Engineer

The Brian Setzer Orchestra

Guitar Slinger (1996)	Engineer, Mixing
Dirty Boogie (1998)	Engineer

Frank Sinatra

L.A. Is My Lady (1984)	Engineer, Assistant Engineer, Mixing Assistant

Stone Temple Pilots

No. 4 (1999)	Engineer

Sarah Vaughan with Milton Nascimento

Brazilian Romance (1987)	Mixing

Narada Michael Walden

Ecstasy's Dance: The Best of Narada Michael Walden (1996)	Mixing

Was (Not Was)

What Up, Dog? (1988)	Engineer, Mixing

Original Score

Dead Man Walking [Original Score] (1996)	Mixing, Recording Technician
Trespass (1992)	Engineer, Mixing
Groundhog Day (1993)	Engineer
Hope Floats [Original Soundtrack] (1998)	Engineer
Love Actually (2003)	Engineer, Mixing

Kris Solem . . . .

Bone Thugs N Harmony

Collection, Vol. 1 (1998)	Mastering

Compton's Most Wanted
Represent (2000)   Mastering
DJ U-Neek
Ghetto Street Pharmacist (1999)   Mastering
Kool G Rap
Roots of Evil (1998)   Mastering
Donna De Lory
Bliss (2000)   Mastering
Mo Bee
Now or Never: Odyssey 2000 (2000)   Mastering
Lizzy Borden
Deal with the Devil (2000)   Enhanced CD Audio Creation
Ricky Martin
Shake Your Bon-Bon [US Single] (2000)   Mastering
MC Eiht
Tha8t'z Gangsta (2001)   Mastering
Motley Crue
Dr. Feelgood (1989)   Mastering
Mötley Crüe (1994)   Remastering
Greatest Hits (1998)   Remastering
Supersonic and Demonic Relics (1999)   Mastering
Live: Entertainment or Death (1999)   Mastering
Motörhead
Snake Bite Love (1998)   Mastering
The Presidents of the United States of America
Freaked Out and Small (2000)   Mastering
Shabaz
Shabaz (2001)   Mastering
Shadowfax
Live (1995)   Mastering, Digital Assembly
Strunz & Farah
Stringweave (2001)   Mastering
Yes
House of Yes: Live From House of Blues (2000)   Mastering

Paul Stubblebine ....

Oscar Alemán
Swing Guitar Masterpieces 1937- 1957 (1998)   Mastering
Ustad Salamat Ali Khan
Breath of the Rose (1993)   Digital Mastering
Red Allen
Bluegrass Reunion (1991)   Mastering
Red Allen And Frank Wakefield
Kitchen Tapes (1994)   Mastering
Vishwa Mohan Bhatt
Gathering Rain Clouds (1993)   Digital Mastering
Tommy Castro
Live at the Fillmore (2000)   Mastering

Gene Clark	
This Byrd Has Flown (1995)	Remastering
Ry Cooder & V.M. Bhatt	
Meeting by the River (1993)	Digital Mastering
Dick Dale	
Tribal Thunder (1993)	Mastering
French-Frith-Kaiser-Thompson	
Live Love Larf & Loaf (1987)	Remastering
Jerry Garcia	
Jerry Garcia & David Grisman (1991)	Mastering
Jerry Garcia/David Grisman	
Not for Kids Only (1993)	Mastering
Shady Grove (1996)	Mastering
So What (1998)	Mastering
David Grisman	
Tone Poems (1994)	Mastering
Tone Poems 2 (1995)	Mastering
DGQ-20 (1996)	Mastering
John Wesley Harding	
Awake: The New Edition (2001)	Mastering
Mickey Hart, with Flora Purim	
Planet Drum (1991)	Mastering
John Lee Hooker	
Don't Look Back (1997)	Mastering
J.B. Hutto	
Masters of Modern Blues (1995)	Mastering
Dick Hyman	
From the Age of Swing (1994)	Digital Mastering
Swing Is Here (1996)	Mastering
In Recital (1998)	Editing, Mastering
Ladysmith Black Mambazo	
Gift of the Tortoise (1994)	Engineer
Taj Mahal	
Mo' Roots (1974)	Engineer
Mississippi Fred McDowell	
My Home Is in the Delta (1964)	Mastering
Amazing Grace (1966)	Transfers, Remastering
Holly Near	
Simply Love: The Women's Music Collection (2000)	Mastering
Edge (2000)	Mastering
Negro Fife and Drum Bands	
Traveling Through the Jungle (1995)	Mastering
The Neville Brothers	
Live on Planet Earth (1994)	Digital Editing
Old & In the Way	
That High Lonesome Sound (1996)	Mastering
Breakdown: Live Recordings 1973 (1997)	Mastering
San Francisco Gay Men's Chorus	
Naked Man (1996)	Mastering
ExtrABBAganza (1997)	Mastering

Santana
Swing of Delight (1980)   Mastering
Pete Sears & Friends
Watchfire (1988)   Producer, Engineer
Long Haul (2001)   Producer, Engineer, Mastering, Mixing
Tuck & Patti
Taking the Long Way Home (2000)   Digital Transfers
Doc Watson
Doc & Dawg (1997)   Mastering
Official Soundtrack
Grateful Dawg (2001)   Mastering
Apocalypse Now Redux (2001)   Mastering

Bruce Swedien ·

Barbara Acklin
Love Makes a Woman (1968)   Engineer
Patti Austin
Every Home Should Have One (1981)   Engineer, Mixing
George Benson
George Benson Anthology (2000)   Engineer, Mixing
Peabo Bryson w/ Roberta Flack
Born to Love (1983)   Engineer
Natalie Cole
This Will Be: Natalie Cole's… (1997)   Engineer
Tyrone Davis
Can I Change My Mind (1969)   Engineer
Turn Back the Hands of Time… (1970)   Engineer
Roberta Flack
I'm the One (1982)   Engineer
Herbie Hancock
Gershwin's World (1998)   Mixing
Eddie Harris
Best of Eddie Harris (1965)   Engineer, Remixing
Instant Death (1971)   Engineer
James Ingram
Greatest Hits: Power of Great Great Music (1991)   Engineer, Mixing
The Jacksons
Victory (1984)   Engineer, Mixing
Michael Jackson
Off the Wall (1979)   Engineer, Mixing
Thriller (1982)   Sound Effects, Engineer, Mixing
Bad (1987)   Drums, Engineer, Speech/Speaker/Speaking Part, Mixing
Dangerous (1992)   Percussion, Arranger, Drums, Keyboards, Vocals, Vocals (bckgr),
                                             Producer, Engineer, Mixing
History: Past, Present and Future (1995)   Percussion, Drums, Special Effects, Engineer
Michael Jackson & Janet Jackson
Scream/Childhood (1995)   Engineer, Mixing
Quincy Jones
I Heard That! (1969)   Engineer

Roots (1977)	Engineer
Sounds & Stuff (1978)	Engineer, Mixing
Back on the Block (1989)	Drums, Special Effects, Drums (Snare)
From Q with Love (1999)	Drums, Engineer, Mixing

Jennifer Lopez

Jenny from the Block [Australia CD] (2002)	Mixing
This Is Me… Then Jennifer Lopez (2002)	Engineer, Mixing
I'm Glad [CD5] (2003)	Engineer, Mixing
Reel Me [Bonus EP] (2003)	Engineer, Mixing
Get Right (2005)	Engineer, Mixing
Rebirth (2005)	Engineer, Mixing

Michael McDonald

Very Best of Michael McDonald (2001)	Engineer, Mixing, Original Recording Producer

Sergio Mendes & Brasil '66

Classics (1987)	Associate Producer
Brasileiro (1992)	Arranger, Mixing

Missing Persons

Best of Missing Persons (1987)	Producer

Lee Morgan & Wayne Shorter

Complete Vee Jay Lee Morgan-Wayne Shorter Sessions (2000)	Engineer

Rufus & Chaka Khan

Masterjam (1979)	Engineer, Mixing

Barbra Streisand

Till I Loved You (1988)	Engineer, Mixing

Donna Summer

Donna Summer (1982)	Engineer, Mixing

Muddy Waters

Live at Mister Kelly's (1971)	Engineer

Original Soundtrack

Color Purple (1985)	Engineer, Executive Producer, Mixing

Sam Taylor . . . .

Atomic Opera

For Madmen Only (1994)	Producer, Engineer, Photography

The Galactic Cowboys

Galactic Cowboys (1991)	Producer
Space in Your Face (1993)	Producer

Pat Hunter

Life Lessons (2005)	Guitar (Rhythm), Vocals (bckgr), Producer

King's X

Out of the Silent Planet (1988)	Producer
Gretchen Goes to Nebraska (1989)	Organ, Piano, Producer
Faith Hope Love (1990)	Organ, Producer
King's X (1992)	Producer

Original Soundtrack

Bill & Ted's Bogus Journey (1991)	Producer

David Thoener . . . .

AC/DC
For Those About to Rock We Salute You (1981)   Engineer, Mixing
Aerosmith
Toys in the Attic (1975)   Assistant Engineer
Pandora's Box (1991)   Mixing
Get a Grip (1993)   Engineer
Big Ones (1994)   Engineer
Box of Fire (1994)   Remixing
Allgood
Kickin' & Screamin' (1994)   Producer
The Blues Brothers
Made in America (1980)   Engineer
Michael Bolton
Time, Love & Tenderness (1991)   Mixing
Brooks & Dunn
Red Dirt Road (2003)   Mixing
Roseanne Cash
Retrospective (1995)   Producer, Engineer, Mixing
Cheap Trick
Sex, America, Cheap Trick (1996)   Mixing
Rodney Crowell
Greatest Hits (1993)   Engineer
Houston Kid (2001)   Mixing
Celine Dion
All the Way: A Decade of Song (1999)   Engineer
Bob Dylan
Bob Dylan 30th Anniversary Concert (1993)   Mixing
Alecia Elliott
I'm Diggin' It (2000)   Engineer
The Features
Exhibit A (2004)   Mixing
Peter Frampton
Shine On: A Collection (1992)   Engineer, Mixing
J. Geils Band
Love Stinks (1980)   Engineer, Mixing
Freeze Frame (1981)   Engineer, Mixing
Sammy Hagar
I Never Said Goodbye (1987)   Producer, Engineer, Mixing
Heart
Private Audition (1982)   Engineer, Mastering, Mixing
Jars of Clay
Who We Are Instead (2003)   Engineer
Billy Joel
River of Dreams (1993)   Producer, Mixing
Kiss
Killers (1982)   Engineer
k.d. lang
Live by Request (2001)   Mixing

John Lennon
Walls and Bridges (1974)   Assistant Engineer
Menlove Ave. (1986)   Engineer
Courtney Love
America's Sweetheart (2004)   Mixing
Ricky Martin
Sound Loaded (2000)   Mixing
matchbox twenty
Mad Season (2000)   Engineer, Mixing
EP (2003)   Mixing
Meat Loaf
Very Best of Meatloaf (1998)   Mixing
John Cougar Mellencamp
Best That I Could Do (1978-1988) (1997)   Engineer
Willie Nelson
Rainbow Connection (2001)   Engineer, Mixing
Santana
Supernatural (1999)   Mixing
Rob Thomas
Something to Be [Dual Disc] (2005)   Engineer, Mixing
John Waite
Essential (1992)   Producer
Original Soundtrack
Horse Whisperer (1998)   Engineer, Mixing
Armageddon (1998)   Engineer, Mixing
Patch Adams (1998)   Mixing
Songcatcher (2001)   Engineer, Mixing

Brent Truitt. . . . .

Gail Davies
Greatest Hits [Koch] (1998)   Mandolin
Dixie Chicks
Top of the World Tour: Live (2003)   Mandolin, Vocals (bckgr)
Matt Flinner
View from Here (1998)   Engineer
Latitude (2001)   Engineer
David Grier
Panorama (1997)   Engineer
Michael Reno Harrell
Ways To Travel (1997)   Mandolin
Second Wind (2000)   Producer
Chris Jones
Follow Your Heart (1999)   Mixing
Irene Kelley
Simple Path (2001)   Mandolin, Mixing
Alison Krauss
Two Highways (1989)   Mandolin
Now That I've Found You: A Collection (1995)   Mandolin

The Lonesome River Band
One Step Forward (1996)   Engineer
Molasses Creek
Citybound (2000)   Mandolin, Producer, Engineer
The Nitty Gritty Dirt Band
Welcome to Woody Creek (2004)   Overdubs
Dolly Parton
Halos & Horns (2002)   Mandolin
Live and Well [DVD] (2004)   Mandolin
Jon Randall
Willin' (1999)   Guitar (Acoustic), Mandolin, Percussion, Guitar (Electric), Organ (Hammond),
                            Producer, Engineer, Harmony Vocals, Mastering
Riders in the Sky
Public Cowboy #1: The Music of Gene Autry (1996)   Producer, Engineer, Mixing
Yodel the Cowboy Way (1998)   Engineer
Great Big Western Howdy from Riders In The Sky (1998)   Guitar, Mandolin, Engineer
Christmas the Cowboy Way (1999)   Engineer
Woody's Roundup: A Rootin' Tootin' Collection (2000)   Engineer
Monsters, Inc. Scream Factory Favorites (2002)   Engineer
Pair of Kings (2002)   Engineer
Engineer Silver Jubilee (2003)   Engineer
Strings of Fire
Acoustic Tribute to Guns N Roses (2000)   Mandolin, Producer, Engineer, Mixing, Papoose
Victor Wooten
Yin-Yang (1999)   Assistant Engineer
Frankie Yankovic
Songs of the Polka King, Vol. 2 (1997)   Guitar, Mandolin

Leanne Ungar . . . .

Laurie Anderson
Big Science (1982)   Engineer, Vocals (bckgr)
Mister Heartbreak (1984)   Engineer
Home of the Brave [Video] (1986)   Engineer
Home of the Brave (1986)   Engineer
Talk Normal: The Laurie Anderson Anthology (2000)   Engineer
Joy Askew
Tender City (1996)   Engineer
Perla Batalla
Perla Batalla (1994)   Producer, Engineer
Mestiza (1998)   Engineer, Mixing
Heaven and Earth: The Mestiza Voyage (2000)   Engineer, Mixing
Carlene Carter
Hindsight 20/20 (1996)   Engineer
Ray Charles
My World (1993)   Engineer
Leonard Cohen
New Skin for the Old Ceremony (1974)   Assistant Engineer
Various Positions (1985)   Engineer
Future (1992)   Producer, Engineer, Mixing

Cohen Live (1994)	Producer, Engineer
More Best of Leonard Cohen (1997)	Producer, Engineer
Field Commander Cohen: Tour of 1979	Producer, Engineer
Ten New Songs (2001)	Engineer, Mixing
Dear Heather (2004)	Producer, Engineer
Holly Cole	
Don't Smoke in Bed (1993)	Engineer
It Happened One Night (1995)	Engineer
Guster	
Goldfly (1997)	Engineer
Joe Henderson	
Porgy and Bess (1997)	Engineer
Janis Ian	
Night Rains (1979)	Engineer
Billy Joel	
Greatest Hits, Vol. 1, 2 & 3 (2000)	Recorder, Engineer
Shepard	
Radical Light (1992)	Engineer
Bill Staines	
First Million Miles (1989)	Mixing
First Million Miles, Vol. 2 (1998)	Mixing
Cat Stevens	
Numbers (1975)	Engineer
Paul Winter Consort	
Canyon (1985)	Engineer, Mixing
Concert for the Earth (1985)	Mixing
Wolf Eyes (1988)	Engineer
Paul Winter	
Anthems (1992)	Engineer
Greatest Hits (1998)	Engineer
Original Soundtrack	
Passion Fish (1993)	Engineer
Solaris (2002)	Engineer

Tony Visconti . . . .

The Alarm	
Best of the Alarm & Mike Peters (1998)	Producer, Engineer, String Arrangements
Altered Images	
I Could Be Happy: The Best of Altered Images (1997)	Producer
Adam Ant & The Ants	
Antmusic: The Very Best of Adam & The Ants (1994)	Producer
Adam Ant	
Super Hits (1998)	Producer
Badfinger	
Magic Christian Music (1970)	Arranger, Producer
Bob Geldof & the Boomtown Rats	
Great Songs of Indifference: The Best of Bob Geldof & The Boomtown Rats (1997)	Producer
David Bowie	
Space Oddity (1969)	Bass, Flute, Arranger, Recorder, Producer, Mixing

Man Who Sold the World (1970)	Bass, Guitar, Piano, Bass (Electric), Guitar (Bass), Producer, Remixing
David Live (1974)	Producer, Engineer
Diamond Dogs (1974)	Strings, Arranger, Mixing
Young Americans (1975)	Arranger, Producer, Mixing
Low (1977)	Producer
Heroes (1977)	Bass, Vocals (bckgr), Wind, Producer, Engineer
Stage (1978)	Producer, Engineer
Lodger (1979)	Bass, Guitar, Mandolin, Guitar (Rhythm), Vocals (bckgr), Producer, Engineer
Scary Monsters (And Super Creeps) (1980)	Guitar (Acoustic), Guitar, Vocals (bckgr), Producer, Engineer
Ziggy Stardust (1982)	Producer, Remixing
Joe Cocker	
With a Little Help from My Friends (1969)	Guitar, Mixing
D. Generation	
Through the Darkness (1999)	Guitar (Acoustic), Producer
Brian Eno	
Eno Box I: Instrumentals (1994)	Producer
Gentle Giant	
Gentle Giant (1970)	Producer, Liner Notes
Acquiring the Taste (1971)	Producer
John Hiatt	
Living a Little, Laughing a Little (1996)	Producer
Mary Hopkin	
Earth Song, Ocean Song (1971)	Vocals, Producer
Bert Jansch	
Moonshine (1973)	Bass, Percussion, Arranger, Bass (Electric), Recorder, Vocals, Shaker, Tubular Bells, Vocal Harmony
Luscious Jackson	
Electric Honey (1999)	Producer, Engineer
Paul McCartney	
Press to Play (1986)	Orchestral Arrangements
Mercury Rev	
All Is Dream (2001)	Flute, Mellotron, Orchestration, String Arrangements
The Moody Blues	
Other Side of Life (1986)	Producer, Engineer
Sur La Mer (1988)	Programming, Producer, Engineer, Mixing
Keys of the Kingdom (1991)	Producer, Engineer, String Arrangements, Mixing
Time Traveler (1994)	Programming, Producer, Engineer, Mixing
The Move	
Move (1968)	Strings, Brass, Woodwind
Sparks	
Indiscreet (1975)	Producer
Big Beat (1976)	Producer
In the Swing (1993)	Producer
Plagiarism (1997)	Arranger, Conductor, Vocal Arrangement, Orchestral Arrangements
The Strawbs	
Grave New World (1972)	Producer
Halcyon Days (1997)	Arranger, Producer, Engineer, Mixing

Thin Lizzy
Dedication: The Very Best of Thin Lizzy (1991)   Producer
Tyranosaurous Rex
Unicorn (1969)   Piano, Producer
Beard of Stars (1970)   Piano, Producer
T. Rex
T. Rex (1970)   Piano, Producer, String Arrangements
Electric Warrior (1971)   Piano, Producer
Slider (1972)   Producer
Tanx (1973)   Producer
T. Rextasy: The Best of T. Rex (1985)   Bass, Arranger, Vocals (bckgr), Producer, String Arrangements
U2
Wide Awake in America (1985)   Producer
Wakeman
Voyage: The Very Best of Rick Wakeman (1997)   Producer
Original Soundtrack
Moulin Rouge (2001)   Vocals
Various Artists
Secret Policeman's Third Ball: The (1987)   Producer

Bil VornDick ·

Acoustic Syndicate
Crazy Little Life (2000)   Producer, Engineer
Terra Firma (2003)   Producer, Engineer, Mixing
Trace Adkins
Big Time (1997)   Engineer
Asleep At The Wheel
Wheel Keeps on Rollin' (1995)   Engineer
Alison Brown
Out of the Blue (1998)   Engineer, Mixing
T-Bone Burnett
Criminal Under My Own Hat (1992)   Engineer
Vassar Clements
Grass Routes (1991)   Producer, Engineer, Mixing
Cornerstone
Out of the Valley (1994)   Producer, Engineer, Mastering, Mixing
Lonesome Town (1995)   Producer, Engineer, Mastering, Mixing
Jerry Douglas
Under the Wire (1986)   Producer, Engineer
Restless on the Farm (1998)   Engineer, Mixing
Lookout for Hope (2002)   Engineer
Béla Fleck
Double Time (1984)   Engineer
Deviations (1984)   Engineer
Béla Fleck & The Flecktones
Béla Fleck & The Flecktones (1990)   Mixing
Flight of the Cosmic Hippo (1991)   Engineer, Mixing
Live Art (1991)   Mixing
UFO Tofu (1992)   Engineer

Bluegrass Sessions: Tales From the (1999)	Engineer, Mixing
Bluegrass Sessions: Tales from the Acoustic Planet, V (2001)	Recorder, Engineer, Mixing
Drive [Bonus Track] (2005)	Mixing
Tony Furtado	
Within Reach (1992)	Engineer
Full Circle (1994)	Engineer
Clive Gregson	
I Love This Town (1996)	Engineer
Alison Krauss	
Two Highways (1989)	Producer, Engineer
I've Got That Old Feeling (1990)	Producer, Engineer, Editing, Mastering
Now That I've Found You: A Collection (1995)	Producer, Engineer, Mixing
Doyle Lawson & Quicksilver	
Heaven's Joy Awaits (1988)	Engineer
Hymn Time in the Country (1988)	Engineer
I Heard the Angels Singing (1989)	Engineer
My Heart Is Yours (1990)	Engineer
Del McCoury	
Deeper Shade of Blue (1993)	Engineer, Mixing
Cold Hard Facts (1996)	Engineer, Mixing
Edgar Meyer	
Love of a Lifetime	Engineer
The Nashville Bluegrass Band	
My Native Home (1985)	Engineer
Idletime (1987)	Engineer
Nashville Bluegrass Band (1987)	Engineer
Boys Are Back in Town (1990)	Engineer
Home of the Blues (1991)	Engineer
Waitin' for the Hard Times to Go (1993)	Engineer
The New Grass Revival	
Friday Night in America (1989)	Engineer
Maura O'Connell	
Just in Time (1988)	Engineer
Helpless Heart (1989)	Engineer
Stories (1995)	Engineer, Mixing
Wandering Home (1997)	Mixing
Mark O'Connor	
Heroes (1993)	Engineer
Peter Rowan	
New Moon Rising (1988)	Engineer
Dust Bowl Children (1990)	Engineer
Peter Rowan & Jerry Douglas	
Yonder (1996)	Engineer, Mixing
Ralph Stanley	
Back to the Cross (1992)	Engineer, Mixing
Saturday Night & Sunday Morning (1992)	Engineer, Mixing
Stanley Blues (2002)	Producer, Engineer, Mixing
Ralph Stanley & Friends	
Clinch Mountain Country (1998)	Producer, Engineer, Mixing

Rhonda Vincent

If Heartaches Had Wings/One Step Ahead Of The Blue (2003)	Engineer, Mastering
One Step Ahead (2003)	Engineer

Doc Watson

Portrait (1988)	Engineer
On Praying Ground (1990)	Engineer, Remixing
My Dear Old Southern Home (1991)	Engineer

Michael Wagener ·

Accept

Restless & Wild (1983)	Engineer, Mixing
Balls to the Wall (1984)	Mixing
Predator (1997)	Producer, Engineer, Mixing

Sebastian Bach

Bring 'em Bach Alive (1999)	Producer, Engineer, Mixing

Alice Cooper

Freedom for Frankenstein: Hits & Pieces 1984-1997 (1998)	Producer

Dokken

Tooth and Nail (1984)	Mixing
Under Lock and Key (1985)	Producer, Engineer, Mixing
Beast from the East (1988)	Engineer
Back in the Streets (1989)	Producer, Engineer, Mixing
Long Way Home (2002)	Mixing

Extreme

Extreme II: Pornograffitti (1990)	Producer

Janet Jackson

Black Cat [US Single] (1989)	Mixing
Design of a Decade: 1986-1996 (1995)	Remixing

Megadeth

So Far, So Good…So What! (1988)	Mixing

Metallica

Master of Puppets (1986)	Mixing

Motley Crue

Too Fast for Love (1981)	Mixing
Decade of Decadence (1991)	Remixing, Mixing

Ozzy Osbourne

No More Tears (1991)	Mixing
Live & Loud (1993)	Engineer, Mixing
Ozzman Cometh: Greatest Hits (1997)	Engineer, Mixing

Poison

Look What the Cat Dragged In (1986)	Mixing

Queen

Stone Cold Crazy (1991)	Remixing, Mixing

Saigon Kick

Saigon Kick (1988)	Producer, Engineer, Mixing

Skid Row

Skid Row (1989)	Producer, Engineer, Mixing
Slave to the Grind (1991)	Producer, Mixing

The Sons of the Pioneers
Tumbling Tumbleweeds [MCA 1995] (1987)   Producer, Engineer, Mixing
Stryper
Soldiers Under Command (1985)   Producer, Engineer
Testament
Low (1994)   Mixing
Live at the Fillmore (1995)   Producer, Mixing
Demonic (1997)   Mixing
Very Best of Testament (2001)   Mixing
Titanium Black
Bleed for You (2005)   Producer, Mixing
W.A.S.P.
Inside the Electric Circus (1986)   Mixing
Warrant
Dog Eat Dog (1992)   Producer, Engineer, Liner Notes, Mixing
White Lion
Pride (1987)   Producer, Engineer, Mixing
Big Game (1989)   Producer, Engineer, Mixing
X
Wild Thing (1984)   Producer, Engineer, Mixing
Ain't Love Grand! (1985)   Producer, Engineer

Shelly Yakus . . . .

Herb Alpert
Keep Your Eye on Me (1987)   Producer
The Band
Music from Big Pink (1968)   Engineer
Blue Öyster Cult
Agents of Fortune (1976)   Engineer
Spectres (1977)   Engineer
Booker T. & the MG's
Melting Pot (1971)   Engineer
Alice Cooper
Billion Dollar Babies (1973)   Engineer
Dire Straits
Making Movies (1980)   Engineer
Eurythmics
Be Yourself Tonight (1985)   Recorder
Aretha Franklin
Who's Zoomin' Who? (1985)   Engineer
Grand Funk Railroad
All the Girls in the World Beware (1974)   Engineer
Heart
Private Audition (1982)   Engineer
Don Henley
End of the Innocence (1989)   Engineer, Mixing
Actual Miles: Henley's Greatest Hits (1995)   Engineer, Mixing
B.B. King
King of the Blues [Box] (1992)   Remixing

John Lennon

Walls and Bridges (1974)   Engineer

Menlove Ave. (1986)   Engineer

Imagine: John Lennon [Original… (1988)   Engineer

Van Morrison

Moondance (1970)   Engineer

Stevie Nicks

Wild Heart (1983)   Engineer, Mixing

Rock a Little (1985)   Engineer

Tom Petty & the Heartbreakers

Damn the Torpedoes (1979)   Producer, Engineer

Hard Promises (1981)   Engineer

Long After Dark (1982)   Engineer, Remixing

Southern Accents (1985)   Engineer

Pack up the Plantation: Live! (1986)   Engineer

Playback (1995)   Engineer, Mixing

The Raspberries

Raspberries (1972)   Engineer

Fresh (1972)   Engineer

Return to Forever

Hymn of the Seventh Galaxy (1973)   Engineer

Where Have I Known You Before (1974)   Engineer

No Mystery (1975)   Producer

Bob Seger

The Distance (1982)   Engineer

Like a Rock (1986)   Engineer

Patti Smith Group

Easter (1978)   Mixing

Dream of Life (1988)   Mixing

Masters [Box] (1996)   Mixing

Mavis Staples

Have a Little Faith (2004)   Mastering, Mixing

U2

Under a Blood Red Sky (1983)   Engineer

Rattle and Hum (1988)   Mixing

Desire [US 3 Track CD] (1988)   Mixing

Best of 1980-1990 (1998)   Remixing, Mixing

Best of 1980-1990 [Japan] (1998)   Remixing, Mixing

Suzanne Vega

Solitude Standing (1987)   Mixing

Warren Zevon

I'll Sleep When I'm Dead (An Anthology) (1996)   Mixing

Original Soundtrack

Armageddon [Original Soundtrack] (1998)   Engineer

David Z. . . . .

Tab Benoit

Fever for the Bayou (2005)   Producer

Big Head Todd & the Monsters
Sister Sweetly (1993) — Guitar, Percussion, Producer, Engineer, Mixing
Tinsley Ellis
Kingpin (2000) — Producer, Recorder, Mixing, Guitar, Percussion, Keyboards
Fine Young Cannibals
Finest (1996) — Producer
The Go-Go's
Greatest (1990) — Producer
Gov't Mule
Deep End, Vol. 1 (2001) — Producer, Engineer
Buddy Guy
Heavy Love (1998) — Producer
Etta James
Let's Roll (2003) — Mixing
Mixing Blues to the Bone (2004) — Mixing
Syl Johnson
Bridge to a Legacy (1998) — Producer, Remixing
Jill Jones
For Love (1987) — Producer
G-Spot (1987) — Producer
Mia Bocca (1987) — Producer
Leo Kottke
Standing in My Shoes (1997) — Celeste, Sitar, Producer, Engineer, Drum Programming
Leo Kottke & Mike Gordon
Clone (2002) — Mixing
Jonny Lang
Lie to Me (1997) — Vocals (bckgr), Producer, Engineer
Wander This World (1998) — Producer, Engineer, Mixing
John Mayall & Friends
Along for the Ride (2001) — Guitar (Rhythm), Producer, Engineer, Mixing
Prince
Crystal Ball (1998) — Engineer
Kenny Wayne Shepherd
Ledbetter Heights (1995) — Producer, Engineer
Jimmy Thackery
Healin' Ground (2005) — Engineer, Mixing
Jody Watley
Jody Watley (1987) — Producer
You Wanna Dance with Me? (1990) — Producer
Greatest Hits (1996) — Producer

Index

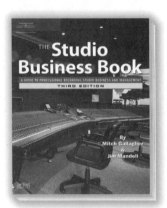
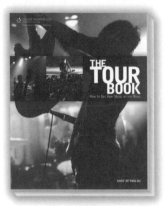
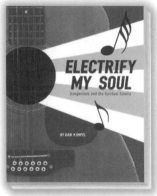
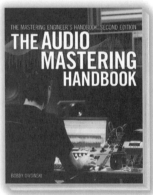
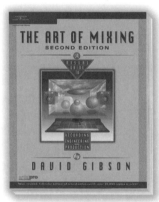

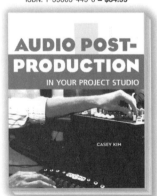